Land Grabbing and Global Governance

Land grabbing per se is not a new phenomenon, given its historical precedents in the eras of imperialism. However, the character, scale, pace, orientation and key drivers of the recent wave of land grabs is a distinct historical event closely tied to the changing dynamics of the global agri-food, feed and fuel complex.

Land grabbing is facilitated by ever greater flows of capital, goods, and ideas across borders, and these flows occur through axes of power that are far more polycentric than the North-South imperialist tradition. Land grabs occur in the context of changes in the character of the global food regime, formerly anchored by North Atlantic empires; the integrated food-energy complex seems to be headed towards multiple centres of power, especially with the rise of the BRICS and the proliferation of middle income countries participating in many of the land transactions.

Land Grabbing and Global Governance offers insights from leading scholars and experts on contemporary land grabs. This volume examines land grabs in direct relation to a global economy undergoing profound change and the role of new configurations of actors and power in governance institutions and practices.

This book was published as a special issue of *Globalizations*.

Matias E. Margulis is Assistant Professor of International Studies at the University of Northern British Columbia. His current book project explores the global regulation of agricultural trade and food security. He is a former Canadian trade policy advisor and has worked on global food security policy at several multilateral organizations.

Nora McKeon studied history at Harvard and political science at the Sorbonne before joining the Food and Agriculture Organization (FAO) of the United Nations where she became responsible for the overall direction of FAO's policy and programme interaction with civil society. She now divides her time between research, teaching and activism around food systems, peasant farmer movements and UN-civil society relations.

Saturnino M. Borras Jr is Associate Professor at the International Institute of Social Studies (ISS) in The Hague, Adjunct Professor at the College of Humanities and Development Studies (COHD) of China Agricultural University in Beijing, and a Fellow of the Amsterdam-based Transnational Institute (TNI) and of the California-based Food First.

Rethinking Globalizations

Edited by
Barry K. Gills, University of Newcastle, UK
Kevin Gray, University of Sussex, UK

This series is designed to break new ground in the literature on globalization and its academic and popular understanding. Rather than perpetuating or simply reacting to the economic understanding of globalization, this series seeks to capture the term and broaden its meaning to encompass a wide range of issues and disciplines and convey a sense of alternative possibilities for the future.

Land Grabbing and Global Governance

Edited by
**Matias E. Margulis, Nora McKeon and
Saturnino M. Borras Jr**

LONDON AND NEW YORK

First published 2014
by Routledge
2 Park Square, Milton Park, Abingdon, Oxon, OX14 4RN

Simultaneously published in the USA and Canada
by Routledge
711 Third Avenue, New York, NY 10017

Routledge is an imprint of the Taylor & Francis Group, an informa business

British Library Cataloguing in Publication Data
A catalogue record for this book is available from the British Library

ISBN 13: 978-0-415-62834-1

Typeset in Times New Roman
by Taylor & Francis Books

Publisher's Note
The publisher accepts responsibility for any inconsistencies that may have arisen during the conversion of this book from journal articles to book chapters, namely the possible inclusion of journal terminology.

Disclaimer
Every effort has been made to contact copyright holders for their permission to reprint material in this book. The publishers would be grateful to hear from any copyright holder who is not here acknowledged and will undertake to rectify any errors or omissions in future editions of this book.

Contents

CONTENTS

Citation Information

The chapters in this book were originally published in *Globalizations*, volume 10, issue 1 (February 2013). When citing this material, please use the original page numbering for each article, as follows:

Chapter 1
Introduction: Land Grabbing and Global Governance:
Critical Perspectives
Matias E. Margulis, Nora McKeon &
Saturnino M. Borras Jr
Globalizations, volume 10, issue 1 (February 2013)
pp. 1–24

Chapter 2
Land Grabs Today: Feeding the Disassembling of National
Territory
Saskia Sassen
Globalizations, volume 10, issue 1 (February 2013)
pp. 25–46

Chapter 3
Land Grabbing as Security Mercantilism in International
Relations
Philip McMichael
Globalizations, volume 10, issue 1 (February 2013)
pp. 47–64

Chapter 4
Governing the Global Land Grab: Multipolarity, Ideas, and
Complexity in Transnational Governance
Matias E. Margulis & Tony Porter
Globalizations, volume 10, issue 1 (February 2013)
pp. 65–86

Chapter 5
The Governance of Gulf Agro-Investments
Eckart Woertz
Globalizations, volume 10, issue 1 (February 2013)
pp. 87–104

Chapter 12
The Minimum Human Rights Principles Applicable to Large-Scale Land Acquisitions or Leases
Priscilla Claeys & Gaëtan Vanloqueren
Globalizations, volume 10, issue 1 (February 2013)
pp. 193–198

Chapter 13
Private Governance and Land Grabbing: The Equator Principles and the Roundtable on Sustainable Biofuels
Ariane Goetz
Globalizations, volume 10, issue 1 (February 2013)
pp. 199–204

Chapter 14
Restrictions to Foreign Acquisitions of Agricultural Land in Argentina and Brazil
Nicolás Marcelo Perrone
Globalizations, volume 10, issue 1 (February 2013)
pp. 205–209

Please direct any queries you may have about the citations to
clsuk.permissions@cengage.com

INTRODUCTION

Land Grabbing and Global Governance: Critical Perspectives

MATIAS E. MARGULIS*, NORA McKEON** &
SATURNINO M. BORRAS JR***

*University of Northern British Columbia, Prince George, Canada & Max Planck Institute for the Study of Societies, Cologne, Germany
**Roma Tre University, Rome, Italy
***International Institute of Social Studies, The Hague, The Netherlands

ABSTRACT Land grabbing has emerged as a significant issue in contemporary global governance that cuts across the fields of development, investment, food security, among others. Whereas land grabbing per se is not a new phenomenon, having historical precedents in the era of imperialism, the character, scale, pace, orientation, and key drivers of the recent wave of land grabs is a distinct historical phenomenon closely tied to major shifts in power and production in the global political economy. Land grabbing is facilitated by ever greater flows of capital, goods, and ideas across borders, and these flows occur through axes of power that are far more polycentric than the North–South imperialist tradition. In this introduction we argue that land grabbing speaks to many of the core questions of globalization studies. However, we note scholars of globalization have yet to deeply engage with this new field. We situate land grabbing in an era of advanced capitalism, multiple global crises, and the role of new configurations of power and resistance in global governance institutions. The essays in this collection contribute to identifying land grabbing as an important and urgent topic for theoretical and empirical investigations to deepen our understanding of contemporary globalization and governance.

Introduction

Over the last few years, land grabbing has become a well-established phenomenon. There are varying estimates of the quantity of lands that have changed hands during recent years, from a low of 45 million hectares (World Bank, 2010) to a high of 227 million hectares (Oxfam, 2012), although how the counting was done in these estimates is not always clear. This global land rush is characterized by transnational and domestic corporate investors, governments, and local elites taking control over large quantities of land (and its minerals and water) to produce food, feed, biofuel, and other industrial commodities for the international or domestic markets. Such land deals are often associated with very low levels of transparency, consultation, and respect for the rights of local communities living off the land (Borras and Franco, 2010; Cotula, 2012; Zoomers, 2010). In response to concerns over the real and massive experiences of dispossession, violence, and social exclusion, land grabbing has been elevated to an issue of world political significance around which local and transnational resistance has swelled and for which new global governance instruments are being created. The importance of land grabbing as a topic in global governance is well established. This salience is confirmed by events in the real world: land grabbing is on the agenda of the Group of Eight (G8)/Group of Twenty (G20); it is at the core of the World Bank's new global development agenda; several new global governance instruments have been negotiated to address land grabbing; global civil society and transnational social movements are mobilizing around this phenomenon; and investors and corporations are intensifying their acquisitions and global competition for land.

The idea of a land grab has a long intellectual history dating back to the writings of Karl Marx. The study of land and agrarian change has been integral to our understanding of the development of capitalism and the contemporary world order (Araghi and Karides, 2012; Peluso and Lund, 2011). We recognize that land grabs today are deeply shaped by past practices and historical legacies and exhibit continuities from the past but also diverge in significant ways, and are riddled with contradictions and tensions. Our emphasis here, however, is on the specific contemporary context that is giving rise to land grabbing on a global scale. There is a burgeoning academic literature that has so far examined land grabbing from the perspective of agrarian political economy (Peluso and Lund, 2011; White et al., 2012) and political ecology (Fairhead et al., 2012), as well as around the issues of food security (Robertson and Pinstrup-Anderson, 2010), food sovereignty (Rosset, 2011), labor (Li, 2011), human rights (De Schutter, 2011), gender relations (Berhman et al., 2012; Chu, 2011; Julia and White, 2012), land use change (Friis and Reenberg, 2010), the role of the state (Borras et al., 2013b), water grabbing (Allan et al., 2012; Mehta et al., 2012), and neoliberalism (Araghi and Karides, 2012).

With some exceptions scholars of globalization in general have been absent from the debate on this emerging issue. This is unfortunate because land grabbing is emblematic of contemporary globalization and speaks to many of the big questions that concern scholars of globalization. Land grabbing is facilitated by ever more extensive and rapid flows of capital, goods, and ideas across borders and these flows occur through axes of power that are far more polycentric than the North–South imperialist tradition. In addition, land grabbing is occurring in the context of late capitalism and global multiple food–energy–climate–finance crises in which we can see the changing character of global production and consumption, including an integrated global food–energy complex. Land grabbing is a global-scale phenomenon that is occurring in all regions and parts of the world, and not only in Africa as is assumed to be the case (see Visser and Spoor, 2011, on post-Soviet Eurasia; Borras et al., 2012b, on Latin America; Borras and Franco, 2011, on Southeast Asia). Whereas land grabbing per se is not a new phenomenon, having historical precedents in the eras of colonialism and imperialism (Alden Wily, 2012), the drivers, scale, and pace of the recent wave of land grabs are distinct from previous eras. As Saskia Sassen, explains (2013, this volume), unlike in the eras of colonialism and imperialism the current wave of land grabs occurs in a world of sovereign states exercising territorial control at least formally. Transborder flows of capital, property rights, and agricultural production go through, rather than bypass, multiple layers of formal governance mechanisms ranging from investment and trade treaties to financial markets. Therefore, contemporary global land grabbing displays properties specific to our era of advanced economic globalization. Land grabbing is an important site of new transnational political struggles for authority and control over resources and governance. These struggles go beyond who should control the land, and are contests largely about what should be grown on it, how, by whom, for what markets, hence the future of global agriculture. Thus the stakes being fought over in the struggles in the global land grab are massive and are likely to reshape the future course of globalization, partly by producing openings and/or closing off avenues for global policies and practices that provide those that live off the land with autonomy, including a degree of protection from global economic forces, to decide future life courses.

In this introductory essay, we raise the point of the need for globalization studies to address more systematically the issue of global land grabbing. As suggested above, the global land grab reveals strongly many aspects of economic globalization. In the same instance, contemporary globalization cannot be fully understood without a deeper understanding of land grabbing. It is useful to develop a more nuanced understanding of new and important sets of transborder flows, power relations, and political struggles that converge where land grabbing occurs and in global-scale governance institutions and practices. These global aspects have remained largely under-studied and under-theorized but are precisely the terrain for inquiry where globalization scholars are most strongly situated to engage with questions concerning territory, power, authority, and resistance.

This collection is a preliminary effort seeking to bring a lens from globalizations studies to land grabbing. Our purpose is twofold. One is to offer initial analyses of land grabbing from a globalization perspective in order to bring land grabbing to the attention of scholars interested in globalization and transnational governance. Our hunch is that given that land grabbing cuts across so many core areas of globalization research—territorialization, financialization, trade, human rights, crises, and so on—readers will quickly start to see the links between their work and the ideas presented here, and in the process we hope to stimulate new questions and lines of investigation in the field. A second purpose is to foster greater dialogue between scholars of globalization with the burgeoning literature on land grabbing spearheaded by agrarian political economy and political ecology scholars. These latter fields of study, which now provide an extensive set of case studies of land grabbing, would be enriched by the global-scale theoretical contributions of globalization and transnational governance studies. This can lead to more robust analysis of global–local interactions behind land grabbing. One starting point for such cross-fertilization is to consider how local land struggles are likely to be altered by changes in the global policy environment, such as the entrance of foreign investors that is permitted by the burden of the debt regime affecting most developing countries—as Sassen (2013, this volume) explains—but also by global governance instruments aimed at defending the rights of those who live off the land (Künnemann and Monsalve Suárez, 2013, this volume; McKeon, 2013, this volume). Studies of globalization and governance also stand to benefit from a deeper engagement with agrarian political economy and political ecology analysis of land grabbing because the latter have produced deep knowledge of the social, economic, and political effects of the multiple food–energy–climate–finance crises *on the ground*. Globalization and transnational governance scholars have disproportionately paid attention to the recent global financial crisis with little consideration of the other related political economy processes. It is not our point that one crisis (i.e. financial, food or climatic) is more important than another one. Instead our point is that knowledge of globalization in the twenty-first century is most likely to be enhanced only when we start from the standpoint that these crises are mutually affected world historical events.

This collection is organized around the transnational contestation of land grabbing and its governance. This is because the global/transnational scales are sites of new and significant governance activity. This volume offers a perspective that examines land grabbing and its governance as embedded within a larger international political economy context. The collection offers critical perspectives in the sense that most authors in this collection are concerned by land grabbing and its negative social and ecological consequences. Hence, this collection is sympathetic to a global social justice agenda. It is in this context that we also purposely include knowledge and experiences from outside the academy: several of the essays in this volume are written by activists situated in global civil society who have participated in the negotiation and resistance politics of emergent global land governance. This coming together of academic and activist researchers enriches this collection immensely, and is important for the co-production and -mobilization of knowledge.

Global Governance and Land Grabbing

One of the notable developments that followed public awareness of a global land grab in 2008 was the rapid elevation of land grabbing onto the global governance agenda and a flurry of global rule-making projects at various scales involving a multiplicity of actors to regulate land grabbing. Land grabbing has been taken up in the work of the United Nations (UN) system and Bretton Woods institutions—but most actively at the UN Food and Agriculture Organizations (FAO), the Committee on World Food Security (CFS) and the World Bank, at the G8 and G20 summits, at the European Commission (i.e. in discussion about the indirect effects of its biofuel mandate), and in the African Union's work on a regional land policy framework. The well known, flagship global rule-making projects are the recently negotiated UN *Voluntary Guidelines on the Responsible Governance of Tenure of Land, Fisheries and Forests* (herein 'Voluntary Guidelines'; see Seufert, 2013, this volume) and the ongoing transnational negations to develop rules for responsible agricultural investment (see Stephens, 2013, this volume). Many other projects have been spawned by the food crisis that impact on global governance and are directly related to land grabbing, such as the Global Agriculture and Food Security Program (a new multi-donor trust fund that encourages public and private investment in agriculture), the G8's so-called New Alliance for Food Security and Nutrition, a development assistance program now spearheaded by the Obama administration, and the World Economic Forum's 'Grow Africa' initiative. All of these projects share the objective of promoting large-scale private-sector led investments in developing country agriculture and highlighting the weight of investments relative to that of policies. Meanwhile, dozens of countries are revisiting and reforming national and local land planning and tenure laws as well as their bilateral/multilateral trade, investment, and development cooperation arrangements—and depending on the local politics, doing so to either facilitate (Borras et al., 2013b) or limit (Murmis and Murmis, 2012; Perrone, 2013, this volume; Wilkinson et al. 2012) land grabbing domestically.

'Global governance' is a term that is widely used to refer to the modern practice of governing transborder problems and to the institutions, rules, actors, and ideologies that govern the global political economy (we include here the social and biophysical). Global governance as an academic concept and field emerged in the 1990s in response to new global-scale problems such as HIV/

AIDs, climate change, and international migration that came to be understood as beyond the capacity of any single nation-state to manage on their own (Roseneau, 1995). The field of global governance was also deeply influenced by shifting power at the global level and its implication for international cooperation; this included at first the fall of the Soviet Union and what this meant for US unipolarity and multilateralism and, more recently, the focus on emerging countries as new players in multilateralism. Today the term global governance is widely used by academics and the general public in a variety of ways and meanings, including reference to the 'practices of governance without government' (Roseneau and Czempiel, 1992); a 'normative goal' (Weiss, 2000); a 'discourse' (Brand, 2005); the inclusion of actors other than nation-states (McKeon, 2009) and the 'institutionalization of the neoliberal globalization project' (Cox, 1993). Like other scholars, we recognize the complexity and contradictions bound up with this term/concept and empirical reality (see Kahler and Lake, 2003; Wilkinson and Hughes, 2002). In our view, a critical approach to global governance is required to make sense of the new global rule-making projects around land grabbing. This includes identifying the actors, interests, and ideologies driving particular governance initiatives but also the international political economy context in which such initiatives arise.

Land and Territoriality

Land at first glance does not easily fit the type of singular issue areas commonly associated with contemporary global governance. Unlike other fields of global governance such as climate change, HIV/AIDs, and terrorism that are framed as global-scale problems that are broadly recognizable as such by the global imagination—climate change with (negative) ecological change, HIV/AIDs with high mortality rates, terrorism with unpredictable violence—land does not slot easily into existing socially constructed categories of a global-scale 'problem'. Unlike earlier moments of world history the contemporary period of world order is one defined by nation-states as the primary forms of political organization. As such, in the current era land and its control have tended to be equated with state practices. This conception of land as integral to sovereign territory and authority is affirmed by most international practices, such as international legal recognition of state borders and territorial authority (i.e. the spatial demarcation of where a state's land and water borders begin and end). In the postcolonial era, land is regarded as a thing belonging to a national state. In general, land has not figured as a significant issue area of global governance with the exceptions of instances of where land is invaded by an occupying force. Land as sovereign territory is a key international norm and framework critical to understanding the politics of global land governance. This particular norm and discourse that the land belongs to the state is especially strong in postcolonial states where the state owns most of the land. Rolf Künnemann and Sofía Monsalve Suárez (2013, this volume) note that land tenure governance regimes in the Global South mirror their colonial antecedents in that they provide the state with far-reaching control over the land. They contend that while contemporary land grabbing may be driven by global economic actors, the importance of national legal frameworks should not be overlooked because these have actually made it easier for states to facilitate land grabbing. Closely related to the argument made by Künnemann and Monsalve Suárez (ibid.), Borras et al. (2013, this volume) explain that states actively facilitate land grabs through a combination of the following tasks that only national governments have absolute authority to perform, namely, (1) 'invention/justification' of the need for large-scale land investments; (2) 'definition, reclassification and quantification' of what is 'marginal, under-utilized and empty' lands; (3) 'identification' of these particular types of land; (4)

'acquisition/appropriation' of these lands; and (5) 'reallocation/disposition' of these lands to investors. Much of what is being grabbed is within the legal-administrative-military control of national states.

The global land grab raises deeper questions about territoriality in the era of advanced economic globalization. In her contribution to this collection, Saskia Sassen (2013, this volume) explains that the global land grab suggests a larger structural transformation at play that is 'producing massive structural holes in the tissue of national sovereign territory'. For Sassen, the global land grab reveals an 'active making of an increasingly large number of partial, often highly specialized, cross-border spaces and arrangements' occurring during a moment of massive systematic change; land is shifting from sovereign national territory to a commodity for the global market. Land is highly demanded by capitalism that is leading to the rapid commodification and financialization of land on a world scale and 're-purposing' of national territory along the lines of the demands and purposes of foreign firms and governments (Sassen, 2013, this volume). This, according to Sassen, does not signal the end of the state but a transformation of the state that is ever more inserting itself into transnational processes that operate according to other (non-national) logics. However, such transformation can be highly destructive to society and citizenship: 'Foreign land acquisitions include vast stretches of national territory articulated through villages, smallholder agriculture, rural manufacturing districts, and through the actors that make these economies and reproduce them—whether or not this is recognized by the state. Much of this politico-structural complexity is today being evicted from that territory due to those acquisitions. At the extreme we might ask what is citizenship when national territory is downgraded to foreign-owned land for plantations and the rest is evicted—floras, faunas, villages, smallholders' (Sassen, 2013, this volume).

In his contribution to this collection, Philip McMichael's (2013, this volume) reading of the global land grab through a 'food regime' lens similarly identifies the global grab as a paradox, where '"re-territorialization" via investment in offshore lands for agro-exporting of food, fuel and bio-economic products, and "de-territorialization" as host states surrender land and water for export to states defined (through market measures or policy) as food-dependent'. Indeed, the global land grab signals a major shift in the global agri-food system because the process of 're-territorialization' is a strategy by certain states and investors 'to avoid dependence on markets, or more particularly, market intermediaries' that he labels as an incipient form of 'security mercantilism' that is overriding the World Trade Organization (WTO)/corporate food regime with a set of bilateral arrangements organized by states and/or sovereign wealth funds (ibid.).

A Short History of Global Land Governance and Structural Changes in the Global Political Economy

The current efforts to construct land grabbing as a sphere of global governance need to be put in the historical context of global land politics. The postwar interstate system dominated by the US actively sought to keep the land question out of formal international governance institutions and practices. This was largely a response to quash leftist and socialist states that sought to create international instruments to reinforce land reform and/or collectivization at home. Land reform, especially the nationalization of privately held lands and land redistribution from elites to peasants/landless poor, has long been a highly ideological and politicized struggle. Land reform was a very contentious issue of international significance during the Cold War. In the 1960s, under the Alliance for Progress, the US supported land reform on a selective basis, providing bilateral assistance to countries where it regarded land reform, if not adequately addressed, would result in communist revolutions. An early effort to establish formal international governance for land took place at the World Conference on Agrarian Reform and Rural Development (WCARRD) convened by FAO in 1979. The aim of this conference was to establish an international framework (in the context of the Cold War) for land reform and rural development. Despite political momentum in advance of the conference, WCARRD was unsuccessful in reaching this objective. As Nora McKeon (2013, this volume) explains, the international land agenda lost further steam, as it fell 'victim in the 1980s to the introduction of structural adjustment and a general disenchantment with agriculture as a motor for development'. Whereas land reform was pulled out of oblivion in the 1990s as part of the World Bank-led implementation of a market-led agrarian reform approach, land had receded in importance for states as an issue requiring international deliberation. It is partly the lack of political progress at the international level to advance social justice-oriented redistributive land policies that eventually led to the conditions that gave birth to the 'Global Campaign for Agrarian Reform' by La Via Campesina and its allies. Launched in 1999 originally as an anti-market-assisted land reform campaign, the campaign later evolved into a more comprehensive agrarian reform agenda (Borras and Franco, 2009). This campaign has contributed to the revival of agrarian reform in the international official agenda, especially at the FAO. In turn, this led to what is essentially a second version of WCARRD, the International Conference on Agrarian Reform and Rural Development (ICARRD) in March 2006, organized by FAO and hosted by the Brazilian government and held in Porto Alegre.

The ICARRD initiative paved the way for states and rural social movements to articulate a new normative basis for future international land governance that included, among others, the recognition of collective land rights and acknowledged the cultural and social dimensions of land (see ICARRD, 2006; McKeon, 2009, 2013, this volume). This event was critical in that it brought land issues back on the official agenda of the FAO's deliberative bodies. Around this time, bilateral and multilateral agencies initiated and passed their own land and development policies, including the European Union (EU) in 2004, the International Food and Agricultural Development (IFAD) in 2009, the Swedish International Development Agency (SIDA) in 2009, and the United Kingdom's Department for International Development (DFID) in 2010. One of the most concrete outcomes of ICARRD has been the decision by the FAO, supported by civil society organizations, to start a process for possible voluntary guidelines on land tenure. However, political consensus on negotiating international rules proved elusive and crawled along until the global land grab (on the heels of the global food crisis) put the negotiations under the global spotlight. As the global land grab became a matter of public knowledge and concern, it provided the political impetus and sense of urgency to move forward on global land governance. The outcome of this was the negotiation and adoption in 2012 of the Voluntary Guidelines in the newly reformed CFS (which is itself an innovative experiment in global governance). Taking the long view, the global land grab proved to be a significant tipping point in the politics of land that has ushered in land governance at the global scale.

Land grabbing also signals shifts in *world order*. Land grabbing already points to a transition towards new world political, economic, and biophysical conditions with the emergence of the BRICs and middle-income countries, global biofuels complex, and green grabbing (McMichael, 2012). Key aspects of this shift include the geographic sites and modes of agricultural production with the Northern grain-based food regime being supplanted with 'the emergence of new players wanting to gain power in terms of reshaping international rules that govern the production, distribution and consumption of food and other closely related commodities embedded within the ongoing reconfiguration of key hubs of global capital' (Borras et al., 2013, this volume). These new players include the BRICS countries, powerful middle-income countries, new OECD countries such as South Korea, and the Gulf states. However, new and old powers pursue different ends through land grabbing. In his contribution to this collection, Eckart Woertz drives home the point that Gulf states are quite different from the other players in contemporary land grabbing because of their unique political economy conditions. They are rentier states highly dependent on imported food and aware of the historical legacy of the failed 1970s pan-Arab breadbasket strategy that involved land grabbing in Sudan and Egypt (Woertz, 2013, this volume). This time around, and also in response to the depth of the global food crisis, Gulf states are creating new institutions to coordinate food security policies and land investments, including a mix of public and private ventures. A key but less well understood phenomenon is the importance of crops and commodities with multiple and flexible uses across food, feed, and biofuel complexes and industrial commodities; much land grabbing is for what Borras et al. (2013, this volume) call the 'flex crops and commodities' sector. A second important aspect is the shift towards multi-polarity evidenced by the replacement of the G8 with the G20 and the ascent of emerging countries in the governance architecture for finance, trade and climate change (see McMichael, 2013; Margulis and Porter, 2013, this volume). As Margulis and Porter argue in their essay, the global land grab cannot be reduced only to core–periphery relations. Even though Chinese activity in land acquisitions in rural Africa display 'asymmetries of power and patterns of exploitation very closely resembling core–periphery relations . . . Chinese land acquisitions in rural Australia are not captured well by a core–periphery label' (Margulis and Porter, 2013, this volume). Indeed the same applies to *land grabbed-land grabbers* such as Brazil and Argentina which are both major players in land acquisitions across South America but are also major targets of foreign land acquisitions (see, Perrone, 2013, this volume; see also Borras et al., 2012a; Galeano, 2012; Murmis and Murmis, 2012; Urioste, 2012). To a certain extent, land grabbing reveals important shifts in global political power but also in production of resources and goods that may be more vital to a future global political economy where the ecological considerations become more paramount.

Governance and Authority

A number of concepts from global governance scholarship are relevant for the study of land grabbing. The first is the concept of *authority* which is closely related to the idea of governance; which actors have authority to regulate a particular sphere of activity? Global governance scholarship has shown that authority has flowed in two principal ways over the past decades that differ from the postwar international system of governance.

First, there has been a *shift of authority delegated from the state to international institutions.* International institutions play a greater role in managing interstate affairs than previously; this is most prominent in the case of the EU, the WTO, and the International Criminal Court (ICC), which can take decisions that are binding on states and constrain a state's policy space. Emerging global land governance at first glance does not appear to involve a formal delegation of land governance from the state to supranational institutions. None of the transnational governance mechanisms—the Voluntary Guidelines or principles for responsible agriculture investment—are taking the form of legally binding international treaties. However, multilateral institutions are the key sites for the new politics of addressing land grabbing. In particular, we can observe different actors enrolling different multilateral institutions to advance alternative objectives. The G8 countries have enrolled the World Bank as their preferred site for the creation and implementation of emergent global land governance. The World Bank's official policy supports large-scale investments in lands as a means of improving agricultural productivity and economic growth that fit well within its new agricultural development strategy that has become the core of its activities since 2008. Simply put, the G8 countries have sought to provide the World Bank with the authority to be the leading agent in this new sphere of governance, and they have continued to provide it with resources and entrust it to manage a spate of new global agricultural development programs. Global civil society and transnational rural movements have instead enrolled the FAO and the CFS to serve as a key arena for emergent global land governance. The FAO and the CFS are global policy spaces that have been much more open to incorporating human rights and exploring food sovereignty as an alternative paradigm for global agricultural policy. The CFS, in particular following the 2008 global food crisis, has been reformed and has taken on a more central role in global agricultural and food policy debates (McKeon, 2011; Margulis, 2012, 2013). For many, including McKeon (2013, this volume) the CFS has filled, partially, a governance gap that existed for transnational political deliberation over food security and rural development. But, the CFS is not the only important arena in which transnational agrarian movements try to construct global governance in their favor. They engage in other strategic undertakings through multilateral institutions, such as the Human Rights Council (HRC) for Via Campesina's advocacy for a UN Peasants' Charter (Edelman and Carwil, 2011).

Global governance scholarship also has examined the *shift of authority to non-state actors*. Non-state actors have taken on governance functions in existing policy fields but also in new areas of activity. The first group includes private actors that play a greater role of governing transnational financial transactions and economic flows often through modes of self-regulation, including the use of standards and benchmarking, as well as private international arbitration of financial and investment deals (Cutler et al., 1999; Hall and Biersteker, 2002). NGOs and transnational social movements too have increased authority in global governance, and this is seen in diverse areas ranging from fair trade labeling and certification to developing industry standards for humanitarian relief to the monitoring and reporting of human rights and environmental abuses. The rise of non-state authority should not be seen as a zero-sum game where states compete with non-state actors for authority in governance. The situation is more nuanced. Many private forms of governance require explicit consent from the state, especially legal approbation of private practices at the national level and for their global operations (Brathwaite and Drahos, 2000). In practice, states always retain some regulatory oversight even if they choose to exercise it lightly. There is also a trend toward hybrid forms of global governance, where even industry-led initiatives involve states and NGOs as stakeholders in governance practices and implementation such as at the International Standards Organization (Clapp, 1998) or the Global Fund for Aids, Tuberculosis and Malaria (Hein and Kohlmorgen, 2008). Non-state actors also exert authority outside of formal global governance arrangements. For example, credit rating agencies' assessment of the state's credit worthiness (i.e. in the form of bond ratings) has a significant influence on the state's financial affairs. Transnational business lobbies also work to influence global rules such as in the creation of the intellectually property rights regime at the WTO (Sell, 2003). NGOs and transnational social movements have contested global economic governance such as mobilizing against the policies of multilateral institutions like the WTO, the World Bank, and the International Monetary Fund, producing what O'Brien et al. (2000) identify as a 'complex multilateralism' whereby multilateral institutions seek to respond to pressure from transnational social movements and other non-state actors.

Transnational social movements and NGOs are highly visible in the politics of emerging global land governance. NGOs were the first to bring the global land grab to public attention (GRAIN, 2008). Moreover, NGOs and transnational agrarian movements were also quick to mobilize transnationally against the global land grab. However, mobilization at the global scale this time around has less to do with organizing mass public protests (as it was in the case against the WTO), but tends to focus on advocacy work in global policy spaces, particularly the CFS. The emphasis on the CFS (in the midst of a relative absence of anti-WTO type of mass mobilizations) is politically relevant, and we argue that NGOs and transnational agrarian movements are contributing to the creation and contesting emergent global land governance (see also Borras and Franco, 2009). McKeon points (2013, this volume) to the importance of the 'reformed' CFS as an open space that was available for transnational agrarian movements and their NGO allies, working through the International Planning Committee (IPC) for Food Sovereignty—today's largest international coalition of rural social movements—to introduce land issues as an item for intergovernmental deliberation at the CFS. According to McKeon (ibid.), '[c]ivil society intervention in the discussions was decisive in obtaining agreement that the Voluntary Guidelines be negotiated within the CFS . . . outcomes were largely attributable to the innovative format of the CFS whereby political decisions are made in plenary sessions in which civil society and social movements are full participants rather than in closed door drafting committees as is normally the case in intergovernmental forums.' The embeddedness of global social movements at the CFS provides a novel experiment in complex multilateralism (see O'Brien et al., 2000).

The participation of global civil society is more than token inclusion; global civil society at the CFS has been relatively successful in advancing its goals and articulating alternative policies that challenge the mainstream policies advanced by the G8 and World Bank. Indeed, the success by global social movements to position the Voluntary Guidelines as a wedge and counter-discourse against the earlier maneuver of the World Bank to place the Principles for Responsible Agricultural Investments (PRAI)—which is essentially a voluntary, corporate self-regulatory instrument—as the centerpiece to regulate land grabbing is indicative of the chessboard politics shaping emergent global land governance (McKeon, 2013, this volume; Margulis and Porter, 2013; this volume).

The heightened presence of global civil society presents its own challenges. At a deeper level is the tension within and between global civil society groups caught between the three political tendencies to governing the land grab identified by Borras et al. (2013, this volume), namely, regulate to facilitate land deals; regulate to mitigate negative impacts and maximize opportunities; and regulate to stop and rollback land grabbing. The position global civil society actors take on this continuum results partly from ideology (i.e. taking an explicit anti-capitalist stance or not), institutional factors (i.e. whether an autonomous coalition of agrarian social movements or a coalition of NGOs, aid donor agencies, and international financial institutions), and differences in strategy and tactics of political work (i.e. dealing with land grabbing in focusing on the 'here and now' issues in specific land cases versus dealing with strategic issues such as the character and orientation of the world's agriculture) (Borras et al., 2013, this volume). These positions are significant because they 'compete with each other in their interpretations of key international governance instruments, how to use these, and for what purposes' and thus the meaning ascribed and how emergent global land governance will be implemented on the ground (ibid.).

Private-sector actors concerned by emergent global land governance were relatively less present than global civil society organizations in the CFS at the outset, but they have engaged increasingly as the political salience of this forum has become more evident, in close alliance with several national delegations to the CFS process. As several authors in this collection note, it is ironic that the initial drive for private self-regulation has been most strongly advanced by the G8 countries and the World Bank but not by private actors themselves (McKeon, 2013, this volume; McMichael, 2013, this volume; Margulis and Porter, 2013, this volume). Indeed, much of the World Bank-proposed PRAI seeks to integrate the numerous transnational private self-regulatory schemes on sustainability (Stephens, 2013, this volume; see also Borras and Franco, 2010). Fortin and Richardson (2013, this volume) argue that private sustainability certifications schemes fall short of providing the protection of land rights its champions suggest. Such schemes cannot ensure sourcing is from poor farmers and that free, prior, and informed consent (FPIC) is respected. In addition, such schemes are not equipped to fully account for intensified competition for land resulting from indirect land-use change (ibid.). Fortin and Richardson suggest that certification schemes do enhance the scrutiny of land deals because of the information made public and through the auditing process provide some leverage to pressure large transnational firms' procurement practices whose brand is closely tied to claims of 'sustainability'. However, they contend certification schemes continue to fall short of providing robust protection of land rights and a pro-poor policy framework to support rural development and livelihoods.

There is already an alliance among the private sector (e.g. World Economic Forum, Bill and Melinda Gates Foundation), the G8, and the World Bank that cooperates in promoting global agricultural development projects. These actors remain highly supportive of promoting private standards and certification as the primarily means to address land grabbing. Even if only some private actors engage in the formal spaces of emergent global land governance, most can choose to operate through backdoor lobbying, aggressive media work to influence governance processes, and low key negotiations especially within other global governance institutions for finance and investment and the World Bank that are less accessible to global civil society (especially the radical elements that now participate in the CFS). In addition, agrifood corporations and large institutional investors engaged in land grabbing can resort to their structural power to advance their agendas (see Clapp and Fuchs, 2009).

Land Grabbing as Struggles for Control Grabbing and Land Authority

We now turn to a discussion about conceptualizing land grabbing. Indeed, one of the central aims of this collection is to explore different approaches to the study of the global land grab from a perspective that takes seriously insights from work on globalization and governance. At the same time, theorization and analysis can be done without complete and perfect information about land grabbing (see discussion on the politics of number below) once we begin to conceive of land grabbing as embedded in wider processes rather than just procedural matters concerning the formal transfer of property rights. Take for example Saskia Sassen's essay in this collection, which argues that land grabs are particularly strong illustrations of the global inserting itself into the local revealing significant contradictions at play; states are simultaneously acting as facilitators of land grabs, which on the one hand is an assertion of national sovereignty, while in the very same instance they are ceding territorial sovereignty (Sassen, 2013, this volume).

For the contributors to this collection land grabbing is marked by *a twofold transnational contest for control over resources and authority over institutions*. Current research has demonstrated that land grabbing reveals a sharp and intensifying global competition for control over land (Peluso and Lund, 2011), including the bundle of productive resources contained in or on the land. This process manifests itself in efforts to control specific pieces of land most visible in the exchange of property rights to a specific piece of land on a permanent or temporary basis. Formal recognition of land control always includes access to a bundle of resources (i.e. water, subsoil minerals, organic and genetic matter, etc.) that may not necessarily be captured in a formalized mode but can affect others' use and access to the productive resources found in or on the land (Ribot, 1998; Ribot and Peluso, 2003; see also Sikor and Lund, 2009).

As such, we follow Borras et al.'s (2012b, p. 405) in framing on land grabbing as *control grabbing,* as follows:

> [C]ontemporary land grabbing is the capturing of control of relatively vast tracts of land and other natural resources through a variety of mechanisms and forms involving large-scale capital that often shifts resource use to that of extraction, whether for international or domestic purposes, as capital's response to the convergence of food, energy and financial crises, climate change mitigation imperatives and demands for resources from newer hubs of global capital.

An accompanying contest can be observed at the level of governance, which is about authority and control of institutions. Land grabbing is making it evident that contests over governance are not limited to the institutions that facilitate specific land deals but in fact are much more expansive and cut across a variety of institutions and practices that go beyond the land registries and the state and extended to transnational actors and global institutions. A distinction we make here with regard to existing work is that the control and authority over land is increasingly deterritorialized by the process of land grabbing. This involves the formal transfer of control to foreign interests, and the increasing interaction among the production practices on the land with other international and transnational governance practices, such as investment, trade, and certification regimes. The latter in turn shape what is produced, how it is produced, and how production moves across borders. Such a diffused concept of authority does not necessarily override national land authority, since states can terminate a lease or sale, however, the fact remains that land control and authority is entangled across various types of governance institutions at multiple scales of which the national is only one part.

The thickening web of governance institutions relevant to a specific land grab will vary considerably, depending on the type of modality of acquisition, commodity type, production process, and final market destination. Two general and interrelated features can be deduced. The first is that the contestation over authority is likely to be more crowded. Investors, states, domestic and global civil society, and transnational, international, and regional institutions are likely to be involved in contesting land control and authority. The second feature is that these contests go beyond the authority over particular pieces of property. The nascent transnational politics of land grabbing points to a more generalized contest over the rules of the global resource accumulation game. However, it is not just rules that are jockeyed over by actors. Control over the norms, discourses, and institutions, as well as specific rules of particular regimes are also being contested. The targeting of global and transnational policy spaces (e.g. FAO, G8/G20, and CFS) by actors positioned across the pro- and anti-land grabbing continuum (see Borras et al., 2013, this volume) illustrates that conflicts over land can occur at vast distances from the land as well as on the spot. It also confirms that such contests over governance and authority at different scales span a range of formal and informal modes of governance. This goes beyond the specific provisions in the Voluntary Guidelines or the World Bank PRAI but a much broader contest over what the global agenda on land grabbing should be about, what the guiding norms and principles should be, the production of legitimizing and delegitimizing discourses and framing which provide the context and meaning for specific rules and governance practices.

Control grabbing and land authority are linked: one cannot happen without the other. For examples, investors cannot make land deals without constant use of international institutions and rules; contemporary land grabbing works through, not against, international and bilateral investment, trade, and development regimes (Künnemann and Monsalve Suárez, 2013, this volume; McMichael, 2013, this volume; Sassen, 2013, this volume). Control grabbing and land authority also make it clear that such transnational contests feature highly asymmetric power relations because actors are endowed with differentiated capacities to create and control governance for land. For example, investors can leverage massive financial resources to acquire land at very favorable terms, can hire the best investment lawyers to draw up contracts that shift the risks on to host states and local peoples, can hire lobbyists and experts to play global rules to their favor, and so on.

The approach to the study of land grabbing and governance offered in this collection takes complexity and indeterminacy as a given. In particular, we recognize that the contestation of specific land deals and local institutions and practices are more likely to be entangled with one another in a more direct way, the overlap of actors much tighter, and developments of such contests to move much more in parallel at the local/national level. Shifting our gaze to the global level, including the manifest global–local interactions and dynamics, means not only that localized land grabs and struggles over global governance are distanced but that the actors will be highly diverse and not necessarily networked or occupy the same global policy spaces. Moreover, global-scale developments are perhaps less likely to move in parallel or interact as directly with events on the ground due to the specific challenges of contesting global governance, including the distance between global rule-making and implementation on the ground, the general underdevelopment of global–local measures to enforce accountability, and the challenge of ensuring cooperation and coordination among highly diverse actors and interests at multiple scales without a centralizing authority. However, these aforementioned challenges are general to other fields of global governance, many of which have been overcome. As such, it is important to remind ourselves that what is in fact occurring through contestation at the local and global levels is the production of new forms of global land governance. This process is highly fluid and the interaction between the local and the global, and the multilayered and multisite contests for control of land and institutions is a key dynamic that is shaping this new field of governance. The novel development is that whereas land contests were more or less understood as localized, these contests are now becoming globalized/globalizing and taking place in a much more congested multiscale terrain of multiple actors, institutions, and frameworks. To sum up, the global land grab is as much about controlling governing institutions as it is about controlling resources. Governance provides a useful additional entry point that brings into focus the contest that is occurring by a myriad of actors to seek control and influence over the institutions that govern land.

The Evolving Terrain of Study

In addition to the themes discussed above, there are developments specific to emerging global land governance that warrant further attention and discussion. These include the complexity of governing land grabbing, terminology and discursive debates, and the politics of numbers and measurement.

Complexity of Global Land Governance

The global governance of land grabbing is marked by a high level of *complexity*. This complexity plays out in several ways. The first is that the phenomenon of land grabbing is itself highly complex and variegated—different types of actors are grabbing land for different reasons in different ways in different countries. As such, there is no 'typical' case of land grabbing (and this is why the concept of control grabbing is a useful conceptualization to organize all this variability). Therefore emergent global land governance at best is targeted to some but not all possible forms of land grabbing. Land is more than a thing (i.e. sovereign territory or a productive economic resource) but inherently multidimensional partly because of its centrality to biophysical and ecological cycles important for human and non-human life. In addition, land has non-material value, for example, when land plays an important role in religious and/or cultural belief systems (see Gentry et al., 2013). The extent to which emergent global land governance can capture the multidimensional character of land is an open question. The peculiar features of 'flex crops and commodities' introduce more complexity from the perspective of potential practices to regulate land grabbing. Flex crops straddle multiple commodity sectors, geographic spaces, and international political economy categories and lead to a blurring of sectoral boundaries and transnational governance mechanisms that 'are generally structured by sector or theme, namely, food, feed, energy/fuel, forestry, climate change mitigation strategies' (Borras et al., 2013, this volume). As a result, flex crops not only make understanding the global land grab a more difficult challenge but this also 'fragments the political space and makes single-issue focus advocacy campaigns more difficult' (ibid.).

The issue of complexity in overlapping and/or competing global governance institutions and instruments is manifested also in two other types of control grabbing, namely, *green grabbing* and *water grabbing*. Grabbing for environmental ends, or green grabbing, is a phenomenon distinct to the contemporary era of land grabbing as much of it has something to do with climate change. The Reducing Emissions through Deforestation and Forest Degradation (REDD) and its successor regime is a fast expanding global policy regime which, under certain circumstances, can lead to enclosure and dispossession (Fairhead et al., 2012) as new schemes such as carbon markets and payment for ecosystem services are integrated into land planning, development, and livelihood policymaking at the international and national level (Corbera and Schroeder, 2011). Meanwhile, Mehta et al. (2012, p. 193) argue that on many occasions, land grabbing is essentially 'water grabbing', which they define, broadly as 'a situation where powerful actors are able to take control of, or reallocate to their own benefits, water resources already used by local communities or feeding aquatic ecosystems on which their livelihoods are based'. In these two types of resource grabbing, global *land* governance shrinks immediately—and a broader lens on governance that incorporates climate change and water governance instruments becomes necessary. Increasingly, therefore, the challenge is twofold: *deepening* and *broadening* our understanding of global land governance.

Thus far emergent global land governance is highly *fluid*. Its development to date has been shaped by its being taken up in very specific sites of global governance, namely the FAO and the World Bank. However, there is no reason to assume that these sites, and the frameworks, logics, and politics specific to each will continue to be the primary conduits for the future development and consolidation of global land governance. Margulis and Porter (2013, this volume) argue that emergent global land governance has developed along a pathway where investment and land tenure policy have dominated the global governance agenda to the exclusion of other considerations. Their essay attempts to peel back the layers of this complexity and they examine the variation across issue areas, the mix of public and private elements, and the mix of local and global elements evident in new global land governance instruments such as the Voluntary Guidelines and the World Bank's PRAI—and the interaction among them. Rather than seeing this complexity as necessarily disabling strategies of resistance by weaker actors to regulate land grabbing, Margulis and Porter (ibid.) suggest that 'smaller and poorer actors will be most successful working through the types of complexity' and 'enrolling transnational actors and networks in efforts to change governance rather than trying to avoid or reverse complexity by focusing more exclusively on solutions at the local level or at the formal intergovernmental level (for instance through treaties)'.

Emergent global land governance may become even more complicated with the appearance of new governance fields on the horizon. In their contributions to this collection, Fortin and Richardson (2013, this volume; see also Goetz, 2013, this volume), explain that the G8, the World Bank, and the corporate agri-food sector favor the inclusion of private standards and certification as part of the global land governance toolbox. International human rights have also gained salience in emergent global land grabbing, not least for the centrality of the right to food in the work of the CFS and in the Voluntary Guidelines. In their contribution to this collection, Rolf Künnemann and Sofía Monsalve Suárez from the Foodfirst Information Action Network (FIAN) suggest that the global land grab may be providing the opportunity for an even bolder human rights approach (see also Claeys and Vanloqueren, 2013, this volume). They argue that there is an important historical opportunity to advance the normative and legal basis for operationalizing the human right to land. They cite the recent and successful experience of global civil society efforts in advancing the international human right to food in the 1990s as evidence of the viability of such an approach. Moreover, they stress the international human right to land must build on recent advances in the understanding of human rights as involving obligations not just for states but also for non-state actors, such as transnational corporations, institutional investors, and multilateral institutions. This is an obligation to protect, respect, and fulfill human rights to fill some of the governance gaps in contemporary international law and postcolonial land regimes that are 'impediments to implementing effective redistributive measures in the Global South and provide a framework for policy reforms conducive towards privatizing and commodifying land' (Künnemann and Monsalve Suárez, 2013, this volume).

All this suggests potential further crowding of emergent global land governance. Such crowding is likely to intensify the already significant asymmetries of power among states, between investors and local peoples, and between states, investors, and global civil society. As such, a strategy for containing or managing emergent global land governance may be desirable. The Künnemann and Monsalve Suárez (ibid.) proposal for the human right to land is a potential organizing principle to address evolving global land governance. However, it is likely that this will be resisted by states and also some civil society actors that see this regime either as unfavorable to their interests or simply too weak. Nevertheless, this suggests that much norm-building and rule-making on global land governance is likely to take place, and be contested, in the years to come.

Terminology and Discursive Debates

In addition to getting a general picture of how much land has been grabbed, it is also important to ask questions about how land grabs are being framed and who is doing the framing. Definitions are useful starting points because they permit for greater analytical precision to the extent it helps simplify for the purpose of research what are very complex processes. At the same time, competing definitions of land grabbing reveal and obscure aspects of the phenomenon, and serve different ends, whether these be academic ends in the sense of shaping a scientific field, or political in the sense of advancing certain political projects. The two can be intertwined.

This tension is most evident in deciding what term to use to label this phenomenon. The use of the term 'large-scale land acquisition' is the most commonly used descriptor. Other commonly used terms in the literature and public discourse include cropland expansion, land grabs, land deals, and the global land rush, to name a few. Each term plays a discursive role. Despite efforts by many actors to present large-scale land acquisitions as a 'descriptive' label, it is important to acknowledge that this term is not a neutral one. The word 'acquire' makes reference only to the actions of those acquiring land and evokes an administrative transaction between those who seek to acquire land and those who give up land. This particular semantic frame can render invisible the existence of, and consequences, for land users, who may not be the party giving up land. The term 'acquisition' is a technical, administrative term. In a lot of ways, wittingly or unwittingly, it depoliticizes contemporary land grabbing. Therefore the term acquisition is part of a legitimizing discourse. This term is especially popular among key policy and governmental actors. This is the term preferred by the World Bank, (inter)governmental institutions, as well as by the International Land Coalition (ILC), which is a coalition of the international financial institutions (World Bank, IFAD), intergovernmental institutions (e.g. FAO), aid donors, and some NGOs (e.g. Oxfam). By comparison, the term land grab evokes something very different. A 'grab', like a 'power grab', suggests an unfair appropriation of something and this is a cogent reminder of the normative power of discourse and framing. More generally, the term 'land grab' evokes the legacy of colonialism and imperialism. The term 'land grabbing' politicizes and historicizes contemporary land grabs. We consciously use the terms 'land grabs' and 'land grabbing' in this collection to remind us that these actions often occur under conditions of highly asymmetric power relations, access to information, and distribution of benefits and costs, and are often linked back to historical legacies of exclusion and dispossession.

Counting Land Grabs and the Politics of Numbers/Measurement

The situation facing anyone engaged in the global land grabbing debate is a lack of sufficient empirical data. While this may be factually true, it is important to situate the debate about data with regard to the politics of numbers and measurements. Numbers are not objective depictions of reality but implicitly involve political judgments about how phenomena should be measured and results interpreted (see, e.g. Alonso and Starr, 1987; Brysk, 1994). Scholars have recently begun to seriously examine the power of numbers and measurement in global and transnational governance (Hansen and Mühlen-Schulte, 2012; Hansen and Porter, 2012). The importance of international benchmarking, credit-rating, and risk-management techniques, all of which depend on highly sophisticated measurements and indices, for policy decisions illustrates the fact that the 'authority attributed to numerical indicators has enabled various forms of communication and governance at a distance in the global political economy, involving state and non-state actors on different levels' (Hansen and Mühlen-Schulte, 2012, p. 456). We observe such politics of numbers and measurement coursing in the policy and academic debates about land grabbing. Numbers play an important role in mediating the creation of land grabbing as a global political and policy issue. We briefly highlight below some of the hotspots of the politics of numbers/measurement in the context of land grabbing.

The most publicized and contested numbers are those of the various projects of quantifying the global land grab. After land grabbing came to international attention in 2008 following the publication of GRAIN's 'Seized!' report, there was a rush by international organizations and global civil society to provide figures. At that stage, apart from the knowledge of some specific land deals, there was little publicly available information. The first generation of reports were published between 2008 and 2010 (e.g. Cotula et al., 2009; GRAIN, 2008; Von Braun and Meinzen-Dick, 2009; World Bank, 2009) with figures on the land acquired varying considerably. Concerns about the accuracy and reliability of the data were frequently cited. Most important, these initial reports had an important symbolic function of ringing the alarm bell: reports communicated to policymakers and publics that land grabs were in fact occurring, land deals were of significant volumes, and that land deals were on a rapid rise across most regions of the world. Thus, the initial reports confirmed land grabbing was a significant global-scale phenomenon and made a strong case for the need for global governance interventions. Once land grabbing was acknowledged as a global problem, a new demand arose for 'better' numbers, especially by states and international organizations reluctant to support the regulation of land grabbing, in order to better inform and guide global policymaking and global civil society actions. This is not at all surprising, since numbers always create demand for more and better numbers.

The political significance of the data, and who produced the data, has become deeply intertwined with the politics of framing and discourse about land grabbing, although these play out in different ways. The fact that land grabbing is a recent development and the state of knowledge about it so limited creates a situation that affords actors engaged in data construction extraordinary influence in shaping the policy debate. It is important to recall that such data collection practices are a time- and resource-intensive process, so only a limited set of actors has the capacity to do this. Partly because of the general opacity of land grabbing, no matter how good any data is, they will always be viewed by some as suspect and unreliable. This makes the quantification of land grabbing a catch-22—there is a demand by powerful actors for high quality data in order to have evidence-based policymaking, while at the same time these actors are aware that data may never meet the standards they expect in order to have reliable evidence. Indeterminacy becomes a structural condition as actors continue to muddle forward in creating governance while hoping for precision but simultaneously reading the data with a large grain of salt.

The politics of numbers is also at play in other ways beyond the quantification of land grabbing. The World Bank has deployed measures to explain the incidence and location of land grabbing. The Bank has argued that land grabbing is happening in countries with weak governance (Deininger, 2011). Citing multiple examples of questionable land deals in Sub-Saharan Africa, the Bank suggests there is a correlation between undesirable land investments and states where institutions and the rule of law are weak (even though a lot of land grabbing occurs where states are 'strong' such as in Brazil and Australia). To make such a claim the Bank is directly referring its own Worldwide Governance Indicators. These indicators face considerable criticism for their accuracy and political bias (Arndt, 2008; Langbein and Knack, 2009; Thomas, 2010; on power/knowledge, see Löwenheim, 2008). However, for policymakers engaged in global land governance, this is a mere footnote because the Bank's expert authority (and the reverence of the G8 and many G20 officials for the World Bank's data producing prowess) ensure its arguments are heard loud and clear. This also works to confirm many policymakers' pre-existing assumptions and biases because many of them share the World Bank's vision of agricultural-led development. This marshaling of the evidence presents a particular policy problem that suggests land grabbing per se is not the problem but weak governance at the national level. It also partly suggests that solutions to the problem need to be directed at beefing up national institutions rather than cross-border regulation.

In short, there is a major push in global policy circles to produce more credible data. While better figures would certainly be welcome, it is important for scholars to contextualize this exercise as primarily a political one. Ultimately, the differences in quantification methods are rooted in the competing definitions of and political positions on regulating land grabbing.

Conclusion

The contemporary wave of land grabbing is a unique world historical event that reveals a nascent shift in the global political economy towards a more polycentric configuration of power and production. What appears on the surface to be rational responses by states and firms to outsource agricultural production in a context of rising prices and uncertainty about supply is in fact much more. The essays in this collection situate land grabbing as symptomatic (and amplifying) of deeper structural changes that feature simultaneously the de-territorialization and commodification of sovereign national territory across much of the globe, and the partial geographical relocation of global agricultural production that includes significant change in what is grown, for what ends, and for whom. These changes are produced (and reproduced) by the emergence of new centers of power and capital that extend beyond the North to include emerging powers such as China and Brazil as well as less mighty but highly significant ones such as Vietnam, Argentina, South Korea, and the Gulf states. This polycentric order is also evident in the multi-directionality of contemporary land grabbing by states and firms that travel in North–South, South–North, North–North, and South–South directions. The massive shifts in power and production that are driving contemporary land grabbing are thus far flowing through the architecture of advanced neoliberal globalization. Whereas contemporary land grabbing is driven by diverging logics, such as the commodification of land and/or 'security mercantilism' that may have illiberal ends, today's grabs are facilitated by the institutions and practices of neoliberal globalization (i.e. liberalized international investment, finance, and trade regimes, and going forward with sustainability regimes).

The global land grab has catalyzed emergent global land governance. This is an extraordinary development in the historical trajectory and practice of land politics and governance with the explicit reframing of land as a governance issue *at the global scale*. As a result, land governance practices are being reconfigured to recognize and address the interaction between localized and transnational forms of authority. This, of course, has long been a social reality and lived experience for those on the land even if earlier global governance did not always reflect this reality. The most concrete element of emergent global land governance is the new Voluntary Guidelines on land tenure that articulate this global/local nexus. However, by no means do the Voluntary Guidelines capture the full spectrum and diversity of actors, institutions, and practices active and relevant to land. Instead, the Voluntary Guidelines need to be contextualized as the first but not necessarily final word on global land governance.

It is remarkable that land grabbing is prompting contestation largely *within* the global governance institutions rather than outside them. 'Global' issues often have a slow journey of being transformed from local problems to ones of universal relevance. The contestation of land grabbing was immediately recognized as a global-scale challenge. This reading was evident with the G8/G20's inclusion of land grabbing as an issue of global relevance and emphasis placed on land grabbing during the negotiaton of the Voluntary Guidelines in the CFS. As a result, there has been a fairly rapid consensus for global rule-making projects on land (even if there are competing views on the objectives and goals of such projects). The changing terrain of the contestation of land grabbing at the global scale is notable with radical transnational social movements being present and active in global governance of land grabbing from the get-go. Even if one acknowledges that the CFS is only one of the relevant institutions in emerging global land governance, and its authority to make binding rules may be very limited, the manner in which the CFS has taken on the status of a central institution for global deliberation on land governance and the openness of its policy space to social movements are remarkable. This is now acknowledged by the increasing presence of and serious engagement by powerful actors—states and the private sector alike. It may be too early to claim what the long-term significance of the CFS is for 'democratizing' global governance but the content of its work program does suggest that it is unlikely to be a body that will simply rubber stamp the preferences of the most powerful actors. Thus, the CFS's work on land grabbing is likely to contribute to making highly visible and public the political contests for control over land and authority over institutions. It may prove fertile ground for novel experiments to enhance the quality of deliberation, transparency, and legitimacy of global governance around a highly dynamic and explosive issue within a significantly inclusive and diverse setting of actors holding a wide spectrum of political ideologies and goals. In the end, the impact of its global policy decisions will depend in large part on the degree to which they constitute reference points for social movement mobilization and are brought to bear on policies and legislation at national level, an object for future research.

Contemporary global land governance is at an embryonic phase with its future contours not yet discernible. Whereas the Voluntary Guidelines may provide the foundations for a progressive transnational framework for land tenure and rights, there is no reason to assume that future global land governance will develop along these lines. Given the broad shifts in power and production in the global political economy, and the rising tensions this is producing in other areas of global governance such as the WTO and UN climate change talks, we should not necessarily expect global land governance to continue to develop smoothly or in the same manner or form as previous global rule-making projects in other fields. What is clear is that the dynamics of contestation will be important in shaping future global land governance. We expect that future outcomes may be highly determined by the degree to which contestation of global land governance comes to grips with the complexity of land grabbing.

First, our reading is that the prominence of 'flex crops and commodities' in the global land grab suggests that public/private crop-specific sustainability/certification regimes and single-issue transnational advocacy campaigns are insufficient strategies. Yet it is recognized that sustainability/certification schemes are presently *de rigueur* in contemporary governance and such instruments and practices continue to have significant support among many powerful and influential actors across states, the private sector, global civil society, and international organizations. As such, how the contestation of land grabbing can shift the terrain of debate beyond sustainability/certification schemes (or not) will be a critical juncture in the development of global land governance. We expect such political struggles will be galvanized in the upcoming transnational negotiations over responsible agricultural investment in the CFS.

Second, the contestation for control of institutions may not likely remain confined to the present focal points of global political interactions, that is, the CFS (and the FAO where global social movements are most included). As several of the contributions to the collection emphasize, land grabbing encompasses a much broader form of dispossession than access to land—it is deeply tied to financialization of the global economy, changing national policies and patterns of world trade, and to ecological crises, all of which themselves manifest as domains of contested global governance. Therefore, we suspect that the broadening and deepening of global land governance beyond its present agriculture and food security anchoring is inevitable in the future. This suggests to us that even more difficulties will present themselves in the future because there is no framing that would be broadly accepted by all actors to bridge these multiple contested domains.

Acknowledgements

We would like to express our appreciation to Barry Gills for his encouragement and support to pursue this project. We thank the authors for committing and contributing their ideas and time to produce the original essays in this collection. We also wish to recognize the efforts of all the peer reviewers who contributed invaluable feedback that strengthened the quality of this collection.

References

Alden Wily, E. (2012) Looking back to see forward: the legal niceties of land theft in land rushes, *Journal of Peasant Studies*, 39(3–4), pp. 751–775.

Allan, J. A., Keulertz, M., Sojamo, S. & Warner, J. (2012) *Handbook of Land and Water Grabs in Africa: Foreign Direct Investment and Food and Water Security* (Milton Park & New York: Routledge).

Alonso, W. & Starr, P. (1987) *The Politics of Numbers* (New York: Russell Sage Foundation).

Araghi, F. & Karides, M. (2012) Land dispossession and global crisis: Introduction to the special section on land rights in the world-system, *Journal of World-Systems Research*, 18(1), pp. 1–5.

Arndt, C. (2008) The politics of governance ratings, *International Public Management Journal*, 11(3), pp. 275–297.

Behrman, J., Meinzen-Dick, R. & Quisumbing, A. (2012) The gender implications of large-scale land deals, *Journal of Peasant Studies*, 39(1), pp. 49–79.

Borras, S. M. & Franco, J. C. (2009) Transnational agrarian movements struggling for land and citizenship Rights, *IDS Working Paper* 323, pp. 1–44 (Brighton: Institute for Development Studies).

Borras, S. M & Franco, J. C. (2010) From threat to opportunity? Problems with the idea of a 'Code of Conduct' for land grabbing, *Yale Human Rights & Development Law Journal*, 13(1), pp. 507–523.

Borras, S. M. & Franco, J. C. (2011) Political dynamics of land grabbing in Southeast Asia: understanding Europe's role, Discussion Paper (Amsterdam: Transnational Institute).

Borras, S. M., Franco, J. C., Gomez, S., Kay, C. & Spoor, M (2012a) Land grabbing in Latin America and the Caribbean, *Journal of Peasant Studies*, 39(3–4), pp. 845–872.

Borras, S. M., Franco, J. C. & Wang, C. (2013) The challenge of global governance of land grabbing: changing international agricultural context and competing political views and strategies, *Globalizations*, 10(1), pp. 00–00.

Borras, S. M., Gomez, S., Kay, C. & Wilkinson, J. (2012b) Land grabbing and global capitalist accumulation: key features in Latin America, *Canadian Journal of Development Studies*, 33(4), pp. 402–416.

Borras, S. M., Hall, R., Scoones, I., White, B. & Wolford, W. (forthcoming) Governing global land deals: the role of the state in the rush for land, *Development & Change*.

Braithwaite, J. & Drahos, P. (2000) *Global Business Regulation* (Cambridge: Cambridge University Press).

Brand, U. (2005) Order and regulation: global governance as a hegemonic discourse of international politics? *Review of International Political Economy*, 12(1), pp. 155–176.

Brysk, A. (1994) The politics of measurement: the contested count of the disappeared in Argentina, *Human Rights Quarterly*, 16(4), pp. 676–692.

Cashore, B. (2002) Legitimacy and the privatization of environmental governance: how non-state market-driven (NSMD) governance systems gain rule-making authority, *Governance*, 15(4), pp. 503–529.

Chu, J. (2011) Gender and 'Land Grabbing' in Sub-Saharan Africa: Women's land rights and customary land tenure, *Development*, 54(1), pp. 35–39.

Claeys, P. & Vanloqueren, G. (2013) The minimum human rights principles applicable to large-scale land acquisitions or leases, *Globalizations*, 10(1), pp. 193–198.

Clapp, J. (1998) The privatization of global environmental governance: ISO 14000 and the developing world, *Global Governance*, 4(3), pp. 295–316.

Clapp, J. & Fuchs, D. A. (2009) *Corporate Power in Global Agrifood Governance* (Cambridge, MA: Massachusetts Institute of Technology Press).

Corbera, E. & Schroeder, H. (2011) Governing and implementing REDD+, *Environmental Science and Policy*, 14(2), pp. 89–99.

Cotula, L. (2012) The international political economy of the global land rush: a critical appraisal of trends, scale, geography and drivers, *Journal of Peasant Studies*, 39(3&4), pp. 649–680.

Cotula, L., Vermeulen, S., Leonard, R. & Keeley, J. (2009) *Land Grab or Development Opportunity? Agricultural Investment and International Land Deals in Africa* (London: International Institute for Environment and Development).

Cox, R. W. (1993) Gramsci, hegemony and international relations: an essay in method, in S. H. Gill (ed.) *Gramsci, Historical Materialism and International Relations* (Cambridge: Cambridge University Press), pp. 49–67.

Cutler, A. C., Haufler, V. & Porter, T. (1999) *Private Authority and International Affairs* (Albany, NY: State University of New York Press).

De Schutter, O. (2011) How not to think of land-grabbing: three critiques of large-scale investments in farmland, *Journal of Peasant Studies*, 38(2), pp. 249–279.

Deininger, K. (2011) Challenges posed by the new wave of farmland investment, *Journal of Peasant Studies*, 38(2), pp. 217–247.

Edelman, M. & Carwil, J. (2011) Peasants' rights and the UN system: Quixotic struggle? Or emancipatory idea whose time has come? *Journal of Peasant Studies*, 39(1), pp. 81–108.

Fairhead, J., Leach, M. & Scoones, I. (2012) Green grabbing: a new appropriation of nature? *Journal of Peasant Studies*, 39(2), pp. 237–261.

Fortin, E. & Richardson, B. (2013) Certification schemes and the governance of land: Enforcing standards or enabling scrutiny? *Globalizations*, 10(1), pp. 00–00.

Friis, C. & Reenberg, A. (2010) Land grab in Africa: Emerging land system drivers in a teleconnected world, GLP Report No. 1 (Copenhagen: GLP-IPO).

Galeano, L. (2012) Paraguay and the expansion of the Brazilian and Argentinian agribusiness frontiers, *Canadian Journal of Development Studies*, 33(4), pp. 458–470.

Gentry, B. S., Sikor, T., Auld, G., Bebbington, A. J., Benjaminsen, T. A., Hunsberger, C. A., Izac, A. M., Margulis, M. E., Plieninger, T., Schroeder, H. & Upton, C. (2013) Changes in land governance in an urban era, in K. C. Seto & A. Reenberg (eds) *Rethinking Global Land Use in an Urban Era* (Cambridge, MA: MIT Press).

Goetz, G. (2103) Private governance land grabbing: the Equator Principles and the Roundtable on Sustainable Biofuels, *Globalizations*, 10(1), pp. 00–00.

GRAIN (2008) Seized! The 2008 land grab for food and financial security, Grain Briefing (Barcelona: GRAIN).

Hall, R. B. & Biersteker, T. J. (2002) *The Emergence of Private Authority in Global Governance* (Cambridge: Cambridge University Press).

Hansen, H. K. & Mühlen-Schulte, S. (2012) The power of numbers in global governance, *Journal of International Relations and Development*, 15(4), pp. 455–465.

Hansen, H. K. & Porter, T. (2012) What do numbers do in transnational governance? *International Political Sociology*, 6(4), pp. 409–426.

Hein, W. & Kohlmorgen, L. (2008) Global health governance conflicts on global social rights, *Global Social Policy*, 8(1), pp. 80–108.

ICARRD (2006) Final Declaration of the International Conference on Agrarian Reform and Rural Development, http://www.icarrd.org/news_down/C2006_Decl_en.doc.

Kahler, M. & Lake, D. A. (eds) (2003) *Governance in a Global Economy: Political Authority in Transition* (Princeton, NJ: Princeton University Press).

Künnemann, R. & Monsalve Suárez, S. (2013) International human rights and governing land grabbing: a view from global civil society, *Globalizations*, 10(1), pp. 00–00.

Langbein, L. & Knack, S. (2009) The Worldwide Governance Indicators: Six, one, or none? *Journal of Development Studies*, 46(2), pp. 350–370.

Li, T. M. (2011) Centering labor in the land grab debate, *Journal of Peasant Studies*, 38(2), pp. 281–298.

Löwenheim, O. (2008) Examining the state: a Foucauldian perspective on international 'governance indicators', *Third World Quarterly*, 29(2), pp. 255–274.

McKeon, N. (2009) *The United Nations and Civil Society: Legitimating Global Governance—Whose Voice?* (London: Zed).

McKeon, N. (2011) *Global Governance for World Food Security: A Scorecard Four Years after the Eruption of the 'Food Crisis'* (Berlin: Heinrich-Boll-Stiftung).

McKeon, N. (2013) 'One does not sell the land upon which the people walk': land grabbing, rural social movements, and global governance, *Globalizations*, 10(1), pp. 00–00.

McMichael, P. D. (2012) The land grab and corporate food regime restructuring, *Journal of Peasant Studies*, 39(3&4), pp. 681–701.

McMichael, P. D. (2013) Land grabbing as security mercantilism in international relations, *Globalizations*, 10(1), pp. 00–00.

Margulis, M. E. (2012) Global food security governance: the Committee on World Food Security, Comprehensive Framework for Action and the G8/G20, in R. Rayfuse & N. Weisfelt (eds) *The Challenge of Food Security: International Policy and Regulatory Frameworks* (Cheltenham, UK: Edward Elgar), pp. 231–254.

Margulis, M. E. (2013) The regime complex for food security: implications for the global hunger challenge, *Global Governance*, 19(1), pp. 53–67.

Margulis, M. E. & Porter, T. (2013) Governing the global land grab: multipolarity, ideas, and complexity in transnational governance, *Globalizations*, 10(1), pp. 00–00.

Mehta, L., van Veldwisch, G. & Franco, J. C. (2012) Introduction to the special issue: water grabbing? Focus on the (re)appropriation of finite water resources, *Water Alternatives*, 5(2), pp. 193–207.

Murmis, M. & Murmis, M. R. (2012) Land concentration and foreign land ownership in Argentina in the context of global land grabbing, *Canadian Journal of Development Studies*, 33(4), pp. 490–508.

O'Brien, R., Goetz, A. M., Scholte, J. A. & Williams, M. (2000) *Contesting Global Governance: Multilateral Economic Institutions and Global Social Movements* (Cambridge, UK: Cambridge University Press).

Oxfam (2012), Land and power: the growing scandal surrounding the new wave of investments in land, http://www.oxfam.org/sites/www.oxfam.org/files/bp151-land-power-rightsacquisitions-220911-en.pdf.

Peluso, N. L. & Lund, C. (2011) New frontiers of land control, *Journal of Peasant Studies*, 38(4), pp. 667–681.

Perrone, N. M (2013) Restrictions to foreign acquisitions of agricultural land in Argentina and Brazil, *Globalizations*, 10(1), pp. 00–00.

Ribot, J. C. (1998) Theorizing access: forest profits along Senegal's Charcoal Commodity Chain, *Development and Change*, 29(2), pp. 307–341.

Ribot, J. C. & Peluso, N. L. (2003) A theory of access, *Rural Sociology*, 68(2), pp. 153–181.

Robertson, B. & Pinstrup-Andersen, P. (2010) Global land acquisition: neo-colonialism or development opportunity? *Food Security*, 2(3), pp. 271–283.

Rosenau, J. N. (1995) Governance in the twenty-first century, *Global Governance*, 1(1), pp. 13–43.

Rosenau, J. N. & Czempiel, E. O. (eds) (1992) *Governance Without Government: Order and Change in World Politics* (Cambridge: Cambridge University Press).

Rosset, P. (2011) Food sovereignty and alternative paradigms to confront land grabbing and the food and climate crises, *Development*, 54(1), pp. 21–30.

Sassen, S. (2006) *Territory, Authority, Rights: From Medieval to Global Assemblages* (Princeton, NJ: Princeton University Press).

Sassen, S. (2010) A savage sorting of winners and losers: contemporary versions of primitive accumulation, *Globalizations*, 7(1–2), pp. 23–50.

Sassen, S. (2013) Land grabs today: feeding the disassembling of national territory, *Globalizations*, 10(1), pp. 00–00.

Sell, S. K. (2003) *Private Power, Public Law: The Globalization of Intellectual Property Rights* (Cambridge: Cambridge University Press).

Seufert, P. (2013) The FAO Voluntary Guidelines on the Responsible Governance of Tenure of Land, Fisheries and Forests, *Globalizations*, 10(1), pp. 00–00.

Sikor, T. & Lund, C. (2009) Access and property: a question of power and authority, *Development and Change*, 40(1), pp. 1–22.

Stephens, P. (2013) The Principles for Responsible Agricultural Investment, *Globalizations*, 10(1), pp. 00–00.

Thomas, M. A. (2010) What do the Worldwide Governance Indicators measure?, *European Journal of Development Research*, 22(1), pp. 31–54.

Urioste, M. (2012) Concentration and 'foreignization' of land in Bolivia, *Canadian Journal of Development Studies*, 33(4), pp. 439–457.

Visser, O. & Spoor, M. (2011) Land grabbing in post-Soviet Eurasia: the world's agricultural land reserves at stake, *Journal of Peasant Studies*, 38(2), pp. 299–323.

Von Braun, J. & Meinzen-Dick, R. (2009), 'Land grabbing' by foreign investors in developing countries: risks and opportunities, IFPRI Policy Brief 13 (Washington DC: International Food Political Research Institute).

Weiss, T. G. (2000) Governance, good governance and global governance: conceptual and actual challenges, *Third World Quarterly*, 21(5), pp. 795–814.

Wilkinson, J., Reydon, B. & di Sabbato, A. (2012) Concentration and foreign ownership of land in Brazil in the context of global land grabbing phenomenon, *Canadian Journal of Development Studies*, 33(4), pp. 417–438.

Wilkinson, R. & Hughes, S. (2002) *Global Governance: Critical Perspectives* (New York: Routledge).

White, B., Borras, S. M, Hall, R., Scoones, I. & Wolford, W. (2012) The new enclosures: critical perspectives on corporate land deals, *Journal of Peasant Studies*, 39(3&4), pp. 619–647.

Woertz, E. (2013) The governance of Gulf agro-investments, *Globalizations*, 10(1), pp. 00–00.

Wolford, W., Borras, S. M., Hall, R., Scoones, I. & White, B. (forthcoming) Governing global land deals: the role of the state in the rush for land, *Development and Change*.

World Bank (2009) *Large-scale Acquisition of Land Rights for Agricultural or Natural Resource-based Use* (Washington, DC: World Bank).

World Bank (2010) *Rising Global Interest in Farmland: Can It Yield Sustainable and Equitable Results?* (Washington, DC: World Bank).

Zoomers, A. (2010) Globalisation and the foreignisation of space: seven processes driving the current land grab, *Journal of Peasant Studies*, 37(2), pp. 429–447.

Matias E. Margulis is Assistant Professor of International Studies at the University of Northern British Columbia and a postdoctoral fellow at the Max Planck Institute for the Study of Societies. He is currently writing a book on the global politics of international trade and food security. He is a former Canadian trade policy advisor and has worked on global food security policy at several multilateral organizations.

Nora McKeon studied history at Harvard and political science at the Sorbonne before joining the Food and Agriculture Organization (FAO) of the United Nations where she became responsible for the overall direction of FAO's policy and program interaction with civil society. She now divides her time between research, teaching, and activism around food systems, peasant farmer movements, and UN–civil society relations. She is the author of *Peasant Organizations in Theory and Practice* (with Michael Watts and Wendy Wolford, UNRISD, 2004), *The United Nations and Civil Society: Legitimating Global Governance—Whose Voice?* (Zed, 2009), and *Global Governance for World Food Security* (Heinrich-Boll Foundation, 2011).

Saturnino M. Borras, Jr is Associate Professor at the International Institute of Social Studies (ISS) in The Hague, a fellow of the Transnational Institute (TNI) and Food First, and Adjunct Professor at the College of Humanities and Development (COHD) of China Agricultural University (CAU) in Beijing. He is co-coordinator of the Land Deal Politics Initiatives (LDPI; http://www.iss.nl/ldpi) which is an international network of academics doing research on global land grabbing. He is co-editor, together with Marc Edelman and Cristobal Kay, of the book *Transnational Agrarian Movements Confronting Globalization* (Wiley-Blackwell, 2008).

Land Grabs Today: Feeding the Disassembling of National Territory

SASKIA SASSEN

Columbia University, NY, USA

ABSTRACT   *This essay focuses on the larger assemblage of elements that promoted and facilitated the sharp increase in foreign land acquisitions by governments and firms since 2006. The concern is not to document the empirics of foreign land acquisition. Conceptually the essay negotiates between the specifics of the current phase of land acquisitions, on the one hand, and, on the other, the assemblage of practices, norms, and shifting jurisdictions within which those acquisitions take place. This assemblage of diverse elements does not present itself explicitly as governance. But I argue it is a type of governance embedded in larger structural processes shaping our global modernity; in fact, it may have had deeper effects on the current phase of land acquisitions than some of the explicit governance instruments for regulating land acquisitions. This mode of analysis is based on the conceptual and methodological work I developed in my book,* Territory, Authority, Rights *(Sassen, 2008); put succinctly it proposes that to explain the x (in this case, foreign land acquisitions) requires a focus on the non-x (in this case, that larger assemblage of elements that amounts to a structural enablement and embedded governance). This deeper structural level is also what makes the current phase of land acquisitions potentially deeply consequential, to the point of signaling the further disassembling of national territory. Such disassembling can enable the rise of a new type of global geopolitics, one where national sovereign territory increasingly is subject to non-national systems of authority—from familiar IMF and WTO conditionality to elementary controls by diverse foreign actors over growing stretches of a country's land.*

Introduction

The acquisition of land by foreign governments and foreign firms is a centuries' old process in much of the world. But we can detect specific phases in these long and diverse histories. One large-scale phase is the shift in the meaning and the modes of such land acquisitions by foreign actors once the world was mostly, though not completely divided into putatively independent nation-states. States resisted at times, including the US in the 1970s when it passed legislation preventing foreign investors aiming to buy land in the American Midwest from doing so; at that time these were mostly from the Gulf states and Europe, who had up till then bought mostly firms, hotels, office buildings, Hollywood cinema studios, and more.

In this essay I focus on the most recent phase in this long history: the rapid and sharp increase in foreign land acquisitions that took off in 2006 (what has come to be known as the global land grab). While this can be seen merely as a continuation of an old practice, the available evidence (Anseeuw et al., 2012b; Borras et al., 2011; Cotula, 2011; Deininger et al., 2011; De Schutter, 2011, p. 257; FAO, 2011; Land Matrix, 2012; UNTCAD, 2009) points to significant change in the curve describing the size of overall acquisitions. From 2006 to 2010 over 70 million hectares of land were bought or leased for which we can establish both buyers and sellers; this figure jumps to over 200 million hectares if we consider only reported sales (Anseeuw et al., 2012b; Cotula, 2011; Land Matrix, 2012; see Margulis et al., 2013, this volume). What concerns me here is this sharp change in the curve of acquisitions: it points to a break in a long-term trend that might indicate a larger structural transformation in an old practice. Analytically, and in terms of this essay, I see this sharp rise as of 2006 as more significant to understand the current period than the long-term trend towards acquiring foreign land, e.g. Japan's acquisitions of land in Asia and Brazil beginning in the 1960s (see Sassen, 1991, chapter 4) or older imperial histories of land appropriation. From a substantive historical perspective, this long history is enormously important from many different angles, an issue I address at length elsewhere (Sassen, 2008, see chapters 3 and 4).

My aim here is to situate this sharp growth of foreign land acquisitions in a larger context. The aim is not to document the fact itself of land acquisitions, a subject that has received much attention in the last few years with excellent critical and empirical studies (e.g. besides those already cited, see the recent special issues of the *Journal of Peasant Studies*) and I examine at great length elsewhere (Sassen, 2013). Nor is the aim to document the reasons behind foreign land acquisition. It is a well-known and generally accepted fact that the key reason for this growth is rapid development in several parts of the world and ongoing demand from highly developed countries (e.g. Land Matrix, 2012). The larger context within which this growth takes place is characterized by changes in the global economy and in financial markets, and, at a deeper level, changes in the larger interstate system, still the basic frame for cross-border transactions. Further, the financializing of commodities has brought new potentials for profit-making to the primary sector, from food to minerals and metals, thus stimulating speculative investments in land.

The organizing proposition for my inquiry here is that the assemblage of practices, norms, technologies, and shifting jurisdictions within which both the financial crisis and rise in land acquisitions take place all point to a deep disjuncture. It is that the simultaneous privatizing and globalizing of market economies is producing massive structural holes in the tissue of national sovereign territory. And one instance is, precisely, that of massive foreign land acquisitions that re-purpose that acquired land for their own aims. This also brings with it a shift of that acquired land from 'national sovereign territory' to the commodity 'land' for the global market. In other words, a weakening of a complex category that *at its best* brought with it a formal enabling of the state's authority and inhabitants' rights to make the state accountable (Sassen, 2008). The issue here is not one of nationalism versus globalism, but one of complexity: where once there was a prospect of democratic decision-making, now there is an expansion of opaque transnational networks that control the land.

The Partial Disassembling of National Territory

Land, broadly understood, has become one of the major new needs of advanced capitalism—for food and industrial crops, for underground water tables, for traditional and new types of mining. I use the term traditional economies here to refer to smallholder economies, and generally the absence of financialized commodification and of corporatization; thus I do not include 100-years-old plantations, even if they are old. Clearly these definitions of 'traditional' economies are approximations to complex and mixed realities, subjects I addressed in earlier work (e.g. Sassen, 1988) and more recently (Sassen, 2010). At a time of extreme financialization and systemic transformation, the growing demand for those material resources has ascended in importance and visibility, and has stimulated their financializing.

This demand and what it takes to fulfill it, is part of the systemic deepening of the current phase of capitalism. It comes down to an expansion of the operational space for advanced capitalism through the expulsion of people from a range of institutional settings in both the Global South and North, with specific modalities in each (Sassen, 2013). The sharp increases in displaced peoples, poverty, illnesses that kill even though curable, are part of this new phase; they are not anomalies. So is the widespread hunger and starvation even though there is plenty of food produced. Nor are these types of juxtapositions new. They have happened in other phases of the development of capitalist economies.

One specificity of the current era that matters to my analysis here is the formal apparatus through which land acquisitions take place, and, secondly, the fact that the context is one where most of the world is organized into *formally* sovereign nation-states. Formal sovereignty can easily coexist with coloniality, that is, post-historic colonialism (e.g. Maldonado-Torres, 2007; Mignolo, 2007; Quijano, 2000, 2007; see also Frank, 1971; Bravo, 2011). Yet formal sovereignty here helps make visible the substantive assemblage of elements that need to come together in order to execute some of these large-scale acquisitions of land in a foreign country. In considering formal sovereignty on its terms, I can trace the transformations that need to take place in order for these acquisitions and associated investments to be negotiated by foreign parties and a national government. It helps me recover the work of acquiring large amounts of land in a foreign country.

In my reading, this can easily lead to a shift from sovereign national territory to land. One way of conceiving of this shift is as a partial and specialized reassembling of bits and pieces of territory, authority, and rights once ensconced in the formation that is the nation-state, which now begin to shift towards a novel formation. The massive increase in land acquisitions by foreign buyers/leasers after 2006 is one such reassembling of bits once fully part of national sovereign territory. It is, then, also an accelerated disassembling of national sovereign territory. And it is an instance of what I refer to as the endogenizing of the global into the national—in this case, a very material and visible one.

If the global is in good part constituted inside the national, as I argue, then globalization in its many different forms directly engages a key assumption in the social sciences and far beyond, including international relations, diplomacy, media, and more: The implied correspondence of national territory and national institutions with the national, including national sovereign territory. That is to say, if a process or condition is located in a national institution or in national territory, it must be national. This assumption describes conditions that have held, albeit never fully, throughout much of the history of the modern state, especially since World War I, when the modern secular state achieves its most developed form; to some variable extent, it has continued to be such well into the global era that took off in the 1980s. But by the end of the 1990s, with the neoliberal project thoroughly installed in a large part of the world, these conditions—the correspondence of national territory and national institutions with the national—began to be actively unbundled. This active unbundling does not mean that nation-states disappear. Rather, I argue, we see emergent denationalization processes that are part of the formation of the global. In the case of the post-2006 foreign land acquisitions, it is their scale and the unequal power of the actors involved that can be interpreted as an accelerated denationalization of national territory.

Thus the fact that a process or entity is located within the territory of a sovereign state and encased in national policies and institutions does not necessarily mean it is a national process or entity, nor that it can be assumed to be encompassed by national sovereign territory. Today it is an empirical question. While most such entities and processes are likely to be national, we need empirical research to establish whether it is for a growing range of localizations of the global and, perhaps more difficult to establish, for components of the global that are becoming endogenous to the national. Much of what we continue to code as national today may well be a sufficiently transformed condition to barely qualify as national—the national here understood as a historically constructed condition. Developing the theoretical and empirical specifications that allow us to accommodate such conditions is a difficult and collective effort. Again, I think of large-scale foreign land acquisitions as having a particularly strong capacity to make the global endogenous to the national; it does so in the form of widening structural holes in the tissue of national sovereign territory.

The larger conceptual landscape within which the specifics of this article need to be situated is the active *making* of an increasingly large number of partial, often highly specialized, cross-border spaces and arrangements. The International Monetary Fund (IMF) and World Bank restructuring programs launched in the 1980s are an early instance of this. These programs take on new and expanded forms through the IMF conditionalities and later the World Trade Organization (WTO) rules launched in 1995 to secure open borders for global firms and privatization of erstwhile public sectors (see also McMichael, 2013, this volume). These types of arrangements disassemble particular components of the nation-state and of the formal state apparatus from the inside. In this process, also, lie the elements for enabling national actors, including governments, to operate in global spaces. These operations have mostly been guided by narrow economic and geopolitical interests, resulting in negative outcomes for much of the world's population in both so-called rich and poor countries, and some fast movers in between. Nonetheless, there have also been some promising initiatives aimed at the global common good, such as the International Criminal Court (ICC) and less formalized global civil society initiatives; these lack power but they matter because they point to the feasibility of common-good global governing (see also McKeon, 2013, this volume).

Neither the proliferation of these partial assemblages nor the denationalizing of key components of the national necessarily entails the end of national states. In fact, in my reading of the evidence (e.g. Sassen, 2008, chapters 4 and 5), the national state, most particularly the executive branch of government, has played a significant role in the development of the current global corporate economy. But that proliferation and denationalizing do dislodge bits and pieces of national and interstate governance out of their traditional institutional settings (whether national or international) and shift them to novel settings.[1] The case of massive foreign land acquisitions is a particularly material and visible instance of this dislodging of traditional government functions, a process which today mostly takes more elusive, though powerful, forms; for instance, the installing of a private interest in national law, making it appear as a public-interest norm in old or new national law, such as has happened with finance (Sassen, 2008, chapter 5).

These novel assemblages capture partial, often highly specialized, elements of diffuse national orders and reorient them to particular utilities and purposes. The vast foreign land acquisitions illustrate a range of such reorientations, including: growing food for a foreign country's vastly expanded middle classes, access to abundant water supplies for manufacturers of mass-consumption sodas, developing palm plantations for making biofuels, and the constructing of large ports and roads to access minerals. What was once part of national sovereign territory is increasingly repurposed for a foreign firm or government.

More generically, but still including the case of massive foreign land acquisitions, these cross-border systems amount to particularized assemblages of bits of territory, authority, and rights that used to be part of more diffuse institutional domains *within* the nation-state and the traditional supranational system. The tendency is toward a mixing of constitutive rules once solidly lodged in the nation-state project. They can privatize what was once public regulation, as is the case with the Lex Constructionis, or they can constitute jurisdictions that cut across the borders of nation-states, as is the case with the ICC and with WTO's Agreement on Trade-Related Intellectual Property Rights (TRIPS). The case of massive foreign land acquisitions includes both of these.

Their emergence and proliferation have consequences even though this is a partial, not an all-encompassing development. They are potentially profoundly unsettling of what are still the prevalent institutional arrangements—nation-states and the supranational system. They promote a multiplication of diverse spatiotemporal framings and diverse normative orders where once the dominant logic was toward producing unitary national spatial, temporal, and normative framings. The concern here is not to protect these systems, but that these are now among the few that provide some protections and legal grounds for claim-making to those without power and at risk of losing the little they have. Again, all of these features apply to the case of land grabs.

Repositioning Territory in the Global Division of Functions

The extent of land acquisitions in the Global South by foreign governments and foreign firms and investors over the last few years marks a new phase. It is not the first time in modern times: this is a recurrent dynamic that tends to be part of imperial realignments. China's acquiring of mines in Africa is linked to its rise as a global power. Britain, France, the US, and others all did this in their early imperial phases and in many cases have owned vast stretches of land in foreign countries for hundreds of years. But each phase has its particularities. One key feature of the current period is that unlike past empires, today's world consists largely of nation-states recognized as sovereign, no matter how feeble this sovereign power is in many cases. Rather than imperial grab through force, the mechanism is foreign direct investment or direct buying/leasing. Buyers include governments, sovereign wealth funds, foreign firms, nationally based foreign corporations and investment banks, or some combination of these.

What is actually being measured in general descriptions of these acquisitions can vary considerably depending on the study. I have chosen the collectively generated data of the Land Matrix project in collaboration with International Land Coalition (Anseeuw et al., 2012a,

2012b; Land Matrix, 2012), a major contribution to the subject.[2] According to their definition the pertinent types of land acquisitions included have the following characteristics:

- They entail a transfer of rights to use, control, or own land through sale, lease, or concession.
- They imply a conversion from land used by smallholders, or for important environmental functions, to large-scale commercial use.
- They are 200 hectares or larger and were not concluded before the year 2000 when the FAO food price index was lowest.

The Land Matrix Database contains information about two types of data covering respectively acquisitions 'reported' (200 million plus hectares) and 'cross-referenced' (70 million hectares). 'Reported' data cover deals presented in published research reports and media reports and government registers where these are made public. 'Cross-referenced' data refer to those reported deals that are referenced from multiple sources; the cross-referencing process involves an assessment of the reliability of the source of the information, triangulation with other information sources, and, if necessary, confirming with in-country partners in the networks of the Land Matrix partners. Media reports are not considered sufficient for cross-referencing. Research reports based on fieldwork, confirmation by known in-country partners, or official land records have been considered sufficient evidence.

While the much reported explosion in food demand and in its prices was certainly a key factor in this new phase of land acquisitions, it is biofuels that account for most of the acquisitions.[3] Cross-referenced data from the Land Matrix show biofuel production accounts for 40% of land acquired. In comparison, food crops account for 25% of cross-referenced deals, followed by 3% for livestock production, and 5% for other non-food crops. Farming broadly understood accounts for 73% of cross-referenced acquisitions. The remaining 27% of land acquired is for forestry and carbon sequestration, mineral extraction, industry, and tourism (see Figure 1).

A second major pattern is the massive concentration of foreign acquisitions in Africa. Of the publicly reported deals, 948 land acquisitions totaling 134 million hectares are located in Africa; 34 million of these hectares have been cross-referenced. This compares with 43 million hectares reported for Asia (of which 29 million hectares have been cross-referenced) and 19 million hectares in Latin America (of which 6 million hectares have been cross-referenced). The remainder (5.4 million hectares reported and 1.6 million hectares cross-referenced) is in other regions, particularly Eastern Europe and Oceania (see Figure 2).

A few examples signal the range of buyers and of locations. Africa is a major destination for land acquisitions. South Korea has signed deals for 690,000 hectares and the United Arab Emirates (UAE) for 400,000 hectares, both in Sudan. Saudi investors are spending $100 million to raise wheat, barley, and rice on land leased to them by Ethiopia's government; they received tax exemptions and export the crop back to Saudi Arabia.[4] China secured the right to grow palm oil for biofuels on 2.8 million hectares of Congo, which would be the world's largest palm oil plantation, and is negotiating to grow biofuels on 2 million hectares in Zambia (*The Economist*, 2009; Hall, 2011; Putzel et al., 2011). Perhaps less known than the African case is the fact that privatized land in the territories of the former Soviet Union, especially in Russia and Ukraine, is also becoming the object of much foreign acquisition. In 2008 alone, these acquisitions included the following: a Swedish company, Alpcot Agro, bought 128,000 hectares in Russia; South Korea's Hyundai Heavy Industries paid $6.5 million for a majority stake in Khorol Zerno, a company that owns 10,000 hectares in eastern Siberia. Gulf investors are planning to acquire Pava, the first Russian grain processor to be floated on the financial markets to

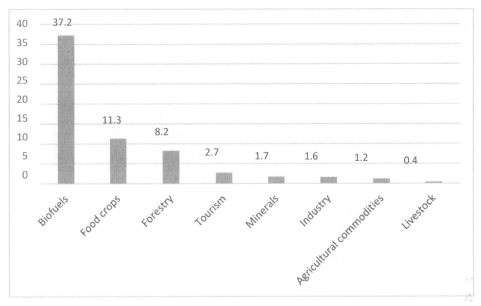

Table 1. Global land acquisitions by sector, 2011 (in millions of hectares), 2011.
Source: Anseeuw et al., 2012. p. 24.

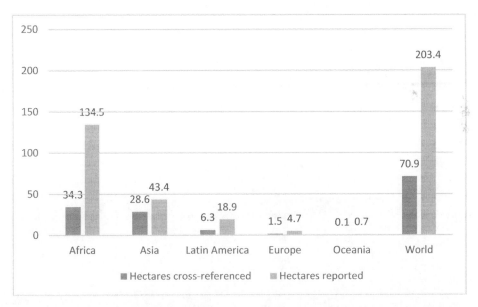

Table 2. Regional distribution of land acquisitions (in millions of hectares), 2011.
Source: Anseeuw et al., 2012, p. 23.

sell 40% of its landowning division, giving them access to 500,000 hectares. Also less noticed than the African case is that Pakistan is offering half a million hectares of land to Gulf investors with the promise of a security force of 100,000 to protect the land.

In what follows I focus briefly on one set of countries. The aim here is to illustrate the range of foreign actors involved in acquiring land. It is merely one small window into a large and varied reality.

Six Destinations for Acquiring Land: A Snapshot

In an analysis of 180 large land acquisitions in Africa, Friis and Reenberg (2010) categorize major investors into four main groups: (1) oil-rich Gulf states (Saudi Arabia, UAE, Qatar, Bahrain, Oman, Kuwait, and Jordan; (2) populous and capital-rich Asian countries such as China, South Korea, Japan, and India; (3) Europe and the US; (4) private companies from around the world. Investors are mostly energy companies, agricultural investment companies, utility companies, finance and investment firms, and technology companies.

Using the Friis and Reenberg (2010) data presented in their report, I constructed the following graphs (Figure 3) to represent this geography by focusing on the top six sellers in Africa and their investors. These graphs aim at visualizing the important data Friis and Reenberg (2010) provide. Squares indicate the top six land sellers in Africa and circles indicate buyers; the thickness of the line between a seller and a buyer is measured by the reported size of land acquisition in hectares. The top six African land sellers are Ethiopia, Madagascar, Sudan, Tanzania, Mali, and

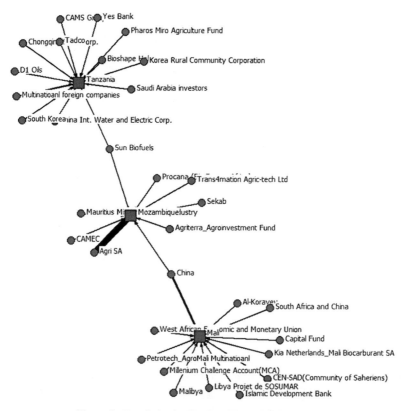

Figure 1. Top six land sellers in Africa and their investors

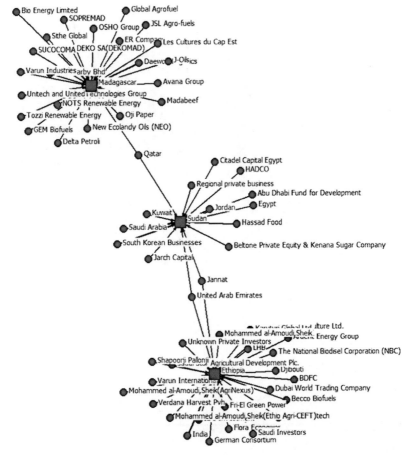

Figure 1. Continued

Mozambique—all Sub-Saharan, and all, except Mali, in East Africa. In all these countries both private investors and government agencies have acquired land.

No specific investor dominates in five of these six top-selling countries. The exception is Mozambique, where Agri SA, the South African farmers' association, is the largest buyer, and overwhelmingly so. When we measure by national origin, each seller does have a dominant country in terms of size of acquisitions: India in Ethiopia, South Korea in Madagascar, Saudi Arabia in Sudan, China in Mali. In Tanzania, it is a multinational group. There are few cross acquisition cases; here are some cases: Sun Biofuels[5] bought land in Tanzania and Mozambique; China, in Mozambique and Mali; Qatar, in Madagascar and Sudan; UAE and Jannat, in Sudan and Ethiopia.

Overall there are a total of 47 different country origins among investors in these six countries. Among the countries with the most diverse group of investors by country of origin are Madagascar, with 24 foreign investors from 15 countries, and Ethiopia, with 26 investors from 12 countries. Asian countries (China, South Korea, India, and Japan) make up almost 20% of investors, as distinct from investments, in these six countries. Middle Eastern countries (Saudi Arabia, UAE, Egypt, Jordan, Qatar, Lebanon, and Israel) account for almost 22% of investors. European

Ethiopia
By investor

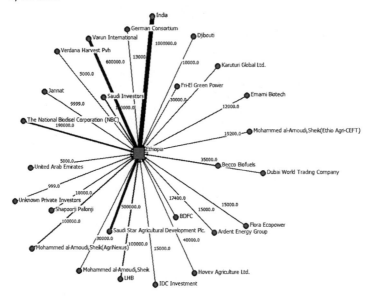

By nationality

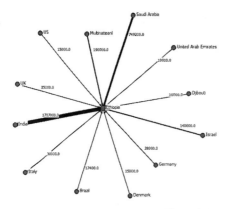

Figure 1. Continued

countries (UK, Sweden, Netherlands, Germany, Italy, Denmark, and France) account for 30% of investors. African countries (South Africa, Mauritius, Libya, and Djibouti) account for about 10% of investors. The remaining investors are from Australia, Brazil, and the United States.

As for investments, three countries dominate. The United States, United Kingdom, and Saudi Arabia together account for 25% of all investments in these six countries, and each has investments in four countries.

Madagascar
By investor

By nationality

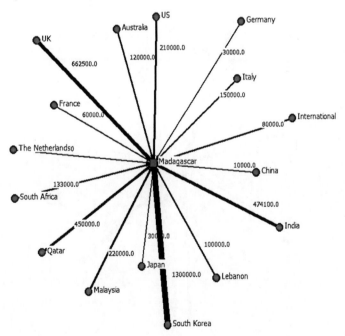

Figure 1. Continued

Sudan

By investor

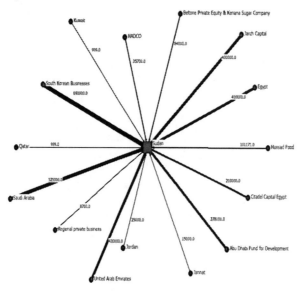

By nationality

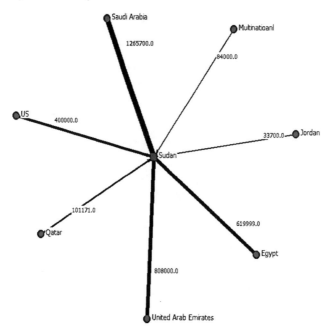

Figure 1. Continued

Tanzania
By investor

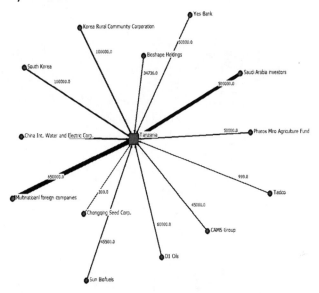

By nationality

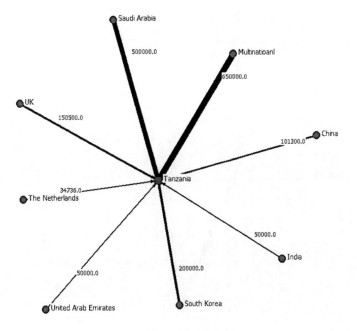

Figure 1. Continued

Mali
By investor

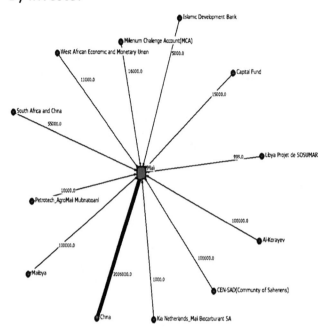

By nationality

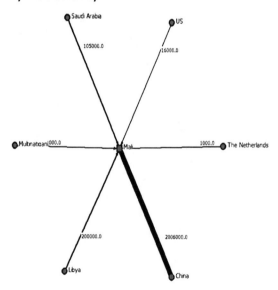

Figure 1. Continued

Mozambique

By investor

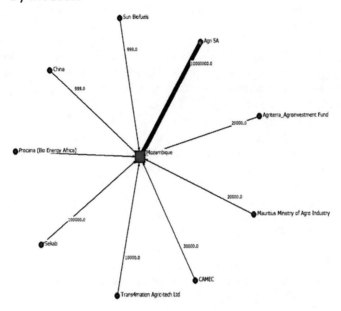

By nationality

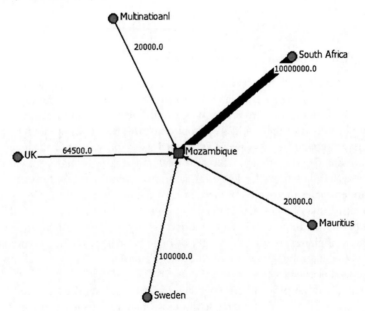

Figure 1. Continued

Land Acquisitions Are Part of a Larger Story

The actual mix of material practices that underlies these acquisitions vary enormously depending on how the land will be used. I am interested in these material practices: they transform sovereign national territory into a far more elementary condition—land for usufruct. This process brings with it a degrading of the governments that sold and leased the land. It evicts farmers and craftspeople, villages, rural manufacturing districts, smallholder agriculture districts, all of which degrades the meaning of citizenship for local people. And when there are no long-term inhabitants, these acquisitions often include uses that poison water, air, and land. Such material practices reconstitute parts of national territory.

These investments in land have crowded out investments in mass manufacturing and other sectors that can generate good jobs and feed the growth of a middle class. And it happened at a time when several countries of the Global South were beginning to experience significant growth in mass manufacturing, and much foreign direct investment was in this sector. This is the type of development that can contribute to the growth of a middle class and a strong working class. If we just consider Africa, for instance, the data show a sharp decline in foreign direct investment (FDI) in manufacturing. South Africa and Nigeria, Africa's top two FDI recipients accounting for 37% of FDI stock in Africa by 2006, have both had a sharp rise in FDI in the primary sector and a sharp fall in the manufacturing sector.[6] This is also the case in Nigeria, where foreign investment in oil has long been a major factor: the share of the primary sector in inward FDI stock stood at 75% in 2005, up from 43% in 1990. Other African countries have seen similar shifts. Even in Madagascar, one of the few (mostly small) countries where manufacturing FDI inflows began to increase as recently as the 1990s and onwards, this increase was well below that of the primary sector.[7] Overall, the current phase of land acquisitions dwarfs investments in manufacturing.

Preparing the Ground for Foreign Land Buying: Debt as a Disciplining Regime

The key empirical trend in the preceding section that matters for the larger argument of this article is the sharp growth in foreign land acquisitions after 2006, and the rapid international diversifying of those doing the acquiring. It is not the fact of foreign acquisition per se, as these have long been part of the world's economic history. But it is not enough to invoke that long history. Every epoch has its specificities, an issue I have examined at length (Sassen, 2008, chapters 3 and 5). Thus today, what also matters is that this sharp growth is happening in an interstate system based on the sovereign authority of the state over its territory. In other words, there are obstacles that were not there in earlier imperial phases. Even if such authority is merely formal for many countries, it makes cross-border land acquisition a different transaction from what it was in an empire. Let me mention two elements here that are a contrast with earlier imperial phases: one is the weight of internationally accepted contractual formats, and the other is the enormous diversity of those acquiring land. These are all obstacles to the ease of foreign land acquisition.

The empirical aspect developed here concerns the IMF and World Bank restructuring programs and, secondly, their effect in reconditioning land for its insertion in today's novel global corporate circuits.[8] The direct and indirect expulsion of people and the destabilizing of a large number of Global South governments via debt restructuring were key mechanisms in this process of reconditioning.

The core conceptual move is to see these programs as a disciplining regime, not simply as a banking transaction, and, secondly, as making the executive branch of government beholden to international and particular foreign national actors (both governments and firms of powerful countries). The initial aims of IMF and World Bank restructuring programs in their many diverse manifestations may have had specific aims that diverge somewhat from the shapes and contents they had taken on by the 1990s. After decades of operation this regime has had the effect of disassembling particular components of a growing number of Global South nation-states. Whether this may (Bello, 2004) or may not (Krueger, 1993) have been the aim, that disassembling took place as a structurally complex, often contingent, development; these features also made it easy to attribute the failures to bring about development to the particularities, i.e. flaws, of each country rather than IMF, World Bank, or WTO policies. The language of failed states, the commonest way to describe these weakened, often devastated nation-states, leaves out many of the locally specific issues that concern me here (e.g. Carrington, 2011; Colchester, 2011; Molnar et al., 2011). Such language represents the facts of these states' decay as set in a historic vacuum, a function of their own weaknesses and corruptions. These states are indeed weak, they are mostly corrupt, and they have cared little about the wellbeing of their citizens. But it is important to remember that it is and was often the vested interests of foreign governments and firms that enabled the corruption and the weakening of these states; and good leaders who resisted Western interests did not always survive, notably the now-recognized murder of Patrice Lumumba by the United States government. Further, the process of foreign land acquisitions now under way cannot be understood simply as caused by the corruption and weakness of host states.

As I have described at greater length in an earlier special issue of *Globalizations* on the financial crisis (Sassen, 2010), IMF and World Bank restructuring programs prepared the ground for the systemic deepening of advanced capitalism. I do agree with the well-known critiques of restructuring programs. But here I want to focus on something that has received less attention: The often devastating socio-economic effects of those programs prepared the ground for the ease with which foreign buyers can get land, in addition to assets like de-nationalized companies, water, and other public services, in many of the countries subjected to the IMF and World Bank restructuring programs. There are (at least) two vectors through which we can identify this bridging. One is the debt regime as one factor contributing to weaken and impoverish national governments in much of the Global South; this in turn has often been one factor stimulating governments' extreme corruption and disregard of the nation's wellbeing in many resource-rich countries. The other is the debt regime as a strong and 'legitimate' point of entry (by the IMF, the World Bank, and so many other international agencies) into a sovereign national state; this in turn enabled extensive disciplining and prioritizing payment of the foreign debt over national priorities, such as education and health. To put it bluntly, it is easier for rich foreign governments, sovereign wealth funds, and corporate investors to buy vast stretches of land in Sub-Saharan Africa and parts of Latin America and Asia, if they have to deal with weakened and/or corrupt governments which function as 'comprador bourgeoisies' (Bravo, 2011; Brautigam and Xiaoyang, 2011; Frank, 1998; Galeano, 1997; Ravanera and Gorra, 2011) and a population left with little and no political representation in the government.

Debt and debt servicing problems have long been a systemic feature of the developing world. But it is the particular features of IMF negotiated debt rather than the fact of debt per se that concerns me here. Further, the gradual destruction of traditional economies prepared the ground, literally, for some of the new needs of advanced capitalism, notably the demand for land—for food and fuels, and for access to water, metals, and minerals. While each of these components is familiar and has happened before, my argument is that they are now part of a new organizing logic that changes their valence and their macro-level effects. This notion or proposition is based on a methodological and interpretation practice I develop at length elsewhere (Sassen, 2008), though I regularly invoke some of its elements in this article.[9]

With few exceptions, poor countries subjected to the restructuring regime that began in the 1980s now have larger shares of their populations in desperate poverty and less likely to enter the 'modern' economy via consumption than they did even 20 years ago. Many of the Sub-Saharan countries had functioning health and education systems and economies, and less destitution than today. Even resource-rich countries have had expanded shares of their people become destitute, with Congo and Nigeria the most familiar cases. The dominant dynamic at work for these populations is, to a good extent, the opposite of the Keynesian period's valuing of people as workers and as consumers. This expelling has given expanded space to criminal networks, to people trafficking, and greater access to land and underground water resources to foreign buyers, whether firms or governments. Systemically, the role of rich donor countries has also shifted: overall they give far less in foreign aid for development than 30 years ago. As a result, the remittances sent by mostly low-income immigrants are larger than foreign aid. Since the late 1990s an increasing share of foreign aid comes through NGOs and philanthropic organizations, further marginalizing the role of governments in the work of development. One extreme outcome is governments that are effectively downgraded to predatory elites.

These systemic shifts contribute to explain a complex difference that can be captured in a set of simple numbers. Generally, the IMF asks heavily indebted poor countries (HIPCs) to pay 20% to 25% of their export earnings toward debt service. In contrast, in 1953, the Allies cancelled 80% of Germany's war debt and only insisted on 3% to 5% of export earnings for debt service. They asked 8% from Central European countries in the 1990s. In comparison, the debt-service burdens on today's poor countries are extreme. It does suggest that the aim for Europe was its re-incorporation into the capitalist world economy—at the time, for Germany, and more recently, for Central Europe. In contrast, the aim for the Global South countries in the 1980s and 1990s was more akin to a disciplining regime, starting with forced acceptance of both restructuring programs and loans from the international system. After 20 years of this regime, it became clear that it did not deliver on the basic components for healthy development. The discipline of debt-service payments was given strong priority over infrastructure, hospitals, schools, and other people-oriented development goals. The primacy of this extractive logic became a mechanism for systemic transformation that went well beyond debt-service payment—the devastation of large sectors of traditional economies, often the destruction of a good part of the national bourgeoisie and petty bourgeoisie, the sharp impoverishment of the population and of the state, except for the executive branch as it often benefits from extraction-based economies.

Even before the economic crises of the mid-1990s that hit a vast number of countries as they implemented neoliberal policies, the debt of poor countries in the South had grown from US$507 billion in 1980 to US$1.4 trillion in 1992.[10] Debt-service payments alone had increased to $1.6 trillion, more than the actual debt. From 1982 to 1998, indebted countries paid four times their original debts, and at the same time, their debt stocks went up by four times. These countries had to use a significant share of their total revenues to service these debts. For instance, Africa's payments reached $5 billion in 1998, which means that for every $1 in aid, African countries paid $1.40 in debt service in 1998. Debt to GNP ratios were especially high in Africa, where they stood at 123% in the late 1990s, compared with 42% in Latin America and 28% in Asia.[11] As of 2006, the poorest 49 countries (i.e. low-income countries with less than $935 per capita annual income) had debts of $375 billion. If to these 49 poor countries we add the 'developing countries', we have a total of 144 countries with a debt of over $2.9 trillion and $573 billion paid to service debts in 2006 (Jubilee Debt Campaign (JDC) UK, 2009). Additional negative elements for these countries are the falling terms of trade and the limits of the HIPC initiative, an issue I elaborate on in Sassen (2010).

Generally, IMF debt management policies from the 1980s onwards can be shown to have worsened the situation for the unemployed and poor (UNDP, 2005, 2008). Much research on poor countries documents the link between hyper-indebted governments and cuts in social programs. These cuts tend to affect women and children in particular through cuts in education and health care, both investments necessary to ensuring a better future (for overviews of the data, see UNDP, 2005, 2008; World Bank, 2005, 2006).

Conclusion

There is a larger history in the making. It includes a repositioning of growing areas of Africa, Latin America, and Asia in a massively restructured global economy. Weakened governments that function as 'comprador bourgeoisies', and the destruction of smallholder economies, have launched a new survival phase in expanding parts of the world.

The key empirical trend that matters for the larger argument in this article is the sharp growth in foreign land acquisitions after 2006, and the rapid international diversifying of those doing the acquiring. It is not the fact of foreign acquisition per se, as these have long been part of the world's economic history. Thus what also matters today is that this sharp growth is happening in an interstate system based on the sovereign authority of the state over its territory. And even if such authority is more formal than substantive for much of the world, it makes cross-border land acquisition a different transaction from what it was in an empire.

Emphasizing the juxtaposition of formal sovereign authority and growing foreign land acquisitions leads to two conceptual issues easily by passed if we simply emphasize the power asymmetry between those acquiring land and host governments.

One of these is to recover the destructive role of IMF and World Bank restructuring, eventually amplified by WTO rules, in weakening the economies, social development, and governments of program countries. This is a larger complex of trends and conditions that actually facilitated the massive foreign land acquisition that took off after 2006. They prepared the ground for the sudden rise in acquisitions, for the relative ease of formal execution of the contracts, and for the rapid diversification of those doing the acquiring.

The other is the repositioning of national sovereign territory resulting from the sharp rise in foreign land acquisitions. National territory is not merely land. Foreign land acquisitions include vast stretches of national territory articulated through villages, smallholder agriculture, rural manufacturing districts, and through the actors that make these economies and reproduce them—whether or not this is recognized by the state. Much of this politico-structural complexity is today being evicted from that territory due to those acquisitions. At the extreme we might ask what is citizenship when national territory is downgraded to foreign-owned land for plantations and the rest is evicted—floras, faunas, villages, smallholders.

In their aggregate, these large-scale land acquisitions contribute to produce a global operational space that is partly embedded in *national* territories. This produces a partial denationalization deep inside nation-states, a structural hole in the tissue of national sovereign territory. I see foreign land acquisitions as one of several such processes that partly disassemble national territory. They become capabilities of an organizing logic that is disarticulated from the national state even as they operate deep inside its territory. Further, in so doing, they often go against the interests not only of much of a country's people but also of national capital. It is important to note, that such denationalizing logics can also be positive, notably human rights compacts and environmental sustainability compacts. But these are as yet weak and ineffective.

Against this larger context, the materiality and visibility of foreign land acquisitions become heuristic: they tell us something about a larger process that is often not as visible and material as land and the direct participation of the executive branch of government in the execution of contracts. This is a very different way of representing economic globalization than the common notion of the whole state as victim. Indeed, to a large extent it is the executive branch of government that is getting aligned with global corporate capital, both in the Global South and in the Global North. This becomes highly visible in the case of foreign land acquisitions. At the same time, in my reading, a key implication of this strategic participation of states in global processes is that guided by different interests, states *could* reorient their goals away from the global corporate agenda and towards global arrangements concerning the environment, human rights, social justice, climate change.

Notes

1   Elsewhere I develop the notion that both these developments feed into a new mode of state authority that remains insufficiently recognized and theorized (Sassen, 2008, chapters 4 and 5), and, secondly, on a more promising note, an opening up of the domain of *global* politics to *nation*-based actors such as citizens and local social movements (Ibid., chapters 7–9).

2   It is important to note that acquisitions in OECD countries are generally not reflected in the data, as private transactions between one commercial user and another that do not involve a conversion of tenure system or away from smallholder production are not included in the Land Matrix. It is, of course, the case that this definition of land acquisitions would not be the most common in Europe. See also Margulis et al. (2013, in this volume) on the issue of measurement.

3   Food commodification and the financializing of these commodities is a major growth sector. The Economist index of food prices rose 78%; soya beans and rice both soared more than 130%. Meanwhile, food reserves slumped. In the five largest grain exporters, the ratio of stocks to consumption-plus-exports fell to 11% in 2009, below its 10-year average of over 15%. Beyond price, trade bans and crises pose a risk even to rich countries that rely on food imports.

4   On the other side, the World Food Program spent $116 million to provide 230,000 tons of food aid between 2007 and 2011 to the 4.6 million Ethiopians it estimates are threatened by hunger and malnutrition. This coexistence of profiting from food production for export and hunger famines, with the taxpayers of the world providing food aid, is a triangle that has repeated itself starting in the post-World War II decades (Sassen, 1988).

5   Sun Biofuels actually failed in Tanzania and shut down in 2011, which led to severe and sudden shocks to the local economy.

6   The share of the primary sector (which includes prominently mining and agriculture) in inward FDI stock increased to 41% in 2006, up from 5% in 1996. In contrast, the share of the manufacturing sector almost halved to 27% from 40% over that period (UNCTAD, 2008).

7   For comprehensive data, see UNCTAD (2008).

8   We see parallel developments, though very different mechanisms, in the Global North. I (2009) have used this lens to analyze the sub-prime mortgage crisis that began in the early 2000s and exploded in 2007 in the US and largely hit modest income households. Most of the attention has gone, and rightly so, to the massive losses for the individuals and families who were sold these mortgages, losses that will continue for years since many of the 'interest-free' periods of these mortgages only expire after 2014. In this case my argument is, again, that beyond the logics of extraction in the form of mortgage payments and mortgage agents' fees, also here we can detect a more foundational dynamic in the form of the systemic deepening of advanced/decaying capitalism and, further, that the instrument is one that can easily expand into the global market represented by *c.* 2 billion modest middle-class households in the world.

9   See Sassen (2008, chapters 1, 8, and 9) for a development of the theoretical, methodological, and historical aspects.

10   This section is based on a larger research project that seeks to show how the struggles by individuals, households, entrepreneurs, and even governments are micro-level enactments of larger processes of economic restructuring in developing countries launched by the IMF and World Bank Programs, as well as in WTO law implementation during the 1990s and onwards.

11   By 2003, debt service as a share of exports only (not overall government revenue) ranged from extremely high levels for Zambia (29.6%) and Mauritania (27.7%) to significantly lowered levels compared with the 1990s for Uganda (down from 19.8% in 1995 to 7.1% in 2003) and Mozambique (down from 34.5% in 1995 to 6.9% in 2003).

References

Anseeuw, W., Alden Wily, L., Cotula, L. & Taylor, M. (2012a) *Land Rights and the Rush for Land: Findings of the Global Commercial Pressures on Land Research Project* (Rome: International Land Coalition), http://www.landcoalition.org/sites/default/files/publication/1205/ILC%20GSR%20report_ENG.pdf.

Anseeuw, W., Boche, M., Breu, T., Giger, M., Lay, J., Messerli, P. & Nolte, K. (2012b) *Transnational Land Deals for Agriculture in the Global South: Analytic Report based on the Land Matrix Database International Land Coalition* (Bern/Montpellier/Hamburg: CDE/CIRAD/GIGA), http://www.landcoalition.org/publications/transnational-land-deals-agriculture-global-south.

Bello, W. (2004) *Deglobalization: Ideas for a New World Economy* (London: Zed Books).

Borras, S. M., Jr, Hall, R., Scoones, I., White, B. & Wolford, W. (2011) Towards a better understanding of global land grabbing: an editorial introduction, *Journal of Peasant Studies*, 38(2), pp. 209–216.

Brautigam, D. & Xiaoyang, T. (2011) *African Shenzhen: China's Special Economic Zones in Africa* (Cambridge: Cambridge University Press).

Carrington, D. (2011) UK firm's failed biofuel dream wrecks lives of Tanzania villagers, *The Guardian*, 30 October, http://www.guardian.co.uk/environment/2011/oct/30/africa-poor-west-biofuel-betrayal.

Colchester, M. (2011) Palm oil and indigenous peoples in South East Asia, FPP contribution to ILC Collaborative Research Project on Commercial Pressures on Land (Rome: ILC).

Cotula, L. (2011) The outlook on farmland acquisitions, IIED contribution to ILC Collaborative Research Project on Commercial Pressures on Land (Rome: ILC).

Deininger, K., Byerlee, D., Lindsay, J., Norton, A., Selod, H. & Stickler, M. (2011) Rising global interest in farmland: can it yield sustainable and equitable benefits? (Washington, DC: World Bank).

De Schutter, O. (2011) How not to think of land grabbing: three critiques of large-scale investments in farmland, *Journal of Peasant Studies*, 38(2), pp. 249–279, http://dx.doi.org/10.1080/03066150.2011.559008.

Dossou, P. J. (2011) Evolution and impacts of coastal land use in Benin: the case of the Sèmè-Podji Commune, VADID contribution to ILC Collaborative Research Project on Commercial Pressures on Land, (Rome: ILC).

Economist, The (2009) Outsourcing's third wave, 21 May, http://www.economist.com/node/13692889.

Food and Agriculture Organization (FAO) (2011) Land grabbing: case studies in 17 countries of Latin American and the Caribbean, (New York: United Nations), http://www.tni.org/sites/www.tni.org/files/download/borras_franco_kay__spoor_land_grabs_in_latam__caribbean_nov_2011.pdf.

Frank, A. G. (1971) *Sociology of Development and Underdevelopment of Sociology* (London: Pluto Press).

Frank, A. G. (1998) *Re-orient: Global Economy in the Asian Age* (Berkeley, CA: University of California Press).

Friis, C. & Reenberg, A. (2010) *Land Grab in Africa: Emerging Land System Drivers in a Teleconnected World,* GLP Report No. 1 (Copenhagen: GLP-IPO), http://farmlandgrab.org/wp-content/uploads/2010/08/GLP_report_01.pdf.

Galeano, E. H. (1997) *Open Veins of Latin America: Five Centuries of the Pillage of a Continent* (New York: Monthly Review Press).

Globalizations (2010) Special Issue: Globalization and Crisis, *Globalizations*, 7(1–2), http://www.tandfonline.com/toc/rglo20/7/1-2.

Hall, R. (2011) Land grabbing in Africa and the new politics of food, *Future Agricultures*, Policy Brief 041.

Jubilee Debt Campaign (JDC) UK (2009) How big is the debt of poor countries?, http://www.jubileedebtcampaign.org.uk/2%20How%20big%20is%20the%20debt%20of%20poor%20countries%3Ff2647.twl.

Krueger, A. O. (1993) *Economic Policy at Cross-Purposes: The United States and the Developing Countries* (Washington, DC: Brookings Institute).

Krueger, A. O. (ed.) (2002) *Economic Policy Reforms and the Indian Economy* (Chicago: University of Chicago Press).

Land Matrix (2012) *The Land Matrix, Beta version: The online public database on land deals* (ILC/CIRAD/CDE/GIGA/GIZ), http://landportal.info/landmatrix.

McKeon, N. (2013) 'One does not sell the land upon which the people walk': land grabbing, rural social movements, and global governance, *Globalizations*, 10(1), pp. 105–122.

McMichael, P. (2013) Land grabbing as security mercantilism in international relations, *Globalizations*, 10(1), pp. 47–64.

Maldonado-Torres, N. (2007) On the coloniality of being, *Cultural Studies*, 21(2), pp. 240–270.

Margulis, M. E., McKeon, N. & Borras, S. M. (2013) Land grabbing and global governance: critical perspectives, *Globalizations*, 10(1), pp. 1–23.

Mignolo, W. (2007) Delinking: the rhetoric of modernity, the logic of coloniality, and the grammar of de-coloniality, *Cultural Studies*, 21(2), pp. 449–514.

Molnar, A., Barney, K., De Vito, M., Karsenty, A., Elson, D., Benavides, M., Tipula, P., Soria, C., Sherman, P. & France, M. (2011) Large acquisition of rights on forest lands for tropical timber concessions and commercial wood plantations, Rights and Resources Initiative (RRI) contribution to ILC Collaborative Research Project on Commercial Pressures on Land (Rome: ILC).

Putzel, L., Assembe-Mvondo, S., Bilogo Bi Ndong, L., Banigouila, R. P., Cerutti, P., Chupezi Tieguhong, J., Djeukam, R., Kabuyaya, N., Lescuyer, G. & Mala, W. (2011) Chinese trade and investment and the forests of the Congo Basin: synthesis of scoping studies in Cameroon, Democratic Republic of Congo and Gabon, Working Paper 67 (Bogor, Indonesia: CIFOR).

Quijano, A. (2000) Coloniality of power, Eurocentrism and Latin America, *Nepantla: Views from the South*, 1(3), pp. 533–580.

Quijano, A. (2007) Coloniality and modernity/rationality. *Cultural Studies*, 21(2–3), pp. 168–178.

Ravanera, R. & Gorra, V. (2011) Commercial pressures on land in Asia: an overview, IFAD contribution to ILC Collaborative Research Project on Commercial Pressures on Land (Rome: ILC).

Rawat, V. B., Bhushan, M. B. & Sujata, S. (2011) The impact of special economic zones in India: a case study of Polepally SEZ, SDF contribution to ILC Collaborative Research Project on Commercial Pressures on Land (Rome: ILC).

Sassen, S. (1988) *The Mobility of Labor and Capital* (Cambridge: Cambridge University Press).

Sassen, S. (1991) *The Global City: New York, London, Tokyo* (Princeton, NJ: Princeton University Press).

Sassen, S. (2008) *Territory, Authority, Rights: From Medieval to Global Assemblages,* revised 2nd ed. (Princeton, NJ: Princeton University Press).

Sassen, S. (2009) When local housing becomes an electronic instrument: the global circulation of mortgages—a research note, *International Journal of Urban and Regional Research*, 33(2), pp. 411–426.

Sassen, S. (2010) A savage sorting of winners and losers: contemporary versions of primitive accumulation, *Globalizations*, 7(2), pp. 23–50.

Sassen, S. (2013) *Expulsions: When Complexity Produces Elementary Brutalities* (Cambridge, MA: Harvard University Press).

United Nations Conference on Trade and Development (UNCTAD) (2008) *World Investment Directory Volume X: Africa* (New York: United Nations).

UNCTAD (2009) Investment report: transnational corporations, agricultural production and development (New York: United Nations), http://unctad.org/en/docs/wir2009_en.pdf.

United Nations Development Programme (UNDP) (2005) *A Time for Bold Ambition: Together we can Cut Poverty in Half: UNDP Annual Report* (New York: UNDP).

UNDP (2008) *Human Development Report 2007–2008, UNDP Annual Report* (New York: UNDP).

Wiener Bravo, E. (2011) The concentration of land ownership in Latin America: an approach to current problems, CISEPA contribution to ILC Collaborative Research Project on Commercial Pressures on Land (Rome: ILC).

World Bank (2005) *Increasing Aid and Its Effectiveness, in Global Monitoring Report: Millennium Development Goals: from Consensus to Momentum* (Washington, DC: World Bank).

World Bank (2006) *Global Economic Prospects: Economic Implications of Remittances and Migration* (Washington, DC: World Bank).

Saskia Sassen is the Robert S. Lynd Professor of Sociology and Co-Chair, The Committee on Global Thought, Columbia University (http://www.saskiasassen.com). Her recent books are *Territory, Authority, Rights: From Medieval to Global Assemblages* (Princeton University Press, 2008) and *A Sociology of Globalization* (W.W. Norton, 2007). Her books are translated into over 20 languages. Her newest book is *Expulsions: When Complexity Produces Elementary Brutalities* (Cambridge University Press, 2013).

Land Grabbing as Security Mercantilism in International Relations

PHILIP McMICHAEL

Cornell University, New York, USA

ABSTRACT *International studies routinely consign agri-food relations to the analytical margins, despite the substantive historical impact of the agri-food frontiers and provisioning on the structuring of the interstate system. As a case in point, current restructuring of the food regime and its global political-economic coordinates is expressed through the process of 'land grabbing'. Here, the crisis of the WTO-centered corporate food regime, which has neoliberalized Southern agriculture while sustaining Northern agro-food subsidies, is manifest in a new form of mercantilism of commandeering offshore land for supplies of food, feed, and fuel. This article examines the content and implications of this new 'security mercantilism', which both affirms and contradicts a neoliberal order, anticipating a shift in international relations around resource grabbing.*

Introduction

Conceptions of the modern world order, anchored in an international state system, focus on industrial development, and therefore military capacity, as the key determinant of state power in the state system (see, e.g. Giddens, 1987; Kössler, 2003; Shaw, 1994). But this relation omits the significance of agriculture as the source of food and raw materials upon which industry and its labor force depends, as well as the power associated with control over the supply of agricultural products. The omission informs much of social theory, which disembeds analysis of sociopolitical relations from their agroecological foundations. And it is not simply the significance of the agricultural base, but agricultural productivity and/or cost-reducing access to frontier lands and their ecological bounty that lower costs of labor and other inputs in the process of industrialization and the accumulation of power (Moore, 2012). This much world systems analysis allows, in representing world ordering around a single division of labor within which regions and states form, compete, and stratify (Wallerstein, 1974). Even so, hegemonic relations privilege industrial and finance capital, with agriculture in shadow (but see Arrighi, 2007).

A corrective to the industrial-centric perspective on the trajectory of the state system comes from food regime analysis. The 'food regime' concept situates the global ordering of international food production, circulation, and consumption relations within specific institutional arrangements corresponding to a hegemonic organizing principle in the state system (Friedmann and McMichael, 1989). Thus far, food regimes have been associated with British, US, and corporate hegemony (McMichael, 2009). The recent, corporate food regime was institutionalized via WTO rules and protocols, privileging agro-exporters from the US and Europe in global food markets, served by states. Arguably, this arrangement is in transition. While the 'land grab' is multifaceted, that part of it focusing on agricultural land (and water) enables the shift of food and fuel production to new 'offshore' agro-export zones—complementing and rivaling Northern 'granaries'. From this perspective, land grabbing performs a specific function at this historical moment. That is, while land grabbing is a time-honored practice, it serves particular interests and provides particular resources in particular times. For example, it may be appropriate to view elements of land grabbing today as re-colonization, but how and why it is recurring on such a significant scale, on so many fronts, is a question requiring historicization—arguably via the 'food regime' lens.

Accordingly, this essay examines land grabbing as an expression of the changing geopolitical coordinates of the food regime in context of a combination of food, energy, financial, and climate crises. The key shifts involve (1) an emergent 'agro-security mercantilism' by which certain states seek to guarantee access to food and biofuels via sponsoring direct acquisition of lands offshore, and (2) a proliferation of governance mechanisms to justify and enable a new phase of land investments. By mercantilism I refer to land grabbing that overrides the multilateral trading system governed by WTO rules, substituting direct access to productive land for food and fuel supplies rather than relying on market access. Evolving governance mechanisms simultaneously deepen the privatization of states and land-use. In other words, while the latter is consistent with neoliberal doctrine, the former violates its trade fetishism with security mercantilism. Another way of capturing this seeming paradox is by characterizing the land grab as pivoting on a dialectic: of 're-territorialization' via investment in offshore lands for agro-exporting of food, fuel, and bio-economic products, and 'de-territorialization' as host states surrender land and water for export to states defined (through market measures or policy) as food-dependent (see also Sassen, 2013, pp. 25–46). As I suggest elsewhere (McMichael, 2012), the land grab opens a new chapter in the redistribution of power across an increasingly multi-centric global food system, with rising agro-export powers in middle-income countries (as expressed in the formation of the Group of Twenty (G20)).[1]

Food Crisis, Land Grab, and Food Regime Restructuring

The land grab stems from a longer-term agrarian crisis linking the British-centered food regime to the current process of restructuring of the corporate food regime as the land grab takes hold. Karl Kautsky identified the agrarian crisis of metropolitan agriculture in the late nineteenth century as a consequence of the competitive impact on European farmers from cheap grains from the New World (1988 [1899], p. 243; and see Friedmann, 1978). Grains and meat from the settler states reduced European wage costs, constituting an important value relation sustaining the expansion of industrial capitalism in the late nineteenth century (Araghi, 2003). Pressure on European farmers was suppressed for a time in the early to mid-twentieth century via a protectionist interlude, which shaped the US-centered food regime emerging in the postwar period (when GATT removed farm sectors from trade liberalization measures to resuscitate the world economy). In the US, state-managed commodity stabilization schemes restored and extended industrial agriculture, generating substantial food surpluses for export to Third World states via a concessional PL-480 food aid program (Friedmann, 1982). Aid promoted agro-export based trade relations, emulated in the 1970s by European producers adopting the US agribusiness model and also exporting food to the Global South. Alongside of this North–South trade in foodstuffs, agro-exporting internationalized in the 1980s via a combination of transnational investments and structural adjustment mandates.

Over the long run, therefore, late nineteenth-century settler state agro-exporting anticipated a general offshoring of industrial agriculture, as the US-centered food regime morphed into a corporate food regime, anchored by the WTO (1995) as it institutionalized liberal trade and investment relations. It is this trajectory that has laid the foundations for the contemporary offshore land grab. Karl Kautsky's account of the agrarian crisis of a century earlier foresaw the (current) relocation of agro-industrial zones from Global North to South as new frontiers of cheap land (and water) attract financial investment and replace eroding (and therefore increasingly expensive) Northern resources:

> Those tropical countries which are not suited to wheat cultivation—Central America, Northern Brazil, large parts of Africa, India, South Eastern Asia—would then also join the ranks of the European grain farmers' competitors. Eventually, this competition will have to lose its ruinous character. The surface of the earth is finite . . . And if the capitalist burdens which once depressed agriculture in Western Europe now begin to do the same to its competitors in the USA, Russia, and so on, this is not proof that the crisis in Western European agriculture is coming to an end. It simply proves that the crisis is extending its grip. (Kautsky, 1988 [1899], p. 252)

The tropical regions identified by Kautsky are targeted in the land grab as agro-export zones. Offshoring of agriculture via the land grab alters the geography of the corporate food regime, compounding Northern agro-exporting to Southern markets with expanding exports of food, feed, and agrofuels from new agro-industrial zones proliferating across regions of the Global South and Eastern Europe (see, e.g. Visser and Spoor, 2011). Such export flows include raw material inputs for the lucrative globalized trade in processed foodstuffs, which now comprise 80% of the food trade (De Schutter, 2011, p. 13).

The food price spike of 2007–2008 signaled the extended grip of the agrarian crisis, which was always about the management of capital's value relations. This crisis now takes three forms. First, capital faces a general crisis of accumulation, with rising costs of production (energy) and reproduction (wage-foods). Second, investment initiative has passed to finance capital, as neoliberalism's redistributive (vs. productive) dynamic (Araghi, 2009) has shrunk investment opportunity in non-agricultural sectors, leaving agro-futures as the new axis of speculation as food and land prices inflate—in turn driving the land grab and further land inflation (Kaufman, 2010; McMichael, 2012). And third, the 'food' crisis is compounded by the corporate food regime's 'crisis of low prices' (Rosset, 2008), precipitating a general deflation of small producer economy across the world during the 1990s and 2000s that, along with steeply rising input costs, undermined potential benefits (or increased production) from rising crop prices (Patnaik, 2008).

From the latter, we might say that the agrarian crisis is no longer a crisis of metropolitan farming alone, but a general agrarian crisis insofar as no social form of agriculture is particularly stable. Weis has noted that about half of global grain production is consumed directly as food grain, while 35% feeds livestock and 17% is dedicated to biofuel production: '(t)he surge in the latter two comes at a time when the yield gains associated with the Green Revolution have effectively maxed out, and the volume of per capita grain production on a global scale has been level since peaking in 1986' (Weis, 2010, p. 327). In consequence, capital's reproductive relations now include a rising land grab for resources (with potential for raising yields) and speculative returns, with the resulting enclosures compromising the (socio-ecological) reproductive relations of world peasantries. Oxfam estimates almost 230 million hectares of land (space of Western Europe) acquired primarily by foreign investors since 2001, with most occurring since the food price crisis of 2008 (Zagema, 2011).

Thus, while agro-industrialization has historically concentrated in the Global North, powering a cheap (corporate) food regime, declining sustainability and rising costs have encouraged off-shoring to exploit cheap inputs. Just as industrial agriculture has experienced a declining bio-physical productivity, with soil depletion and a drop in efficiency of nitrogen use from 60% to 20% from the 1950s to the 1990s (van der Ploeg, 2010, p. 100), the expense of 'biophysical override' (Weis, 2007) rises with the price of commodity inputs exacerbated by increased energy and irrigation requirements due to declining efficiency (Holt-Giménez, 2007, p. 10; van der Ploeg, 2010, p. 100). As agri-capital centralized in response to these trends, augmented by financialization, it prefigured the land grab. In addition, given the *conjunction* of crises at the end of the first decade of the twenty-first century, capitals from other sectors (auto, chemical, biotechnology, energy) have combined to take advantage of cost-reducing investments in Southern land, water, and labor, spurred by financial speculation and anticipation of the risk evident in climate change.[2] In other words, the crisis of the neoliberal agro-industrial food regime finds expression in a spatial restructuring process, implicating the state system and its multilateral arrangements.

Food Regime Re-Territorialization: the New 'Security Mercantilism'

The 'food crisis' turning point of the late 2000s expressed the contradictions of the corporate food regime—namely, an intensification of high-energy chemical agriculture, state-mandated investments in food-displacing industrial agrofuels, concentration and centralization of agribusiness and retailing capitals, and a declining capacity and stability of small and medium farming. In the vortex of food inflation and export bans by key grain-exporting countries, and the growing recognition of future limits on arable land and food supplies, and energy sources, a new wave of enclosure via 'land grabbing' ensued. While attention has been focused on the targeting of lands in the Global South, the land grab phenomenon has been quite universal, and quite differentiated in its forms—for cropland, forests, conservation, urbanization, tourism, military bases, speculative investment, and so on (Zoomers, 2010). For the purposes of this analysis, land acquisition for food, feed, and agrofuels has reformulated food regime mercantilism. That is, while WTO rules have protected farm subsidies for Northern agro-exporters (via green and amber boxes), allowing a form of institutionalized mercantilism in otherwise 'free' international commodity trade, land grabbing entails a direct 'security mercantilism'.

The land grab presages a *new territorialization*, to secure offshore land for the purpose of repatriating agricultural products to investing states. Unlike the 'ghost acres' phenomenon, by which food grown offshore is commandeered through market mechanisms managed by trading companies, the recent form of land grabbing is hardly ghost-like, especially when the Chinese government, for example, expatriates Chinese farmers to grow food and fuel crops off-shore, and Middle Eastern states reverse unsustainable cropping on home-lands and directly commandeer resources overseas to supply their rising food needs (affluent consumers and a migrant labor force). Saudi Arabia is currently managing the relocation of wheat production to land offshore as its water resources decline, and the Gulf Cooperation Council (GCC) has a planned expansion of associated food imports. In addition, the African Union (AU), which, through the 2003 Maputo Declaration, has established a Comprehensive African Agricultural Development Programme with the goal of directing 10% of member-government investment in agriculture—some funding for this initiative being provided by land acquisitions (Committee on World Food Security, 2011, p. 19).

A recently released data set by NGO GRAIN (2012) documents over 400 land grabs, a substantial portion of which are initiated by states or state companies, constituting the new 'security mercantilism' (termed 'developmental outsourcing' by Hofman and Ho, 2012). These include: China's state-owned largest farming company Beidahuang investing in soy, maize, and other crops in Argentina, the Philippines, and Australia; Japan's Sojitz Corporation backed by the state to invest in Argentina, Brazil, and other South American countries; China's state-owned Shaanxi Kingbull Livestock Co. investing in Australian cattle; Hassad Food (financed by Qatar's sovereign wealth fund) investing in Australia, Sudan, Turkey, Vietnam, Pakistan, and India; the Chinese National Complete Import and Export Corporation investing in sugarcane and cassava in Jamaica, Benin, and Sierra Leone; China's Chongquin Grain Group state corporation investing in soybeans in Bahia, Brazil, and eventually oilseed rape in Canada and Australia, rice in Cambodia and palm oil in Malaysia; China's Tianjin State Farms Agribusiness Group investing in maize, alfalfa, and sunflower in Bulgaria and Colombia; Djibouti's state-owned Société Djiboutienne de Sécurité Alimentaire investing in wheat in Sudan, Ethiopia, and possibly Malawi; Egypt's National Bank investing in cereals in Sudan; joint state ventures between the governments of Ghana and Qatar to produce food crops in Ghana for Qatar, between those of Laos and Kuwait to produce rice in Laos for Kuwait, and between the Korean and Philippine governments for private investment in the Philippines; Saudi Arabia investing in Pakistani farmland; Abu Dhabi's Al Dahra Agricultural Company investing in feed and food crops in Europe, the US, South Asia, and North Africa to supply the UAE; the Brunei Investment Authority investing in Mindanao; the Oman Ministry of Agriculture investing in rice in the Philippines; the Korean state-owned Jeonnam Feedstock investing in feed crops in Mindoo; the Malaysian government's Federal Land Development Authority investing in oil palm in Sierra Leone, and so on.

This kind of 're-territorialization' is designed to avoid dependence on markets, or more particularly, market intermediaries. Thus: 'China wants to cut out the soy middlemen. It clearly does not trust the large American-owned commodity traders like Cargill and Bunge. Leading the way is Beidahuang Land Cultivation Group, a giant state-owned farming business . . . In 2011 it secured a deal with the governor of Rio Negro in Argentina to lease some 570,000 acres. It also tied up a long-term agreement with domestic Argentine land giant Credus, which controls more than 2 million acres of farms. Beidahuang said it would also build a new port to export the soy' (Pearce, 2012, p. 202). In Africa, Beijing has 1.5 million nationals, building infrastructure and 'digging water canals and pursuing irrigation schemes in Mali . . . manning seed labs in South Africa . . . tilling soil from Senegal to Mozambique' (Ibid., p. 203). Meanwhile, in 2008, at the height of the food price crisis, Saudi Arabia launched the King Abdullah Initiative, geared to supporting offshore investment in land to produce rice, wheat, barley, corn, sugar, green fodders, and livestock, and enabled by substantial sovereign wealth funds (Green, 2012). This initiative facilitates private Saudi companies 'seeking land and agricultural investments overseas, providing funds, credit and logistics, establishing government relations, signing agreements and conducting investigations into water resources, quality of land, availability of labour, facility of FDI and transparency, which it then avails to its domestic companies' (Ibid.). Interestingly enough, the governments of neighboring states United Arab Emirates and Qatar are more directly involved in acquiring agricultural land, rather than facilitating private acquisition.

The recent Land Matrix report (Anseeuw et al., 2011) shows that 66% of the demand for agricultural land is by Middle Eastern investors, in order to reduce market dependence, with Egypt following suit. A parallel report by the International Land Coalition and the Oakland Institute claims 'agricultural investment is increasingly becoming an important asset class not just for the Gulf states, but also the BRIC nations and other emerging markets that can see their domestic food supplies insufficient for their growing population' (Middle East Business News, 2012). There is also evidence to suggest that such offshore investments are not solely driven by 'security mercantilism', but also anticipate supplying other markets in the longer run (Ibid.; Pearce, 2012, p. 202)—underscoring the parallel proliferation of food/feed supply zones and circuits that mark a significant transition in the geography of the food regime (McMichael, 2012). For example, in a recent Brazil–Mozambique land deal, 6 million hectares, at a symbolic price, will underpin an offshore agro-export operation—as the Mato Grosso Cotton Producer Association president noted: 'Mozambique is like Mato Grosso in the middle of Africa, with free land, without so many environmental obstacles, with a much cheaper shipment cost to China. Nowadays, as well as land being extremely expensive in Mato Grosso, it is impossible to get a license to clear the area' (quoted in MercoPress, 2011).

Within this transition, there is of course the expanding role of agrofuels in the global land grab as well as in the content of commodity circuits in the food/fuel regime—some of this is driven by EU (mercantilist) green fuel mandates stimulating palm oil expansion in Malaysia and Indonesia, and Guatemala and Colombia. And, as with food exporting, agrofuel production is not simply driven by foreign investments, as local states and private investors participate in developing food/fuel export complexes geared to provisioning states and global markets (Borras et al., 2012, p. 863; McMichael, 2009).

Under the arrangements of 'security mercantilism', WTO multilateral trading arrangements are overridden by direct land acquisition to secure food/feed/fuel supplies for designated national consumers. Instead of market rule under WTO auspices, organized by TNCs around the principle of 'comparative advantage' (including Northern subsidies), the food regime geography associated with this part of the land grab approximates a set of bilateral arrangements organized by states and/or sovereign wealth funds. Approximates is the operative word because despite the World Bank's report finding agribusiness and investment funds as the principle land acquirers (Deininger et al., 2011), as Lorenzo Cotula points out: '. . . the divide between private and government-backed land deals should not be overestimated. The home country governments of investors can play a major supportive role for private-sector led initiatives, providing diplomatic, financial and other support to private deals . . . Also the very borderline between public and private investors may be fluid, as the implementation of deals signed between governments may be driven by private operators' (2012, p. 660).

Since the land grab *also* involves financial houses with no particular geopolitical attachments the resulting global agro-export complex intensifies the corporate food/fuel regime along multicentric lines (no longer dominated by North–South trade relations). In either case, the redirection of food flows registers agricultural offshoring to deepen the agro-export complexes promoted by the WTO-driven corporate food regime. Geographical reconfiguration of the food regime depends on the progressive relocation of industrial agriculture from Global North to rising agro-exporters in South America, Southeast Asia, and Eastern Europe, and to the so-called 'empty lands' of Africa dramatized by a renewed phase of land grabbing. The new investment patterns in the Global South favor bulk commodities—thus, for Southeast Asia, '83% of the farmland being acquired or leased on a long-term basis is dedicated to the production of major row crops (soft oilseeds, corn, wheat and feed grains)' (Borras and Franco, 2010, p. 31).[3] While agribusiness and retailing corporations continue to organize much of the production, the growing involvement of sovereign wealth funds and state and multi-state investor alliances (e.g. the GCC, the AU) restructures supply chains as 'extra-market relations'.

In spite of some government attempts to link biofuel investment to smallholder inclusion (e.g. Tanzania, Brazil), in general, large-scale land investments in Africa 'follow a simple model of concentrated production using a plantations system' (Committee on World Food Security, 2011, p. 34; Wilkinson and Herrera, 2008). Justifying such developments, World Bank lead-economist Deininger and co-author Byerlee note three factors contributing to the increased farm size associated with recent 'land acquisitions': new technology, labor limitations of frontiers, and integrated supply chains requiring produce certification (2011, p. 13). Eschewing previous claims in the economics literature, including the World Bank's *World Development Report, 2008*, for the responsiveness and superior efficiency of family farms, they note:

> Recent innovations in crop breeding, tillage, and information technology may make labor supervision easier and reduce diseconomies of scale of large operations. Pest-resistance and herbicide-tolerant varieties facilitated broad adoption of zero tillage and, by reducing the number of steps in the production process and the labor intensity of cultivation, allowed management of larger areas. . . . The scope for substituting crop and pest models and remotely sensed information on field conditions for personal observation also reduces the advantage of local knowledge and experience in tactical farm decisions while climate change and the associated greater variability of climatic conditions reduces the value of traditional knowledge. Private operators in Argentina and Ukraine assert that, with modern technology, good managers can effectively supervise units of 10,000 to 15,000 ha for grain and oilseeds. (Ibid., pp. 13–14)

In relation to this blueprint for the large scale, the 2008 report of the EU's High Level Group on the Competitiveness of the Agro-Food Industry (HLGCAI) underlines an important dimension of the land grab: the scale production of inputs for the food processing industry (80% of world trade). The feedstuff inputs for the EU's livestock industry, for example, amount to 70% of its production costs (Fritz, 2011, p. 74). Animal feed is the EU's largest agricultural product import, providing 75% of EU consumption of protein-rich feedstuffs, and the EU is 'by far the world's largest importer of soymeal and the second largest importer of soybeans after China . . . soymeal imports experienced strong growth in the last years, increasing from 13 million tonnes in 1997 to 23 million tonnes today' (Ibid., p. 77). Brazil and Argentina provide 80% of the EU's soybean and soymeal imports (Ibid., p. 81) and soy monocultures in these countries (in addition to Paraguay, Bolivia, and Uruguay), continue to expand (driven also by Chinese demand for soy products)—thereby intensifying the land grab. And Europe's domestic protein crop has been decimated by cheap soy imports. Thus, in context of the land grab, the *Coordination Paysanne Européene* (CPE) maintained that European farmers can grow the protein Europe needs via crop rotation of legumes that would benefit soil fertility and biodiversity and reduce carbon emissions in the process (Fritz, 2011, p. 87), and warned that without a European agricultural policy production will continue to move offshore (CPE, 2006).

In this regard, the EU's initiation of the HLGCAI (including representatives from agribusiness, transnational food corporations, the European Commission, member states, and some civil society organizations (CSOs)) was a regional response to the 'food crisis', and the prospect of a shifting geography of the food regime. The HLG report notes rising competition from Brazil, China, Argentina, Thailand, Indonesia, and Malaysia on the one hand, and insufficient access to cheap raw materials on the other (Fritz, 2009, p. 9). In other words, as anticipated by Kautsky, the European agro-export complex nurtured by the WTO regime is losing its world market share as food exporting relocates to middle-income countries, fueling public and private interest in accessing cheaper food and fuel supplies offshore. While the report affirms WTO multilateralism, it recommends completion of 'bilateral trade negotiations between the EU and, *inter alia*, India, Ukraine, Andean, ASEAN and Central American countries as well as further talks with China, Russia, Mercosur and Mediterranean countries' (Fritz, 2011, p. 10). Such bilateral trade deals facilitate the exporting of agricultural commodities arising from land grabbing.

European embrace of bilateral trade deals signals the restructuring underway in the food regime. As suggested, the WTO-sponsored food regime enabled Northern investment in transnational supply chains (beyond the pattern of 'dumping' of Northern food surpluses in Southern markets), anticipating the offshoring associated with the land grab. But herein lies a difference between Europe and the predominantly Asian and MENA states sponsoring offshore production via land grabbing. European offshoring of food and feed production by transnational firms has been enabled by WTO liberalization and investment protocols. Thus French food retailer Carrefour has invested significantly in high-value agro-exporting from the 'new agrarian districts' of Brazil's Sao Francisco Valley (Marsden, 2003, pp. 30, 57). In 2002 the Doux group, the foremost French and European poultry producer, purchased Frangosul, the fourth largest poultry producer in Brazil, reducing its production costs by two-thirds (Herman and Kuper, 2003, pp. 21–22). Sales by small ranchers in the Amazon to Brazilian slaughterhouses are now replaced by large commercial ranchers producing directly for supermarkets—European supermarkets dominate the beef export market with extensive cattle ranching, and Europe and the Middle East account for 75% of Brazil's beef exports (French, 2004, p. 148). And from the UK, Tesco and Marks and Spencer dominate the green bean export crop in Kenya, where almost 90% of horticulture is destined for Europe, especially the UK (Dolan, 2004).

Northern states have a substantial network of corporate supply chains already in place—e.g. Carrefour has 15,600 in 34 countries (Fritz, 2011, p. 11), now complemented by offshore land grabs by banks, funds, and philanthropists. However, Asian and MENA states depend more on sovereign wealth funds and government firms and banks to compete for land offshore, as a matter of material security, whether for immediate or longer-term purposes. For example, South Korea, a major food importer, is mobilizing for direct access to offshore food supplies:

> It imports almost 90% of its wheat and corn. And it is growing uncomfortable about that. In 2008, Korean food companies suddenly found that key foreign suppliers were banning exports in order to feed their own people. In Seoul, the government established a National Food Strategy to subsidize national corporations willing to annex foreign land to secure key supplies. . . . So, but 2030, South Korea wants to grow a quarter of its food on foreign soil owned or leased by Korean companies. The executives of Daewoo and the other industrial corporations that made South Korea rich are now on a new mission—to scour the world for land to feed their nation. (Pearce, 2012, pp. 204–205)

In addition, South Korea plans to 'bypass the large international trading firms by buying grain directly from US farmers', via an office in Chicago, eventually supplemented with grain elevators to allow 'multiyear delivery contracts with farmers, agreeing to buy specified quantities of wheat, corn, or soybeans at a fixed price' (Brown, 2011).

Governing the New Security Mercantilism

While the WTO is the forum for multilateral trade liberalization, its Agreement on Agriculture has sustained a contradictory mercantilism, whereby 'elite northern interests strategized to create and use the WTO as a tool to preserve their own subsidy regimes, while at the same time enforcing liberalization on the rest of the world' (Pritchard, 2009, p. 302). The fact that the WTO is authored by states but also accountable to them, or at least their competitive relations (McMichael, 2000), has fueled a paralyzing contention (by key Southern states) in the as yet unresolved Doha Round. One key issue concerned continuation of farm subsidies in, and support for agricultural exports from, the US and the EU; the G-21 (representing more than two-thirds of the world's rural population) led the challenge in the name of protecting their farmers, with India in particular contesting tariff reduction on imported foodstuffs, and West African states demanding the elimination of US cotton subsidies. Paralysis of the Doha Round has essentially immunized the WTO from land grabbing questions, which now occupy the attention of other international forums such as the FAO and its Committee on Food Security, as well as agencies such as the World Bank (as addressed in the following section).

Agricultural trade tensions are now complicated by a rising 'security mercantilism', centered on Southern state sponsorship of land grabbing. Such re-patterning of food/fuel circuits reframes the contours of the food regime—qualifying the WTO architecture of 'liberalized' commodity flows. Given the centrality of agro-exporting, direct annexation of supply zones deepens the corporate regime (with state complicity in commodification of land and water) rather than necessarily transitioning to a successor regime (McMichael, 2012).

From a food regime perspective, this new 'security mercantilism' defies the architecture of the WTO's Agreement on Agriculture. While previous patterns of food trading continue, new patterns of direct supply from annexed land are forming. That is, whereas the WTO trade rules require lowering of agricultural protections to encourage Northern food exporting and institutionalize export agriculture (with IMF support), now a parallel infrastructure of private and voluntary rules and protocols via soft laws facilitates land grabbing (non-trade based food circulation). This infrastructure is in turn enabled by international legal protections that have deepened during the era of political-economic liberalization. Thus: 'a burgeoning number of treaties (over 2,600 by 2010) and growing state consent for settling disputes through international arbitration rather than through domestic courts have considerably strengthened international safeguards for foreign acquirers of land' (Anseeuw et al., 2011, p. 53). In contrast, international conventions regarding land rights for indigenous peoples and communities are considerably weaker than investment law (Ibid., p. 54).

The emerging land grab infrastructure follows several decades of dismantling of public capacity in the Global South (particularly in Sub-Saharan Africa) as a consequence of structural adjustment mandates—rendering states more vulnerable to *reformulation of land policy* to accommodate private and/or foreign interests. Between 1980 and 2006, public expenditure on agriculture in the Global South fell 50% from US$7.6 to $3.9 billion (*The Economist*, 2008). Structural adjustment 'dismantled the elaborate system of public agencies providing farmers with access to land, credit, insurance inputs and cooperative organization' (World Bank, 2007, p. 138). In addition to eroding smallholder farming and public support of the agrarian economy, neoliberal policies have 'privatized' state policy, such that states hosting land investment (whether onshore or offshore) lack substantial protective regulations, which are further compromised by interstate competition for foreign capital, lowering investor requirements. Thus the Ethiopian government offers five-year tax holidays and very low land fees—a practice widespread among African states (Anseeuw et al., 2011, p. 33), even though states may experience divisions 'between those who tend to prioritize political legitimacy and those who prioritize capital accumulation, and these cleavages run between and within ministries and levels of governance' (Borras et al., 2011, p. 44). And rent seeking among state officials is common (see, e.g. Anseeuw et al., 2011, pp. 48–49; Colchester et al., 2007; Fairbairn, 2011). Land governance, then, is essentially organized to accommodate powerful private interests. As a recent International Land Coalition report, noting considerable legal variability across states, observes:

> Legal dispossession may occur through compulsory acquisition of privately titled lands or, far more commonly, through the appropriation of land and other resources that are possessed by local communities under customary form of tenure but are not given formal legal recognition as being owned by them . . . [and where] traditional leaders are recognized as trustees of lands traditionally owned by communities, and where such local elites coerce or manipulate access to these lands on behalf of investors and speculators . . . The overall result . . . is that governments in many Asian and African countries are not only the main legal landowners but also the legal controllers of land disposition over most of the lands traditionally owned and used by their citizens. This makes it perfectly legal for governments to sell or lease out lands on which their citizens live or which they use. This is important to prospective land acquirers . . . (Anseeuw et al., 2011, pp. 50–52)

Under these conditions, then, Southern states (to greater or lesser extent) transition from organizing farm sectors for national development, or trade (via the WTO), to *reorganizing* land and water use for a global resource grab, enabled by international financial institutions and financiers, and an emerging set of soft laws parameterizing land acquisition within a normative developmentalist framework.

Leading the way is the consensus emerging from the food-crisis inspired High Level Conference on World Food Security at the FAO, June 2008. This consensus affirmed the neoliberal preference for market solutions to modern problems, but in turn laid the foundations for land acquisition on a large scale to be organized and governed through private mechanisms. The canonical text was perhaps the World Bank's *World Development Report*, 2008, which declared (after a quarter century of neglect and undermining of Southern farm sectors): 'it is time to place agriculture afresh at the center of the development agenda' (2007, p. 1), with the 'new agriculture' to be 'led by private entrepreneurs in extensive value chains linking producers to consumers' (2007, p. 8). FAO Secretary General Jacques Diouf echoed this vision, in a May 2008 press release that 'high food prices represent an excellent opportunity for increased investments in agriculture by both the public and private sectors to stimulate production and productivity,' adding that '(g)overnments, supported by their international partners, must now undertake the necessary public investment and provide a favourable environment for private investments' (quoted in Urquhart, 2008).

The urgency of the food and energy crises refocused the attention of the global political-economic elite on mobilizing agricultural resources to offset food, water, and fuel shortages. Agricultural land in the Global South, in particular, is targeted for 'productivity increase' via technification. For example, Susan Payne, CEO of Emergent Asset Management (a UK investment fund planning to spend $50 million on African land) declared: 'Farmland in sub-Saharan Africa is giving 25% returns a year and new technology can treble crop yields in short time frames . . . Agricultural development is not only sustainable, it is our future. If we do not pay great care and attention now to increase food production by over 50% before 2050, we will face serious food shortages globally' (quoted in Vidal, 2010). 'Agricultural development' of course needs physical as well as a politico-legal infrastructure facilitating private property relations and market rule. As such, it represents a new claim for territorialization in the (normalized) interest of 'feeding the world' (cf. Peluso and Lund, 2011, pp. 673–674).

In Africa and Asia much of the land is state land but communally held, and as such is subject to government designation as 'idle' land, given potential commercial rewards, in addition to windfall revenues for indebted states. A case in point is the passage in December 2011 of a Land Acquisition Bill in Indonesia, which, according to the Deputy Secretary General of the Asian Peasant Coalition (APC), 'will heighten land grabbing in Indonesia [at the expense of traditional land rights]. Although the bill only applies to government projects, it will benefit privately operated projects on government-bought land. The government is relying on about $150 billion of private investment between 2010 and 2014 to overhaul its roads, railways and ports,' (APC, 2011). Here, the public/private nexus foreshadowed in government land grabbing by reclassification contributes to the infrastructure of 'security mercantilism'. Unsurprisingly, international development and financial institutions are working with governments on privatizing land relations to enable and attract foreign investment in African land. US investment, for example, is encouraged by the US government's Millennium Challenge Corporation (MCC), which disburses money in the form of grants to particular states on condition that they meet certain neoliberal economic criteria. Most MCC Compacts signed with African countries focus on agriculture, with a central land privatization component, supporting 'market-based solutions to food security' (GRAIN, 2010).

Global land grabbing is promoted by, among other organizations, the World Bank, its International Finance Corporation (IFC), the International Rice Research Institute (IRRI) of the Consultative Group on International Agricultural Research (CGIAR), the European Bank for Reconstruction and Development (IBRD), and others, with particular focus on Sub-Saharan Africa. The IFC's partner, the Foreign Investment Advisory Service (FIAS), targets 'investment climates' in foreign markets, creating land registries, and easing the process of land titling, leasing, and foreign investment—made easier where, as the International Institute for Environment and Development (IIED) found that 'many countries do not have sufficient mechanisms to protect local rights and take account of local interests, livelihoods, and welfare' (Daniel, 2009, p. 17). A new FIAS initiative, Investing Across Borders (IAB), has conducted project surveys in 87 countries in 2009, targeting information regarding technical regulatory and licensing only, discounting human impact. The information compares investment climates and opportunities for competition—thus the IFC/FIAS compiled 'A Diagnostic Checklist for Land Markets' itemizing questions about land holding customs, law, power struggles, state capacity to protect investments, and so on (Daniel, 2010, pp. 17–18).

The proliferation of these development 'services' deepens the informal infrastructure of global enclosure. This infrastructure has both ideological and material dimensions. It recycles the trope of 'feeding the world' informing the new investment rules. It also includes a multifaceted complex: in addition to legal and technical assistance from the development agencies, and soft law procedural guidelines for land investments, there are Roundtables to certify soy and oil palm production in the name of environmental sustainability, and climate protocols such as the EU's Emissions Trading Scheme (ETS), Kyoto's Clean Development Mechanism (CDM), and Reduced Emissions from Degradation and Deforestation (REDD)—all geared to incentivize land acquisitions, offsets, and set-asides in the name of greenhouse gas emission management (see Fortin and Richardson, 2013, pp. 141–159; Margulis and Porter, 2013, pp. 65–86).

With respect to emergent soft law procedural guidelines, the food regime incorporates a private framework with voluntary codes of conduct proposed by the development agencies (World Bank and FAO) to legitimize and facilitate the restructuring associated with land grabbing. Whereas WTO rules enabled dumping of Northern food in Southern markets, and the rise of new agro-exporting states (e.g. Brazil, Argentina, Thailand), the new land acquisition protocols foreshadow global enclosure in the name of commodification. First, patterns of circulation are *reconstituted*, as land grabs capitalize new agro-export zones. Second, the commodities circulating are increasingly *fungible* as food, feed, fuel, and processed foods. Third, circulating commodities embody the cheap land, water, and labor resources captured by land deals effected by a state-finance capital nexus dedicated to constructing *new frontiers* of accumulation. And fourth, this restructuring regime embodies a normative vision of *agricultural modernization*, enhanced food production, smallholder incorporation into value chains, rural employment, and smart agro-technologies (McMichael and Schneider, 2011).

Land Governance Contention

New initiatives in land (grabbing) governance include the 'infrastructural' protocols listed above, and especially the voluntary codes of conduct. With respect to these codes, the difference between the World Bank-led Responsible Agricultural Investment (RAI) and the recent *Voluntary Guidelines on the Responsible Governance of Tenure of Land, Fisheries and Forests in the Context of National Food Security* (herein 'Voluntary Guidelines') of the FAO's Committee on Food Security's (CFS) regarding the social implications of land grabbing is striking. The difference centers on the politics of the 'agricultural footprint' of foreign investors. Whereas the RAI sanctions the agro-exporting model associated with the WTO regime, deepened by 'security mercantilism', the Voluntary Guidelines tilt in the opposite direction, strengthening recognition of customary property tenure and gender equity on the land, and supporting the principle of 'food sovereignty' (Patel, 2009).

The RAI emerged from closed-door discussions by the Bank and other multilaterals, reproducing a developmentalist model, focusing on investment protocols rather than on land rights (Borras and Franco, 2010, p. 511). Because of its investment focus it has been rejected by the International Planning Committee for Food Sovereignty (IPC) network and other CSOs in favor of a(n ongoing) consultative process under CFS auspices, regarding the impact of land investment on the rights of inhabitants on targeted lands. Key to this initiative are two alternative policy frameworks: the Voluntary Guidelines (designed to strengthen recognition of customary property tenure and address gender inequity) and the Minimum Human Rights Principle proposed by the UN Special Rapporteur for the right to food, Olivier De Schutter (see Claeys and Vanloqueren, 2013, pp. 193–198).

The juxtaposition of these codes reflect the tensions in the food/fuel regime in transition, as land grab investors and governments face rising opposition from CSOs and in public forums (see *The Economist*, 2011). Thus in October 2011 the Pan-African Parliament Committee on Rural Economy, Agriculture, Natural Resources and Environment proposed a moratorium on new large-scale land acquisitions, pending implementation of land policies and guidelines on good land governance (see http://farmlandgrab.org/post/view/19457). And in May 2012, Friends of the Earth International (FOEI) released a report entitled 'Land, life and justice: How land grabbing in Uganda is affecting the environment, livelihoods and food sovereignty of communities' on the eve of the World Bank's conference on land and poverty. The report details Bank assistance for land grab projects that force people to 'give up their livelihoods, food supply and access to water', and how Uganda and other developing countries, 'desperate to create jobs and eradicate poverty, . . . are increasingly being duped by multinational corporations and financial investors to give away large tracts of land for commercial farms that these players are exploiting to whet their food needs, energy supplies and investment at the expense of locals' (Matsiko, 2012). Lester Brown (2011) locates tensions in 'food nationalism' (that is, 'security mercantilism'), suggesting that it 'may help secure food supplies for individual affluent countries, but it does little to enhance world food security. Indeed, the low-income countries that host land grabs or import grain will likely see their food situation deteriorate.' De Schutter, in characterizing the RAI as 'responsibly destroying the world's peasantry', notes that because the RAI principles 'ignore human rights, they neglect the essential dimension of accountability' (2010).

The CFS's Voluntary Guidelines address accountability directly through a membership that gives voice (beyond states and financial institutions) to CSOs (such as FoodFirst Information and Action Network/FIAN, Oxfam, Action Aid International, the Action Group on Erosion, Technology and Concentration/ETC, and the Asian NGO coalition for Agrarian Reform and Rural Development). The Voluntary Guidelines also 'represent the first negotiated agreement . . . [to] . . . create an international standard' which matters 'because the CFS has a comprehensive mandate—which is the only way governments will be able to transform agriculture and food systems to eradicate hunger and ensure sustainable production . . .' (Murphy, 2012; also Seufert, 2013, pp. 181–186). Whether and to what extent the Voluntary Guidelines will gain traction in regulating land grabbing remains to be seen, but it does represent an alternative approach to RAI agnosticism regarding investment source, product destination, and social implications of enclosure. As the Special Rapporteur on the right to food notes: 'It is precisely because the links between trade and the realization of the right to food are complex that human rights impact assessments should be conducted before free trade agreements are agreed upon' (De Schutter, 2012, p. 5). Ultimately, contention centers on the meaning of 'the right to food'. In this particular conjuncture, *land grabbing includes an alternative (investor-driven) 'right to food' appropriating the vision of the human 'right to food'*.

The question of the right to food now drives FAO deliberations, in particular via the recent reform of the CFS (2009) (McKeon, 2013, pp. 105–122). In addition to revitalizing the one-country-one-vote structure, CSOs were recognized by member states as critical to the reform and action plans. The International Planning Committee for Food Sovereignty (IPC) played a key role in securing the right to food as a central objective, and shifting the center of gravity of participants from the international financial institutions towards CSOs representing a variety of key 'stakeholders' including smallholding farmers, artisanal fisherfolk, pastoralists, landless, urban poor, agricultural and food workers, women, youth, consumers, indigenous peoples, and related NGOs (Wilson, 2010, p. 20). The CFS thus 'provides for a totally unprecedented level and quality of participation by non-state actors, with particular attention to organizations representing small food producers and poor urban consumers . . . [and recognizes] the right of civil society organizations to autonomously establish a global mechanism to facilitate their participation in the CFS' (McKeon, 2011, p. 15).

The CFS ontology, unlike that of the WTO, does not equate food security with markets (McMichael, 2003). It is predisposed to addressing 'reality on the ground' where supporting farming populations (the majority of the world's poor) is integral to the alleviation of hunger. De Schutter observes that adopting 'a human rights framework . . . may guide the redefinition of the policy priorities triggered by the current crisis. The question "for whose benefit?" is at least as important as the question "how to produce more?"' (2008). The subsequent consolidation of this ontology through the CFS consultative process has enabled the CFS to make 'important strides in being recognized as a significant forum'—especially in developing an alternative framework to that of the RAI (McKeon, 2011, p. 16).

While the CFS intervention is in a formative stage, there has been a discursive shift within the development community, as neoliberal claims for food security via the market have been compromised by the continuing food crisis, and the majority interests of smallholding food producers have found an institutional voice in the FAO, at least. Borras et al. note, cautiously: 'to date we have not witnessed . . . a spark of multi-level protests from the same groups of civil society organizations with scale and intensity that is anywhere close to the anti-WTO campaign. . . . There are scattered mobilizations, including those in the arena of the UN Committee on Food Security (CFS)' (2011, p. 43). It is in this forum that the claim for the implementation of domestic food security measures is taking hold, and it represents an institutional beachhead for resistance to land grabbing and its mercantilist footprint.

Conclusion

This essay claims that contemporary land grabbing represents a challenge to the ordering of trade relations via the WTO-based corporate food regime. The latter depended on a contradictory structure of free trade among member states, allowing dominant agro-exporters (in particular the US and the EU) to manage global 'food security' via world 'granaries'. Current trends indicate a restructuring trajectory as land investments driven by security concerns on the part of East Asian and Middle Eastern states capitalize new agro-export zones 'offshore' alongside other forms of land grabbing driven by financial and agribusiness and energy companies. Catalyzed by the food price inflation of 2007–2008, land grabbing seeks to secure food supplies and speculative gains on the one hand, and a more fundamental shifting of geo-economic relations on the other. Geo-economic shifts involve a double diversification, of (1) *supply zones* in rising middle-income agro-exporters and on (primarily African) frontiers comprised of unprotected smallholders and common lands, and (2) *fungible agricultural products*: food, feed, and fuel.

As suggested, Northern states are losing their centrality in organizing and dominating the food/fuel regime—not only because of the G20 challenge to WTO rules, but also because certain states (especially Asian and Middle Eastern states) are overriding the WTO multilateralism in directly commandeering agricultural supplies. Such commandeering may even assume a liberal face—such as the agreement signed in August 2012 by Bangladesh to take a 10-year lease on South Sudanese land to *jointly* produce food crops (*Daily Star*, 2012). One might argue that the 'land grab' is really the opening round of a more profound scramble for high ground, so to speak, as energy descent and climate catastrophe intensifies (cf. Parenti, 2011). It is possible that codes of conduct will cease to provide the veneer they provide today of 'responsibly destroying the world's peasantry' (De Schutter, 2010), and may cease altogether if the state system is unable to curb an intensifying resource competition, exemplified in recent forms of 'security mercantilism' that defy the embedded liberalism of the WTO.

An alternative scenario is preferable (and possible)—one that matches a global anti-land grab mobilization (on the ground and in institutions like the FAO/CFS) with growing recognition of the rationality of recognizing the greater resilience and democratic consequence of land, energy, water, and food sovereignty initiatives. Given the crisis of industrial agriculture, and the growing international consensus regarding the superior knowledge-intensive, environmentally restorative, and climatic sustainability of small and medium-sized diverse farming (Altieri, 2010; Badgley and Perfecto, 2007; IAASTD, 2008; Pretty et al., 2006), there is a chance that such 'scaling down and out' will deepen. In order to secure this outcome, there are perhaps two related organizational frameworks. First is the kind of democratic multilateral scenario proposed by French activist, Jose Bové, for a reformed UN (embodied in reform of the CFS) and alternative multilateral institutions such as a Convention on Food Sovereignty and Trade in Food and Agriculture and a World Commission on Sustainable Agriculture and Food Sovereignty (Bové and Dufour, 2001, p. 165), and symbolized in the global campaign for a UN Peasants' Charter (Edelman and James, 2011). The second is the formation of bioregional scales of political organization, centered on agroecosystems as the solution to human survival in a climate-challenged planet (Duncan, 1996). The journey towards this outcome, where 'territory' acquires a biophysical rather than simply a political form, begins with politicization of land grabbing.

Acknowledgement

The author is grateful for the helpful suggestions of two anonymous reviewers for revisions to the original draft of this article.

Notes

1   This observation is echoed in Borras et al. (2011, pp. 25–26), describing 'an emerging polycentric food-energy regime—in contrast to previous food regimes anchored by empires on either side of the North Atlantic', and in Dauvergne and Neville (2009). It is notable that a substantial part of land grabbing concerns bringing land into production of domestic food and fuel crops, which registers a rising global middle class in BRICS countries in particular and across the Global South in general (cf. Cotula, 2012, p. 664).

2   Thus a GRAIN researcher notes: 'Rich countries are eyeing Africa not just for a healthy return on capital, but also as an insurance policy. Food shortages and riots in 28 countries, declining water supplies, climate change and huge population growth have together made land attractive' (Vidal, 2010).

3   Cotula's research suggests that some contracts (e.g. Sudan, Mali) 'appear to create no safeguards to ensure that local food security needs are met'—at odds with claims by host governments to improve domestic food security (Cotula, 2011, p. 37).

References

Altieri, M. (2010) Scaling up agroecological approaches for food sovereignty in Latin America, in H. Wittman, A. A. Desmarais & N. Wiebe (eds), *Food Sovereignty. Reconnecting Food, Nature and Community* (Halifax: Fernwood), pp. 120–133.

Anseeuw, W., Alden Wily, L., Cotula, L. & Taylor, M. (2011) *Land Rights and the Rush for Land: Findings of the Global Commercial Pressures on Land Research Report* (Rome: ILC).

Araghi, F. (2003) Food regimes and the production of value: some methodological issues, *The Journal of Peasant Studies*, 30(2), pp. 337–368.

Araghi, F. (2009) Accumulation by displacement: global enclosures, the food crisis, and the ecological contradictions of capitalism, *Review*, 32(1), pp. 113–146.

Arrighi, G. (2007) *Adam Smith in Beijing: Lineages of the Twenty-First Century* (London & New York: Verso).

Asian Peasant Coalition (APC) (2011) Indonesia's land acquisition bill will intensify landgrabbing, says Asian peasant group, *Farmlandgrab*, 17 December. http://farmlandgrab.org/post/view/19785.

Badgley, C. & Perfecto, I. (2007) Can organic agriculture feed the world? *Renewable Agriculture and Food Systems*, 22(2), pp. 80–85.

Borras, S. M., Jr. & Franco, J. (2010) From threat to opportunity? Problems with the idea of a 'code of conduct' for land-grabbing, *Yale Human Rights and Development Law Journal*, 13(2), pp. 507–523.

Borras, S. M., Jr., Franco, J. C., Kay, C. & Spoor, M. (2011) *Land Grabbing in Latin America and the Caribbean Viewed from Broader International Perspectives* (Chile: FAO Regional Office).

Borras, S. M., Jr., Franco, J. C., Goméz, S., Kay, C. & Spoor, M. (2012) Land grabbing in Latin America and the Caribbean, *Journal of Peasant Studies*, 39(3/4), pp. 845–872.

Bové, J. & Dufour, F. (2001) *The World Is Not For Sale* (London: Verso).

Brown, L. (2011) The new geopolitics of food, *Foreign Policy*, May/June, http://www.foreignpolicy.com/articles/2011/04/25/the_new_geopolitics_of_food.

Claeys, P. & Vanloqueren, G. (2013) The minimum human rights principles applicable to large-scale land acquisitions or leases, *Globalizations*, 10(1), pp. 193–198.

Colchester, M., Aik Pang, W., Chuo, W. M. & Jalong, T. (2007) *Land is Life: Land Rights and Oil Palm Development in Sarawak* (Bogor: Sawit Watch & Moreton-in-Marsh: Forest Peoples Programme).

Committee on World Food Security (CFS) (2011) *Land Tenure and International Investments in Agriculture: A Report by The High Level Panel of Experts on Food Security and Nutrition*, July (Rome: Committee on World Food Security (FAO)).

Cotula, L. (2011) *Land Deals: What's in the Contracts?* (London: IIED).

Cotula, L. (2012) The international political economy of the global land rush: a critical analysis of trends, scale, geography and drivers, *Journal of Peasant Studies*, 39(3/4), pp. 649–680.

Coordination Paysanne Européene (CPE) (2006) *For a Legitimate, Sustainable, and Supportive Common Agricultural Policy*, 15 November, http://www.cpefarmers.org.

Daily Star (2012) Bangladesh to lease Sudanese farmland, *Daily Star*, 3 August, http://farmlandgrab.org/post/view/20869.

Daniel, S. (2009) *The Great Land Grab: Rush for World's Farmland Threatens Food Security for the Poor* (Oakland, CA: The Oakland Institute).

Daniel, S. (2010) *(Mis)Investment in Agriculture: The Role of the International Finance Corporation in Global Land Grabs* (Oakland, CA: The Oakland Institute).

Dauvergne, P. & Neville, K. J. (2009) The changing North-South and South-South political economy of biofuels, *Third World Quarterly*, 30(6), pp. 1087–1102.

De Schutter, O. (2008) Building resilience: a human rights framework for food and nutritional security, 8 September, A/HRC/9/23 (New York: United Nations).

De Schutter, O. (2010) Responsibly destroying the world's peasantry, 4 June, http://farmlandgrab.org/13528.

De Schutter, O. (2011) The World Trade Organization and the post-global food crisis agenda, Briefing Note 04, November (Rome: FAO/United Nations).

De Schutter, O. (2012) Submission to the consultation on the First Draft of the Global Strategic Framework for Food Security and Nutrition of the Committee on World Food Security, 8 May (Rome: FAO/United Nations).

Deininger, K. & Byerlee, D. (2011) The rise of large farms in land abundant countries: do they have a future? Policy Research Working Paper 5588 (Washington, DC: World Bank Development Research Group Agriculture and Rural Development Team).

Deininger, K., Byerlee, D., Lindsay, J., Norton, A., Selod, H. & Stickler, M. (2011) *Rising Global Interest in Farmland: Can It Yield Sustainable and Equitable Benefits?* (Washington, DC: World Bank).

Dolan, C. S. (2004) On farm and packhouse: employment at the bottom of a global value chain, *Rural Sociology*, 69(1), pp. 99–126.

Duncan, C. (1996) *The Centrality of Agriculture: Between Humankind and the Rest of Nature* (Montreal: McGill-Queen's University Press).

Economist, The (2008) The new face of hunger, 17 April, http://www.economist.com/node/11049284.

Economist, The (2011) Evidence is piling up against acquisitions of farmland in poor countries, 5 May, http://farmlandgrab.org/post/view/18564.

Edelman, M. & James, C. (2011) Peasants' rights and the UN system: Quixotic struggle? Or emancipator idea whose time has come? *Journal of Peasant Studies*, 38(1), pp. 81–108.

Fairbairn, M. (2011) Indirect dispossession: how domestic power imbalances mediate foreign demand for land in Mozambique, Presentation to LDPI Land Grab conference, University of Sussex, April.

Fortin, E. & Richardson, B. (2013) Certification schemes and the governance of land: enforcing standards or enabling scrutiny? *Globalizations*, 10(1), pp. 141–159.

French, H. (2004) Linking globalization, consumption, and governance, in Linda Starke (ed.), *State Of the World, 2004: The Consumer Society* (Washington, DC: The WorldWatch Institute), pp. 144–163.

Friedmann, H. (1978) World market, state, and family farm: social bases of household production in an era of wage labor, *Comparative Studies in Society and History*, 20(4), pp. 545–586.

Friedmann, H. (1982) The political economy of food: the rise and fall of the postwar international food order, *American Journal of Sociology*, 88S, pp. 248–286.

Friedmann, H. & McMichael, P. (1989) Agriculture and the state system: the rise and fall of national agricultures, 1870 to the present, *Sociologia Ruralis*, 29(2), pp. 93–117.

Fritz, T. (2011), Globalizing Hunger: Food Security and the EU's Common Agricultural Policy (CAP). Transnational Institute (draft).

Giddens, A. (1987) *The Nation-State and Violence* (Cambridge: Polity Press).

GRAIN (2010) Turning African farmland over to big business: the US's Millennium Challenge Corporation, *Seedling*, 3–5 April.

GRAIN (2012) GRAIN releases data set with over 400 global land grabs, 23 February, http://www.grain.org/fr/article/entries/4479-grain-releases-data-set-with-over-400-global-land-grabs.

Green, A. R. (2012) Africa: Saudi Agricultural Minister enticed by continent land, *This is Africa*, 8 June, http://farmlandgrab.org/post/print/20619.

Herman, P. & Kuper, R. (2003) *Food for Thought: Towards a Future for Farming* (London: Pluto Press).

Hofman, I. & Ho, P. (2102) China's 'developmental outsourcing': a critical examination of Chinese global 'land grabs' discourse, *Journal of Peasant Studies*, 39(1), pp. 1–48.

Holt-Giménez, E. (2007) Exploding the biofuel myths, *Le Monde diplomatique*, July, pp. 10–11.

International Assessment of Agricultural Knowledge, Science and Technology for Development (IAASTD) (2008) Executive summary of the synthesis report, http://www.agassessment.org/docs/SR_Exec_Sum_280508_English.pdf.

Kaufman, F. (2010) The food bubble: how Wall Street starved millions and got away with it, *Harper's Magazine*, July, pp. 27–34.

Kautsky, K. (1988 [1899]) *The Agrarian Question* (Vol. 2) (London: Zwan Publications).

Kössler, R. (2003) The modern nation state and regimes of violence: reflections on the current situation, *Ritsumeikan Annual Review of International Studies*, 2, pp. 15–36.

McKeon, N. (2011) *Global Governance for World Food Security: A Scorecard Four Years After the Eruption of the 'Food Crisis'* (Berlin: Heinrich-Böll-Stiftung).

McKeon, N. (2013) 'One does not sell the land upon which the people walk': land grabbing, rural social movements, and global governance, *Globalizations*, 10(1), pp. 105–122.

McMichael, P. (2000) Sleepless since Seattle: what is the WTO about? *Review of International Political Economy*, 7(3), pp. 466–474.

McMichael, P. (2003) Food security and social reproduction, in S. Gill & I. Bakker (eds), *Power, Production and Social Reproduction* (Basingstoke, UK: Palgrave MacMillan), pp.

McMichael, P. (2009) A food regime genealogy, *Journal of Peasant Studies*, 36(1), pp. 139–170.

McMichael, P. (2012) The 'land grab' and corporate food regime restructuring, *Journal of Peasant Studies*, 39(3/4), pp. 681–701.

McMichael, P. & Schneider, M. (2011) Food security politics and the Millennium Development Goals, *Third World Quarterly*, 32(1), pp. 119–139.

Margulis, M. E. & Porter, T. (2013) Governing the global land grab: multipolarity, ideas, and complexity in transnational governance, *Globalizations*, 10(1), pp. 65–86.

Marsden, T. K. (2003) *The Condition of Rural Sustainability* (Wageningen: Van Gorcum).

Matsiko, H. (2012) World Bank under attack for aiding land grabs in Uganda, *The Independent*, 6 May, http://farmlandgrab.org/post/view/20446.

MercoPress (2011) Mozambique offers Brazilian farmers 6 million hectares to develop agriculture, *MercoPress*, 16 August, http://en.mercopress.com/2011/08/16/mozambique-offers-brazilian-farmers-6-million-hectares-to-develop-agriculture

Middle East Business News (2012) Great resource rush, 7 May, http://farmlandgrab.org/post/view/20448.

Moore, J. (2012) Cheap food & bad money: Food, frontiers, and financialization in the rise and demise of neoliberalism, *Review*, 33(2–3).

Murphy, S. (2012) Governments agree on voluntary rules to control land grabs, *IATP*, 16 March, http://www.farmlandgrab.org/post/print/20191.

Parenti, C. (2011) *Tropic of Chaos. Climate Change and the New Geography of Violence* (New York: Nation Books).

Patel, R. (2009) What does food sovereignty look like? *Journal of Peasant Studies*, 36(3), pp. 663–706.

Patnaik, P. (2008) The accumulation process in the period of globalization, *Economic and Political Weekly*, 28, pp. 108–113.

Pearce, F. (2012) *The Land Grabbers: The New Fight Over Who Owns the Earth* (Boston: Beacon Press).

Peluso, N. L. & Lund, C. (2011) New frontiers of land control: introduction, *The Journal of Peasant Studies*, 38(4), pp. 667–681.

Pretty, J., Noble, A. D., Bossio, D., Dixon, J., Hine, R. E., Penning de Vries, F. W. T. & Morison, J. I. L. (2006) Resource conserving agriculture increases yields in developing countries, *Environmental Science & Technology*, 40(4), pp. 1114–1119.

Pritchard, B. (2009) The long hangover from the second food regime: a world-historical interpretation of the collapse of the WTO Doha Round, *Agriculture and Human Values*, 26(4), pp. 297–307.

Rosset, P. (2008) Food sovereignty and the contemporary food crisis, *Development*, 51(4), pp. 460–463.

Sassen, S. (2013) Land grabs today: feeding the disassembling of national territory, *Globalizations*, 10(1), pp. 25–46.

Seufert, P. (2013) The FAO Voluntary Guidelines on the Responsible Governance of Tenure of Land, Fisheries and Forests, *Globalizations*, 10(1), pp. 181–186.

Shaw, M. (1994) *Global Society and International Relations: Sociological Concepts and Political Perspectives* (Cambridge: Polity Press).

Urquhart, S. (2008) Food crisis, which crisis? Our crisis or theirs? The battle over the world's food supply relocates to Rome, *Guerilla News Network*, 2 June, http://gnn.tv/articles/3718/food_crisis_which_crisis.

Van der Ploeg, J. D. (2010) The food crisis, industrialized farming and the imperial regime, *Journal of Agrarian Change*, 10(1), pp. 98–106.

Vidal, J. (2010) How food and water are driving a 21st-century African land grab, *The Observer*, 7 March.

Visser, O. & Spoor, M. (2011) Land grabbing in post-Soviet Eurasia: the world's largest agricultural land reserves at stake, *Journal of Peasant Studies*, 38(2), pp. 299–324.

Wallerstein, I. (1974) *The Modern World-System: Capitalist Agriculture and the Origins of the European World-Economy in the Sixteenth Century* (New York: Academic Press).

Weis, T. (2007) *The Global Food Economy: The Battle for the Future of Farming* (London & New York: Zed Press).

Weis, T. (2010) The accelerating biophysical contradictions of industrial capitalist agriculture, *Journal of Agrarian Change*, 10(3), pp. 315–341.

Wilkinson, J. & Herrera, S. (2009) *Agrofuels in Brazil: what is the outlook for its farming sector?* (Rio de Janeiro: Oxfam International), http://www.globalbioenergy.org/uploads/media/0811_WilkinsonHerrera_-_Agrofuels_in_Brazil.pdf.

Wilson, J. B. (2010) *The Reformed Committee on World Food Security: A Briefing Paper for Civil Society* (Bilbao: International Planning Committee for Food Sovereignty).

World Bank (2007) *World Development Report 2008: Agriculture for Development* (Washington, DC: World Bank).

Zagema, B. (2011) Land and power: the growing scandal surrounding the new wave of investments in land, *Oxfam Briefing Paper* (Oxford, UK: Oxfam International).

Zoomers, A. (2010) Globalisation and the foreignisation of space: seven processes driving the current global land grab, *Journal of Peasant Studies*, 37(2), pp. 429–448.

Philip McMichael is a Professor of Development Sociology at Cornell University. His research is on the contemporary agrarian question, including land grabbing and its legitimating discourses, and agrarian resistances. He has authored *Development and Social Change: A Global Perspective* (Sage, 2012, 5th edn.) and edited *Contesting Development: Critical Struggles for Social Change* (Routledge, 2010). He has also worked with the FAO, UNRISD, the IPC for Food Sovereignty, and La Vía Campesina.

Governing the Global Land Grab: Multipolarity, Ideas, and Complexity in Transnational Governance

MATIAS E. MARGULIS* & TONY PORTER**

*University of Northern British Columbia, Prince George, Canda & Max Planck Institute for the Study of Societies, Cologne, Germany
**McMaster University, Hamilton, Canada

ABSTRACT   *Since 2008, a series of new regulatory initiatives have emerged to address large-scale land grabs. These initiatives are occurring simultaneously at multiple levels of social organization instead of a single, overarching institutional site. A significant portion of this activity is taking place at the transnational level. We suggest that transnational land governance is indicative of emerging shifts in the practice of governance of global affairs. We analyze such shifts by asking two related questions: what does land grabbing tell us about developments in transnational governance, particularly with regard to North–South relations, and what do these developments in transnational governance mean for regulating land grabbing?*

Introduction

Since 2008, a series of new regulatory initiatives and global institution-building projects have emerged to address large-scale land grabs. These are occurring simultaneously at multiple levels of social organization instead of a single, overarching institutional site. The range of actors operating in this web is considerable and highly diverse and we see states, multilateral organizations, global civil society, corporate actors, and peasant farmers engaging in and demanding diverse modes of governance. Taken together, these signal the emergence of what might be termed transnational land governance.

We develop four propositions about the complexity of transnational land governance that, in our view, have not been accorded sufficient attention in the literature on land grabbing and permits for a more critical study of land grabbing and global governance. The first proposition is that the institutional arrangements associated with US dominance and the earlier colonial period of land grabbing are being replaced by more complex, polycentric ones operating in an increasingly multipolar global political economy, rendering the previous North–South and West–East cleavages less relevant. The second proposition is that the ideational and the material aspects of transnational governance are becoming more directly entangled and complex as we approach or surpass the earth's physical ability to sustain our civilization and a multiplicity of actors mobilize normative beliefs and scientific knowledge to address intensified resource challenges and land conflicts. The third proposition is that conflict and collaboration among states and other actors will play out through the informal complex of transnational land governance arrangements rather than undermining or replacing them, for instance by developing purely local or more formal, legalized international solutions. The fourth proposition is that the best chance for protecting vulnerable populations, often subject to illegal and violent dispossession of their land, is for concerned transnational advocacy networks and states to work through and seek to orchestrate the informal complex of transnational land governance towards social justice ends. The next section of the essay develops the theoretical aspects of the above propositions. The following sections then examine the relevance of our propositions to land grabbing.

Theorizing New Developments in Transnational Governance

There is a widespread sense that the pace of change in global affairs is accelerating, perhaps even catastrophically. Scholars have made important advances in understanding the significance of these changes, moving us well beyond older models of international affairs such as state-centric realism. It is important to build on these insights from studies of global and transnational governance to know how best to regulate or challenge land grabbing. In this section, we draw on insights from existing studies to develop our four propositions.

Beyond Older Colonial and Unipolar Power Relations

The global financial and economic crisis that began in 2007 revealed most clearly significant shifts in the balance of power among key international actors. The replacement of the Group of Eight (G8) by the Group of Twenty (G20) at the Heads of State level and the incorporation of the G20's developing country members into all the significant institutions in the international financial architecture marked decisively the arrival of new participants at the table of great powers. This was reinforced by the damage the crisis did to the US and European economies and to the credibility of their economic models, and the strength displayed by other economies, such as China's or Brazil's. These shifts in the balance of power are not confined to global finance but demonstrable across diverse governance fields, including international trade (Narlikar and Tussie, 2004; Narlikar and Wilkinson 2004), climate change (Barros-Platiau 2010; Hochstetler and Viola, 2012; Vihma, 2011; Williams, 2005), money (Bowles and Wang, 2008), energy (Lesage et al., 2010; Victor and Yeuh, 2010) and oceans (Suárez de Vivero and Rodríguez Mateos, 2010). Exceptions remain, such as emerging powers limited inroads at the IMF and World Bank evident in these countries' minor voting shares (Wade, 2011). However the power shift is evident even within these institutions, as the increased prominence of emerging powers in foreign aid is changing the theory and practice of global development and no longer the exclusive remit of the North (see Dauvergne and Farias, 2012; de Haan, 2011;

Tan-Mullins et al., 2010; Walz and Ramachadran, 2011). This change has been called a 'silent revolution' in global development (Woods, 2008).

Our point is not to claim that the US has been dislodged from its privileged position. Clearly, the US remains a dominant actor. Nevertheless the US is experiencing a relative erosion of power, introducing new dynamics to the global system and making possible future trajectories in transnational governance that may not have been imaginable previously. Consequently, talk of US empire or unipolarity, which had been fashionable earlier in the decade, is less useful today to the extent it renders invisible, or implicitly makes secondary, the power dynamics of multipolarity.

Two lessons from international relations theory for understanding multipolarity are clear. The first is that governance is likely to be more complicated with larger numbers of major players at the table with ever more diverse interests (see Lake, 1993). A second, discussed further below, is that polarity is only one among many factors that shape transnational governance, and other forms of power and order than the conventional state capabilities that theories of polarity focus on are also important. These changes are highly relevant to land grabbing, and lead to our first proposition: the political and economic institutions associated with colonialism and US unipolarity are being supplanted by a more complex set of relationships, in which old cleavages that separated North and South or a capitalist West and a state-centric East are no longer as relevant.

The Ideational, the Material, and the Earth's Limits

Two quite different aspects of transnational governance have displayed increased prominence in recent years: its ideational and material aspects. Inspired by the 'cultural turn' in the social sciences, the increased importance of the ideational aspect is evident in a long list of theoretical innovations in the study of international relations and global governance, including epistemic communities (Haas, 1989), soft power (Nye, 2005), constructivism (Wendt, 1995), post-structuralism (de Goede, 2006), cultural political economy (Jessop, 2004), and legitimacy (Cashore, 2003; Zürn, 2004). The increased complexity of materiality in transnational governance is evident in the major concerns that have assumed a higher priority in global public policy, including sustainable development and climate change, which reference the material limits of the earth; global health issues which concern the materiality of the body; and global poverty alleviation, which involves material standards of living.

While initially much of the focus of ideational research programs within international relations was on whether ideas could shape the interactions among states, it is increasingly urgent today to understand better the more direct power relationships between transnational ideas and the materiality of the earth and its life forms. The mediating role of states in this relationship can still be important. However many of these material/ideational interactions do not run through states, for instance when new private sector ideas like genetic engineering have direct material effects on the earth and its life forms. Risk has become increasingly important in managing the interactions between humans and our environment, including in specific interactions that are some distance from traditional centralized state policies (Aradau and Van Munster, 2007; Power, 2007).

This leads to our second proposition: normative beliefs and scientific knowledge are important not only because they influence states, but also because they directly interact with the intensified resource challenges and land conflicts that accompany the earth's diminishing physical ability to sustain our civilization.

The Complexity of Transnational Governance

A great deal of scholarly work has been done to illuminate the complexity of transnational governance.[1] State principals delegate to non-state agents or intergovernmental organizations that they do not fully control. Business and other non-state actors produce and implement rules and operations that states would have provided in previous times. One theme in this literature is that the local, national, and global interact in complex ways.

An emerging theme in this literature is that it is important to analyze both the autonomy of particular regimes or clusters of institutions and their interactions with one another. This contrasts, for instance, with an earlier research program on international regimes that focused on one regime at a time and sought to analyze its relationship with the states involved in it (Krasner, 1982). A growing number of studies have shown that interaction among regimes and/or clusters of institutions is deepening and producing uncertainty for actors (Raustiala and Victor, 2004). Heightened uncertainty may lead to new cooperation and coordination problems, such as constraining or chilling effects by one institution on another (Axelrod, 2011; Conca, 2000; Eckersley, 2004; Oberthür and Gehring, 2006; Veggeland and Borgen, 2005) or 'spillover' effects that can reinforce fragmentation and regime integration/separation dynamics (Biermann et al., 2009; Johnson and Urpelainen, 2012). Uncertainty also creates opportunities for policy entrepreneurs and new ideas to enter global policy spaces that may set governance along new pathways.

Alter and Meunier (2009) for instance identify the systemic effects of complexity, such as an increase in *chessboard politics* where states manipulate complexity, for instance through forum shifting, but they also create relatively *autonomous small group environments* because states engage in a series of smaller forums instead of a few large universal intergovernmental organizations. Abbott and Snidal (2009) treat this as a shift from *old governance*, which is top down, to *transnational new governance* in which states orchestrate a variety of institutions that may be formal or informal, public or private. Jessop and Sum (2006, p. 267) call this *metagovernance* (setting the rules for other governance bodies) and *collibration* (working to modify the balance of power among them). This is similar as well to the use by Braithwaite and Drahos (2000) of the concept of *enrolment* from actor-network theory, where even weaker actors can enhance their power by creating programs that attract adherence from decentralized networks that they do not definitively control. 'Orchestration', 'collibration', and 'enrolment' are similar concepts in their emphasis on the importance for successful outcomes of strategic engagement with a loosely defined set of relatively autonomous zones of governance, rather than reliance on rules emanating from a single center of control. However, 'enrolment' is best suited to the identification of opportunities for weak or non-state actors to initiate and benefit from such engagement.[2]

This leads to our third proposition: the types of informal mediating governance institutions that have proliferated will continue to grow, and the altered balance of power will play out through them, rather than undermining them. This development is particularly salient for understanding emergent transnational land governance because we suggest that new regulatory initiatives are likely to interact and overlap with a wider constellation of regimes and clusters of institutions. Those actors that do not recognize the significance of these interactions are likely not to respond effectively to the governance opportunities and challenges that accompany them.

Strategies for Protecting the Vulnerable

Our analysis leads us to formulate a fourth and more practical proposition: that smaller and poorer actors will be most successful in achieving social justice-oriented goals, including the revalorization of collective/communal land rights and small-scale agriculture, by working through these types of complex transnational governance rather than trying to avoid or reverse them, for instance by focusing more exclusively on solutions at the local level or at the formal intergovernmental level (for instance through treaties). This view is consistent with research by Braithwaite and Drahos (2000), who have proposed a number of ways that weaker actors can prevail over stronger actors in transnational governance by making use of its complex and normative character, successfully enrolling other actors and networks. Such strategies have worked in various governance fields. Take, for instance, transnational advocacy for human rights (Keck and Sikkink, 1998), access to medicines (Sell and Prakash, 2004), and digital copyright (Dobusch and Quack, 2012). Our view is also consistent with research on the experience of developing countries in transnational networks by Martinez-Diaz and Woods (2009). Therefore, a transnational governance framework is useful to the extent that it can demonstrate how weak and strong actors can use formal and informal enrolment strategies to influence decision-making at multiple scales. It is also important to understand dynamics that lead to the 'disenfranchisement' (Fisher and Green, 2006) of weaker actors in transnational governance in order to develop strategies to prevent this. These approaches challenges more state-centric and rationalist views that would see these complex and fragile networks being undermined by interstate conflict, by a decline in the support provided them by US hegemony, ideology, or business, or by a resurgence of territorially based nationalism or regionalism. It also challenges Drezner's (2009, p. 66) more pessimistic view that sees the undermining of formal legal obligations that the growth of these informal institutions represent as beneficial to powerful states.

Land Grabbing, North–South Relations, and Complexity in Transnational Governance

We now begin to assess the relevance of these propositions for the issue of land grabbing. Land grabbing has generated a global debate over whether such large-scale investment in agriculture can promote pro-poor economic growth and sustainable development or whether instead it will exacerbate food insecurity, ecological deterioration, and political instability in developing countries (Cotula et al, 2009; HLPE, 2011). Scholarship has primarily focused on the local and national case studies where land grabbing is occurring and how it is being resisted. Links to global-level processes, such as the interplay with the political economy of biofuels, land reform, and agricultural restructuring in developing countries (Borras et al., 2010; Zoomers, 2010) are becoming better understood.

Like the other contributors to this volume, our view is that we need to pay more attention to the transnational dimensions of land grabbing and its governance. The proliferating literature on land grabbing is providing us a clearer view of its scale, location and characteristics albeit with big gaps in knowledge related to the lack of transparency and public disclosure of most transactions.[3] Rather than reproduce those overviews here, we proceed directly to our analysis of the three new developments in transnational governance that we discussed above.

Beyond Older Colonial and Hegemonic Power Relations

We suggest the utility of comparing the balance of state power across historical periods to highlight the political and economic institutions associated with land grabbing and how such institutions have shaped North–South relations. For our purposes, it is important to recognize that the current land grab is a massive and growing trend (Anseeuw et al., 2011; Oxfam, 2012;

World Bank, 2009).[4] However, this section will show that despite some similarities with earlier periods, current global power relations differ significantly from earlier ones.

In the era of colonialism, European sovereign states—Spain, the Netherlands, France, and Great Britain—were the drivers of the land grab in the pursuit of expanding their national wealth and empires (Weaver, 2003). During this period core–periphery relations dominated with imperial powers administering social, economic and political exchanges within the colonial territories. Core–periphery exchanges facilitated the transfer of wealth from colonies to serve the interests of an imperial power (Hobsbawm, 1987; Wallerstein, 1974).

After World War II the role of land in the developing world began to change. Formal colonialism began to disappear and US hegemony became a dominant feature of the global political economy (Ruggie, 1982). The US and its allies were not primarily concerned with the direct acquisition of land in the Global South. An important exception is the ownership of plantations such as those of the United Fruit Company, including the notorious case of CIA involvement in the 1954 overthrow of the Guatemalan government when it threatened that firm's interests in that country (Immerman, 1983). However, the general trend during this period was towards nationally oriented agricultural production, which, with the input of imported fertilizer and mechanized technology corresponded to the form of production that has been labeled Fordism (Busch and Bain, 2009; McMichael, 2009). Multinational corporations like Cargill and Monsanto dominated agri-food processing and trade that resulted but did not focus on direct foreign investment in land. In the socialist East and in many developing countries the state would often claim ownership of part or all of the farmland. Global institutions relevant to agriculture, such as the food aid regime that assisted in the disposal of Northern agricultural surpluses, or the exclusion of agriculture from the General Agreement on Tariffs and Trade (GATT), reflected these overall aspects of the post-World War II political economy of agriculture, and the pre-eminent role of the US in organizing it (Friedmann, 1992).

Present land grabs are characterized by complex and polycentric relationships that do not easily fit a core–periphery framework. Certainly many land grabs do have some characteristics of core–periphery relations. For example, Chinese land acquisitions in rural Africa suggest significant asymmetries of power and patterns of exploitation very closely resembling core–periphery relations associated with the era of imperialism given China's recent ascendency in global affairs (see Ayers, 2012). However, these do not come with formal colonial control, and elsewhere the situation is even more complex. For instance, substantial Chinese land acquisitions in rural Australia are not captured well by a core–periphery label. Brazilian investors are major players in the purchase of farmland across South America (Borras et al., 2012, p. 24; Dauvergne and Neville, 2010) and increasingly in Africa, which is a major target of Brazilian foreign and commercial policy (White, 2010). This policy of outward investment has strong and active support from the Brazilian state because it is increasing its firms profile in the agri-food sector, in which it is a global leader. Yet Brazilian land is also a target of foreign commercial interests and investment, which has prompted the Brazilian Congress to reform land ownership laws in order to curb speculative foreign investment (on 'land grabbed land grabbers', see Borras et al., 2013, pp. 161–179; Perrone, 2013, pp. 205–209).

During the colonial era, land was most often acquired by direct violent means and its legal ownership held by the titled monarchs of Europe in perpetuity (and later in common public trusts during the emergence of modern nation-states in the former colonies). Contemporary land grabs involve negotiated transfer of legal property rights between government or traditional land owners to investors. We recognize that the legitimacy and legality of many transactions remain deeply contested, that sporadic violence continues to occur and that land grabbing has increased the insecurity of many communities. Nevertheless, current land grabs are primarily mediated through formal practices (e.g. contracts, memoranda of understanding) sanctioned by the governance practices of national and subnational authorities and by transnational economic actors that have legal personality (Alden Wily, 2012).

The political economy of land in the earlier period of US hegemony differs in four additional ways from contemporary land acquisitions. First, the sources of capital for foreign direct investment in the food–feed–fuel complex are more varied then before, including private investors that have not otherwise specialized in agriculture and sovereign wealth funds or state-owned enterprises from emerging developing countries. Second, current land grabs are taking place in the context of a broader shifts in the agri-food industry where deregulated global trade, financialization, and advances in biotechnology and production methods are rapidly reorganizing the sector, precipitating a decline of the relative power of traditional agri-food corporations such as Cargill in favor of retailers such as Walmart and agri-food transnationals from the Global South (e.g. Brazil's JBS now boasts the status as the world largest producer of beef) (Clapp and Fuchs, 2009; Hopewell, 2012; McMichael, 2012). Third, there is an upswing in interest in direct foreign investment in land as a new asset class, notably by new actors such as private and public (i.e. national) pension funds estimated to be over $US5 billion (GRAIN, 2011, 2012). Such investment in land relates to its speculative value and the hopes of mitigating risk through its 'safe haven' status (Savills, 2012) and hopes for new sources of profit from biofuels, new agricultural technologies, or higher quality branded produce and processed food for which its origins and the conditions of its production matter. Fourth, developing countries are actively courting and facilitating direct foreign investments after decades of public disinvestment in agriculture, reflecting the reorientation of national policy towards a greater emphasis on the agricultural sector (see Borras et al., forthcoming; CAADP, 2010). This practice is supported by changes in the global policy and governance terrain such as the new global development paradigm of agricultural investment-led poverty reduction that has emerged as a major component of the G8/G20's response to the 2008 global food crisis, such as the L'Aquila Food Security Initiative and the New Alliance for Food Security and Nutrition and the World Bank's global food security fund (Margulis, 2012).

Overall then our proposition fits well with contemporary land grabbing. More complex sets of relationships are replacing older power relationships between North and South or between a US-led capitalist West and state-centric regions elsewhere.

The Ideational, the Material, and the Earth's Limits

There are numerous ways that land grabbing is related to a new and significant presence of material systemic threats to the earth and its life forms (see Foley et al., 2005). The search for land is driven to a significant degree by concerns that the earth's cultivable land is running out (Bringezu et al., 2012; Harvey and Pilgrim, 2011; Lambin and Meyfroidt, 2011). The same applies to its usable water (Barlow, 2007; Mehta et al., 2012; Smaller and Mann, 2009). In part, this is evident in the prominence in land grabbing of those countries where land is already scarce or highly degraded, who fear for their own food security, such as the Gulf states (Woertz, 2013, pp. 87–104). It is also evident in the anticipation of investors with long time horizons (such as sovereign wealth funds that run on commercial principles) that land prices are going to rise as scarcity increases.[5] Climate change, which may seriously damage the productivity of existing agricultural land, exacerbates the risks associated with shortages of land. The proliferation of 'green grabs' are important here as actors invest in land in hopes of slowing and/or repairing ecological damage but also in creating global markets for the selling and trading of carbon and 'ecosystem services' (Fairhead et al., 2012). The prominent place of biofuels as a driver of land grabbing reflects the exhaustion of another of the earth's resources: fossil fuels (see, e.g. Borras et al., 2010). This is now an integrated global threat, tied together by prices in global markets, and by the use of agriculture to produce energy, which is as central to our industrial civilization as food. Struggles likely will intensify between countries with dwindling resources and countries with the remaining stocks.

The materiality of resource scarcities does not make them self-evident. On the contrary, both the problem and its solution have crucial contested ideational dimensions that involve far more complexity than a more traditional supply of ideas to policymakers by lobbyists or experts. For example, the impact of biofuel production on land in Africa can be influenced simultaneously by European voter preferences on legislation requiring the use of biofuels in vehicles, the calculations of scientists who are assessing the climate change problem and the viability of biofuel technologies, the expectations of transnational investors investing in a particular plot of land, and the knowledge involved in the practical implementation challenges for small farmers or agricultural workers growing a new biofuel crop such as jatropha (see, e.g. Hunsberger, 2010). This complexity provides a great many locations at which the systems driving land grabbing can and must be challenged if it is to be altered. In contrast to earlier models of international politics where it was easier to address international problems by influencing decision-makers in a few powerful states, or by altering the text of a key treaty, today large expanses of the transnational flows of power and knowledge that shape the material practices involved in land grabbing do not run directly through the state at all.

These complex entanglements of ideas and materiality are also evident in the way that the signals of scarcity are also mediated through highly imperfect financial markets. Capital and financial markets especially are oriented towards the estimation of the present value of a future revenue stream (Nitzan and Bichler, 2009). The 2008 financial crisis and the problems of carbon trading (Chan, 2009) have starkly revealed the shortcomings of financial markets in trying to connect investors to new investment frontiers. Nevertheless promoters of investment in farmland, very much like promoters of sub-prime mortgage investments earlier, solicit investments by projecting future trends based on contestable measures of past performance. For instance Savills, a global real estate services provider, has created a *Global Farmland Index*, which is used to construct a measure for global land prices 'showing positive growth in many established and emerging markets' (Savills, 2012, p. 4). While Savills acknowledges some measurement problems in the construction of its index, the overall effect is to obscure the severity of these problems and the uncertain political conflicts over land that the future may bring. If US sub-prime mortgages or carbon derivatives are opaque, agricultural contracts in Sudan, where law is weak or absent, are worse. The contracts in the current wave of land acquisitions primarily promise long-range benefits such as the construction of infrastructure or the generation of employment, in exchange for very cheap or even free rights to the land (usually in the form of long-term leases). Even some advocates of large-scale land acquisitions, such as the World Bank, have found a shocking lack of evidence that these long-run benefits will materialize. There are many examples of land being held for its speculative value (e.g. World Bank, 2009, p. 45), reducing its current use for agriculture by expropriating those currently working the land or by making the land unaffordable to them.

The ideational and material interface is also present in the recent structural upward shift in food prices. Rising world food prices are not a simple reflection of supply and demand but reflect the increasingly complex interplay between actors and ideas across global financial, energy, and food markets (Clapp and Helleiner, 2012). Developing countries have for decades been competing in world food markets under declining terms of trade. The current commodities 'boom' is widely regarded as an exciting and dynamic conjuncture with perceptions among private and public actors of the untapped opportunity and profitability this affords taking on the status of conventional economic wisdom (Deutsche Bank, 2009; *Financial Times*, 2010). Land, and the potential to overcome the agricultural 'yield gap' with the incorporation of modern biotechnology, is increasingly viewed as an underexploited asset and driving actors to invest in the sector with a clear herd-like mentality.

Another complex interaction between ideas and materiality is highlighted by the very prominent place that transparency plays in the World Bank's influential report (2009, pp. vii, 26) on land grabbing:

> a major conclusion of the report is that access to a basic set of good information is essential for all stakeholders . . . As long as property rights to land and, where necessary water, are well-defined and a proper regulatory framework to prevent externalities is in place, productivity- and welfare-enhancing transactions can occur without the need for active intervention by the state.

This prioritization of information provision matches the interests of the writers of the report, who are advocating more of what they themselves do. Transparency has been promoted as a solution to a wide range of governance problems, including in finance (Best, 2005) and the extractive sector (Haufler, 2010). However, this reliance on transparency is seriously problematic in two overlapping ways. First, it advocates reliance on a process of information dissemination which obscures the deficiencies of that process itself. These deficiencies include especially the influence of power differentials on what information is produced, who can disseminate it, and who can access it. Second, it obscures the significance of material and political practices that operate independently of the information dissemination process. The idea of transparency can operate like ideology in obscuring, legitimizing, and therefore helping to produce exploitative material practices associated with land grabbing.

More specifically, the emphasis on transparency obscures the massive asymmetries in 'voluntary' contracting between large investors, such as sovereign wealth funds, and those at risk in the land acquisition, such as someone whose family has engaged in pastoral agriculture for generations without formal legal title to the land or any resources to produce or defend such a title (Cotula, 2012). There are also gender dimensions to these asymmetries with many land deals failing to take the needs and interests, and differentiated consequences of men and women (Behrman et al., 2012). Case studies from Sub-Saharan Africa (Chu, 2011) and Indonesia (Julia and White, 2012) show that where land titles are more often held by men than women, even though women make up the disproportionate share of the agricultural work force, women continue to face significant institutional, legal, and social barriers to equal access to land rights (Cotula, 2011). As Borras and Franco (2010, p. 519) emphasize, transparency is not the same as accountability; transparency does not ensure transactions are accountable to the interest of the rural poor.

The World Bank report itself provides many examples of outright failures to consult, proforma consultations, or consultations with some stakeholders and not others—particularly with men and not the women who are most affected (World Bank, 2009, pp. 49–50). Disclosure policies and the framework of prior and informed consent—as compared to more stringent regulations—can shift risk towards those who are presently using the land, unfairly legitimizing and empowering those with resources who wish to acquire land, and leaving existing exploitative market practices intact (Gupta, 2010, pp. 34–35).

Despite these problems, the complex interaction of ideas and materiality does not always work relentlessly against vulnerable actors. Most present land acquisitions are leases, which legally could be terminated if the investor does not follow through on commitments—or even if domestic politics changes. Local protests and the transnational support mechanisms for these create intangible but materially significant investment risks that provide incentives for foreign investors to address the concerns of critics.

The Complexity of Transnational Governance

In this section we will see that the complexity of the transnational governance institutions that are addressing land grabbing matches the complexity that we discussed in the previous two sections. As noted in our earlier theoretical discussion, this complexity, which trumps the shifting balances of power among states, is evident along three axes: by issue area; by the varying mix of public and private elements; and by the mix of local and global elements. We also discuss here the autonomy of new regulatory instruments for land grabbing and the interaction among them and with other governance instruments across scales and issue areas.

We start the discussion by examining the two recent transnational instruments that have been advanced for regulating land grabbing: the *Principles for Responsible Agricultural Investment that Respects, Livelihoods, and Resources* (PRAI) and the *Voluntary Guidelines on the Responsible Governance of Tenure of Land, Fisheries and Forests in the Context of National Food Security* (hereafter 'Voluntary Guidelines'). Complexity is evident in the differences in the issue areas that they express: the first is more concerned with investment, and the second with land tenure. Each instrument is embedded in distinct principles, norms, rules, cognitive frames, and discourses. The land grabbing phenomena is pulling these two regimes, including their rules and constituent actors, into a closer orbit. This process is increasing the diversity and density of actors engaged in global rule-making over land. These include state and non-state actors that have access to and participate in these and related regimes, but which may have not previously operated in the same governance spaces, such as the International Planning Committee for Food Sovereignty and the World Bank are now doing at the FAO's Committee on World Food Security (CFS) (McKeon, 2013, pp. 105–122).

Situating these instruments within an issue area permits us to contextualize the actors, interests, and ideas in these new global rule-making projects. Recall that it was the G8, not investors, that tasked multilateral organizations to develop an international framework for responsible investment in agriculture at its 2009 Summit (G8, 2009, para. 113b; Vidal, 2009). Whereas PRAI is often referred to as a form of private governance (i.e. it is intended to provide socially responsible investment by private actors), its development has been primarily an exercise of consultation and deliberation among experts from international institutions. In fact, multi-stakeholder consultation processes will only start to shape a new framework for responsible agriculture investment significantly after several years of work by international public officials.

The World Bank has demonstrated significant intellectual and organizational leadership in the PRAI project. PRAI has been presented by its creators to the outside world as a set of evidenced-based codes and best practices assembled to guide and inform decision-making by investors (and host states when courting investment in agriculture). The primary objective of the PRAI is clear: it is to encourage and intensify private investment in agriculture and to enhance the commercial viability of such investments by reducing investor risk (PRAI, 2010, pp. 2–14). It is very much part of the regulate to facilitate camp in the land grabbing governance debate (see Borras et al., 2013, this volume). Very importantly, PRAI lacks a normative basis for weighing the different type of risks and emphasizes a procedural approach where transparency and disclosure are pre-eminent.

The second initiative, the Voluntary Guidelines, traces it origins to the 2006 UN *International Conference on Agrarian Reform and Rural Development* (ICARRD) and longer-term concerns about land tenure and land reform in developing countries (McKeon, 2013, this volume; Seufert, 2013, pp. 181–186). Multi-actor negotiations, involving states and representatives from international institutions, global civil society, and the private sector, began in April 2011 and completed recently in May 2012. This is an important difference to PRAI because global civil society participation has been significant, and has elevated the perceived legitimacy of the Voluntary Guidelines. The Voluntary Guidelines, initially endorsed by the FAO's CFS, have been further endorsed and legitimized by the G20 Heads of State, who 'encouraged' its implementation (G20, 2012). Work on the Voluntary Guidelines has shifted towards devising a plan for implementation, including mechanisms to monitor and evaluate the guidelines, seeking financial support from donors and other multilateral institutions, and assisting individual developing countries to codify the Voluntary Guidelines in domestic law and practices. In contrast to the investment focus of PRAI, the primary objective of the Voluntary Guidelines is to enhance the tenure security of landholders and users, and increase access to land and productive resources by poor rural households. In emphasizing its concern with 'the benefit of all, with an emphasis on vulnerable and marginalized people' it has a more explicit normative emphasis than PRAI (FAO, 2010, p. 5). The guidelines resonate with alternative visions of the relationship between the economy, people, and the earth (Ibid., p. 13). Unlike PRAI's unquestioned approach of integrating rural farmers with global finance and agri-food chains,[6] the guidelines seek to maintain the viability of smallholder production and autonomy of rural and indigenous communities. Global civil society groups and transnational peasant movements continue to support the Voluntary Guidelines as an important bulwark against land grabbing (Civil Society Mechanism, 2011, p. 4; Global Witness, 2010). As such, the Voluntary Guidelines were clearly part of a significant norm-generating exercise in transnational governance. The diffusion of these norms to the ground-level is the present challenge.

A new dimension of complexity has to do with increasing interaction between PRAI and the Voluntary Guidelines. As discussed above, each instrument developed in a unique way, addresses a different issue, and has been supported by a different set of actors. Yet increasingly these instruments are not independent of one another. First, the final text of the negotiated Voluntary Guidelines includes provisions on 'responsible investment' and more direct reference to large-scale land acquisitions (FAO, 2011, pp. 23–25). Second, there is now a concerted effort to bridge the PRAI and Voluntary Guidelines by creating a new set of principles. These principles, while taking into account the work to date on PRAI, would be more 'extensive'. They would involve multi-stakeholder negotiation under the auspices of the CFS and ensure that they are consistent and complementary with the Voluntary Guidelines (FAO, 2011). Such convergence is highly contentious, because global civil society actors see PRAI as a threat to protecting land rights of the poor and as a guise for a long-term corporate takeover of rural people's farmlands (GCAR, 2010). However, this regime/forum-shifting (Helfer, 2004) of the negotiation of the principles to the CFS away from the G8 supported inter-agency process may be regarded as a step towards enhancing inclusiveness, participation and legitimacy, and it signals some partial success in the orchestration strategy by global civil society. The CFS certainly lends a gloss of legitimacy to the idea of PRAI that was previously lacking. This will also put greater pressure on global civil society to achieve its ends because it will likely necessitate the greater inclusion of private actors. Research has shown that private actors use their technical expertise very effectively in the creation of new transnational governance (Cutler et al., 1999) and that this, in turn, intensifies asymmetries in the negotiation process that favors actor with higher levels of expertise and material resources (Quack, 2010).

Global complexity is also intensified by the overlap between the principles and guidelines discussed so far with a broader set of international and regional regulatory frameworks, codes, and informal rules at the international, national, and subnational levels. The Voluntary Guidelines refer and build upon a variety of other codes, rules, and agreements, including ICARRD, international human rights law (e.g. right to food, land, and of indigenous peoples), and regional initiatives such the African Union's recent land policy framework (AU, 2010). With respect to global investment rules already in place, these include the OECD's Policy Framework for Investment (PFI), OECD Guidelines for Multinational Enterprises (the MNE Guidelines), and the OECD Risk Awareness Tool for MNEs in Weak Governance Zones (WGZ Tool) to name a few (OECD, 2010). The principles explicitly build on existing codes of conduct and best practices. However, actors negotiating the principles at the CFS are not necessarily linked to the existing transnational public and private networks that monitor and implement these and other finance and investment related governance instruments. It is important to note that the latter instruments are not fixed but are themselves quite fluid. Any future 'principles' are unlikely to be wholly determined by the actors formally involved in the negotiation at the CFS on the specifics. They will also be indirectly influenced by events and actors at other institutions, such as the OECD and other mechanisms of financial governance. Consequently, this situation increases the complexity of the task facing the CFS: to establish meaningful principles that are seen as legitimate by investors (which are the primary target of such rules), that can build upon existing monitoring systems for investment useful for naming and shaming purposes, and that can foster the 'ratcheting up' of standards across the investment regime. This is a tall order but one that may be less onerous if transnational advocacy groups concerned with land grabbing can establish coalitions with other global civil society, institutional actors and sympathetic policy elites already active on global investment issues.

The complexity of the public–private dimension also plays out in the Voluntary Guidelines and PRAI. Take the Voluntary Guidelines, which are focused on land tenure that is foremost a national public responsibility, but whose negotiation involved significant input from global civil society (and to a much lesser extent from the private sector). The PRAI on the other hand, were formulated primarily by supra-national public authorities, but that only have meaning if incorporated by investors. PRAI's vision involves a more prominent role for the private sector with private standards and other benchmarks as the building blocks of effective governance. Private governance is also evident in other institutions that complement the above two instruments. These include certification schemes such as the Roundtable on Sustainable Palm Oil or the Roundtable on Sustainable Biofuels (World Bank, 2009, pp. 96–97; see also Fortin and Richardson, 2013, pp. 141–159), and the UN Global Compact.

Indeed, the blurring of the public–private axis is likely to become more pronounced in the implementation stage for both these new instruments. Non-state actors such as global civil society organizations or private hedge funds also play an important role in influencing the two initiatives as they continue to develop, although this influence remains contested. Certainly some states continue to strongly assert their sovereignty. As a government official in the Office du Niger put it in response to criticisms of land grabbing, 'We are responsible for developing Mali. If the civil society does not agree with the way we are doing it, they can go jump in a lake' (MacFarquhar, 2010). Yet as Ruggie (2008) and others have argued, simple state authority is increasingly insufficient to legitimize and enable the operations of foreign investors in host countries—there is a social license to operate, the terms of which are heavily shaped by local and transnational civil society.

The interaction between public and private is also evident in the micro-level practices of the private contracts between small farmers and larger firms that may rent them their land, purchase their crops, and provide inputs or marketing services. These are heavily influenced by the existing capacities of the actors involved, the legal regime within which they are operating, and the physical characteristics of the plants and machinery involved (World Bank, 2009). A similar point can be made about gender relations within the household, which govern the differing allocations of individuals' engagements with the land, the modes of mobility that shape their daily and seasonal movement across the land, and their capacities to engage with the legal regime that constitutes property rights and contracts, blurring the boundary between a 'private' household space and a larger public sphere,

These micro-level factors also highlight the global/local axis of complexity. Countries vary in land ownership and property rights transfer rules. Present land ownership patterns are often a result of specific historical patterns and the internal political dynamics of countries. For instance, ironically Brazil's anachronistic constitutional rules may help it control the amount of land that can be purchased by foreign companies. In many poor countries of the South such capacity is weaker, making them vulnerable to asymmetrical power relations.

Struggles between globality and localness are evident at all scales. PRAI's reference to global principles of environmental sustainability (PRAI, 2010, p. 18) only has meaning in its implementation at the most local, micro-level, including, for instance, the interaction between the roots of a plant and the nutrients of the soil, which can either be sustainable, or a form of 'soil-mining' where the foreign investor takes the nutrients without compensation, destroying the land. Virtual water exports where scarce water is exploited in developing countries by exporting water-intensive crops is similar (Barlow, 2007). Determining which is occurring and acting on it requires an engagement of science with that particular crop, land, and farmer. The enforcement of the transnational governance instrument therefore requires a chain of capacities, rules, and practices that interactively link the transnational principles with the farmer and the local ecosystem. National institutions are important in this chain, but only one part of it, and not necessarily the most decisive one.

Land grabbing is also linking states and rural peoples situated at the local to new global commercial commodity chains, including the complex mix of investment, trade, and private rules that undergird these exchanges. As recent acquisitions suggest, there is a strong economic incentive to outsource parts of the food, feed, and biofuel production process. This has to do with shifting the burden of costs of production to poor developing countries were wages are cheaper, land is 'under-utilized' (often claimed falsely by governments and investors to be so), and where environmental governance and enforcement is weak. Much of this facilitated by international, bilateral, and regional investment and trade agreements as well as economic cooperation partnerships.

To sum up, new regulation of land is linked across multiple governance regimes at the transnational, regional, national, and local levels. The governance of land grabbing certainly cannot be reduced to PRAI or the Voluntary Guidelines. Conflicts reveal characteristics of chessboard politics that were discussed earlier. Non-state actors such as multilateral institutions and global civil society are also maneuvering in this political chessboard. PRAI and the Voluntary Guidelines rest upon multiple clusters of governance practices, all of which operate under of the authority of diverse and distant configurations of state and non-state actors. They go far beyond the simpler shift in the balance of power signified by the replacement of the G8 by the G20 or the decline in US dominance. While newly powerful states such as China and the Gulf states may be less attentive to these complex set of transnational institutions, they too must work through them to some degree, especially in needing to interact with host states and other local actors that in turn are connected in complex ways to the transnational institutions.

Strategies for Protecting the Vulnerable

Our fourth proposition was that that smaller and poorer actors will be most successful working through the types of complexity we have discussed above and enrolling transnational actors and networks in efforts to change governance rather than trying to avoid or reverse complexity by focusing more exclusively on solutions at the local level or at the formal intergovernmental level (for instance through treaties). There is already some support in the discussion above for this: the sheer complexity of the challenges makes it impossible for any one actor to manage them. No single formal intergovernmental organization can manage this complexity either. Treaties are simply too slow.

There are three main additional reasons why local responses alone will not work. *First*, by avoiding transnational engagements important economic and social benefits may be lost. Chronic poverty, food insecurity, limited access to credit and technology, ecological constraints, and political disfranchisement are serious challenges facing many of the world's rural poor. Economic globalization increases the pressures on these populations as demand for natural resources and agricultural output intensifies, producing what Sassen (2010, 2013, pp. 25–46) refers to as the 'savage sorting of losers'. At the same time, it is important to keep in mind that urbanization and transitioning of the rural poor from a global majority to minority may in the long-term further diminish their political voice. These are very real challenges for the formulation of socially just land governance. These larger forces suggest the importance for rural people and their advocates to develop bottom-up 'best practices', that reflect the needs, knowledge, and aspirations of existing land users, but that also can engage and enroll other powerful transnational actors and steer projects towards relatively more beneficial forms that respect existing and/or desired land arrangements.

Second, transnational developments will continue to impinge on the local, even if strong local prohibitions on land grabbing were in place. This includes climate change and the destruction of water sources far from the local farm. *Third*, local power relations may be even more unfavorable to poor users of land than transnational ones. This includes gender relations in the family, local authorities that do not listen to their constituents, and national states that serve the interests of urban skilled elites. For instance in northern Argentina, local states officials, landowning elites, and foreign investors have clear-cut over 60,000 hectares for soybean production destined for China. This has occurred in an area where rural communities have earned their livelihoods by small-scale sheep herding on customary used land. Large-scale land deals between the Ethiopian state and foreign investors are producing high tech mega-farms, including the acquisition by the Indian firm Karuturi Global of 300,000 hectares. Media reports local workers earn income below the extreme poverty threshold and, more recently, allegations of forced evictions, murder, and rape of villagers have surfaced concerning this deal (Bloomberg News, 2009). The World Bank's own research suggests that much of the land grabbing is being carried out by domestic investors, often with privileged access to the state (Deininger et al., 2011). Even though this claim is not fully supported by all studies, it provides a reminder that the shocking lack of transparency in the documentation and accountability mechanisms for investment is not only due to lack of state capacity in host countries, but also officials' desires to be unaccountable.

There are significant opportunities for the poorest farmers to obtain greater protection if the various elements in the transnational arrangements that might be helpful to them are successfully orchestrated. The efforts by global civil society and peasant organizations to support the Voluntary Guidelines and subsume PRAI is one example. Firms reliant on financial and product markets in democracies can be held accountable through a variety of mechanisms, including public regulation, private litigation, reputational damage to their brand, and organized protests. International campaigns and consumer boycotts against blood diamonds, use of sweatshop labor, or cooperation with authoritarian regimes have shifted private actors' perceptions of the importance of responsible behavior to safeguard reputations and profits. New scientific studies have challenged the purported benefits of biofuels. The fragility and interdependence of the financial system amplifies the risks that investors face in engaging in land grabbing and make them more vulnerable to transnational pressures.

These varied types of responses to the problem of land grabbing have less impact on authoritarian countries, but those countries too have reputational costs that they must consider. For instance, in 2013 the Gulf states must act with great care in addressing their citizens' demands lest they lose vital support from the US. Even China consented to the rapid referral of the Libyan case to the International Criminal Court, indicating its sensitivity to certain international responses to problems of local violence. In conflicts with the US over exchange rates and other matters vital to China, its human rights reputation, at home and abroad, plays a role in the alliances with the US and others that it can sustain, or even its access to foreign investment opportunities in countries like Canada. Much Chinese investment is through sovereign wealth funds that are operating sufficiently on market principles so that losses from disruptions or reputational damage to the value of the agricultural assets that they hold will be unwelcome.

Conclusion

Our first three propositions argued that the land grab illustrates three key changes in the global political economy: changing balance of power and decreasing relevance of framing global relations around either East–West or North–South axes; the direct interaction between ideas and material systemic threats; and the complexity of transnational governance. Our fourth proposition argued that these complex transnational institutions can be helpful for protecting the poorest users of the land. We address these in turn.

First, it is clear that the balance of power has changed. The case of land grabbing does not correspond to earlier cases of North–South conflicts dominated by the European colonial powers or the US. Southern states are major players, as investors, in protecting or abusing their own populations, and in negotiating strong or weak international rules. This introduces more complex dynamics into the transnational political process: Southern states are not 'victims' seeking to rebuff the North. Rather, human beings in certain parts of the South are being victimized by a plurality of actors: by states and investors from the South and North but also by local elites. Traditional concepts of South–South solidarity or other traditional forms of interstate political conflict are therefore less relevant to understanding the type of global politics of land grabbing.

Second, the global character of the interaction between ideas and material systemic threats to the earth and its life forms is evident in land grabbing. Much of the transnational politics associated with land grabbing can obscure and complicate the broader ecological clash that is at play. This is in part because the two key transnational governance instruments that have been developed under the guidance of the G8/G20, a club of powerful states, and the FAO, a food and agriculture policy institution with universal memberships and with a long history of deep engagement with non-state actors, and a concern with growing production. The process has not engaged the climate change regime, which in any case is a relatively new and weak regime. We, like others, view the land grab as part of a wider transformation of the relationship between people and the earth as much as it is about organizing economies and polities. Agriculture is a major source of greenhouse gas emissions and ecosystem degradation, and also the solution to the current risk that the planet cannot support its human population. Since the vulnerable are the most susceptible yet also the least resourced to respond to the destruction of ecosystems and climate change risks, and since agriculture is asked to sustain the life of the world's population that does not live on the land, the environmental/ecological aspects of governance will be critical going forward. The interactions of scientific knowledge and ideas about the environment with material practices, many of which do not directly involve states, will be important in this. We recognize this aspect will be highly contested by actors; this is already evident in current policy debates on agroecology, smart agriculture, and ecosystem services as approaches to address the ecological crisis, most notably in the case of green grabs.

Third, it is clear that the interaction of land grabbing with the complexity of transnational governance highlights the significance of each of these for the other. This complexity is evident in the way that the land grab involves new relations between food, fuel, feed, and finance that expose communities of persons, which have historically been the most exploited and least able to benefit from the process of wealth generation in the global economy, to ever greater systemic and personal risks. This includes risk to their material wellbeing (i.e. livelihoods by loss of land) but also the security of persons when rural people are faced with forced evictions and violence. In the context of a global economy mediated by the belief in price signals, mechanisms are required to the shift the burden of risk more squarely onto the shoulders of investors, who presently often reap most of the rewards, and who are better capitalized to absorb such risks compared to the rural poor.

Fourth, the complexity of the problem requires complex solutions. Local, national, or transnational solutions alone cannot be effective. Nor can purely public or purely private solutions, nor solutions that focus on one issue such as efficiency or investor protection at the expense of the human right to food or the protection of the earth's ecosystems. Thus all three axes of complexity that we have identified are important. In seeking to defend the rights of poor people threatened by land grabbing it is helpful to work with, expand, strengthen, and alter complex transnational linkages, rather than to try to reduce or cut them. No single governance initiative by itself can be effective. Notions such as chessboard politics, enrolment, and the highlighting of linkages of land regulation to relatively autonomous and distant governance and knowledge practices and flows of power are useful in conceptualizing strategic responses to this complexity.

Acknowledgements

We thank two anonymous reviewers and Claire Cutler for their comments. An earlier version of this paper was presented at the 2011 International Studies Association annual conference in Montréal, Canada.

Notes

1   The relevant literatures are large. See for instance Biermann et al. (2009); Braithwaite and Drahos (2000); Djelic and Sahlin-Andersson (2007); Hawkins et al. (2006); Hooge and Marks (2003); Jessop (2004); Levi-Faur (2005); Morgan (2006); Ong and Collier (2005); Raustiala and Victor (2005); Sassen (2006); Young et al. (2010).

2   The most extensive development of the opportunities for weak actors to make use of enrolment in global business regulation is provided by Braithwaite and Drahos (2000). An early well-known development of the concept of enrolment in actor-network theory is provided by Callon (1986). For an application of actor-network theory to transnational governance, see also Porter (2012).
3   The current state of scholarship can be found in the pages of *Journal of Peasant Studies* 39(2); 39(3–4), *Development* 54(1), *Water Alternatives* 5(2), *Development & Change* (forthcoming), and the *Canadian Journal of Development Studies* (forthcoming).
4   We recognize the exact scale of land grabs, and debate about the best suited methods, remain hotly contested However, it is also important to contextualize the politics of measurement as one aspect of the ideational contests at play in the transnational governance of land grabs (see Margulis et al., 2013, pp. 1–23).
5   Take for example, Savills, a global real estate service provider, which has developed a Global Farmland Index that tracks farmland values in 14 key markets. These developments further confirm the creation of a *global land market*.
6   This approach is consistent with the World Bank's new agriculture agenda. See Akram-Lodhi (2008).

References

Abbott, K. & Snidal, D. (2009) Strengthening international regulation through transnational new governance: overcoming the orchestration deficit, *Vanderbilt Journal of Transnational Law*, 42, pp. 501–578.

African Union (AU) (2010) *Land Policy in Africa: A Framework to Strengthen Land Rights, Enhance Productivity and Secure Livelihoods* (Addis Ababa: AUC-ECA-AfDB).

Akram-Lodhi, H. (2008) (Re)imagining agrarian relations? The World Development Report 2008: agriculture for development, *Development and Change*, 39(6), pp. 1145–1161.

Alden Wily, L. (2012) Looking back to see forward: the legal niceties of land theft in land rushes, *Journal of Peasant Studies*, 39(3–4), pp. 751–775.

Alter, K. & Meunier, S. (2009) The politics of international regime complexity, *Perspectives on Politics*, 7(1), pp. 13–24.

Anseeuw, W., Alden Wily, L., Cotula, L. & Taylor, M. (2011) *Land Rights and the Rush for Land: Findings of the Global Commercial Pressures on Land Research Project* (Rome: International Land Coalition).

Aradau, C. & Van Munster, R. (2007) Governing terrorism through risk: taking precautions, (un)knowing the future, *European Journal of International Relations*, 13(1), pp. 89–115.

Axelrod, M. (2011) Savings clauses and the 'chilling effect': regime interplay as constraints on international governance/law, in S. Oberthür & O. S. Stokke (eds) *Managing Institutional Complexity: Regime Interplay and Global Environmental Change* (Cambridge, MA: MIT Press), pp. 87–114.

Ayers, A. J. (2012) Beyond myths, lies and stereotypes: the political economy of a 'New Scramble for Africa', *New Political Economy*, available as iFirst.

Barlow, M. (2007) *Blue Covenant: The Global Water Crisis and the Coming Battle for the Right to Water* (Toronto: McLelland & Stewart).

Barros-Platiau, A. F. (2010) Quando países emergentes reformam a governança global das mudanças climáticas: o Brasil sob Lula, *Revista Brasileira de Política Internacional*, 53, pp. 73–90.

Behrman, J., Meinzen-Dick, R. & Quisumbing, A. (2012) The gender implications of large-scale land deals, *Journal of Peasant Studies*, 39(1), pp. 49–79.

Best, J. (2005) *The Limits of Transparency: Ambiguity and the History of International Finance* (Ithaca, NY: Cornell University Press).

Biermann, F., Pattberg, P., van Asselt, H. & Zelli, F. (2009) The fragmentation of global governance architectures: a framework for analysis, *Global Environmental Politics*, 9(4), pp. 14–40.

Bloomberg News (2009) Ethiopian farms lure investor funds as workers live in poverty, 29 December, http://www.bloomberg.com/apps/news?pid=newsarchive&sid=aeuJT_pSE68c.

Borras, S. M & Franco, J. (2010) From threat to opportunity? Problems with the idea of a 'Code of Conduct' for land grabbing, *Yale Human Rights & Development Law Journal*, 13(1), pp. 507–523.

Borras, S. M., McMichael, P. & Scoones, I. (2010) The politics of biofuels, land and agrarian change: editors' introduction, *Journal of Peasant Studies*, 37(4), pp. 575–592.

Borras, S. M., Franco, J. C., Gomez, S., Kay, C. & Spoor, M. (2012) Land grabbing in Latin America and the Caribbean, *Journal of Peasant Studies*, 39(3–4), pp. 845–872.

Borras, S. M., Franco, J. C. & Wang, C. (2013) The challenge of global governance of land grabbing: changing international agricultural context and competing political views and strategies, *Globalizations*, 10(1), pp. 00–00.

Borras, S. M., Hall, R., Scoones, I., White, B. & Wolford, W. (forthcoming) Governing global land deals: the role of the state in the rush for land, *Development & Change*.

Bowles, P. & Wang, B. (2008) The rocky road ahead: China, the US and the future of the dollar, *Review of International Political Economy*, 15(3), pp. 335–353.

Braithwaite, J. & Drahos, P. (2000) *Global Business Regulation* (Cambridge: Cambridge University Press).

Bringezu, S., O'Brien, M. O. & Schütz, H. (2012) Beyond biofuels: Assessing global land use for domestic consumption of biomass: A conceptual and empirical contribution to sustainable management of global resources, *Land Use Policy*, 29(1), pp. 224–232.

Busch, L. & Bain, C. (2009) New! Improved? The transformation of the global agrifood system, *Rural Sociology*, 69(3), pp. 321–346.

Callon, M. (1986) Some elements of a sociology of translation: domestication of the scallops and the fisherman of St. Brieuc Bay, in J. Law (ed.) *Power, Action and Belief: A New Sociology of Knowledge?* (London: Routledge and Kegan Paul), pp. 196–233.

Cashore, B. (2003) Legitimacy and the privatization of environmental governance: how non-state market-driven (NSMD) governance systems gain rule-making authority, *Governance*, 15(4), pp. 503–529.

Chan, M. (2009) Subprime carbon? Re-thinking the world's largest new derivative market, (Washington, DC: Friends of the Earth).

Chu, J. (2011) Gender and 'land grabbing' in Sub-Saharan Africa: women's land rights and customary land tenure, *Development*, 54(1), pp. 35–39.

Civil Society Mechanism (CSM) (2011) CSO Consolidated Comments on Zero Draft, 10 April, http://cso4cfs.files. wordpress.com/2010/11/cso-comments-zero-draft-10-05-11-2.pdf.

Clapp, J. & Fuchs, D. (eds) (2009) *Corporate Power in Global Agrifood Governance* (Cambridge, MA: MIT University Press).

Clapp, J. & Helleiner, E. (2012) Troubled futures? The global food crisis and the politics of agricultural derivatives regulation, *Review of International Political Economy*, 19(2), pp. 181–207.

Comprehensive African Agriculture Development Program (CAADP) (2010) *Renewing the African Commitment to Agriculture* (Nairobi: African Union).

Conca, K. (2000) The WTO and the undermining of global environmental governance, *Review of International Political Economy*, 7(3), pp. 484–494.

Cotula, L. (2011) *Land Deals in Africa: What Is in the Contracts?* (London: International Institute for Environment and Development).

Cotula, L. (2012) *Human Rights, Natural Resource and Investment Law in a Globalized World: Shades of Grey in the Shadow of the Law* (London: Routledge).

Cotula, L., Vermeulen, S., Leonard, R. & Keeley, J. (2009) *Land Grab or Development Opportunity? Agricultural Investment and International Land Deals in Africa* (London: International Institute for Environment and Development).

Cutler, A. C., Haufler, V. & Porter, T. (1999) *Private Authority and International Affairs* (Binghamton: SUNY Press).

Dauvergne, P. & Neville, K. J. (2010) Forests, food, and fuel in the tropics: the uneven social and ecological consequences of the emerging political economy of biofuels, *Journal of Peasant Studies*, 37(4), pp. 631–660.

Dauvergne, P. & Farias, D. B. (2012) The rise of Brazil as a global development power, *Third World Quarterly*, 33(5), pp. 903–917.

De Goede, M. (2006) *International Political Economy and Poststructural Politics* (Basingstoke, UK: Palgrave).

De Haan, A. (2011) Will China change international development as we know it?, *Journal of International Development*, 23(7), pp. 881–908.

Deininger, K., Byerlee, D., Lindsay, J., Norton, A., Selod, H. & Stickler, M. (2011) *Rising Global Interest in Farmland: Can it Yield Sustainable and Equitable Benefits?* (Washington, DC: World Bank).

Deutsche Bank (2009) *Investing in Agriculture: Far-Reaching Challenge, Significant Opportunity* (London & New York: Deutsche Bank Group).

Djelic, M. L. & Sahlin-Andersson, K. (eds) (2007) *Transnational Governance: Institutional Dynamics of Regulation* (Cambridge: Cambridge University Press).

Dobusch, L. & Quack, S. (2012) Framing standards, mobilizing users: copyright versus fair use in transnational regulation, *Review of International Political Economy*, forthcoming. doi:10.1080/09692290.2012.662909.

Drezner, D. W. (2009) The power and peril of international regime complexity, *Perspectives on Politics*, 7(1), pp. 65–70.

Eckersley, R. (2004) The big chill: the WTO and multilateral environmental agreements, *Global Environmental Politics*, 4(2), pp. 24–50.

Fairhead, J., Leach, M. & Scoones, I. (2012) Green grabbing: a new appropriation of nature? *Journal of Peasant Studies*, 39(2), pp. 237–261.

Fisher, D. R. & Green, J. F. (2004) Understanding disenfranchisement: civil society and developing countries' influence and participation in global governance for sustainable development, *Global Environmental Politics*, 4(3), pp. 65–84.

Food and Agriculture Organization of the United Nations (FAO) (2010) *Voluntary Guidelines for Responsible Governance Voluntary of Land and Natural Resources: Zero Draft* (Rome: FAO).

FAO (2011) *Voluntary Guidelines for Responsible Governance Voluntary of Land and Natural Resources: Zero Draft Final* (Rome: FAO).

Financial Times, The (2010) Business and food sustainability special report, 27 January.

Friedmann, H. (1992) Distance and durability: shaky foundations of the world food economy, *Third World Quarterly*, 13(2), pp. 371–383.

Foley, J., DeFries, R., Asner, G. A., Barford, C., Bonan, G., Carpenter, S. R., Chapin, F. S., Coe, M. T., Daily, G. C., Gibbs, H. K., Helkowski, J. H., Holloway, T., Howard, T. A., Kucharik, C. J., Monfreda, C., Patz, J. A., Prentice, I. C., Ramankutty, N. & Snyder, P. K. (2005) Global consequences of land use, *Science*, 309(5734), pp. 570–574.

Fortin, E. & Richardson, B. (2013) Certification schemes and the governance of land: enforcing standards or enabling scrutiny?, *Globalizations*, 10(1), pp. 00–00.

Global Campaign for Agrarian Reform (CGAR) (2010) *Why We Oppose the Principles for Responsible Agricultural Investment*, http://www.fian.org/resources/documents/others/why-we-oppose-the-principles-for-responsible-agricultural-investment.

Global Witness (2010) How the FAO's Voluntary Guidelines can effectively address governance of large-scale land acquisitions, http://www.landcoalition.org/cpl-blog/wp-content/uploads/100706-gwpaper-for-july-2010-fao-meeting-final.pdf

GRAIN (2011) Pension funds: key players in the global farmland grab, http://www.grain.org/article/entries/4287-pension-funds-key-players-in-the-global-farmland-grab.pdf.

Group of Eight (G8) (2009) *Responsible Leadership for a Sustainable Future* (L'Aquila: G8).

GRAIN (2012) Pension funds table as of June 2012, http://www.grain.org/attachments/2520/download.

Group of Twenty (G20) (2012) G20 Leaders Declaration, http://g20.org/images/stories/docs/g20/conclu/G20_Leaders_Declaration_2012_1.pdf

Gupta, A. (2010) Transparency as contested political terrain: who knows what about the global GMO trade and why does it matter?, *Global Environmental Politics*, 10(3), pp. 32–52.

Haas, P. M. (1989) Do regimes matter? Epistemic communities and Mediterranean pollution control, *International Organization*, 43(3), pp. 377–403.

Harvey, M. & Pilgrim, S. (2011) The new competition for land: food, energy, and climate change, *Food Policy*, 36(Supplement 1), pp. S40–S51.

Haufler, V. (2010) Disclosure as governance: The Extractive Industries Transparency Initiative and resource management in the developing world, *Global Environmental Politics*, 10(3), pp. 53–73.

Hawkins, D. G., Lake, D., Nielson, D. L. & Tierney, M. J. (2006) Delegation under anarchy: States, international organizations, and principle-agent theory, in D. G. Hawkins, D. Lake, D. L. Nielson & M. J. Tierney (eds) *Delegation and Agency in International Organizations* (Cambridge: Cambridge University Press), pp. 3–38.

Helfer, L. R. (2004) Regime shifting: the TRIPS agreement and new dynamics of international intellectual property lawmaking, *Yale Journal of International Law*, 29(1), pp. 1–83.

High Level Panel of Experts (HLPE) (2011) *Land Tenure and International Investments in Agriculture: A Report by the High Level Panel of Experts on Food Security and Nutrition of the Committee on World Food Security* (Rome: FAO).

Hobsbawm, E. J. (1987) *The Age of Empire, 1875–1914* (New York: Pantheon Books).

Hochstetler, K. & Viola, E. (2012) Brazil and the politics of climate change: beyond the global commons, *Environmental Politics*, 21(5), pp. 753–771.

Hooge, L. & Marks, G. (2003) Unraveling the central state, but how? Types of multi-level governance, *American Political Science Review*, 97(2), pp. 233–43.

Hopewell, K. (forthcoming) New protagonists in global economic governance: the rise of Brazilian business at the WTO, *New Political Economy*.

Hunsberger, C. (2010) The politics of jatropha-based biofuels in Kenya: convergence and divergence among NGOs, donors, government officials and farmers, *Journal of Peasant Studies*, 37(4), pp. 939–962.

Immerman, R. H. (1983) *The CIA in Guatemala: The Foreign Policy of Intervention* (Austin, TX: University of Texas Press).

Jessop, B. (2004) Multi-level governance and multi-level metagovernance, in Bache, I. & Flinders, M. (eds) *Multi-Level Governance* (Oxford: Oxford University Press), pp. 49–74.

Jessop, B. & Sum, N. L. (2006) *Beyond the Regulation Approach: Putting Capitalist Economies in their Place* (Cheltenham, UK: Edward Elgar).

Johnson, T. & Urpelainen, J. (2012) A strategic theory of regime integration and separation, *International Organization*, 66(4), pp. 645–677.

Keck, M. E. & Sikkink, K. (1998) *Activists Beyond Borders* (Ithaca, NY: Cornell University Press).

Krasner, S. D. (1982) Structural causes and regime consequences: Regimes as intervening variables, *International Organization*, 36(2), pp. 185–205.

Lake, D. A. (1993) Leadership, hegemony, and the international economy: naked emperor or tattered monarch with potential?, *International Studies Quarterly*, 37(4), pp. 459–489.

Lambin, E. F. & Meyfroidt, P. (2011) Global land use change, economic globalization, and the looming land scarcity, *Proceedings of the National Academy of Sciences*, 108(9), pp. 3465–3472.

Lesage, D., Van de Graaf, T. & Westphal, K. (2010) *Global Energy Governance in a Multipolar World* (Farnham, UK: Ashgate).

Levi-Faur, D. (2005) The global diffusion of regulatory capitalism, *The Annals of the American Academy of Political and Social Science*, 598, pp. 12–32.

MacFarquhar, N. (2010) African farmers displaced as investors move in, *New York Times*, 21 December.

McKeon, N. (2013) 'One does not sell the land upon which the people walk': land grabbing, rural social movements, and global governance, *Globalizations*, 10(1), pp. 105–122.

McMichael, P. (2009) A food regime genealogy, *Journal of Peasant Studies*, 36(1), pp. 171–196.

McMichael, P. (2012) The land grab and corporate food regime restructuring, *Journal of Peasant Studies*, 39(3&4), pp. 681–701.

McMichael, P. (2013) Land grabbing as security mercantilism in international relations, *Globalizations*, 10(1), pp. 47–64.

Margulis, M. E. (2012) Global food security governance: the Committee on World Food Security, Comprehensive Framework for Action and the G8/G20, in R. Rayfuse & N. Weisfelt (eds) *The Challenge of Food Security: International Policy and Regulatory Frameworks* (Cheltenham, UK: Edward Elgar), pp. 231–254.

Margulis, M. E., McKeon, N. & Borras, S. M. (2013) Land grabbing and global governance: critical perspectives, *Globalizations*, 10(1), pp. 1–23.

Martinez-Diaz, L. & Woods, N. (2009) Introduction: developing countries in a networked global order, in L. Martinez-Diaz & N. Woods (eds) *Networks of Influence? Developing Countries in a Networked Global Order* (Oxford: Oxford University Press), pp. 1–18.

Mehta, L., Veldwisch, J. V. & Franco, J. (2012) Introduction to the special issue: water grabbing? Focus on the (re)appropriation of finite water resources, *Water Alternatives*, 5(2), pp. 193–207.

Morgan, B. (2006) Turning off the tap: urban water service delivery and the social construction of global administrative law, *European Journal of International Law*, 17(1), pp. 215–246.

Narlikar, A. & Tussie, D. (2004) The G20 at the Cancun ministerial: developing countries and their evolving coalitions in the WTO, *World Economy*, 27(7), pp. 947–966.

Narlikar, A. & Wilkinson, R. (2004) Collapse at the WTO: a Cancun post-mortem, *Third World Quarterly*, 25(3), pp. 447–460.

Nitzan, J. & Bichler, S. (2009) *Capital as Power: A Study of Order and Creorder* (New York and London: Routledge).

Nye, J. S., Jr (2005) *Soft Power: The Means To Success In World Politics* (New York: Public Affairs).

Oberthür, S. & Gehring, T. (2006) Institutional interaction in global environmental governance: the case of the Cartagena Protocol and the World Trade Organization, *Global Environmental Politics*, 6(2), pp. 1–31.

Ong, A. & Collier, S. J. (2005) *Global Assemblages: Technology, Politics and Ethics as Anthropological Problems* (Malden, MA: Blackwell).

Organization for Economic Cooperation and Development (OECD) (2010) *Freedom of Investment Process: Responsible Investment in Agriculture. Note by the Secretariat* (Paris: OECD).

Oxfam (2012) Land and power: the growing scandal surrounding the new wave of investments in land, http://www.oxfam.org/sites/www.oxfam.org/files/bp151-land-power-rights-acquisitions-220911-en.pdf.

Perrone, N. M (2013) Restrictions to foreign acquisitions of agricultural land in Argentina and Brazil, *Globalizations*, 10(1), pp. 00–00.

Porter, T. (2012) Making serious measures: numerical indices, peer review, and transnational actor-networks, *Journal of International Relations and Development*, 15(4), pp. 532–557.

Principles for Responsible Agricultural Investment that Respects, Livelihoods, and Resources (PRAI) (2010) *Extended Version* (Washington, DC: World Bank).

Quack, S. (2010) Law, expertise and legitimacy in transnational economic governance: an introduction, *Socio-Economic Review*, 8(1), pp. 3–16.

Raustiala, K. & Victor, D. (2004) The regime complex for plant genetic resources, *International Organization*, 58(2), pp. 277–309.

Ruggie, J. G. (1982) International regimes, transactions, and change: Embedded liberalism in the postwar economic order, *International Organization*, 36(2), pp. 379–415.

Ruggie, J. G. (2008) Protect, respect and remedy: a framework for business and human rights, *Innovations: Technology, Governance, Globalization*, 3(2), pp. 89–212.

Sassen, S. (2006) *Territory, Authority, Rights: From Medieval to Global Assemblages* (Princeton, NJ: Princeton University Press).

Sassen, S. (2010) A savage sorting of winners and losers: contemporary versions of primitive accumulation, *Globalizations*, 7(1–2), pp. 23–50.

Sassen, S. (2013) Land grabs today: feeding the disassembling of national territory, *Globalizations*, 10(1), pp. 25–46.

Savills (2012) Going with the grain: why international farmland is becoming an increasingly sought after investment, International Farmland Focus 2012, Savill Research Rural, http://pdf.euro.savills.co.uk/global-research/international-farmland-focus.pdf.

Sell, S. K. & Prakash, A. (2004) Using ideas strategically: the contest between business and NGO networks in intellectual property rights, *International Studies Quarterly*, 48(1), pp. 143–175.

Seufert, P. (2013) The FAO Voluntary Guidelines on the Responsible Governance of Tenure of Land, Fisheries and Forests, *Globalizations*, 10(1), pp. 181–186.

Smaller, C. & Mann, H. L. (2009) *A Thirst for Distant Lands: Foreign Investment in Agricultural Land and Water* (Winnipeg: International Institute for Sustainable Development).

Suárez de Vivero, J. L. & Rodríguez Mateos, J. C. (2010) Ocean governance in a competitive world: the BRIC countries as emerging maritime powers—building new geopolitical scenarios, *Marine Policy*, 34(5), pp. 967–978.

Tan-Mullins, M., Mohan, G. & Power, M. (2010) Redefining 'Aid' in the China–Africa context, *Development and Change*, 41(5), pp. 857–881.

Veggeland, F. & Borgen, S. O. (2005) Negotiating international food standards: the World Trade Organization's impact on the Codex Alimentarius Commission, *Governance*, 18(4), pp. 675–708.

Victor, D. G. & Yueh, L. (2010) The new energy order, *Foreign Affairs*, 89(1), pp. 61–73.

Vidal, J. (2009) Fears for the world's poor countries as the rich grab land to grow food, *The Guardian*, 3 July, http://www.guardian.co.uk/environment/2009/jul/03/land-grabbing-food-environment.

Vihma, V. (2011) India and the global climate governance: between principles and pragmatism, *The Journal of Environment & Development March*, 20(1), pp. 69–94.

Wade, R. H. (2011) Emerging world order? From multipolarity to multilateralism in the G20, the World Bank, and the IMF, *Politics & Society*, 39(3), pp. 347–378.

Wallerstein, I. (1974) The rise and future demise of the world capitalist system: concepts for comparative analysis, *Comparative Studies in Society and History*, 16(4), pp. 387–415.

Walz, J. & Ramachandran, V. (2011) Brave new world: a literature review of emerging donors and the changing nature of foreign assistance, Center for Global Development Working Papers, http://cgdev.org/files/1425691_file_Walz_Ramachandran_Brave_New_World_FINAL.pdf.

Weaver, J. (2003) *The Great Land Rush and the Making of the Modern World, 1650–1900* (Montreal: McGill-Queens University Press).

Wendt, A. (1995) Constructing international politics, *International Security*, 20(1), pp. 71–81.

White, J. & White, B. (2012) Gendered experiences of dispossession: oil palm expansion in a Dayak Hibun community in West Kalimantan, *Journal of Peasant Studies*, 39(3–4), pp. 995–1016.

White, L. (2010) Understanding Brazil's new drive for Africa, *South African Journal of International Affairs*, 17(2), pp. 221–242.

Williams, M. (2005) The Third World and global environmental negotiations: interests, institutions and ideas, *Global Environmental Politics*, 5(3), pp. 48–69.

Woertz, E. (2013) Gulf states and the governance of agro-investments, *Globalizations*, 10(1), pp. 87–104.

Woods, N. (2008) Whose aid? Whose influence? China, emerging donors and the silent revolution in development assistance, *International Affairs*, 84(6), pp. 1205–1221.

World Bank (2009) *Large-Scale Acquisition of Land Rights for Agricultural or Natural Resource-based* (Washington, DC: World Bank).

Young, O. R., Chambers, W. B. & Kim, J. (2008) & ten Have, C, *Institutional Interplay: Biosafety and Trade* (New York: United Nations University Press).

Zoomers, A. (2010) Globalisation and the foreignisation of space: seven processes driving the current global land grab, *Journal of Peasant Studies*, 37(2), pp. 429–447.

Zürn, M. (2004) Global governance and legitimacy problems, *Government and Opposition*, 39(2), pp. 260–287.

Matias E. Margulis is Assistant Professor of International Studies at the University of Northern British Columbia and a postdoctoral fellow at the Max Planck Institute for the Study of Societies. He is currently writing a book on the global politics of international trade and food security. He is a former Canadian trade policy advisor and has worked on global food security policy at several multilateral organizations.

Tony Porter is Professor of Political Science at McMaster University in Hamilton, Canada. His books include *Globalization and Finance* (Polity Press, 2005), *The Challenges of Global Business Authority: Democratic Renewal, Stalemate, or Decay?* (SUNY Press, 2010), coedited with Karsten Ronit, and *Transnational Financial Associations and the Governance of Global Finance: Assembling Power and Wealth* (Routledge, 2013), coauthored with Heather McKeen-Edwards.

The Governance of Gulf Agro-Investments

ECKART WOERTZ

Barcelona Centre for International Affairs (CIDOB), Barcelona, Spain

ABSTRACT   *In the wake of the 2008 global food crisis and export restrictions imposed by major food exporters, Gulf states announced plans for foreign agro-investments, including major land deals, in the name of national of food security. Media reporting has often conveyed an inaccurate picture of these land deals since project implementation has lagged far behind official announcements. This essay analyzes Gulf states' land deals against the backdrop of domestic politics, strategic vulnerabilities, and earlier agro-investments in the Sudan during the 1970s. Approaches among Gulf states diverge considerably, most notably in the case of Saudi Arabia and Qatar that have created new governance institutions to coordinate food security policies and land investments. Gulf states have also increased their profile on the world stage and now their prominent role in the global land grab requires them to navigate new political spaces, including engagement with global civil society, water politics in countries where they are investing, and in emerging global governance initiatives related to food security and investment in land.*

Introduction

Gulf states are one of three primary actors in the field of land acquisitions. In addition to Asian nations and financial investors, Gulf states have striven to acquire long-term rights to land in the wake of the 2008 global food crisis. Unlike the general trend in the global land grab they are not interested in land deals for biofuel production, Gulf states have focused on land acquisitions for food. Despite their prominence in the global land grab debate, Gulf states have been treated as black boxes. Indeed, their historical motivation for such investments, capacity to achieve them, geopolitical vulnerabilities and their domestic political economy of food are rarely discussed. Crucial differences between them are under-examined in the literature. Many existing studies are written from the perspective of the target countries for investment (see Deininger et al., 2011; Deng, 2011; FIAN, 2010; Horne et al., 2011). As far as Gulf states figure, accounts are based on secondary sources in the English speaking media. The magnitude of agro-investments is often inflated, and uncorroborated news items are at times reiterated, such as the claim that 'many projects include contracts to provide oil and gas supplies in exchange for land' (Zurayk et al., 2011, p. 131; see also GRAIN, 2008). In fact, no evidence for such arrangements exists. And if Gulf states sought them in a crisis situation then they would hardly look to food net-importing countries, but to established food exporters with a track record and the institutional set-ups to deliver (see Wikileaks, 2009a).

This essay analyzes the governance of Gulf agro-investments in land, as far as it is yet discernible. In addition to available literature, this study draws from archival sources, grey literature, local media reporting, and interviews with government and business elites in the Gulf region and Sudan. Media reports are often unreliable and, because of the autocratic nature of rule and lack of bureaucratic capacities, Gulf institutions do not produce public statements and position papers with the same frequency and quality like OECD countries. This needs to be kept in mind when approaching the topic. The first section analyzes the reaction of Gulf states to the 2008 global food crisis against the backdrop of domestic politics, strategic vulnerabilities, and earlier investment attempts to outsource food production to Sudan in the 1970s. This is followed by a discussion of the varied approaches among Gulf states to acquire land and grow food abroad, most notably those of Saudi Arabia and Qatar. For example, Gulf states have created new governance institutions to coordinate food security policies and agricultural investments between various state agencies and the private sector. In contrast, the United Arab Emirates (UAE), Kuwait, Bahrain, and Oman do not have a comparable degree of institutionalization. The last section considers possible future scenarios. It outlines how international relations of Gulf states could be affected by their agro-investments, how they might engage with global civil society, navigate the water politics in target countries, and engagement with global governance initiatives to govern food security and land grabbing.

The Gulf States and the Global Food Crisis of 2008

Memories of Vulnerability

The 2008 global food crisis rang alarm bells in the Gulf states. While rising food prices were a concern, ample oil revenues ensured that imports remained affordable. The real concern for Gulf states were the food export restrictions imposed by their food suppliers such as Argentina, Russia, India, and Vietnam (Al-Alami, 2009; Al-Attiya, 2011; Kingdom of Saudi Arabia, 2010a). The fear emerged that petrodollars might not alone buy food some day in the future and evoked memories of threatened food supplies. During World Wars I and II, the region was at the mercy of respective world powers for crucial food imports (Schatkowski-Schilcher, 1992; Tell, 2000; Wilmington, 1971). In the 1970s, the US threatened to use the 'food weapon' in retaliation against the Arab oil boycott. At that time, a grain embargo was rejected for reasons of impracticality alone; Arab oil exporters were less dependent on US grain deliveries than the US was dependent on oil imports. And given the Gulf states' limited population size at that time, they would have easily found alternative suppliers (US Congress, 1973).

Still, the mere threat of a food embargo was enough to worry Gulf policymakers. Like oil importers, Gulf states were concerned about diversity of supply and transport security. They contemplated oil for food barter deals with alternative suppliers like Australia, developed the vision of Sudan as an Arab breadbasket, and finally cast their lot with a massive expansion of subsidized domestic agriculture that relied on unsustainable mining of fossil water aquifers (Woertz, 2013).

The Gulf states' Sudan 'breadbasket' strategy was in many ways a precursor to today's agro-investment drive. The Kuwait-based Arab Fund for Economic and Social Development (AFESD), a multilateral donor institution of Gulf states that was established in 1971, first formulated it, and the Sudanese authorities adopted it (AFESD, 1976; Government of Sudan, 1977). Tripartite cooperation was a core idea with the Gulf providing the capital, Sudan the land, and Western joint venture partners the know-how and the project management. It built on a controversial expansion of mechanized rain fed farming that was spurred by the Sudanese government at that time. The expansion was often in conflict with customary land rights of smallholders and pastoralists and contributed to erosion and desertification (O'Brien, 1985).

However, the breadbasket plan never came to fruition. When the Arab Authority for Agricultural Investment and Development (AAAID) was created in 1976, pledges by Arab governments were only about a tenth of the initial AFESD proposal. By 1978, Sudan faced a balance of payment crisis and Gulf states rapidly lost interest thereafter. Commercially, agricultural projects in the Sudan never paid off (Interagency Intelligence Memorandum, 1980). Beside political unrest, the notorious corruption of the Nimeiri regime proved to be a major impediment. The Kenana Sugar Company 270 kilometers southwest of Khartoum was the only larger project where Gulf states really invested, and that only after securing extensive assurances, like guaranteed off-take agreements in hard currency. Otherwise, they never ventured beyond pilot plants, or else became mired in feasibility considerations (Oesterdiekhoff and Wohlmuth, 1983).

Agro-Investments Back on the Agenda

Agro-investments abroad are back on the agenda in Gulf states. Gulf states share a set of peculiar motivations that set them apart from other international investors. Factor endowment, geographical location, and the role of affordable food for political legitimacy weigh in the balance. In the case of Saudi Arabia, the decline of a domestic agro-business class that looks for new business opportunities plays a role as well; fossil water aquifers in Saudi Arabia are facing depletion and the country has decided to phase out its subsidized wheat production by 2016. International agro-investments are regarded as one pillar of a food security strategy. Others include strategic storage, food subsidies, a reorientation of domestic agriculture towards more water efficiency, and the management of import dependence through diversification of supplies (Al Riyadh, 2009; Kingdom of Saudi Arabia, 2010a, 2010b).

Given their preoccupation with food security, the focus of Gulf states has been on staple foods like wheat and rice, feedstock for their livestock industry like barley and alfalfa, and meat production. They have not eyed projects for industrial input factors like cotton or rubber, as they do not have the industries that would require the respective feedstock. Except for sugar, tropical crops have not ranked high in their investment plans. Gulf states have no interest in biofuels. This is remarkable, as biofuel projects have constituted a whopping 58% of all announced international land acquisitions according to Anseeuw et al. (2012, p. 24). The Kenana Sugar Company, about half of which is owned by Kuwait and Saudi Arabia, produces ethanol for European markets, but this is an outlier. The idea is to enhance the value of molasses by-products, biofuels are not regarded as a core activity.[1] As large oil producers, Gulf states have sought to downplay the environmental impacts of their products and are wary of potential competition. In the past, the Saudi oil minister has slammed biofuels for unfavorable economics and dubious environmental claims, promoting solar energy for electricity production instead (*Gulf News*, 2008).

This time around, Gulf states have announced agro-investments on a global scale in faraway places like Australia, Vietnam, Ukraine, or Brazil. Yet, the most popular target countries are geographically close, like Sudan, Pakistan, and Ethiopia (Al-Rasheed, 2012, p. 128). Established political ties and cultural affinities have also played a role. Most of these countries are net food importers themselves. Some of them, like Pakistan and Egypt, have serious water scarcity problems similar to those of the Gulf states. Not surprisingly, investments in these states have been controversial. Governments in developing countries have been eager to attract Gulf capital to modernize their agricultural sectors, build up infrastructure, and improve their sources of revenues, but dealings have not been transparent. Advocacy groups have accused Gulf states of violating customary land rights of smallholders and compromising food security in target countries (GRAIN, 2008; Horne et al., 2011).

Announced Gulf projects have often exceeded 100,000 hectares, and one feels reminded of the gigantic AFESD vision of the Sudan breadbasket in the 1970s. However, contrary to widespread media perception, many have yet to get off the ground. Funding constraints after the global financial crisis, difficult framework conditions, and political backlash in target countries have been among the impediments (Woertz, 2011). A World Bank report about large land deals in general showed that only one-fifth of analyzed projects farming operations had actually begun (Deininger et al., 2011). A considerable implementation gap was also confirmed by other fieldwork-based reports, even though they were highly critical of land investments (Deng, 2011; FIAN, 2010; Horne et al. 2011).

The issue of reliability of media reports was highlighted in April 2012 when the International Land Coalition (ILC), German consultancy GIZ, and research centers in Hamburg, Montpellier, and Bern released the Land Matrix. The Land Matrix was advertised as the world's largest and most detailed database about large-scale land acquisitions. It claimed to submit media reports to a rigorous verification process consisting of cross-checking of various sources and surveys in host countries. Based on this verification it assigned reliability codes to land acquisitions (Anseeuw et al., 2012b; Land Matrix, 2012). Only news items with some triangulation like research reports or press releases by investors and governments were included, even though the individual reliability codes for each project were not made public at the release of the website. There is also the possibility to declare projects as failed and remove them from the database, although it is unclear what is required for that to happen. The verification process is ongoing and as a work in progress there might be improvements over time, but at its release the Land Matrix gave a distorted image of international land acquisitions. It reported deals over millions of hectares as fact that never materialized like announced projects by South Korean Daewoo in Madagascar and Chinese ZTE in the Republic of Congo. While South Sudan figured prominently with deals that have never made it beyond the announcement stage, the database did not mention any of the projects in north and central Sudan, where some implementation has actually taken place. Thus, it involuntarily underlined the very problem it had set out to resolve: the unreliability of media reports (Brautigam, 2012a, 2012b; Rural Modernity, 2012)

Even on the projects in north and central Sudan, important qualifications are in order as project implementation is in its early stages, or has only occurred on a fraction of the announced scale based on several interviews between 2008 and 2012.[2] The project in Abu Hamad of Qatar's Hassad Food and a wheat and alfalfa project in Berber of the Saudi-based Al-Rajhi Group would be examples of this. On some older projects cultivation has actually declined dramatically compared to earlier times and it remains to be seen whether rehabilitation is feasible. This is the case with the Zayed al-Khair project of the Abu Dhabi-based Al-Anhar Group which was established in 1999 and the Agadi dry farming scheme of the AAAID in Blue Nile province which has been around since the early 1980s.

There is a major lack of data about Gulf land deals beyond basic press releases and newspaper reports. This lack can not only be attributed to the recent nature of the phenomenon (Margulis and Porter, 2013, pp. 65–86), but also to a general lack of transparency in the region. The Gulf states are 'rentier states'; while in advanced 'production states', i.e. industrialized countries, society supports the state via tax revenues, in the rentier state governments support themselves and their societies via distribution of the oil rent. In exchange for supply of welfare services and job guarantees in the public sector, the state expects political acquiescence—no taxation and no representation (Luciani, 1987). Major transmission mechanisms of transparency are therefore missing: accountability of companies towards the tax man, and of democratically elected governments towards their constituencies. Company accountability to their shareholders is also in a nascent stage and there is no widespread culture of Corporate Social Responsibility that would engage with non-company stakeholders. Many companies are either owned by the government (e.g. the national oil companies) or members of the royal family. Others are non-listed family enterprises. Even among listed companies, most of the larger ones have the state as a majority shareholder (Woertz, 2007). The scarcity of data also applies to target countries, especially documents with contract details are not available (Cotula et al., 2009).

The State as Facilitator: Differences Between Gulf States

The state is dominant in formulating foreign agro-investment strategies and tries to pave the way for sovereign wealth funds (SWFs), state-owned companies, or the private sector by negotiating framework agreements in target countries. All three groups of actors have varying degrees of independence from their respective governments. To cope with the requirements of strategic agro-investments, new governance institutions have been established like Hassad Food, a subsidiary of the Qatar Investment Authority. In other cases, existing development funds like AFESD or the Abu Dhabi Fund for Development (ADFD) have taken a more equity-oriented strategic approach that goes beyond dispersed loan financing. Portfolio investors like the Kuwait Investment Authority (KIA) have been tasked with direct investments, a field where they have formerly not been active. In the case of Saudi Arabia, the government aims at public–private partnerships with the domestic farm business. Gulf states have also shown an interest in breathing new life into pan-Arab institutions like the AAAID.

There are notable differences between GCC (Gulf Cooperation Council) countries in terms of targeted countries, investment activity, and institutional set-ups. Saudi Arabia, UAE, and Qatar have been the most active investors, while Kuwait, Bahrain, and Oman have trailed behind. Saudi Arabia has focused on Sudan, Ethiopia, and other countries in East Africa, which are located close to its long coastline along the Red Sea. The UAE has shown a preference for Pakistan for similar reasons of geographic proximity. Qatar's interests have been widely spread, ranging from Australia, to Vietnam and Kenya. Qatar and Saudi Arabia have the most institutionalized approach with bespoke coordinating agencies like the Qatar National Food Security Programme (QNFSP) and the King Abdullah Initiative for Saudi Agricultural Investment Abroad (KAISAIA).

The Qatar National Food Security Programme (QNFSP)

The QNFSP aims to address Qatar's food security concerns in a comprehensive way by coordinating government agencies, international partner agreements, and foreign agro-investments. QNFSP does not solely focus on international agro-investments, but also on domestic agriculture. At the heart of its work is a Master Plan for food security, which it wants to roll out in 2012/2013.

Right at a time when Saudi Arabia is phasing out wheat production, the Master Plan revives the self-sufficiency strategy with the help of technological means like hydroponics and greenhouses that are run with solar-based desalination to make up for the lack of water resources. With such technologies, Qatar hopes to produce up to 70% of its food by 2023, while it currently imports 90% of it (*Gulf Times*, 2011). Backup capacities for cereal production are planned, but overall, cereals are slated for import, while more value added products like poultry and vegetables could be produced locally (Al-Attiya, 2011).

State-owned Hassad Food is the dominant player in foreign agro-investments. The private sector plays a minor role for lack of capacity. Hassad Food now has projects in Australia and Sudan for wheat and livestock. It is in advanced discussions in Brazil, Pakistan, and Georgia for sugar, rice, and wheat production, respectively.[3] Qatar stresses that its projects need to be commercially viable on a standalone basis and comply with international regulations. In the long run, the idea is that Hassad Food will not run the farms itself, but will only issue off-take agreements (Al-Attiya, 2011).

The King Abdullah Initiative for Saudi Agricultural Investment Abroad (KAISAIA)

In January 2009, KAISAIA was launched to coordinate different segments of the bureaucracy and the private sector. Contrasted to the QNFSP, which has a YouTube channel and its own Facebook and Twitter accounts, KAISAIA shies away from the spotlight and does not even have a website. Some information about the Initiative has been released by the relevant ministries and occasional conference presentations. Where QNFSP is eager to attract international attention, Saudi Arabia is sovereign conscious, prefers discreet decision-making, and shuns the limelight. Contrary to other Gulf states, it needs to cater to a vastly more populous constituency and has a substantial segment of poor among its local population. Qatar's strategy of self-sufficiency with new technological means would not be feasible for Saudi Arabia given its population size and the costs involved.

There is a more direct link between the political economy of Saudi Arabia's domestic agriculture and its planned agro-investments abroad. Land distribution and subsidized wheat cultivation have been a means of wealth distribution to royals and regime clients since the 1980s (Chaudhry, 1997; Elhadj, 2006). Cynics argue that international agro-investments serve to open up new avenues for redistribution of oil rent as the old playground of domestic agriculture is downsized for lack of water. The agro-business community has lobbied for soft loans, subsidies, and agreements with the state that include specified quantities and prices. It was argued that without such inducements foreign agro-investments would not be commercially viable (Al Jazirah, 2011). The Riyadh Chamber for Commerce and Industry has proposed three different alternatives for compensating farmers for the phasing out of wheat production by 2016. Beside direct payments and government purchases of idled land, it has suggested that 60% of such purchases could be paid with shares of a public investment company that would invest in agricultural projects abroad (Riyadh Chamber of Commerce and Industry, 2010). The Saudi Company for

Agricultural Investment and Animal Production (SCAIAP) was launched in April 2009 as part of KAISAIA with a capital investment of $800 million. It could be used for such a purpose.

KAISAIA is conceptualized as a public–private partnership. Indeed, the Saudi government wants to facilitate land leases and investment opportunities for the Saudi private sector by political support and co-financing. The board of directors of SCAIAP has three members from the private sector and the Chambers of Commerce and Industry have functioned as a transmission belt to convey the goals of the initiative and take stock of the suggestions of the private sector (Al-Qahtani, 2009, p. 34). KAISAIA has a complex governance arrangement that is grafted on top of existing domestic and interagency politics. The Ministry of Commerce and Industry (MoCI) leads the initiative and is purportedly anxious that projects will be financially viable without significant subsidies by the state. SCAIAP is owned by the Public Investment Fund (PIF), which falls under the responsibility of the equally budget-conscious Ministry of Finance, which is less convinced by the need for as excessive state support as the industry is requesting. The Ministry of Agriculture (MoA), a stalwart of the domestic agro-lobby, has a deputy role in the initiative, but is less influential in the overall Saudi bureaucratic framework. An Undersecretary of State represents the Ministry of Foreign Affairs. After rumors that the lead role would move from MoCI to MoA (Al Eqtisadiah, 2012), the Minister of Agriculture announced plans to hand over the KAISAIA file from the ministries to SCAIAP in order to streamline procedures (*Arab News*, 2012). This would mean a major upgrade of SCAIAPs role, which has delayed disbursing funds yet to the great dismay of the business community. Only recently has the Saudi Cabinet given the final green light for KAISAIA, specifying a maximum government share of 60% in the financing of projects. It also stipulated that target countries must allow at least 50% of the crops for export back to Saudi Arabia (Saudi Gazette, 2012).

KAISAIA aims at investments in countries with agricultural potential, low-cost labor, good administrative governance, investor protection, and tax relaxation for input factors. In an interview with the daily *Al-Riyadh*, the Saudi Minister of Agriculture identified financial framework conditions as the largest threat to agro-investments, citing unfavorable property rights and taxation laws, hampered repatriation of profits, and exchange rate depreciation. Unanticipated changes to host states land and investment laws once projects have been implemented are of particular concern (Al-Rasheed, 2010, pp. 171–178; *Al Riyadh*, 2011). Other goals of KAISAIA are low-cost transport of food to the Kingdom, free choice of crops, and extended rights to the land, either via ownership or long-term lease contracts. The Saudi Cabinet has drafted a model agreement, which is not public, to safeguard private sector investments via Bilateral Investment Treaties (BITs). The first of this kind was signed in February 2010 with the Philippines (*Arab News*, 2011).

Gulf states have possibilities to reduce transaction costs in some target countries via established ties that are not open to other investors. Yet the preferences they are reeling off are not very different from internationally promoted standards for foreign direct investments and they use such measures like the World Bank's Ease of Doing Business Index to gauge the attractiveness of target countries (Al-Qahtani, 2009). However, this does not prevent them from announcing investments in developing countries with weak governance where such measures are uniquely low. This contradiction might be explained by perceived potential benefits which outweigh the risks. On the other hand, the interest of Gulf states has increasingly shifted to more markets with more stable legal and regulatory frameworks like Australia, Brazil, Argentina, and Ukraine according to QNFSP (Shah quoted in Reuters, 2010).

Other Gulf Countries

In the UAE, foreign land acquisitions have been more informal. The UAE does not have a centralized governmental task force or institution with authority comparable to that of the QNFSP for example. Its efforts to bridge bureaucratic divides and negotiate between different fiefdoms are more limited than in the case of KAISAIA. Furthermore, its federal structure complicates a unified stance. Real power is not vested in the respective ministries, but with influential royals, their advisors, and associated institutions like the Supreme Petroleum Council. Control by individual emirates can be observed in areas like customs, the police force, transport, or parts of the judiciary. The federal budget is small and common policy implementation at times difficult. Federal funding still depends very much on oil-rich Abu Dhabi, which might press for more centralization in the wake of its bailout of Dubai since 2009 (Woertz, 2012).

Notable players in agricultural investments are formally private companies like Al-Qudra or Al-Dahra that have members of the royal family as shareholders. The state-owned ADFD has been assigned a role to develop a large project in Sudan, but still needs to build up management capacities for agricultural projects or will need to find partners for such an endeavor. The commercially motivated set up of a Dubai World subsidiary for investment in natural resources has yet to yield any agro-investment projects, and is presumably hampered by the strong impact of Dubai's financial crisis.

Kuwait prefers a top-down approach, with the ministries of finance and agriculture and the KIA taking the lead. The KIA considers agriculture as part of its overall investment interest in Asia, where it has good-standing investment relations. Kuwait has the most pronounced rentier state structure in the Gulf, with little diversification efforts and a strong emphasis on redistribution policies. The parliament has a reputation for petty fights and procrastination. This can prolong decision-making processes or jeopardize projects altogether (Gavin, 2009; Teitelbaum, 2009).

Bahrain has also shown a characteristic mixture of government support and private sector involvement. Its ability to engage in overseas investments is more limited because it does not command large oil revenues like Saudi Arabia, UAE, Qatar, and Kuwait. The same is true for Oman, which has abstained from the Gulf drive into agro-investments, apart from a small contribution to the Merowe Dam in Sudan. This comes as a surprise given its traditionally close relationships to East Africa and Pakistan, the very regions that other Gulf states target most. Oman has focused its food security strategy instead on the most developed system of strategic storage in the Gulf region (World Bank and FAO, 2012).

Global Political and Economic Engagements

Agro-investments abroad affect the international relations of Gulf states and pose formidable challenges to their leaders and bureaucracies. Given the nascent state of affairs and the lack of public statements by Gulf states, one needs to rely to a certain extent on legitimate inference and speculation, but some trends are discernible. Gulf states need to enhance their bilateral relations with target countries, interact with international institutions like the Food and Agriculture Organization of the United Nations (FAO) and the World Trade Organization (WTO) more, and increasingly engage with global civil society and grassroots movements whose politics are alien to their autocratic ways of doing business at home. They will also face delicate water politics, most notably in the Nile Valley.

Bilateral Relations

Governments of countries hosting Gulf agro-investments are the first parties to be approached by Gulf states, not only because they seek framework agreements that pave the way for their SWFs and private sector actors, but also because in a lot of host countries the state is formally the owner of land, especially in African countries. Yet relationships with many target countries are not very close. Trading relations of the Gulf states are mainly with manufacturing nations in the OECD and some emerging markets like China or India. Arab states aside, South–South relations are much weaker. Only Saudi Arabia has a significant embassy presence in Africa and Asia. Apart from Sudan and Pakistan, agro-investments in many target countries do not start from a baseline of established broad-based trading relationships and established political dialogue.

Established agro-exporters like Brazil, Argentina, and Thailand have taken steps to limit land ownership by foreigners (Perrone, 2013, pp. 205–209). Like oil in the Gulf states, agriculture is an important earner of foreign exchange in these countries, and there are concerns to keep this resource national. Cooperation in developed agro-markets will often take the form of agreements with local firms and partners, rather than building up farming operations from scratch. Leaders of African countries, on the other hand, have been eager to offer land rights to attract Gulf investment. However, these governments have faced increasing pressure from grassroots movements and advocacy groups who have complained about the detrimental effects of land investments on traditional small-scale farmers.

In the future, Gulf states will interact with their partners in new ways. Indirectly, they might also become involved in controversial water politics concerning the cross-border sharing of water resources (see Allan et al., 2012; Mehta et al., 2012). Gulf agro-investments aim to enhance food production and export capacities. All other things being equal, this will lead to increased water consumption in target countries. The Southeastern Anatolia Project (GAP) and reduced water flows along the Euphrates and Tigris have been a bone of contention between Turkey, Syria, and Iraq. In the 2000s, Pakistan lodged objections to Indian dam projects in the Indus basin (FAO, 2010). In the Nile Valley, successful completion of agro-investments in Ethiopia could put Gulf states at loggerheads with Egypt (Brown, 2011; Horne et al., 2011, p. 51). At its annual conference in 2010, the Egyptian Council for Foreign Affairs, a think tank of diplomats, generals, and other public figures, identified Nile water issues as a strategic concern. Projects financed by Gulf donors and the World Bank were portrayed as a threat (*Al-Ahrar*, 2010).

International Cooperation

Gulf states have historically limited their interaction with international organizations; political capital has often been invested at the regional level and in their relations with the US. Part of the reason for Gulf states' limited international engagement to date has to do with how national institutions operate in these regions and their unique positions in the global economy. Gulf autocrats have a high degree of personal discretion in decision-making at the national level and maintain a preference for personal relationships over formal institutional mechanisms. Consequently, Gulf bureaucracies are top heavy and their capacities to communicate on an institutional level across scales, such as in transnational governmental networks or in diplomatic spheres, are relatively underdeveloped. In a system of 'segmented clientelism', ministries can function as personal fiefdoms of royals, with little interagency communication and a high degree of institutional autonomy (Hertog, 2010, p. 235).

For economic reasons, Gulf states' interaction with international organizations has also been limited. Gulf states as petro-economies have often enjoyed budget surpluses or were able to finance budget deficits through domestic borrowing. Hence, unlike most states of the Global South, Gulf states never had to resort to the International Monetary Fund (IMF) or the World Bank for financing and subordinate themselves to conditionality clauses. If they engaged with the Bretton Woods institutions, it was always on equal footing, as they hired them as paid consultants.

However, Gulf states have at times demonstrated a clear interest in using international institutions, international standards, and joint ventures with international partners to safeguard commercial interests. Gulf states are also conscious of the limits of bilateral engagement in economic relationships. These states are a major source of capital and this puts them in advantageous positions in bilateral economic negotiations; however, they have been wary of imposing strict conditionality in bilateral deals in order to avoid unnecessary political confrontation with recipient countries. This was particularly the case during the Sudan breadbasket episode in the 1970s. For example, when at that time Sudan ran into increasing balance of payments problems and Gulf donors became disillusioned with the corrupt governance of the Nimeiri regime, the Gulf states did not confront the Sudanese directly but instead quietly supported the stiff terms of the IMFs structural adjustment program of 1978 (Spiro, 1989).

Following the 2008 global food crises, Gulf states have taken on a more vocal role in advocating for the interest of food importers at the multilateral level. Historically, the WTO has been preoccupied with trade liberalization and the reduction of import barriers. Export restrictions, which are allowed under current WTO rules, have become a very serious concern for the Gulf states and all other food importing countries (see Sharma, 2011). The Gulf states have backed proposals by Japan and Switzerland at the WTO to discipline export restrictions. At the same time, the Gulf states are clearly not holding their breath for a resolution at the WTO and moving forward with land acquisitions. Yet, the logic of land acquisitions has been challenged by the former Saudi chief trade negotiator, Fawaz al-Alami, who has argued against foreign agro-investments because these will not guarantee food security in times of crisis when exporters are most likely to resort to export restrictions and instead has called for the establishment of strategic food reserves (Al-Alami, 2009).

At present, Gulf states are also implementing food reserves on a national level in response to the events of the 2008 global food crisis. However, the International Food Policy Research Institute (IFPRI) has argued that international-scale solutions would be preferable. The argument being that national food reserves lead to unnecessary and expensive storage and potentially to tighter world markets and rising prices—the very problem reserves are intended to address (von Braun and Torero, 2009). Arab states are hopeful and sceptical at the same time when it comes to debates about an international food reserve. Pan-Arab food security concerns were spurned in the 1970s after the US and other food exporters rejected efforts at the FAO to create an international food reserve, as Hashim Awad, a former Minister of Commerce of Sudan pointed out (in Spiro, 1989, p. 492). Despite the significance of food security concerns, Gulf states have not been as active as one would expect at the WTO or even the G20, where Saudi Arabia is a member, to push for global action on export restrictions and food reserve policies.

Signs of more concerted international engagement by Gulf states are evident in the field of climate change. Qatar is highly influential in launching the intergovernmental Global Dry Land Alliance (GDLA), which seeks to address food security concerns in countries that are predominately arid or semi-arid environments—this would include up to 60 countries and around 2

billion people (*Saudi Gazette*, 2010). The GDLAs principal aim is to improve agricultural productivity by establishing centers of research excellence and provide a mechanism for financing
sustainable development and knowledge and technology transfer. The response of other arid
countries to the intergovernmental initiative and a possible supporting role of the United
Nations are not yet fully clear, but Qatar plans to bring the initiative firmly on track by 2013
(Al-Attiya, 2011; QNFSP, 2011). Qatar is anxious to align itself with international concerns
and avoids portraying its agricultural initiatives as narrowly focused on national food security.
This fits more broadly with Qatar's other efforts to gain an international profile, ranging from the
satellite network Al Jazeera, to international conflict intermediation and hosting of the FIFA
World Cup in 2022. Qatar's international activism has also left an imprint on its national
food security strategy and the GDLA initiative.

Qatar also held the presidency of the 66th UN General Assembly in 2011. Qatar's High Representative to the UN, Nassir Abdulaziz Al-Nasser, who held the presidency, tried to fill this cer-
emonial post with more life than is commonly usual. For example, Al-Nasser raised issues like
the impact of financial speculation on food prices or disaster relief during the meetings of the
General Assembly (United Nations, 2012). Other Gulf states have played prominent roles in
the global response to the 2008 global food crisis. Saudi Arabia gave $500 million to the
WFP at the height of the global food crisis in 2008, the largest one-off donation ever, which
saved it from cancelling its emergency food operation that year. Gulf states committed significant funds again when a famine struck the Horn of Africa in 2011. This could hint at a shift
towards more multilateralism as Gulf states have given a relatively higher share of their GDP
to aid than OECD countries, but usually have preferred bilateral over multilateral distribution
channels (World Bank, 2010).

The importance of trade-related issues and market intelligence is exemplified by Gulf states'
recent strategy to get a foothold in international food trading. International food trade is highly
oligopolistic, dominated by a few large trading companies like ADM, Bunge, Cargill, and
Dreyfus, which enjoy significant market power in the global food system (Murphy et al.,
2012). Abu Dhabi recently announced the establishment of a food trading house. It was also a
major investor in the public offering of the international commodity trader Glencore alongside
other Gulf investors like Saudi Prince Al-Waleed's Kingdom Holding. Glencore went on to
acquire Canada's largest grain trader, Viterra, which is expected to benefit greatly from the
end of the Canadian Wheat Board's monopoly on Canadian grain sales. While privileged bilateral access to food production and national storage exemplify mistrust in the reliability of
markets, Gulf states also try to muscle their way into the controversial institutional set-ups of
grain markets and the virtual water trade that they represent (Sojamo et al., 2012).

One challenge facing the Gulf states is that they lack expertise in overseas agricultural projects. To acquire this type of know-how about crops, farm management, and investment environments, Gulf institutions increasingly find themselves cooperating with international
organizations and companies. Take the FAO, which has recently opened an office in Abu
Dhabi. The QNFSP now has cooperation agreements with the International Center for Agricultural Research in the Dry Areas (ICARDA) and Texas A&M University. Saudi Arabia has
approached the World Bank and the International Rice Research Institute (IRRI) to connect it
with countries in Africa and Central Asia in order to facilitate investments in food production
there (IRRI, 2009).

This points to an overall trend of greater global engagement by Gulf states motivated by food
security concerns. Some of this engagement is in the spirit of cooperation but much of it reflects
a strategy of security mercantilism (McMichael, 2013, pp. 47–64). In light of the end of cheap

food and increasing competition for land, such global engagements will become more frequent. Frictions are already evident. At times, there has been the impression within international public and private consultancy circles that Gulf states are only interested in window shopping and getting a carte blanche for their investment activities. A more refined knowledge of international institutions and their agendas will be required for a successful management of strategic partnerships if Gulf states wish to be serious players in global food security.

Engagements with Global Civil Society

Global civil society, including international NGO and transnational and grassroots peasant movements are important actors in global and national political struggles around land deals (Borras et al., 2013, pp. 161–179; McKeon, 2013, pp. 105–122). Gulf states are ill prepared to engage with them. As authoritarian states, they allow only limited participation at home. There have been cautious steps towards liberalization since the 1990s, with Kuwait and Bahrain at the helm of reform measures, but a backlash has ensued in the wake of the Arab Spring (Ehteshami and Wright, 2008). Gulf states are hardly used to global civil society politics and have long ignored criticism of their domestic abuses of human rights. There is no established process in these states for association from below. At the end of the day domestic civil society require the rulers' explicit approval to operate. A widespread practice is either to crackdown on potential civil society activities or to preempt concerns through the establishment of civil society organization that are loyal to the government. Because of such clientelistic practices, civil society activities are rarely controversial as far as they exist. Outside of the Gulf states' borders, the situation is different. Outlawing or cutting off access to the Internet are not options there.

Global civil society organizations have developed into intricate players in a 'global legitimacy game' (Van Rooy, 2004; see also Demars, 2005). Transnational corporations have to engage with them, otherwise their reputation might be tarnished and their bottom line hurt. For Gulf states, the global civil society challenge is new. Global civil society did not have today's reach and capacity for mobilization during the first wave of Gulf land acquisitions in the 1970s. Gulf governments still operate in very 'old school' ways; leaders are more comfortable with confidential backroom deals than with transparent practices. Gulf states do not have sufficient capacities to engage in a transnational public dialogue with global civil society organization and their constituencies. In an increasingly globalized discourse on legitimacy, this can amount to a serious handicap.

Global civil society organizations such as GRAIN and transnational peasant movements like La Via Campesina have embarked on advocacy campaigns against the legitimacy of land deals. So if a particular state is receptive towards receiving foreign investment in land, this can lead to considerable pressure from below from local civil society and from above when local civil society collaborates with global civil society that can more easily access global publics and bring pressure to bear on investors and their host states. Planned projects by Gulf investors have met with significant resistance in Mauritania, Indonesia, and Kenya, just to mention a few. The Merowe Dam in Sudan, which was partly funded by GCC development funds, required the resettlement of 50,000 people, which led to violent protests. The GCC is also financing the heightening of the Roseires Dam in the Blue Nile region in Sudan, which will also lead to displacement of many people once finished in 2013–2014 (Verhoeven, 2012). Large-scale farm investments in politically unstable countries with dubious human rights track records can come with considerable political baggage for Gulf states and increasing exposure to international criticism, something they are precisely actively seeking to avoid.

These examples are not dissimilar to the widespread negative international publicity the Gulf states have attracted for their treatment of migrant workers, not least in countries that have been singled out for Gulf agro-investments such as the Philippines and Indonesia. Such negative perceptions could develop into a serious problem over time and spill over to the area of agro-investments. They may even trump the importance of religious commonality that Saudi Arabia and the Islamic Development Bank have highlighted in the field of international investments since the 1970s. Gulf states have shown a willingness to change their behavior. For example, they have reacted to the criticisms of Human Rights Watch and wildcat strikes by improving labor regulations or enforcing their implementation. They have also engaged with the UN and other international organizations to improve labor practices to this end (Janardhan, 2011). This suggests that international reputation remains an important pressure point for the Gulf states.

Land investment is starting to look like a field where the Gulf states start to acknowledge the need for multi-stakeholder consultations, something they have avoided in the past. Saudi Arabia participated in the FAO private sector consultations on responsible agricultural investments, even though it signaled this was a low priority by only sending the representative of a hired consultancy, Maxwell-Stamp, and not high-level decision-makers from a firm or a ministry (FAO, 2011). Gulf states have started to acknowledge the interests of host countries by addressing issues such as export quotas and local food security in land deals (Kingdom of Saudi Arabia, 2009). They have also stressed their adherence to international standards like the FAO *Voluntary Guidelines for Responsible Governance of Land Tenure, Fisheries and Forests in the Context of National Food Security* (Al-Attiya, 2011). Qatar's Hassad Food and the AAAID announced that they would aim at investing and partnering with existing agro-companies in host countries rather than acquiring land rights directly and building up farming operations from scratch (Reuters, 2009; Wikileaks, 2009b). As explained by the head of an African NGO in an interview, Saudi Arabia has already contacted local groups that could sort out potential problems of project implementation on a community level. This type of diplomacy on the ground by Gulf states is new and signals an experiment to better navigate local political dynamics. Yet, it is unclear whether the Gulf states have fully realized the problem and whether they have the institutional capacities and links to global civil society to effectively engage with civil society groups on a local level.

Conclusion

Land investments are a major pillar of Gulf states' food security strategies in the wake of the 2008 global food crisis. The role of the state as a facilitator is crucial in all Gulf states and in line with the predominant development paradigm of the rentier state. Yet there are important differences between them. They also differ from other international investors as the lack of interest in biofuels and the focus on food crops show. Bilateral approaches are prevalent, but there are signs of increased engagement at the global level, including with international organizations and global civil society. This may increase in the future but will be a major challenge given the immature institutional capacity for global engagement in the Gulf states. If successful in scaling up such a capacity, Gulf states would be more vocal on the international stage. This would also produce more material in the public domain that would be accessible for researchers to better understand these countries' policy, motives, and actions.

Other trends to watch include the effect of Gulf states' land investments on their international relations and their possible involvement in regional water politics. Gulf states may soon come to realize that there are alternative cooperation models like contract farming and joint ventures that are distinct from the plantation model of full control to which they mostly aspire (Cotula et al., 2009, pp. 84–87). In fact, in the newly privatized Gezira scheme in Sudan, interested Gulf investors now negotiate directly with farmers about joint projects. Gulf investors here would have joint rights to the produce and profits, but no direct ownership of the land.[4]

Future research could try to shed more light on these differences and trends on the side of Gulf investors. Too often, they have been safely assigned the role of the bogeyman in the land grab literature. Taking stock of the political economy of Gulf states and their historic food security sensitivities is indispensable for an adequate understanding of their foreign investment activities, especially of land. More research could provide understanding of the evolving institutional landscape at home. For this in particular there will need to be a greater inclusion of Arabic scholars and sources, especially in the case of Saudi Arabia and Sudan. Case studies on the politics and political economy of land investments and their impact with longer time horizons and with historical comparison are warranted. Sudan would provide a fertile ground. Some of the projects that have been announced since 2008 are in an early stage of implementation, and Sudan has struggling or failed legacy projects of the Sudan breadbasket era that go back to the 1970s. Another case in point could be projects of the Senegal River Development Organization (SRDO) that were financed by Gulf donors in the 1970s and 1980s (Koopman, 2009; Spiro, 1989, p. 478). Mali, Mauretania, and Senegal are again hosts to relatively advanced pilot projects for rice production by the Jeddah-based Foras International Investment Company (GRAIN, 2010).

Gulf states are major players in the global land grabs that diverge considerably from the general pattern because of their explicit focus on food production. These states are confronting a changed landscape for agro-investments that includes more direct competition from other states and investors, scrutiny by global civil society, and the need to engage in global governance as never before.

Acknowledgements

I am grateful to the Oil, Energy and the Middle East Program at Princeton University for supporting the research for this article.

Notes

1 Confidential interview Kenana Sugar Company executive, 28 November 2011.
2 Interviews with politicians and executives at companies and SWFs in the Gulf were conducted on a continuous basis between 2008 and 2012. Interviews in Sudan were conducted in November 2011. They included members of the local Ministry of Agriculture in Gedaref, the AAAID, the Arab Organization for Agricultural Development (AOAD), the Agricultural Revival Program (*al-nahda al-zira'iyya*), and the Ministry of Irrigation and Water Resources in Khartoum, and managers, workers, contractors, and guards of the respective projects. Some impressions can be found on my blog at http://oilforfood.info/?p=97. For interview details, see Woertz (2013).
3 Confidential interview with Hassad Food executive, 16 November 2011.
4 Confidential interview with Gezira Board official, 22 November 2011.

References

Al-Ahrar (2010) Tahaluf ghair mubashir baina duwal al-khalij wa isra'il wa amrika fi manabiʿ al-nil didda masalih misr [Indirect alliance between Gulf states, Israel, and America against the interest of Egypt with regard to the Nile Sources], *Al-Ahrar,* 29 December.

Al-Alami, F. (2009) Hal yanjah al-istithmar al-ziraʿi al-khariji? [Is the foreign agro-investment successful?], *Al-Watan,* 29 December.

Al-Attiya, F. (2011) QNFSP Chairman, personal interview, Doha, 15 November.

Al Eqtisadiah (2012) Fi dirasa ʿuridat ʿala fariq jamiʿat al-bitrawl tatadaman tahdid al-misaha bi 300 'alf hiktar, ʿAl-lajna al-ziraʿiyya' taqtarih rafʿ siʿr al-qamh 80% [A study that was presented by a team of the petroleum university implies an area definition of 300 thousand hectares. 'The agricultural committee' proposes an increase of the wheat price by 80%], Al Eqtisadiah, 24 January, http://www.aleqt.com/2012/01/24/article_619120.html.

Al Jazirah (2011) Raghma mada sanatain ʿala 'itlaq mubadara khadim al-haramain li-l-istithmar al-ziraʿi bi-l-kharij: Mustathmirun wa khubara' yutalibun bi-l-taʿtjil bi insha' al-sharika al-hukumiyya li daʿm al-mubadara [Despite two years have passed since the launch of the initiative of the servant of the two holy places for foreign agricultural investment: Investors and experts demand a speeding up of establishing the state company for the support of the initiative], 12 January, http://www.al-jazirah.com/20110112/ec1d.htm.

Al-Qahtani, S. bin H. (2009) *Al-istithmar al-ziraʿi al-khariji* [The Foreign Agricultural Investment], Occasional Papers Series, Vol. 17 (Riyadh: King Saud University, Department of Agriculture).

Al-Rasheed, T. bin F. (2010) *Al-tabaʿa al-ula* [The First Edition], Riyadh.

Al-Rasheed, T. bin F. (2012) *Agricultural Development Strategies: The Saudi Experience: The Role of Agriculture to Enhance Food Security, Alleviate Poverty and Promote Economic Growth* (Saarbrücken, Germany: LAP Lambert Academic Publishing).

Al Riyadh (2009) Wakil wizarat al-ziraʿa li ʿAl-Riyadh': Mubadarat al mamlaka li-l-istithmar al-ziraʿi al-khariji la yaʿni 'iqaf al-istithmarat al-mahalliya wa ʿadam daʿmiha [Deputy of the Ministry of Agriculture to ʿAl Riyadh': The Kingdom's initiative for agricultural investments abroad does not mean the end of domestic investments and their support], 17 July, http://www.alriyadh.com/2009/07/17/article445235.html.

Al Riyadh (2011) Duktur Balghunaim fi hiwar maʿ ʿAl Riyadh' haula mubadara khadim al-haramain li-l-istithmar al-ziraʿi al-khariji. Qariban: Al-rafʿ li majlis al-wuzara' bi syagha jadida li-l-istratijiyya al-ziraʿiyya 2020 [Doctor Balghunaim in an interview with ʿAl Riyadh' about the initiative of the servant of the two holy places for foreign agricultural investment: Soon there will be a proposal to the cabinet with a new design of the agricultural strategy 2020], 12 January, http://www.alriyadh.com/2011/01/12/article593971.html.

Allan, J. A., Keulertz, M., Sojamo, S. & Warner, J. (eds) (2012) *Handbook of Land and Water Grabs in Africa: Foreign Direct Investment and Food and Water Security* (Abingdon & New York: Routledge).

Anseeuw, W., Boche, M., Breu, T., Giger, M., Lay, J., Messerli, P. & Nolte, K. (2012a) Transnational land deals for agriculture in the Global South, Analytical report based on the Land Matrix Database (Bern, Montpellier, Hamburg: CDE, CIRAD, GIGA, GIZ, ILC).

Anseeuw, W., Alden Wily, L., Cotula, L. & Taylor, M. (2012b) Land rights and the rush for land: findings of the Global Commercial Pressures on Land Research Project (Rome: International Land Coalition (ILC)).

Arab Fund for Economic and Social Development (AFESD) (1976) Basic Programme for Agricultural Development in the Democratic Republic of the Sudan, 1976–1985: summary and conclusions (Kuwait City: AFESD).

Arab News (2012a) Kingdom plans agriculture investment in 27 countries, 16 January, http://www.arabnews.com/node/365628.

Arab News (2012b) Agri firm to handle foreign investments, 8 May, http://www.arabnews.com/%5Btermalias-raw%5D/agri-firm-handle-foreign-investments.

Borras, S. M., Franco, J. C. & Wang, C. (2013) The challenge of global governance of land grabbing: changing international agricultural context and competing political views and strategies, *Globalizations,* 10(1), pp. 161–179.

Brautigam, D. (2012a) Chinese engagement in African agriculture, in T. Allan, J. Warner, S. Sojamo & M. Keulertz (eds) *Handbook of Land and Water Grabs in Africa: Foreign Direct Investments and Food and Water Security* (London & New York: Routledge), pp. 89–101.

Brautigam, D. (2012b) 'Zombie' Chinese land grabs in Africa rise again in new database!, 30 April, http://www.chinaafricarealstory.com/2012/04/zombie-chinese-land-grabs-in-africa.html.

Brown, L. R. (2011) When the Nile runs dry, *New York Times,* 1 June.

Chaudhry, K. A. (1997) *The Price of Wealth: Economies and Institutions in the Middle East,* Cornell Studies in Political Economy (Ithaca, NY: Cornell University Press).

Cotula, L., Vermeulen, S., Leonard, R. & Keeley, J. (2009) Land grab or development opportunity? Agricultural investments and international land deals in Africa, Report (Rome: FAO, IFAD, IEED).

Deininger, K., Byerlee, D., Lindsay, J., Norton, A., Selod, H. & Stickler, M. (2011) *Rising global interest in farmland. Can it yield sustainable and equitable benefits? Agriculture and Rural Development* (Washington, DC: World Bank).

DeMars, W. E. (2005) *NGOs and Transnational Networks: Wild Cards in World Politics* (London & Ann Arbor, MI: Pluto).

Deng, D. K. (2011) The new frontier: a baseline survey of large-scale land-based investment in southern Sudan, Norwegian People's Aid, Generation Agency for Development and Transformation-Pentagon (GADET Pentagon), South Sudan Law Society (SSLS).

Ehteshami, A. & Wright, S. M. (2008) *Reform in the Middle East Oil Monarchies* (Reading, UK: Ithaca Press).

Elhadj, E. (2006) Experiments in Achieving Water and Food Self- Sufficiency in the Middle East: The Consequences of Contrasting Endowments, Ideologies, and Investment Policies in Saudi Arabia and Syria, Ph.D. thesis, History Department, SOAS, London.

FAO (2010) Country profile Pakistan, Aquastat, Version 2010 (Rome: FAO).

FAO (2011) Consultation for the private sector on responsible agricultural investment, 2 March (Rome: FAO).

FIAN (2010) Landgrabbing in Kenya and Mozambique: a report on two research missions—and a human rights analysis of land (Heidelberg: FIAN).

Gavin, J. (2009) Special report: Kuwait—political deadlock hits reform, *MEED,* 19 March.

Government of Sudan (1977) *The Six Year Plan of Economic and Social Development, 1977/78–1982/83* (Khartoum: Ministry of Culture and Information).

GRAIN (2008) Seized! The 2008 land grab for food and financial security, GRAIN Briefing (Barcelona: GRAIN).

GRAIN (2010) Saudi investors poised to take control of rice production in Senegal and Mali? Against the Grain (Barcelona: GRAIN).

Gulf Times (2008) Saudi Arabia's oil minister slams biofuels, favours solar energy, 15 April, http://gulfnews.com/news/gulf/saudi-arabia/saudi-arabia-s-oil-minister-slams-biofuels-favours-solar-energy-1.97977.

Gulf Times (2011) Qatar aims to meet 70% of its food needs in 12 years, 20 February, http://www.gulf-times.com/site/topics/printArticle.asp?cu_no=2&item_no=417179&version=1&template_id=36&parent_id=16.

Hertog, S. (2010) *Princes, Brokers, and Bureaucrats: Oil and the State in Saudi Arabia* (Ithaca, NY & London: Cornell University Press).

Horne, F., Mousseau, F., Metho, O., Mittal, A. & Shepard, D. (2011) Country report: Ethiopia, Understanding Land Investment Deals in Africa (Oakland, CA: Oakland Institute).

Interagency Intelligence Memorandum (1980) Sudan: the Nimeiri regime under pressure, Secret, NLC-6-73-3-8-4, 1 March (Atlanta: Carter Library).

International Rice Research Institute (IRRI) (2009) A summary of the meetings held during the visit of Dr Robert Zeigler, Mr Syeduzzaman, and Abdel Ismail to Saudi Arabia, March 7–8, 2009, Los Baños, Laguna.

Janardhan, N. (2011) *Boom Amid Gloom: The Spirit of Possibility in the 21st Century Gulf* (Reading: Ithaca Press).

Kingdom of Saudi Arabia (2009) King Abdulla's Initiative for Agricultural Investment Abroad, Presentation by Taha A. Alshareef at IPC Conference 'Food and Environmental Security. The Role of Food and Agricultural Trade Policy', Salzburg, Austria, 10–11 May (Riyadh: Ministry of Commerce and Industry).

Kingdom of Saudi Arabia (2010a) King Abdullah's Initiative for Saudi Agricultural Investment Abroad: a way of enhancing Saudi food security, Presentation by Abdullah A. Al-Obaid, Deputy Minister for Agricultural Research and Development Affairs, at the Expert Group Meeting on 'Achieving Food Security in Member Countries in Post-Crisis World', Islamic Development Bank, Jeddah, 2–3 May (Riyadh: Ministry of Agriculture).

Kingdom of Saudi Arabia (2010b) *The Ninth Development Plan (2010–2014)* (Riyadh: Ministry of Economy and Planning).

Koopman, J. E. (2009) Globalization, gender, and poverty in the Senegal River Valley, *Feminist Economics*, 15(3), pp. 253–285.

Land Matrix (2012) http://www.landportal.info/landmatrix.

Luciani, G. (1987) Allocation vs. production states: a theoretical framework, in H. Beblawi & G. Luciani (eds) *The Rentier State: Nation, State, and Integration in the Arab World* (London & New York: Croom Helm), pp.

McKeon, N. (2013) 'One does not sell the land upon which the people walk': land grabbing, rural social movements, and global governance, *Globalizations*, 10(1), pp. 105–122.

McMichael, P. (2013) Land grabbing as security mercantilism in international relations, *Globalizations*, 10(1), pp. 47–64.

Margulis, M. E. & Porter, T. (2013) Governing the global land grab: multipolarity, ideas, and complexity in transnational governance, *Globalizations*, 10(1), pp. 65–86.

Mehta, L., Veldwisch, J. V. & Franco, J. C. (2012) Introduction to the special issue: water grabbing? Focus on the (re)appropriation of finite water resources, *Water Alternatives*, 5(2), pp. 193–207.

Murphy, S., Burch, D. & Clapp, J. (2012) Cereal secrets: the world's largest grain traders and global agriculture, http://www.oxfam.org/sites/www.oxfam.org/files/rr-cereal-secrets-grain-traders-agriculture-30082012-en.pdf.

O'Brien, J. (1985) Sowing the seeds of famine: the political economy of food deficits in Sudan, *Review of African Political Economy*, 12(33), pp. 23–32.

Oesterdiekhoff, P. & Wohlmuth, K. (1983) The 'breadbasket' is empty: the options of Sudanese development policy, *Canadian Journal of African Studies/Revue Canadienne des Études Africaines*, 17(1), pp. 35–67.

Perrone, N. M (2013) Restrictions to foreign acquisitions of agricultural land in Argentina and Brazil, *Globalizations*, 10(1), pp. 205–209.

Qatar National Food Security Programme (QNFSP) (2011) Global Dryland Alliance Brochure (Doha).

Riyadh Chamber of Commerce and Industry (2010) Muqtarahat li Mu'alajat 'Athar Waqf Zira'a al-Qamh [Proposals for the treatment of the termination of wheat farming], 24 December, http://www.riyadhchamber.com/newsdisplay.php?id=1028.

Reuters (2009) Gulf Arab states to launch $2 billion agriculture fund, 11 October, http://farmlandgrab.org/post/view/8187.

Reuters (2010) Qatar in talks to buy Argentina, Ukraine farmland, 13 October, http://farmlandgrab.org/post/view/16289.

Rural Modernity (2012) *The Land Matrix: Much Ado About Nothing,* 27 April, http://ruralmodernity.wordpress.com/2012/04/27/the-land-matrix-much-ado-about-nothing/.

Saudi Gazette (2010) Qatar launches Food Security League, 25 September, http://www.saudigazette.com.sa/Error.html?CFID=38069508&CFTOKEN=24147699.

Saudi Gazette (2012) Cabinet okays agro investments abroad, 12 June, http://www.saudigazette.com.sa/index.cfm?method=home.regcon&contentid=20120612126673.

Schatkowski-Schilcher, L. (1992) The famine of 1915–1918 in Greater Syria, in J. Spagnolo (ed.) *Problems of the Modern Middle East in Historical Perspective: Essays in Honor of Albert Hourani* (Reading: Ithaca Press (for Garnet Publishing Ltd)), pp. 229–258.

Sharma, R. (2011) *Food Export Restrictions: Review of the 2007–2010 Experience and Considerations for Disciplining Restrictive Measures* (Rome: FAO).

Sojamo, S., Keulertz, M., Warner, J. & Allan, Anthony, J. (2012) Virtual water hegemony: the role of agribusiness in global water governance, *Water International*, 37(2), pp. 169–182.

Spiro, D. (1989) Policy Coordination in the International Political Economy: The Politics of Petrodollar Recycling, Ph.D. thesis, Department of Politics, Princeton University.

Teitelbaum, J. (2009) *Political Liberalization in the Persian Gulf* (New York: Columbia University Press).

Tell, T. (2000) Guns, gold, and grain: war and food supply in the making of Transjordan, in S. Heydeman (ed.) *War, Institutions and Social Change in the Middle East* (Berkeley, CA & London: University of California Press), pp. 33–58.

United Nations (2012) Website of the Presidency of the 66th General Assembly, http://www.un.org/en/ga/president/66/.

US Congress (1973) The United States oil shortage and the Arab-Israeli conflict, Report of a Study Mission to the Middle East from October 22 to November 3, pursuant to H. Res. 267. 93rd Congress, First Session. Committee on Foreign Affairs, December 20, 1973 (Washington, DC: US Government Printing Office).

Van Rooy, A. (2004) *The Global Legitimacy Game: Civil Society, Globalization, and Protest,* Palgrave Texts in International Political Economy (Basingstoke & New York: Palgrave Macmillan).

Verhoeven, H. (2012) Water, Civilisation and Power: Sudan's Hydropolitical Economy and the Al-Injaz Revolution, PhD, Department of Politics and International Relations, St. Cross College, Oxford University.

Von Braun, J. & Torero, M. (2009) Implementing physical and virtual food reserves to protect the poor and prevent market failure, IFPRI Policy Brief (Washington DC: IFPRI).

Wikileaks (2009a) Kuwait food security: less than meets the eye . . . (cable 09KUWAIT1170), US Embassy, Kuwait.

Wikileaks (2009b) Qatari food company adapts investment strategy to concerns of partner countries (cable 09DOHA552. 2009), US Embassy, Doha.

Wilmington, M. W. (1971) *The Middle East Supply Centre* (Albany, NY: State University of New York Press).

Woertz, E. (2007) GCC stock markets: managing the crisis, Gulf Papers (Dubai: Gulf Research Center).

Woertz, E. (2011) Arab food, water, and the big landgrab that wasn't, *The Brown Journal of World Affairs*, 18(1), pp. 119–132.

Woertz, E. (2012) Repercussions of Dubai's debt crisis, in E. Woertz (ed.) *GCC Financial Markets: The World's New Money Centers* (Berlin & London: Gerlach), pp. 229–254.

Woertz, E. (2013) *Oil for Food: The Global Food Crisis and the Middle East* (Oxford & New York: Oxford University Press).

World Bank (2010) Arab development assistance: four decades of cooperation (Washington, DC: World Bank).

World Bank and FAO (2012) The grain chain: food security and managing wheat imports in Arab countries (Washington, DC: World Bank).

Zurayk, R., Chaaban, J. & Sabra, A. (2011) Ensuring that potential Gulf farmland investments in developing countries are pro-poor and sustainable, *Food Security*, 3(Supplement 1), pp. 129–137.

Eckart Woertz is senior researcher at the Barcelona Centre for International Affairs (CIDOB). Formerly he was a visiting fellow at Princeton University, director of economic studies at the Gulf Research Center in Dubai, and worked for banks in Germany and the UAE. He is the author of *Oil for Food: The Global Food Crisis and the Middle East* (Oxford, 2013).

'One Does Not Sell the Land Upon Which the People Walk':[1] Land Grabbing, Transnational Rural Social Movements, and Global Governance

NORA McKEON[2]

Roma Tre University, Rome, Italy

ABSTRACT   *Defending their access to land has always been a major motivation for rural people to mobilize locally, nationally, and, more recently, in global struggles against land grabbing. I analyze how rural social movements have built up their capacities as global mobilizers and policy players over the past decade. I assess the success with which they are exploiting the current window of political opportunity opened up by interlinked global food, fuel, climate, and financial crises, accompanied by the highly publicized phenomenon of land grabbing. Particular attention is given to the newly reformed Committee on World Food Security, as the only global policy forum in the UN system in which these actors intervene as full participants, and to the recent negotiation of* Voluntary Guidelines on the Responsible Governance of Land, Fisheries and Forests. *The conclusion identifies challenges that need to be addressed in order for rural social movements to consolidate the gains made.*

Introduction

Restrictions of people's control over the territories they inhabit have taken different forms in different epochs and regions. In recent years, however, they appear to have converged into what is perceived as a global trend both by multilateral institutions who seek to 'govern' it and by social movements who oppose it.[3] For rural people, defending their access to land has always been a major motivation to organize and mobilize locally, nationally, and, more recently, at the more remote global level. The current interlinked food, fuel, climate, and financial crises have opened up a window of political opportunity for them by subjecting dominant paradigms and governance to an unprecedented level of questioning. 'Land grabbing', as a highly publi-cized and particularly outrageous phenomenon, is a powerful symptom of the poverty of main-stream policies. The enhanced capacity as global mobilizers and policy players that rural people's organizations have built up over the past decade places them in a better position today than before to exploit this conjuncture. How their confrontation with the defenders of the neoliberal regime will play out over the coming period merits informed attention and com-mitted concern.

This essay traces the evolution of global institutional spaces for policy dialogue on land issues over the past 25 years, the paradigms on which decision-making has been based, and the efforts of concerned social actors to make their voices heard. I provide an assessment of the success with which rural social movements and civil society organizations (CSOs) are exploiting the current moment of political opportunity and close by identifying challenges that need to be addressed in order to consolidate the gains made.

Land Issues on the International Agenda: Institutional Spaces, Paradigms, and the Growth of Transnational Rural Social Movement Networks

Non-state actor presence in the World Conference on Agrarian Reform and Rural Development (WCARRD) convened by FAO in 1979 was limited to recognized international NGOs, of which the only farmers' organization was the International Federation of Agricultural Producers (IFAP) representing large-scale market-oriented farmers. In any event, the land reform agenda was destined to fall a victim in the 1980s to the introduction of structural adjustment and a general disenchantment with agriculture as a motor for development. It was pulled out of oblivion only in the mid-1990s within a neoliberal paradigm that identified market-led econ-omic growth and global market integration as an infallible recipe for world prosperity. In this context, the land issue was framed as one of promoting formal private landed property rights and was addressed, in operational terms, by the Market-Led Agrarian Reform (MLAR) approach promoted by the World Bank (WB) from the early 1990s on (Borras et al., 2006, pp. 17–18).

At the same time, the decade from the mid 1990s saw an explosion of alternatives to the domi-nant neoliberal, productionist paradigm. The right to food, food sovereignty, and agro-ecology were championed by civil society actors who entered the global governance scene for the first time. The most politically significant were the rural social movements that had begun to organize during the 1980s in reaction to the devastating impact of structural adjustment on agricultural production and rural people's livelihoods. The birth of the global peasant network La Via Campesina in 1993 was triggered by the impending creation of the World Trade Organization (WTO) and the realization that 'agricultural policies would henceforth be determined globally and it was essential for small farmers to be able to defend their interests at that level' (quoted in McKeon and Kalafatic, 2009, p. 3). The regional Network of West African Peasant and Agri-cultural Producers' Organizations (ROPPA) was established in 2000 with similar motivations (McKeon et al., 2004).

The civil society forums held in parallel to the two World Food Summits convened by FAO in 1996 and 2002 gave a strong impetus to global networking by rural social movements. Small food producers and indigenous peoples were in the majority thanks to a system of quotas by regions and type of organization and the mobilization of resources to cover delegates' travel costs. Introduced by the transnational peasant movement, La Via Campesina, in 1996 the prin-ciple of food sovereignty defined as the right of peoples to healthy and culturally appropriate food produced through ecologically sound and sustainable methods, and their right to define their own food and agriculture systems, had become the forum's rallying point by 2002 (Desmarais et al., 2010; IPC, 2002; McKeon, 2009, pp. 82–87; Mulvany, 2007; Patel, 2009; Pimbert, 2009; http://www.nyeleni.org/spip.php?article29). The global network that emerged from the forums—the International Civil Society Planning Committee for Food Sovereignty (IPC)—is strongly rooted in rural movements. Its membership includes focal points for constituencies (peasant farmers, fisher folk, pastoralists, indigenous peoples, agricultural workers, etc.), regions, and themes (NGO networks with particular expertise on priority issues). The IPC does not represent existing organizations but facilitates their dialogue and access to decision-making processes (www.foodsovereignty.org). Since 2003, the IPC has facilitated the participation of over 2,000 representatives of small food producers' organizations in FAO policy forums, championing an alternative paradigm to free trade and green revolution technology (McKeon, 2009, pp. 91–100; McKeon and Kalafatic, 2009, pp. 17–18).

Local peoples' access to land was already a main theme at the 1996 parallel forum and it became one of the four substantive pillars of the action plan adopted in 2002, along with the right to food, agroecology, and trade. The link between land and human rights was an important component of the Global Campaign for Agrarian Reform (GCAR), launched by the La Via Campesina and FoodFirst Information and Action Network (FIAN) in 1999, in an effort to bring local and national struggles to the attention of supportive global networks and forums (Borras, 2008). The IPC has proved to be an excellent global 'home' for the GCAR's concerns because of its espousal of food sovereignty, its capacity to facilitate access to intergovernmental spaces, and its careful distinction between the political role of peoples' movements and the supportive stance of NGOs, an issue to which people's organizations are highly sensitive.

A prime opportunity to exploit international space emerged when the Brazilian government proposed to co-sponsor with FAO the first international conference on agrarian reform to take place since WCARRD. The International Conference on Agrarian Reform and Rural Development (ICARRD), held in Porto Alegre in March 2006, gave the IPC an occasion to exploit the synergies its membership afforded between strong rural peoples' movements and NGOs with expertise in agrarian reform issues. The IPC declined an invitation to participate in the ICARRD Steering Committee in order to avoid co-optation and opted instead for an autonomous civil society forum with well-defined opportunities to interact with the official deliberations. The strategy paid off and rural social movements had a meaningful impact on both the process and the outcome of the conference. Their drafting victories included the recognition of collective rights to land; acknowledgement that land is a cultural, social and historical—as well as economic—asset; reference to 'control of' and not simply 'access to' land; and explicit mention of the right to food and food sovereignty (Borras, 2008; ICARRD, 2006; McKeon, 2009, pp. 98–100). ICARRD brought the issue of agrarian reform back onto the agenda of FAO's normative work, although powerful FAO members like the USA and the European Union (EU) have done their best to slow pedal follow-up in order to leave the initiative with the World Bank's market-led approaches.

To keep the momentum going the IPC network set up an ongoing working group on land. A social movement encounter held in Mali in February 2007, the International Nyéleni Forum on Food Sovereignty, gave an important boost. The ICARRD experience had already contributed to expanding the La Via Campesina/IPC vision of agrarian reform beyond access to land by peasant farmers to include a broader range of social actors (i.e. indigenous peoples, pastoralists, artisanal fisherfolk, urban poor, etc.) and extending the geographic focus beyond Latin America and some areas of Asia. The Nyéleni Forum further deepened the vision by exploring important issues like the responsibility of social movements themselves to address conflicts between different communities that share territories. The voice of the indigenous peoples' participants came through strongly in the exhortation to 'view nature as material and spiritual beings, not as "resources" that exist to be exploited'. Corporate control of food production and distribution received attention as a mounting threat to peoples' control over their territories (Nyéleni, 2007).

Shortly before the social movements gathered in Nyéleni, the 2007 food riots got underway. The global food crisis created a political opportunity that rural social movements were prepared to exploit thanks to a decade of global networking and strategizing (De Schutter, 2009a; GRAIN, 2008a; McKeon, 2011b; McMichael, 2009; Van Der Ploeg, 2010; Wise and Murphy, 2012). The interlinked crises have jolted neoliberal paradigms. The free market has clearly failed to guarantee the food security of developing countries, particularly those that succumbed to World Bank advice to sell their commodities on the world market and purchase 'cheap' food in exchange. Concepts that had been considered taboo or peripheral, such as protection for developing country markets, food reserves and supply management, agroecology as a climate-friendly approach to agricultural production, are now being entertained in global policy discussions.

The global food crisis also revealed a global policy vacuum. In the absence of an authoritative and inclusive global body deliberating on food issues, decision-making in this vital field was being carried out, by default, by international institutions like the WTO and World Bank for whom food security is hardly core business, by groups of the most powerful economies like the G8/G20, and by economic actors like transnational corporations and financial speculators subject to no political control. A strong confrontation emerged between different approaches to filling the governance gap. In April 2008 the Secretary General of the UN established a High Level Task Force on the Food Security Crisis (HLTF) composed of the secretariats of UN offices and agencies, the Bretton Woods institutions, and the WTO. The HLTF is an administrative initiative without intergovernmental oversight. In July 2008 it published a Comprehensive Framework of Action on Food Security (CFA) that was strongly critiqued by CSOs for what they saw as its failure to address the long-term structural causes of the crisis and the danger that its existence could be taken as an alibi for avoiding the negotiation of a political, intergovernmental strategic commitment in the face of the food crisis (FIAN, 2008).

For their part, the Group of Eight (G8) countries threw up what many CSOs viewed as a veritable smoke screen of rhetoric about an elusive 'Global Partnership on Agriculture, Food Security and Nutrition' (GPAFS), promising billions of dollars of new investment in agriculture that never quite materialized. The subtext here was judged as an effort to highlight more investment rather than better policies as the solution to the food crisis, and to keep the initiative in the hands of the rich and the powerful (Peoples' Food Sovereignty Now!, 2009).

An alternative to the GPAFS was championed by a number of governments, from the G77 above all, allied with CSOs and social movements and the FAO. It consisted in transforming the existing Committee on World Food Security (CFS) based at the FAO from an ineffectual talk-shop into an authoritative, inclusive global policy forum deliberating on food security in the name of ensuring the right to food of the world's population. The confrontation over this demand at an international conference held in Madrid in January 2009 was so strong that the UN Secretary General was obliged to give the CFS reform option a chance in order to keep peace in the family (FIAN, 2009; IPC, 2009a).

The CFS reform process got underway in April 2009. It was opened up to concerned stakeholders, thanks to a political intuition of the President of the CFS Bureau, and organizations of small-scale food producers were enabled to interact with governments on an equal basis.

The final reform document (CFS, 2009), adopted on 17 October 2009, includes some important points that social movements and CSOs fought hard to defend against the attacks of those governments that wanted to keep the new CFS as toothless as possible (see Box 1).

Box 1. Committee on World Food Security reform document key points

- Recognizes the structural causes of the food crisis and that the primary victims are small-scale food producers.
- Defines the CFS as 'the foremost inclusive international and intergovernmental platform' for food security. Includes defending the right to adequate food in its mission. Empowers it to take decisions on key food policy issues.
- Enjoins it to adopt a Global Strategic Framework (GSF) for food strategy providing guidance for national food security action plans and other CFS participants and as a reference point for coordination and accountability.
- Names civil society organizations (small-scale food producers and urban movements especially) as full participants. Entitles them to intervene in debate on the same footing as governments and to participate in the governance of CFS activities between annual plenary sessions. Acknowledges their right to self-organize autonomously to relate to the CFS.
- Supports the CFS's policy work by a High Level Panel of Experts in which the expertise of small-scale producers and practitioners is acknowledged.
- Recognizes the principle of subsidiarity and promotes linkages between the global meetings and multi-stakeholder policy spaces at regional and country levels.

While the reformed CFS was taking shape, land issues were beginning to attract increased attention. The civil society statement 'No More "Failures-as-Usual"', released on the eve of an FAO-sponsored summit on the global food crisis in June 2008, demanded an immediate halt to the 'new enclosure movement' that was converting arable, pastoral, and forest lands to fuel production (IPC, 2008a). The 'Terra Preta Forum' held in parallel to the FAO Summit dedicated a thematic working group to land and agrofuels and called for a 'new agrarian reform based on food sovereignty' (Terra Preta, 2008, p. 3). A few months later, in October 2008, GRAIN issued its report, *Seized!* (GRAIN, 2008b), and the phenomenon of land grabbing linked to agrofuel promotion and food-for-export initiatives hit the headlines. The following months saw a series of mobilizations at all levels by social movements around the world.

In parallel FAO had been working on a proposal for the formulation of *Voluntary Guidelines on Responsible Governance of Tenure of Land and Other Natural Resources* (hereafter 'Voluntary Guidelines') intended 'to assist countries wishing to develop a formal policy response to problems of weak land governance and corruption'.[5] FIAN was invited to facilitate civil society participation in this process and agreed to accept in its function as coordinator of the IPC land working group, which set conditions for its participation (see Seufert, 2013, pp. 181–186; Künnemann and Monsalve Suárez, 2013, pp. 123–139). Civil society autonomy and self-organization had to be acknowledged, the methodology and principles of participation adopted at ICARRD applied, and adequate resources made available for meaningful regional consultation. These conditions were accepted and over the following months the IPC organized regional civil society consultations that enabled rural social movements to develop their own ideas about the framing, the scope, the principles, and the content of the guidelines (CSOPNVG, 2011; IPC, 2010). An important IPC lobbying objective was that these positions be brought to the attention of governments in an intergovernmental negotiation and that the Guidelines not be simply the result of a technical consultation among stakeholders.

The Voluntary Guidelines were not a direct reaction to the phenomenon of land grabbing. The Principles for Responsible Agricultural Investment (PRAI) launched by the World Bank, FAO, IFAD, and UNCTAD in January 2010 were. The PRAI attracted the opposition of the organizations networked around the GCAR and the IPC both for their lack of any kind of consultative process and as a 'move to legitimize the long-term corporate (foreign and domestic) takeover of rural people's farmlands' (GCAR, 2010) by positing large-scale investments as the solution to rural poverty and hunger (Borras and Franco, 2010a; De Schutter, 2009b, 2010a, 2010b, 2010c).

The Voluntary Guidelines and the PRAI came together in October 2010 at the first session of the reformed CFS, where 'Land Tenure and International Investment in Agriculture' was a key agenda item. Facilitated by members of the IPC land working group, participants at the civil society forum that took place just prior to the CFS developed a common position (Civil Society Mechanism (CSM), 2010, pp. 48–49). Civil society intervention in the discussions was decisive in obtaining agreement that the Voluntary Guidelines be negotiated within the CFS and that a proposal to rubber stamp the PRAI be rejected. It was decided instead, once the Voluntary Guidelines had been approved, to open up an inclusive consideration of principles that could ensure responsible agricultural investment for food security (CFS, 2010, paragraph 26; Margulis and Porter, 2013, pp. 65–86). These outcomes were largely attributable to the innovative format of the CFS whereby political decisions are made in plenary sessions in which civil society and social movements are full participants rather than in closed door drafting committees as is normally the case in intergovernmental forums.

In growing acknowledgement of the strategic importance of the CFS, the involvement of key actors deepened as the Voluntary Guidelines negotiations evolved from July 2011 to March 2012. The US agreed to chair the process. The Africa Group, largely absent at the outset although their region is a prime target for land grabbing, made a remarkably successful effort to strategize and defend its positions. Latin American countries where tenure laws are in revision and the giant China, where land grabbing is an explosive internal issue, came on board as they realized that they would be obliged to apply the Voluntary Guidelines to their own situations once the ink was dry on the paper. The Middle East galvanized over the issue of tenure rights in occupied territories. The private sector network fought to legitimize and protect foreign investment, in alliance with Canada, Australia, and the US, while the EU tended to defend a rights-based approach and a focus on small-scale producers and indigenous peoples. The civil society negotiation team, basing its engagement on its autonomous vision of the guidelines, agreed on a politically acceptable baseline outcome and laboriously drafted and defended alternative wording. The testimony and proposals brought to the debate by organizations of those most directly menaced by violations of their rights to land and other natural resources were particularly effective.

The final text of the Voluntary Guidelines was formally adopted at a special session of the CFS on 11 May 2012. The assessment of rural social movements that had engaged in the process was cautiously positive, although they often had to contend with the skepticism of their bases. The very fact that, for the first time in history, global guidelines on tenure of land and other resources had been negotiated and adopted in an intergovernmental forum was grounds for satisfaction. Battles had been won on critical issues like protection of customary tenure, strong reference to human rights, strict definitions of what consultation with communities implies, priority to restitution and redistributive reforms, and states' obligations to regulate their corporations' operations beyond their own territorial boundaries. At the same time, the Voluntary Guidelines were 'too weak in prioritizing essential support to small-scale producers,. . . . fail to further protect the rights of indigenous peoples already recognized by international instruments and don't include water as a land resource' (CSOPNVG, 2012b). Above all, CSOs emphasized that the Voluntary Guidelines 'do not explicitly challenge the untruth that large-scale investments in industrial agriculture, fisheries and forests are essential for development' (CSOPNVG, 2012a).

The Voluntary Guidelines negotiations were, of course, only one aspect of the social movement engagement on land issues that took place during that period, the bulk of it outside official conference rooms. The Dakar World Social Forum in February 2011 issued a strong appeal calling for an immediate stop to land grabbing. In a rare reference to the UN system in World Social Forum literature, the appeal spoke in positive terms of the Voluntary Guidelines process and urged the CFS to reject the RAI Principles (Dakar World Social Forum, 2011). Nine months later the International Peasant Conference 'Stop the Land Grab', convened by La Via Campesina and the West African peasant movement, brought together 250 participants—rural social movements, NGOs, academics, and media—to exchange experience and analysis. The Global Alliance against Land Grabbing that emerged focuses on supporting resistance at the base and building links with global institutional spaces and processes like the CFS and the Voluntary Guidelines (La Via Campesina, 2012a; Reisenberger and Monsalve Suárez, 2011). Social movements seemed poised to apply a 'sandwich strategy' (Borras, 2008, p. 115) moving simultaneously from the global and the local levels in their fight against land grabs.

Key Characteristics of Global Civil Society Advocacy and Action on Land Grabbing

Land grabbing is only one of a long list of issues on which CSOs have sought to influence global decision-making, from debt relief to land mines or international trade regimes. What is distinctive about global mobilization around access to land? Three interrelated aspects are key to addressing this question: the social actors involved and the alliances they have formed, the way in which they have framed the issues, and the strategies they have adopted to open up and occupy political space.

Social Actors and Alliances

The configuration of social actors promoting global policy advocacy around land grabbing issues is perhaps the most important qualifier of this movement. Much civil society advocacy targeting global policy forums is dominated by NGOs, who may have cogent positions to advance but are not mandated by those in whose name they appear to speak. Engagement by organizations representing the sectors of the population most directly concerned by the policies under discussion is far less frequent. The reasons for this are evident. NGOs' staff and financial resources, proximity to global forums, decision-making processes, language and analysis capacities, access to strategic information and documentation, all put them in a different league from organizations of peasant farmers, urban poor, migrant workers, pastoralists, and other such constituencies (McKeon, 2009, pp. 175–178; 2011a; McKeon and Kalafatic, 2009).

Global advocacy on access to land offers an exception to the rule of NGO leadership. The World Food Summits of 1996 and 2002 attracted an unprecedented level of attention by rural social actors as compared with other global conferences, since the issues under discussion were at the heart of their concerns.[6] That they are the dominant decision-makers in the IPC mechanism which emerged from these forums is the result of a deliberate political orientation and often laborious efforts to apply it. It has necessitated, for example, respecting the time requirements and the modalities of internal consultation of social movements, at the cost of having to live with slow and cumbersome decision-making processes. It has also required developing a practice of training and preparation for small food producer representatives to enable them to defend their positions in global policy forums and feed back to their bases. The IPC has provided a space in which to build trust among different constituencies, expanding progressively to bring in weaker and less well-organized groups like artisanal fisherfolk and pastoralists. This does not imply that all is peaceful coexistence in the world of rural social movements and their NGO supporters. Borras (2008, 2011) has highlighted the importance of acknowledging the class and ideological differences that exist even within a more homogeneous transnational network like La Via Campesina. The IPC is not immune to such phenomena, but it has provided an arena in which differences and conflicts can be contained and addressed. This result has been facilitated by the IPC's converging agenda around the principle of food sovereignty, its joint analysis that transcends North–South tensions, the value-added it offers at global level, and the fact that it does not seek a representational role or a high public profile. As a participant in an IPC self-evaluation session in 2008 put it, 'The political statement of food sovereignty is what we have in common: This allows us to develop common strategies while respecting the voice of each component' (McKeon, 2009, p. 113).

The social movements and NGOs that work together on land issues in the IPC form a core nucleus of organizations with a shared analysis that have been able to build synergies with broader civil society configurations. Examples are the Right to Food and Nutrition Watch, in which FIAN has teamed up with development NGOs (Right to Food and Nutrition Watch, 2010), and the EuropAfrica coalition of European NGOs and African small farmers' networks that are working together on a common policy advocacy platform of which access to land is an important plank (EuropAfrica, 2011). Thanks to the IPC network's long-term investment, interface with FAO constitutes an interesting variation on the 'inside/outside' alliances strategy that has characterized the stance of movements like La Via Campesina vis-à-vis other multilateral institutions like the WTO and the WB. In the latter cases, alliances have been formed between CSOs that enter into the global forums and networks such as La Via Campesina that have refused to legitimize these institutions with their presence and mobilize essentially on the outside. In the case of the FAO and the reformed CFS, in contrast, La Via Campesina and other rural social movements are both 'inside' the negotiating spaces and 'outside', conducting mobilization and campaigning. As we have seen, the reform of the CFS has institutionalized the preeminent position of organizations representing those sectors of the population most directly concerned.

More than in the case of other issues on the global agenda, rural social movements have built significant alliances with the world of committed academics. They have been facilitated in this by the fact that committed academics concerned with land issues have themselves clustered in networks, of which the most noteworthy are the Land Research Action Network (LRAN), the Transnational Institute (TNI), the Initiatives in Critical Agrarian Studies (ICAS) housed at the International Institute of Social Studies (ISS), and the Land Deal Politics Initiatives (LDPI) which is promoting major academic conferences on land grabbing. The latter three teamed up with the IPC to organize a side event on land grabbing with a deliberately academic flavor during the CFS session in October 2010 in order to provide grounding for the social movement/civil society positions. In addition to offering 'evidence-based' support for activist platforms, the committed academics have made highly appreciated contributions to framing and strategizing by helping to identify blind spots in activist analysis and undertaking systematic analysis of emerging issues.[7]

Rural social movements have succeeded in enrolling committed staff members of international organizations concerned with land issues as allies who can make available strategic information, provide technical support, and help to open doors for social movement advocacy. Particularly important reference points are FAO, IFAD, and the UN Human Rights Council.[8] Their networks of relations with like-minded governments are less extensive. Although they often devote considerable attention to negotiation with their national governments and regional economic organizations, these efforts are not sufficiently articulated with the global level.

Framing the Issues

Capacity to frame their claims in ways that resonate with others and can aspire to impact on the global agenda is a key consideration for transnational social movements (Keck and Sikkink, 1998, pp. 201–204; Tarrow, 2005, pp. 61–62). The evolution of how rural social movements and their NGO allies have framed their 'take' on land issues has been traced in the preceding pages. Over the past 15 years their narrative has come to situate itself within the principle of food sovereignty and has adopted a human rights frame. It has expanded from an initial focus on land redistribution in areas where grossly inequitable land ownership is the most evident problem to take cognizance of the privatization of public common land, the key issue in Africa where land grabs are concentrated. Adopting indigenous peoples' vision of 'territory' has enriched the platform and accentuated its radical differences from dominant concepts that focus almost exclusively on the economic value of natural resources. The frame has broadened from access to and control over land to embrace also its sustainable use through the adoption of agroecological approaches. This has made it possible to relate land issues more intimately to the increasingly diffuse civil society platforms regarding climate change and the green economy (La Via Campesina, 2012b).

The autonomous civil society proposal for Voluntary Guidelines discussed above constitutes a comprehensive attack on, and alternative to, neoliberalism and the corporate-driven model of agriculture. It is not only morally irrefutable and the product of a legitimate process but is also logically and legally sound, an infrequent combination in global civil society advocacy platforms. Being able to refer to a systemic and positive framing of land issues has facilitated a coherent approach by rural social movements and their CSO supporters throughout the negotiation of the Voluntary Guidelines and in their opposition to the RAI Principles.

Opening and Occupying Global Policy Spaces

Organizations networked in the IPC made an early strategic assessment that FAO could constitute a politically interesting alternative intergovernmental policy forum to the Bretton Woods institutions and the WTO due to its more democratic governance, its focus on food and agriculture and mission to eliminate hunger, its strong normative role, and its relative openness to engagement with rural people's organizations. This assessment has periodically been confirmed, despite frustration with FAO's bureaucracy, inefficiency, periodic political marginalization, and apparent incapacity or unwillingness to take decisive stances on issues like trade or genetically modified organisms. It was further validated by the stall of the WTO Doha Round and the renewed centrality of food issues on the global agenda with the advent of the global food crisis.

The IPC has invested considerable energy in opening up meaningful political space within FAO. Following the 2002 Civil Society forum the two parties signed a cooperation agreement which institutionalized the principles of civil society autonomy and self-organization. The negotiation of the voluntary guidelines on the right to food in 2003–2004 introduced the practice of full stakeholder participation in the discussions on the same footing as governments. The ICARRD in 2006 further enlarged FAO's repertoire of participation practices.[9] Building on these advances, the 2009 reform of the CFS opened an unprecedented space for direct negotiation between governments and social movements that reaches beyond FAO to involve the UN system as a whole. This architecture and institutional culture were there to be called upon when land and investment ended up on the agenda of the reformed committee. It is important to note that such space cannot be improvised. It is the result of almost a decade of interaction. The fact that the civil society mechanism undertaking the negotiation has been one in which small-scale food producers are dominant has indisputably contributed to legitimizing the demand for participation.

Borras's presentation of the GCAR (2008, pp. 269–273) undertook an initial assessment of its impact following the five stages suggested by Keck and Sikkink: (1) framing debates and getting issues on the agenda, (2) encouraging discursive commitments from state and other policy actors, (3) causing procedural change at the international and domestic levels (4) affecting policy, and (5) influencing behavior changes in target actors. According to Borras' assessment, the GCAR had scored well on stage 1 at the time of writing, but its impact on the other four had been low to marginal. The scorecard has improved with the reformed CFS. The adoption of the Voluntary Guidelines, despite their voluntary nature and however one may assess their content, represents an advance in the area of discursive commitment. The institutional reform of the CFS constitutes an important procedural change at international level that is gradually being replicated further down the chain.[10] So far as policy and behavior changes are concerned bets can be withheld for the coming period as the Voluntary Guidelines move into the phase of implementation and the CFS consultation on principles for responsible investment in agriculture gets underway. However, it seems that further advances may be registered.

Conclusions: Challenges for the Future

Whether this happens will be influenced by how rural social movements and their CSO supporters address a certain number of interrelated challenges: maintaining a forceful position in the global policy space which they have opened up, managing the game of alliances in a more complex field of actors, and building links between local struggles and global policy spaces.

Keeping Heads Up in Global Policy Space

The CFS's authority as a global policy space has been considerably enhanced over the past two years. One sign of this is that the big players are coming back. The WTO, absent from the first session, showed up at the second. The Group of Twenty (G20) under the French presidency made serious efforts to build synergies between CFS and G8/G20 deliberations. The US, having sought to minimize the policy role of the CFS during the reform process, agreed to preside over the Voluntary Guidelines negotiations, and has assumed vice-chairmanship of the CFS Bureau. The World Bank is taking part in CFS discussions, albeit grumpily. Agri-corporations, represented by one middle level staff in 2010, mobilized a team of 44 CEOs for the 2011 session and have developed their own autonomous interface mechanism, which is intervening strongly on investment issues.

Global negotiations in the CFS regarding Voluntary Guidelines implementation and responsible agricultural investment will thus be even more complex and contentious than in the past (Margulis and Porter, 2013, pp. 65–86). Government positions are in rapid evolution (Borras et al., 2013, pp. 161–179). Now that the CFS has become a forum of dissent to be reckoned with there is a real possibility that the staunchest defenders of the global corporate food system may be tempted to clench their figurative fist and squash the disturbers without excessive ceremony. This trend was already evident during the discussions on principles for responsible investment in agriculture in July 2012, when the US, Canada, and Australia ploughed ahead aggressively seeking rapid enshrinement of the private foreign investment-oriented PRAI despite the objections of the African representatives and civil society. Rural social movements will need to continue to back up their card of legitimacy with cogent proposals and to have articulate spokespersons in the room, the growing fatigue of their organizations notwithstanding. What 'bottom lines' should they draw as the most contentious issues come onto the table in order to avoid being co-opted in support of unacceptable outcomes? How to ensure that the debate retains its political status and does not degenerate into technicalities? How to keep a clear idea of strategic priorities and how should these link up across global venues and multiple levels? Capacity building is needed to multiply the number of leaders that can represent small-scale food producers in global policy debate and maintain communication with the base.

Managing the Chessboard of Alliances

The contributions of committed academics and researchers to rural social movement advocacy platforms will be increasingly important over the coming period. As issues of agricultural investment take center stage they will need to be able to address complex evolutions in the global agrofood system and ways in which small-scale producers can be integrated into corporate-controlled value chains on terms that are adverse to them even when their access to land is maintained (McMichael, 2013, pp. 47–64; Borras et al., 2013, pp. 161–179). In this context, the utility of adopting 'land sovereignty' as a broad and pluralistic frame for land issue claims that connects with the already widespread popular demand for food sovereignty has been suggested (Borras and Franco, 2012). Social movements need, of course, to be able to maintain political control over the construction of their platforms and to validate academics' inputs. Individual networks like La Via Campesina and ROPPA have developed ongoing relations of collaboration with researchers in whom they have confidence. Such precedents could be extended at global level in order to develop practices that go beyond popular diffusion of research results to co-production of knowledge, with academics working to agendas co-defined with the social movements and involving them in research and the co-production of knowledge.

Equally important is the need to defend the hard-won principles of the autonomy and self-organization of civil society interaction with global policy forums against efforts to muddy the waters, of which the International Land Coalition (ILC) is an example. Housed in IFAD, the ILC is a network whose members are a mixed bag of CSOs and multilateral institutions including the World Bank, FAO, IFAD, and IFPRI. Whatever the technical quality of its work, its claim to bring civil society views and 'local voices' to bear on global policy discussions undermines the clear definition of the different roles of different actors that is the basis of multi-actor policy dialogue and accountability (ILC, 2011, p. 11). The role of bilateral and multi-lateral donors in this regard is open to critique. The ILC is reported to have mobilized $US18.6 million from its institutional funders through 2006 (Borras, 2010, p. 792). At a meeting on Voluntary Guidelines implementation convened by FAO in July 2012 the EU alone reported that it had funded the ILC to the tune of $US25 million, yet it has declined thus far to fund the IPC's autonomous, rural peoples-controlled efforts. This level of support gives the ILC a clear capacity to influence not only the framing of discourse and the production of knowledge but also, as it suggested at the same meeting, the convening of national platforms on land issues. Yet this is a politically delicate area in which, it could be argued, the initiative should be left with rural peoples' organizations and their governments since it is they—not international coalitions and development partners—who are the legitimate participants in national policy dia-logue (McKeon, 2009, pp. 181–184).

The autonomous CSM (see http://www.cso4cfs.org) is both an opportunity and a challenge from the viewpoint of constructing and clarifying alliances within the world of civil society itself. The CSM is open to all CSOs concerned with food security issues, in all regions and at all levels. It is the recognized channel for civil society input to CFS deliberations. The Mechan-ism's statutes call for special attention to be given to the voices of organizations representing the various constituencies of the food insecure (CSM, 2010, paragraph 10) and these constituencies are numerically dominant in its governance. Nonetheless, it is likely that NGOs will end up playing the leading role, even with the best of intentions, unless people's organizations are able to invest sufficient energy in the CSM to ensure that it is their positions that serve as the foundation for the overall civil society advocacy platforms.

During the decade between the World Food Summit 1996 and the eruption of the food price crisis in 2007 large NGOs had pretty much deserted the halls of FAO and advocacy on food issues was low in their priority list. The picture is different now that food and agriculture have climbed back up on the agenda and that—thanks to the efforts of the rural social movements/ IPC—the CFS has been transformed into an interesting space in the global policy cosmology. As high visibility issues, the food crisis, and land grabbing are attracting the interest of big NGOs for whom advocacy is a public service activity but at the same time an important tool for resource mobilization. Giants like Oxfam and Action Aid have launched campaigns against hunger and land grabbing in which their superior capacity to capture media attention can outshine collective civil society efforts that privilege the visibility of small producers' organizations. Materials produced in the context of Oxfam's GROW and Action Aid's HungerFREE campaigns unequivocally identify the sponsoring NGOs as the central actors in the campaigns' efforts to address the problems at hand and suggest that donations to support their work would be in order. They make little if any reference to initiatives under-taken by organizations of those directly affected by food insecurity and most often promote advocacy agendas defined in the absence of any evident process of consultation with these organizations.[11]

Over the coming period it will be important to find ways to build alliances with the big NGOs but avoid their taking over the agenda and the space. This cannot happen only in the relatively rarified global atmosphere of the CSM. Initiatives like the Dakar Declaration and the Global Alliance against Land Grabbing that emerged from the Mali conference in November 2011 could make a significant contribution in this regard since they place rural peoples' organizations in the lead and set out a basic platform that all adherents are expected to respect. For this poten-tial to be realized, however, it will be necessary for the rural movements to effectively take the initiative to get the alliance up and running, and this has not happened thus far.

Alliance building between small-scale food producers' organizations and governments, in cases where this is politically conceivable, is fundamental and the CFS offers a propitious framework in which to pursue it. The African movements have moved the farthest by establishing an institutionalized dialogue space with the Africa Permanent Representatives to the Rome-based food and agriculture agencies, which foresees exchanges before each CFS session to seek synergies and convergence. During the October 2011 session the two groups teamed up to co-organize a side event on investing in African agriculture that contributed significantly to obtaining official CFS recognition that small-scale producers are responsible for the bulk of investment in agriculture and for most of the food consumed in developing countries (CFS, 2011, paragraphs 25, 26, and 29; EuropAfrica, 2011). As the CFS consultation on principles for agricultural investment gets underway, African government and producer organization representatives are discovering themselves allied in advocating priority attention for national frameworks designed to mobilize and support domestic investment—starting with farmers' own—rather than focusing on foreign corporate investment. Like all of the gains made in the CFS this one now needs to be taken back home, where relations with governments can be dicier than at global level.

Building Links Between Local Struggles and Global Policy Spaces

In fact, rural social movements can justify their investment in global engagement only if it generates support for local struggles and alternatives-building and opens up political space at national level. Internal debates about international policy work range from ideological denunciation of 'selling out to the devil' or moralistic condemnation of 'jet set leaders' to thoughtful reflection on the costs/benefits of the efforts made. More attention needs to be given to understanding what characterizes cases in which productive local–global links have been made and how to multiply them.[12]

One way in which global engagement can incontestably support local struggles is through the 'externalization' of domestic claims, or the 'boomerang' pattern in Keck and Sikkink's terminology (1998, pp. 12–13). A well-known case in which this has worked is that of Daewoo's 90-year lease on 1.3 million hectares of land in Madagascar. Here a winning combination of local rebellion and international outrage contributed to the ousting in March 2009 of the president who had countenanced the deal and its rapid rescinding by his successor (Burgis and Blas, 2009). An important success factor in this case was the existence of a well-organized and articulate peasant movement that was able to communicate what was going on to a supportive global network. Calling governments to account regarding national implementation of their global commitments is another potential global–local bridge-builder. It is a hallmark of the body of international human rights 'soft law' and of the monitoring and appeals machinery of the Human Rights Council. Global human rights conventions have been adopted with particular success by indigenous peoples to defend their rights to their territories thanks to the United Nations Declaration on the Right of Indigenous Peoples and the ILO Convention 169, fruits of decades of determined advocacy, but also by other constituencies (Edelman and Carwil, 2011; Künnemann and Monsalve Suárez, 2013, pp. 123–139).

The CFS tenure guidelines fall into the category of normative 'soft law' that has to be translated into national legislation to become prescriptive. The rapidity with which land deals are proceeding adds urgency to the global–local connection and there is understandable skepticism within rural social movements as to whether the Voluntary Guidelines will make a difference. In December 2010 the president of the national peasant platform in Mali, where a Libyan company had occupied 100,000 hectares of irrigated land in the rice-producing region with the complicity of national capital and authorities, judged that 'the whole thing is moving too fast to be stopped by voluntary guidelines. The only global level action that might make a difference in the immediate would be if the CFS adopted a moratorium on land grabbing and sent a mission to verify the situation.'[13]

Social movements lost their battle to obtain an outright condemnation of large-scale land acquisitions in the Voluntary Guidelines. The adopted text, however, extends to other social categories protection of rights that had previously applied only to indigenous peoples and it opens the door to civil society 'naming and shaming' in CFS plenary sessions. It also encourages states to set up multi-actor platforms and frameworks at local, national, and regional levels in order to implement the Guidelines and monitor their impact on improved governance of tenure, food security, and realization of the right to food (FAO, 2012, paragraphs 26.2 and 26.4). Making this happen in a certain number of countries in each region is a key piece in the Voluntary Guidelines implementation strategy that rural social movements and CSOs are now elaborating, which takes into account the community level-on-up action plan adopted at the Mali 'Stop Land Grabbing Now!' conference (La Via Campesina, 2012a).

The global–local relation is dialectic, not sequential. The WCARRD conference in 1979, prompted by rural unrest in various parts of the world, adopted a progressive *Peasant Charter* that was translated into local languages and brandished by rural movements throughout the agrarian reform doldrums of the 1980s and is still a reference point for them (Saragih, 2005). Rural movements' contestation of MLAR contributed to the convocation of the ICARRD in 2006 which, despite the opposition of powerful FAO members, prompted not insignificant follow-up action like involving small producers' networks in the formulation of the Africa Land Policy Framework Guidelines (McKeon, 2009, p. 100) and the Voluntary Guidelines themselves. The Voluntary Guidelines process, in turn, has fed into the exemplary efforts of Senegalese peasant organizations and their civil society allies to contest land grabbing and to call candidates in the recent presidential election to account on land access issues (CNCR, 2012). Barely 10 days after the adoption of the Guidelines the same national peasant coalition of Mali whose president had expressed doubts about the Voluntary Guidelines' efficacy 18 months earlier was calling on the government to respect their provisions in the national land tenure law, currently being drafted (MADP, 2012). Rights become meaningful when they are claimed, and international normative instruments like the Voluntary Guidelines can potentially serve as important reference points for peoples' claims-making. Realizing this potential is the challenge for social activists committed to global engagement.

Notes

1 Tashunka Witko, a Lakota leader (1840–1877). This citation was used as the slogan for the People's Food Sovereignty Forum in Rome on 13–17 November 2009, held in parallel to the FAO World Summit on Food Security.

2 The author has participated in these evolutions as the FAO officer responsible for civil society relations through 2003 and, subsequently, as a supporter of rural social movements' efforts to gain effective access to FAO policy forums and the reformed CFS. This article draws on her direct experience, which has been documented and analyzed in the cited publications.

3 The literature on institutional reactions to land grabbing is voluminous. On popular resistance see Borras (2008, pp. 261–262; 2010); Borras and Franco (2010b); Matondi et al. (2011); Moyo and Yeros (2005, p. 1); Rosset et al. (2006, pp. 5–19).

4 See Borras et al. (2006, pp. 4–9) for a comprehensive discussion of the history of the land reform agenda. For a detailed and thoughtful review of the land policy and agrarian reform work of FAO, see Monsalve Suárez (2008).

5 Invitation issued by the chief of the Unit on 30 April 2008 to attend a 'partners' meeting on Voluntary Guidelines on Land and Natural Resource Tenure.
6 Mobilization on trade issues in opposition to the WTO is another area in which rural social movements have engaged strongly, but mostly from the outside.
7 Interview with Sofia Monsalve Suárez, January 2011.
8 Particular mention goes to the Special Rapporteur on the right to food, whose courageous, lucid, and articulate positions on land issues have made him a strategic ally in social movement and civil society efforts to defend an alternative paradigm to market-led productivist approaches.
9 See McKeon (2009, pp. 17–120) for a detailed documentation and analysis of the progressive enlargement of political space for civil society engagement with FAO and McKeon (2009, pp. 141–157) and McKeon and Kalafatic (2009, pp. 17–23) for a comparative analysis of UN system global mechanisms for policy interaction with civil society.
10 During the biennial FAO Regional Conferences in 2012, for the first time, civil society spokespersons were enabled to intervene on the same footing as governments on agenda items that concerned issues being treated in the CFS.
11 See, for example, Oxfam's 'Land and Power' report launched on 22 September 2011 (Oxfam, 2011) just before a key Voluntary Guidelines negotiation session. In contrast, the press release issued collectively on 7 October 2011 by the social movements/CSOs participating in the negotiations gave voice to representatives of small-scale producers, artisanal fishworkers, and indigenous peoples. It received considerably less media attention than did the carefully orchestrated Oxfam launch.
12 This could be a fruitful object of social movement–academic collaboration. Case studies and reflection that could be drawn on are located in various areas of inquiry these include those of globalization and global civil society, see Khagram et al. (2002) and Pieterse (2000); on global accountability, see Gaventa and Tandon (2010), Macdonald (2007), Newell and Wheeler (2006), and the burgeoning literature of land grab case studies that the LDPI is stimulating (for a recently published example, see Smalley and Corbera, 2012).
13 Interview with Ibrahima Coulibaly, December 2010.

References

Borras, S. (2008) La Via Campesina and its global campaign for agrarian reform, *Journal of Agrarian Change*, 8(2–3), pp. 258–289.
Borras, S. (2010) The politics of transnational agrarian movements, *Development and Change*, 41(5), pp. 771–803.
Borras, S. & Franco, J. C. (2010a) From threat to opportunity? Problems with the idea of a 'Code of Conduct' for land-grabbing, http://www.tni.org/sites/www.tni.org/files/Yale%20April%202010%20Borras_Franco%20CoC%20paper.pdf.
Borras, S. & Franco, J. C. (2010b), Towards a broader view of the politics of global land grab: rethinking land issues, reframing resistance, Initiatives in Critical Agrarian Studies Working Paper Series No. 1.
Borras, S. & Franco, J. C. (2012) , A 'Land Sovereignty' alternative? Towards a peoples' counter-enclosure, Agrarian Justice Discussion Paper (Hague: Transnational Institute).
Borras, S., Kay, K. & Akram-Lodhi, A. H. (2006), Agrarian reform and rural development: historical overview and current issues. International Institute for Social Studies/UNDP Land, Poverty Reduction and Public Action Policy Paper No. 1.
Borras, S., Franco, J. C., Kay, C. & Spoor, M. (2011) *Land Grabbing in Latin America and the Caribbean Viewed from Broader International Perspectives* (Rome: FAO).
Borras, S. M., Franco, J. C. & Wang, C. (2013) The challenge of global governance of land grabbing: changing international agricultural context and competing political views and strategies, *Globalizations*, 10(1), pp. 161–179.
Burgis, T. & Blas, J. (2009) Madagascar scraps Daewoo farm deal, *Financial Times*, 18 March.
Civil Society Mechanism (CSM) (2010) Proposal for an international food security and nutrition mechanism for relations with CFS, http://www.csm4cfs.org/files/Pagine/1/csm_proposal_en.pdf
Civil society organizations participating in the negotiations on the Voluntary Guidelines on Responsible Governance of Tenure of Land, Fisheries and Forest in the Context of National Food Security (CSOPNVG) (2011) Civil society organizations' proposals to the FAO Guidelines on Responsible Governance of Land and Natural Resources Tenure, http://www.fian.org/news/news/civil-society-organizations-proposals-for-the-fao-guidelines-on-responsible-governance-of-land-and-natural-resources-tenure
CSOPNVG (2012a) Joint political statement of civil society organizations which have actively participated in the process of developing the Voluntary Guidelines, http://www.csm4cfs.org/policy_working_groups-6/land_tenure-6/

CSOPNVG (2012b) Joint press release, 11 May 2012, http://www.csm4cfs.org/policy_working_groups-6/land_tenure-6/

Committee on World Food Security (CFS) (2009) *Reform of the Committee on World Food Security. Final Version* (Rome: FAO).

CFS (2010) *Final Report on the Thirty-sixth Session. Rome 11–14 October and 16 October 2010* (Rome: FAO).

CFS (2011) *Final Report of the Thirty-seventh Session. Rome 17–22 October 2011* (Rome: FAO).

Conseil national de concertation et de coopération des ruraux (CNCR) (2012) *Les candidats interpellés sur le développement rural et la réforme foncière,* http://www.cncr.org/spip.php?article605

Dakar World Social Forum (2011) Dakar appeal against the land grab, http://www.petitiononline.com/dakar/petition.html

De Schutter, O. (2009a) The right to food and the political economy of hunger, 26th McDougall Memorial Lecture, Opening of the 36th Session of the FAO Conference, 18 November.

De Schutter, O. (2009b) *Large-Scale Land Acquisitions Leases: a Set of Minimum Principles and Measures to Address the Human Rights Challenge. Addendum to the Report of the Special Rapporteur on the Right to Food to the Human Rights Council (A/HRC/13/33/Add.2)* (Geneva: Human Rights Council).

De Schutter, O. (2010a) Responsibly destroying the world's peasantry, *Project Syndicate*, 6 April 2010.

De Schutter, O. (2010b), Principles for responsible investment in agriculture, Presented to UNCTAD Commission on Investment, Enterprise and Development, 26 April 2010.

De Schutter, O. (2010c) *Report of the Special Rapporteur on the right to food presented to the 65th General Assembly of the United Nations (A/65/281): Access to land and the right to food* (New York: United Nations).

Desmarais, A., Wiebe, N. & Wittman, H. (2010) *Food Sovereignty: Reconnecting Food, Nature and Community* (Oakland, CA: Food First Books).

Edelman, M. & Carwil, J. (2011) Peasants' rights and the UN system: Quixotic struggle? Or emancipatory idea whose time has come? *Journal of Peasant Studies*, 38(1), pp. 81–108.

EuropAfrica (2011) Africa can feed itself! Summary report of a dialogue between African governments and African family farmers in the context of the 37th Session of the Committee on World Food Security, http://www.europafrica.info/en/news/africa-can-feed-itself-the-summary-report

FAO (2012). Voluntary Guidelines on the Responsible Governance of Tenure of Land, Fisheries and Forests in the Context of National Food Security (Rome: FAO).

FIAN (2008) Time for a human right to food framework of action. FIAN position on the Comprehensive Framework of Action of the UN High Level Task Force on the Global Food Security Crisis, http://www.fian.org/resources/documents/others/time-for-a-human-right-to-food-framework-of-action/pdf

FIAN (2009) Madrid World Food Conference-Outcome, 2 February, http://www.fian.org/news/news/madrid-world-fd-conferene-an-evaluation

Gaventa, J. & Tandon, R. (2010) *Globalizing Citizens: New Dynamics of Inclusion and Exclusion* (London: Zed).

Global Campaign for Agrarian Reform (GCAR) (2010) Why we oppose the Principles for Responsible Investment in Agriculture, http://www.fian.org/resources/documents/others/why-we-oppose-the-principles-for-responsible-agricultural-investment/pdf

GRAIN (2008a) Making a killing from hunger, in *Against the Grain*, (Barcelona: GRAIN).

GRAIN (2008b) *Seized! The 2008 Land Grab for Food and Financial Security,* GRAIN briefing (Barcelona: GRAIN)

International Conference on Agrarian Reform and Rural Development (ICARRD) (2006) *Final Declaration* (Rome: FAO).

International Land Coalition (ILC) (2011) *Strategic Framework 2011–2015* (Rome: ILC).

International Planning Committee for food sovereignty (IPC) (2002) NGO/CSO forum for food sovereignty: A Right for All, 8–13 June, http://www.foodsovereignty.org

IPC (2008a) No More 'Failures-as-Usual'!, http://www.foodsovereignty.org

IPC (2008b) Increased land, territory and water conflicts related to the climate crisis, http://www.foodsovereignty.org

IPC (2009a) Accelerating into disaster: when banks manage the food crisis, http://csa-be.org/IMG/pdf_Statement_Madrid_meeting-EN.pdf

IPC (2009b) Peoples' food sovereignty now! Declaration of the civil society organizations forum parallel to the World Summit on Food Security, 13–17 November, http://peoplesforum2009.foodsovereignty.org

IPC (2010) Call to civil society to participate in the process towards the adoption of Voluntary Guidelines for Land and Natural Resource Tenure by FAO, http://www.foodsovereignty.org

Keck, M. E. & Sikkink, K. (1998) *Activists Beyond Borders* (Ithaca, NY: Cornell University Press).

Khagram, S., Riker, J. V. & Sikkink, K. (2002) *Restructuring World Politics: Transnational Social Movements, Networks and Norms* (Minneapolis: University of Minnesota Press).

Künnemann, R. & Monsalve Suárez, S. (2013) International human rights and governing land grabbing: a view from global civil society, *Globalizations*, 10(1), pp. 00–00.

La Via Campesina (2012a) International Conference of Peasants and Farmers: Stop Land Grabbing! La Via Campesina notebook no.3, http://viacampesina.org/downloads/pdf/en/mali-report-2012-en1.pdf

La Via Campesina (2012b) La Via Campesina's Position on Rio+20, http://www.viacampesina.org/en/index.php?option=com_content&view=article&id=1284:peasants-of-the-world-mobilize-against-green-capitalism-in-rio&catid=48:-climate-change-and-agrofuels&Itemid=75

Macdonald, K. (2007) Public accountability within transnational supply chains: a global agenda for empowering Southern workers? in A. Ebrahim & E. Weisband (eds) *Global Accountabilities: Participation, Pluralism, and Public Ethics* (Cambridge: Cambridge University Press), pp 252–279.

McKeon, N. (2009) *The United Nations and Civil Society: Legitimizing Global Governance—Whose Voice?* (London: Zed).

McKeon, N. (2011a), Including the excluded in global politics: the case of peasants, paper presented at a Building Global Democracy workshop on Including the Excluded in Global Politics, Rio de Janeiro, 13–15 April, http://www.buildingglobaldemcracy.org

McKeon, N. (2011b) *Global Governance for World Food Security: A Scorecard Four Years After the Eruption of the Food Crisis* (Berlin: Heinrich-Böll Foundation).

McKeon, N. & Kalafatic, C. (2009) *Strengthening Dialogue: UN Experience with Small Farmer Organizations and Indigenous Peoples* (New York: UN NGO Liaison Service).

McKeon, N., Watts, M. & Wolford, W. (2004) *Peasant Associations in Theory and Practice* (Geneva: UNRISD).

McMichael, P. (2009) The world food crisis in historical perspective, *Monthly Review* 61(3), http://monthlyreview.org/2009/07/01/the-world-food-crisis-in-historical-perspective

McMichael, P. (2013) Land grabbing as security mercantilism in international relations, *Globalizations*, 10(1), pp. 47–64.

Margulis, M. E. & Porter, T. (2013) Governing the global land grab: multipolarity, ideas, and complexity in transnational governance, *Globalizations*, 10(1), pp. 65–86.

Matondi, P. B., Havnevik, K. & Beyene, A. (2011) *Biofuels, Land Grabbing and Food Security in Africa* (London: Zed).

Ministère de l'Agriculture, de l'Elèvage et de la peche (MADP) (2012) *Rapport de Synthèse de la rencontre préparatoire de la 10ème édition de la Journée du paysan, 27–28 May*, http://www.europafrica.info

Monsalve Suárez, S. (2008) *The FAO and Its Work on Land Policy and Agrarian Reform* (Amsterdam: Transnational Institute & 11.11.11).

Moyo, S. & Yeros, P. (2005) *Reclaiming the Land: The Resurgence of Rural Movements in Africa, Asia and Latin America* (London: Zed).

Mulvany, P (2007) Food sovereignty comes of age, *Food Ethics*, 2(3), p. 19.

Newell, P. & Wheeler, J. (2006) *Rights, Resources and the Politics of Accountability* (London: Zed).

Nyéléni (2007) Nyéléni 2007 Forum for Food Sovereignty, http://www.foei.org

Oxfam (2011) *Land and Power: The Growing Scandal Around the New Wave of Investments in Land* (London: Oxfam).

Patel, R. (2009) Food sovereignty, *Journal of Peasant Studies*, 36(3), pp. 663–706.

Peoples' Food Sovereignty Now! (2009) Who decides? Discussion paper for civil society forum in parallel to FAO World Summit on Food Security, Rome, 13–17 November, http://peoplesforum2009.foodsovereignty.org

Pieterse, J. N. (2000) Globalization and emancipation: from local empowerment to global reform, in B. Gills (ed.), *Globalization and the Politics of Resistance* (New York: Palgrave), pp. 189–206.

Pimbert, M. (2009) *Towards Food Sovereignty* (London: International Institute for Environment and Development).

Reisenberger, B. & Monsalve Suárez, S. (2011) Nyéléni, Mali: a global alliance against land grabbing, http://www.fian.org/news/news/nyeleni-mali-a-global-alliance-against-land-grabbing/pdf

Right to Food and Nutrition Watch (2010) *Land Grabbing and Nutrition: Challenges for Global Governance*, http://www.rtfn-watch.org/en/home/watch-2010/the-right-to-food-and-nutrition-2010/

Rosset, P., Patel, R. & Courville, M. (2006) *Promised Land: Competing Visions of Agrarian Reform* (Oakland, CA: Food First).

Saragih, H. (2005), The world's peasant farmers need a peasant rights convention, http://www.cetim.ch/en/documents/05-onu2-saraghi.pdf

Seufert, P. (2013) The FAO Voluntary Guidelines on the Responsible Governance of Tenure of Land, Fisheries and Forests, *Globalizations*, 10(1), pp. 181–186.

Smalley, R. & Corbera, E. (2012) Large-scale land deals from the inside-out: findings from Kenya's Tana Delta, *Journal of Peasant Studies*, 39(3–4), pp. 1039–1075.

Tarrow, S. (2005). *The New Transnational Activism* (Cambridge: Cambridge University Press).

UN High Level Task Force on the Global Food Security Crisis (HLTF) (2008) *Comprehensive Framework for Action* (Geneva: UN).

Van Der Ploeg, J. D. (2010) The food crisis, industrialized farming and the imperial regime, *Journal of Agrarian Change*, 10(1), pp. 98–106.

Wise, T. A. & Murphy, S. (2012) , *Resolving the Food Crisis: Assessing Food Policy Reforms since 2007,* Global Development and Environment Institute/Institute for Agriculture and Trade Policy, http://www.ase.tufts.edu/gdae/Pubs/rp/ResolvingFoodCrisis.pdf

Nora McKeon studied history at Harvard and political science at the Sorbonne before joining the Food and Agriculture Organization (FAO) of the United Nations where she became responsible for the overall direction of FAO's policy and program interaction with civil society. She now divides her time between research, teaching, and activism around food systems, peasant farmer movements, and UN–civil society relations. She is the author of *The United Nations and Civil Society: Legitimating Global Governance—Whose Voice?* (Zed, 2009).

International Human Rights and Governing Land Grabbing: A View from Global Civil Society

ROLF KÜNNEMANN & SOFÍA MONSALVE SUÁREZ

FIAN International, Heidelberg, Germany

ABSTRACT *The current international responses to the global land grab are insufficient in the sense that they address some aspects of the problem but leave outside their scope important situations of human rights violations and abuses. To address this governance gap, this essay argues for the promotion and application of the right to land as a human right. Globalization in general and the global land grab in particular make it necessary to pay particular attention to the international and transnational dimension of the human right to land. Extraterritorial human rights obligations (ETOs) may turn out to be the missing link for human rights to acquire the conceptual robustness for upholding legal primacy over all other legal regimes such as trade and finance in times of deepening globalization.*

Introduction

Since its inception in 1986, the FoodFirst Information and Action Network (FIAN), an international human rights organization working for the right to adequate food, has investigated land conflicts and supported rural communities worldwide in the defense and struggle for their lands. FIAN was one of the first human rights organizations to systematically apply a human rights approach to land issues and conceptualize access to land and redistributive land reforms as international and national human rights obligations. In particular, FIAN has contributed to developing the concept that access to land is a key component of the human right to food by embedding access to land as part of the 'right to feed oneself' in international human rights law. Indeed, FIAN's contribution to developing the concept of the right to feed oneself was integrated by the United Nations (UN) Committee of Economic, Social and Cultural Rights in its authoritative legal interpretation of the right to food in 1999 (see CESCR, 1999). Later on, FIAN worked to expand this understanding of the right to food and formally participated alongside states in negotiating in 2004 the Food and Agriculture Organization of the United Nations (FAO)'s guidelines to support the progressive realization the right to adequate food (FAO, 2004). These guidelines dedicate an entire guideline (CFS, 2012, see Guidelines No. 8) to the issue of access to resources and assets. More recently, FIAN participated in the process of adoption of the CFS/FAO 'Guidelines on responsible governance of tenure of land, fisheries and forests' (herein the 'Tenure Guidelines'), which will provide specific guidance to states and other actors about how to apply human rights to land tenure issues. It is indeed remarkable for us that in the current global debate about land grabbing, the recognition of land as a human rights issue has gone largely uncontested and has become widely accepted by actors. A short 10 years ago this was barely the case and the shift in where human rights fits into global governance debates at present confirms the consolidating moral and legal force of international human rights.

We argue that the time has come to establish the human right to land under international law and in the practice of global governance. This progressive development in international human rights would be invaluable as a tool for global social justice, in particular, to curb the global land grab. Our position is informed and grounded by FIAN's deep experience in local land struggles in the Global South and as a participant in global and transnational governance. Furthermore, FIAN's work on the right to food over the past decades has made clear to us that advancing a progressive international human rights agenda on the right to food can occur with committed and coordinated political struggle at the local, national, and international levels. A human right to land is not only necessary, it is possible.

We develop our argument as follows. The next section provides a brief overview of the land cases that FIAN has documented and categorizes these into five different types where the involvement of foreign actors and/or an international dimension is significant. This is followed by a more in-depth discussion of why the human right to land is a necessary response to land grabbing. The last section outlines the content and core elements of a human right to land, particularly emphasizing the potential of its extraterritorial dimension to influence the behavior of land grabbers and its facilitating agents. Finally, we draw some conclusions about the usefulness and limitations of the international human rights framework to govern the global land grab.

Different Types of Land Cases with an International Dimension Documented by FIAN

The definition of land grabbing has sparked considerable debate in academic and policy circles (Borras and Franco, 2012; Cotula, 2012a; White et al. 2012; see Margulis et al., 2013, pp. 1–23). Depending on the particular framing of land grabbing, and who is doing the framing, its nature, actors, drivers, and scope will vary significantly, and with this the breadth and depth of the regulatory interventions proposed by different actors. We will return to the definitional debate below, however, we first want to present a brief overview of the land cases that FIAN has documented. These cases go back 25 years, however, we focus on more recent developments that can be situated within the broader land grabbing phenomenon.[1] Our focus is on cases with involvement by foreign actors or with an international dimension, since such cases are critical to understanding land grabbing and its potential governance. For the purposes of our argument, we restrict ourselves here to identifying the main drivers and actors involved. Related human rights violations are also noted. We believe this categorization is important because the emphasis we provide on the human rights abuses experienced by local peoples often goes missing in the typical metrics used to define and measure land grabs. In our view, these states of cases provide a very different picture and hence the potential understanding of land grabbing by global publics and policy-makers compared to what is typically conveyed in the mainstream discourse on governing land grabbing.

The first set of cases with an international dimension are land acquisitions related to mining by companies with headquarters in OECD countries (FIAN and WACAM, 2008). In general, we have observed that mining has heavily intensified in the last few years due to the increased world demand for raw materials, and this has translated into land struggles over areas rich in mineral resources. However, these cases are not limited to the 'usual suspects' in the North. FIAN has also started to document new land struggles caused by the entry of states and mining firms from the Global South that have become major players in extractive industries in the last years. In Mozambique, for instance, we documented the impact of the coal mining operations of the Brazilian corporation, Vale do Rio Doce, on local peasant communities in Tete province; these communities were displaced from prime agricultural lands without being adequately resettled and compensated for their livelihood losses thus putting their right to food at risk (FIAN, 2010b).

The second set of cases relates to large-scale infrastructure development such as the construction of dams for hydropower and irrigation purposes, airports, highways, and harbors. The main international actors involved here are the international financial institutions (IFIs), such as the World Bank, regional development banks, and international banks that provide project support. The IFIs in particular have long promoted the development of large-scale infrastructure projects; developing country states are also eager to for such projects to 'modernize' their economies. Such projects require massive, long-term loans, and the social and ecological costs of such projects have become major points of transnational advocacy (see Goetz, 2013, pp. 199–204). More recently, FIAN has documented the entry of state development banks and private companies from the 'BRICSA' (Brazil, Russia, India, China, and South Africa) group of emerging powers as new players in the world of project finance and major infrastructure. Ecuador is a case in point: the Brazilian construction company Oderbrecht has been involved in the construction of large-scale dams in the Pacific coast area of Ecuador with the financial support of the Brazilian Development Bank (BNDES) and the Inter-American Development Bank (IADB). The construction of the Daule-Peripa dam, for instance, led to the dispossession and displacement of local farmers and fishers from their lands and access to the rivers for the benefit of agribusiness interests seeking to secure sufficient water for irrigation provided by the dam. The projected Baba dam is likely to have similar impacts (FIAN Ecuador, 2007).

The third set of cases comprises cases of foreign investors taking control of people's lands for commercial agricultural production for food, feed, and fuel. In this category FIAN has documented cases of OECD investors acquiring land in Southern countries for the production of agricultural commodities such as coffee (e.g. Mubende region in Uganda), the production of rice (e.g. Yala Swamp area in Kenya), and forest plantations (e.g. Niassa province in Mozambique—see Box 1 below for more detail). FIAN has found that many of these land deals have deprived local communities from their lands and livelihoods. Here too non-OECD countries are becoming more active, and as FIAN has documented, responsible for human rights abuses. Key cases of such violations are the Libyan state-owned company, Malibya, which is leasing lands in Mali for the production of rice (Brot für die Welt et al., 2010), Brazilian soya growers getting control of peasant lands in Paraguay (FIAN, 2006), and South African investors setting up an agrofuels project in Mozambique (FIAN, 2010a). In all these cases, peasant families and communities with different degrees of legal security of land tenure got (or were about to get) dispossessed or displaced from their lands with serious implications for their right to an adequate standard of living.

In the case of Paraguay, this development has been violent compromising also of civil human rights abuses such as the right to physical integrity and to not be arbitrarily detained or deprived from life. Along with this set of cases, FIAN's work also extends to cases where the main actor is a company controlled by national investors in the country where land is grabbed but that company is raising capital for investment either from IFIs (as in the case of Bajo Aguan in Honduras, see APRODEV et al., 2011) and/or from international markets, such as from agricultural investment funds, which can include institutional investors such as pension funds. This has been the case in the Niassa province of Mozambique (FIAN, 2012; Herre, 2010; see Box 1 below), and highlight the links between land grabbing and financialization where investment decisions made by distal actors have negative consequences for rural communities in the Global South.

Box 1. Mozambique: The Human Rights Impacts of Tree Plantations in Niassa Province

Mozambique is one of the poorest countries of the world. Around 35% of Mozambican households are chronically food insecure and 46% of all children below five years are malnourished. Eighty per cent of the population lives in rural areas and depends on subsistence agriculture and the use of natural resources for their livelihoods. Women especially play an important role in guaranteeing sufficient food supply for families.

In order to boost development, the Mozambican government has been actively promoting large-scale private investment in tree plantations for many years. Mozambique's National Reforestation Strategy sets the target of establishing 1.3 million hectares in the next 20 years. Niassa province is in the north of the country and is one of the areas where tree plantations are being developed. According to recent figures, six companies are operating on a total project area of 550,000 hectares, of which around 28,000 hectares are planted with pine and eucalyptus.

One of these companies is Chikweti Forests of Niassa, which is a subsidiary of Global Solidarity Forest Fund (GSFF), a Sweden-based investment fund. Behind the GSFF stand investors from many different countries, including the Netherlands, Norway, and Sweden. Chikweti Forests of Niassa started operating in 2005 and has already acquired around 45,000 hectares of land in the districts of Lago, Lichinga, and Sanga, of which 13,000 have been planted for plantation production.

Chikweti's operations are having severe impacts on local peasant communities in the project area. For peasants in this region family farming is the most important source of livelihoods. Peasants complain about the loss of access to farmland because tree plantations are being set up on lands that they were previously used by local people for food production. In addition to the issues of farmland loss, local people have also lost access to native forests, which have been cut down to make space for the plantations. Forest products are used for several purposes by peasants and local peoples such as for gathering fruits and medicinal plants, home construction, and energy, as well as an additional source of income. Although the Chikweti Forests of Niassa announced that it would provide jobs as part of its investment project, the jobs that have been created are few and scarce, poorly paid and temporary. As such, they do not provide alternative sources of livelihood for locals to 'compensate' for the loss of access to land and forests. Given experiences elsewhere with similar projects, the tree plantations in Niassa will most likely lead to water shortages and water contamination (to date this has not been properly investigated). The tree plantations will also have

---

environmental impacts, which range from destruction of ecosystems to loss of biodiversity and soil degradation.

The introduction of large scale tree plantations has considerable impacts on the enjoyment of human rights by the local population. The partial loss of access to land, forests, and water as consequences of the operations of Chikweti Forests of Niassa impairs the enjoyment of the right to adequate food and the right to water of the peasant communities in the project area. Since thus far only a relatively small part of the areas dedicated to tree plantations are operational, the human rights impacts are likely to increase during the coming years as these projects scale upwards.

Sweden is involved in several ways in the establishment of tree plantations in Niassa region. First, the Swedish government has supported and financed the establishment of large-scale tree plantations in Niassa through its development cooperation agency, SIDA. Second, Sweden is the home state where GSFF is registered and several of the investors in the GSFF, namely the Diocese of Västerås. Other investors outside of Sweden, such as OVF from Norway and the Dutch pension fund Stichting Pensioenfonds ABP, the latter which holds 54.5% of the fund. While the problems with the plantation projects in Niassa had already been recognized and analyzed in a recent report commissioned by SIDA, it remains unclear to what extent the problems have been addressed.

Source: See FIAN (2012). All the sources of the data and evidence cited in this box are provided in this report.

The fourth set of cases relates to land policy reforms and services financed through official development assistance (ODA). Since the 1990s, bilateral donors and IFIs have been active in land policy reforms, sometimes as conditionality for loans. Many of the types of land policies these actors promote, and in some cases are directly involved in the formulation and implementation of, have been found to have negative impacts in the enjoyment of the human right to land of the local population. A case in point is German ODA that has financed the land titling system in Cambodia. There is mounting evidence that this system has denied due process rights to vulnerable households and communities that were seeking legal recognition of their possession rights. The process of land registration (basis for obtaining a formal, legal title to one's land) in Cambodia is considered highly discriminatory due to the fact that the titling process excludes areas that are likely to be disputed or that are considered by the state to be too complicated for the systematic titling process. This exclusion effectively means denying recognition and protection of the possession rights of poor households living in these areas. This has lead to a further weakening of their tenure status as they communities are now more vulnerable to be evicted because their lands are sought after by powerful actors (Brot für die Welt et al., 2011).

The fifth and last set of cases includes cases related to the international regime for investment protection. To further encourage foreign direct investments and protect investors, an array of investment and trade agreements (collectively known as the international investment protection regime) have proliferated in the past 20 years. Such agreements aim at protecting foreign investors (both corporations and individuals) from arbitrary treatment by the host government, such as expropriation or nationalization of investments. Investment treaties strengthen the legal value of individual contracts by making their violation a breach of international law, and give investors direct access to international arbitration when disputes with the host government arise (Peterson,

2009). On several occasions, investors and marginalized groups have contested the same piece of land; investment treaties are tilted towards the interests of investors and can lead to outcomes the can be harmful for local communities. The role of investment treaties in facilitating land grabs is well established (see Cotula, 2012b; Cotula et al., 2009). FIAN has documented how investment treaties can have a chilling effect on land reform. Take the example of the bilateral investment treaty signed between Paraguay and Germany that has been used by German landowners to prevent the Paraguayan government from expropriating lands, which, according to the Paraguayan constitution, are eligible for redistribution for agrarian reform objectives and/or for the return of indigenous peoples to their ancestral territories (Brot für die Welt et al., 2006).

In summary, FIAN has identified many types of cases of land acquisitions that vary by driver and sets of national, international, and transnational actors at play, and which have clear consequences for the enjoyment of human rights. From FIAN's perspective, the most important dimension is whether specific land deals, investments, and/or international policy frameworks result in the loss of access to land by local people. It is worth noting that of the sets of cases that FIAN has worked on, not all cases would be classified as land grabbing in the current use of the term—especially that of land policy reform under ODA or the 'chilling effect' of the international investment regime on land reform. Definitions commonly used by policymakers, NGOs, and scholars tend to take a very narrow view of land grabbing which is mainly descriptive and takes into account only some features of the land grab like size of the land, certain actors, or certain drivers/purposes of the land use change (GRAIN, 2008; ILC, 2011). Even more analytical definitions based on key features which seek to capture the direction of the change in land use and property, and of the change of the relationship between humans and nature to identify who profits or is affected by the changes only go so far (Borras and Franco, 2012a). It is also important to remark that many other human rights organizations have documented other cases of severe human rights violations related to land, such as, for instance, the cases of occupied territories in West Asia and North Africa (HLRN, 2010) which would not classify either as land grabbing as defined in the current literature. This means that human rights organizations such as FIAN and others have been dealing with land cases with involvement of foreign actors or with an international dimension for which existing definitions of land grabbing fail to capture.

The contentious nature of the term land grabbing matters significantly to work on the ground. Indeed, the term land grabbing can also complicate FIAN's work as we have seen in our own advocacy work where land grabbers are trying to strategically attack the very idea of land grabbing by reducing the concept merely to the size at stake or if there is the use of violence in the (forced) removal of people from their lands. For example, a company involved in one of the human rights abuses FIAN has documented was recently complaining that FIAN is unduly calling their investments land grabbing because the size of the land at stake is 'only' 2,000 hectares (many definitions of land grabbing only recognize areas upwards of 5,000 hectares). Another company was claiming that it intends to develop only 1% of the agricultural land of a certain province and because, it deemed this to be a small proportion of land, it claimed it should not be blamed for putting at risk the food security of the communities where the plantations happen to take place. This suggests at least that powerful actors can engage in the politics of measurement for their own ends (Margulis et al., 2013, this volume).

The Need to Defend the Right to Land As a Human Right

The scale, depth, and pace of the current wave of land grabbing gives reason for great concern about the current and future enjoyment of human rights worldwide. The increased interest in land as an economic asset by transnational corporations (TNCs), sovereign wealth and private investment funds, and by state governments is explained by an interplay of several factors, including the changing supply and demand patterns of agricultural commodities (e.g. rising food prices, growing world population, agrofuels, tree plantations, raw materials for industrial use); the financialization of agriculture, which means that land is an attractive investment option not only for agribusiness and energy companies interested in direct production, but also for financial actors interested in increasing returns and lowering risks for their portfolios (see, e.g. Margulis and Porter, 2013, pp. 65–86); the so called 'green economy', which encompasses the appropriation of land and resources for alleged environmental ends such as those implied in the establishment of natural reserves, carbon trade schemes (Fairhead et al., 2012); and the sharp increase of extractive mining, tourism, and urbanization (Borras et al., 2011; Cotula, 2012; White et al., 2012). In addition to these economic factors, states have played a major role in facilitating these developments by changing national legislation in ways that encourage the deepened privatization and commodification of natural resources, dismantle social and environmental regulations of economic activities and by promoting investment and development policies which increase the corporate control over agriculture, mining, and energy (Cotula, 2012a; White et al., 2012).

If not reversed, land grabbing will deprive a significant part of the world's rural population of their access to and control over natural resources (De Schutter, 2011). We share with most critical and radical activists working on food and agriculture issues the position that land grabbing and similar processes will destroy the peasantry, fishing, pastoralists, and forest dweller communities which still are the backbone of local food producing systems. This will also deepen existing patterns of inequality, discrimination, and structural violence against women; the social fabric, stability, and peace of many rural societies are at severe risk. We disagree with those that think that destroying the peasantry is economic progress; policies that promote increasing the number of 'surplus people' are an affront to human dignity and the very idea of human rights (GCAR, 2010).

Many of the international policy responses to land grabbing focus on the land deals themselves, that is, their features and the procedural standards which should be observed during their negotiation (see, e.g. CFS, 2012; De Schutter, 2009; World Bank et al., 2010). However, many of these governance instruments tend to neglect addressing the underlying economic and political drivers of land dispossession—except for the minimum principles formulated by the Special Rapporteur on the right to food (see Claeys and Vanloqueren, 2013, pp. 193–198)—but avoid going so far as establishing binding rules on states and private actors engaged in land deals, without which stopping land grabbing becomes ever more difficult.

The complex nature of land grabbing, which is a point of crystallization of wider socio-economic, political, and cultural developments, tends to cut across local, national, and international actors, norms, and governing institutions, all of which are closely intertwined. As such, it would be naïve to expect one single international institution or policy instrument to be able to regulate the global land grab in a comprehensive manner. On the other hand, any international policy response that cannot address those situations described above which FIAN has identified as threatening human rights (e.g. the case of German ODA and titling programs in Cambodia and the case of bilateral investment treaties and the impediment to expropriate land from foreigners to carry out agrarian reform in Paraguay) must be seen as incomplete.

Therefore, the question we pose is: What would be a more expansive concept around which to build global governance that addresses the full set of challenges posed by the current wave of land grabbing and the increasing interference by international actors and policies in the local enjoyment of land? We argue that making the right to land operational as a human right is the way forward. Indeed, rural and urban people have been de facto claiming this right for long time. La Via Campesina, for instance, has included in its *Declaration on the Rights of Peasants* that peasants, women and men, have a right to land and territory (La Via Campesina, 2009). Demands for a right to land are therefore not new. However, what is new, and should not be underestimated, is the policy space and opportunity for advancing such a progressive project that exists in the present historical moment; land is being discussed at the global level like never before and the successful negotiations of the Tenure Guidelines and the ongoing work at the Committee on World Food Security on the principles on responsible agriculture investment (McKeon, 2013, pp. 105–122; McMichael, 2013, pp. 47–64) confirm that there is some space to create new global governance.

First, there is a normative and legal basis that exists around which to operationalize the human right to land. Take international human rights treaty law that already recognizes the right to land for indigenous and tribal peoples in ILO Convention 169 and the UN Declaration on the Rights of Indigenous Peoples (UNDRIP). Also important, there has been a move in international human rights advocacy and practice to recognize that for all human beings and communities land is indispensable for the enjoyment of various economic, social, and cultural rights, such as the right to food, the right to housing, the right to an adequate standard of living, the right to culture, the right to work, and the right to self-determination and rural women's rights (De Schutter 2009, 2010a, 2010b; Gelbspan and Nagaraj, 2012; Kothari, 2007; OHCHR, 2010).[2]

Despite increased awareness about the inextricable connection between land and several human rights, a clear human rights approach specific to land issues has not been articulated under the existing international human rights framework. The current international human rights treaty framework only refers to the right to land and territory of indigenous peoples. Consequently for non-indigenous peoples this means they cannot directly claim the right to land but instead requires them to take recourse through a multitude of other human rights like food, housing, work, culture, which fragment the arguments. This puts people from communities that are non-indigenous but depending on land in a vulnerable position vis-à-vis states that are depriving them of their lands and territories or failing to protect them against such abuses because they cannot directly claim protection under a right to land but instead indirectly through evoking other multiple rights.

Relying on other human rights to get at the land issue is a risky strategy. The human right to food has been the human rights most referred to with respect to the global governance of land grabbing. However, claiming the right to food alone in the context of land grabbing fails to capture the true scope of related human rights violations. The interpretation of the right to food for example leaves open whether people feed themselves through direct cultivation of lands or through an income and food distribution system. This flexible interpretation has been misused to justify removing people from their lands because they are not using land 'sufficiently/efficiently/sustainably' while claiming that their right to food would be 'better realized' through income gained from promised jobs—which rarely materialize (Li, 2011), or corporate social responsibility/safety net schemes which seldom are little more than charity. A similar argument can be made regarding the right to housing. Even though the right to housing goes beyond the mere buildings, rural communities are vulnerable to losing their communal and agricultural lands or their grazing and seasonally used lands in processes of resettlement because they are compensated for their houses and garden plots only—if this happens at all (FIAN, 2010b).

The state is an important part of the governance equation. A significant share of contemporary land grabbing is occurring on lands which are formally owned by the state and to which occupying communities enjoy different degrees of recognition and protection of their custom-ary/ancestral/informal land rights (Alden Wily, 2012). State authorities—in many cases relying on legal doctrines which were introduced to justify land dispossession by colonial powers—continue to believe that they are vested with power to dispose of these lands at will. Scott (1998) have identified three distinct but interrelated dimensions of state action that can be seen configuring land grabbing: (1) simplification of land-based social relations to render complex social relations 'legible' to state administration and control (i.e. only what it is in the state land records exist, individual property rights are seen as the only land rights enjoying full respect and protection by the state); (2) the assertion of sovereignty and authority over ter-ritory (i.e. right of discovery, terra nullius doctrine, wasteland/vacant lands thesis); and (3) the use of state-sanctioned armed force to ensure compliance, extend territorialization of the nation-state, and broker for private capital accumulation. This type of behavior and the legal land regimes inherited from colonial powers are deep-seated in the structure of many contemporary states, especially in the Global South. Instead of applying policies of restitution and redress of historic land dispossession, of full recognition and protection of customary and ancestral land rights, and of redistribution of private and public lands in cases of widespread landlessness and highly unequal patterns of land ownership, states are facilitating further privatization, com-modification, and (re-)concentration of land in response of the economic drivers mentioned above but also because their legal frameworks makes it easy for them to do so.

The human right to land contributes to challenging this increasing inclination by states, IFIs and investors to treat land and related natural resources as commodities ruled by distant market signals and to concentrate the control of vital resources in the hands of a few. The human right to land provides the necessary political and ethical challenge to the legal doctrines and traditional legal frameworks governing land inherited from colonial states which give unlimited power to the state to dispose over land and do not adequately recognize and protect customary/ancestral/informal land rights, and to policy reforms that encourage further privatizing and commodifying of land. Constitutional and legal frameworks governing land in rural areas have yet to even be reformed on the basis of the right to food or housing. The right to land as human right, however, can be applied successfully to this effect, as indigenous peoples have already done in several countries by referring to ILO Convention 169 (ILO, 2008). The full normative and strategic value of ILO Convention 169 is yet to be fully appreciated and there is a need for further activist and scholarly work and collaboration for using the convention as a model for operationalizing the human right to land.

Applying the right to land as a human right supports the already significant grassroots mobil-ization of the myriad of rural and urban groups defending their lands or demanding access to land. As elaborated in more detail elsewhere (see Monsalve Suárez, forthcoming), the potential of using human rights in agrarian struggles varies at the local and national levels and can range from contributing to the empowerment of oppressed groups to stand up for their rights, decreas-ing violence in land conflicts, changing the way conflicts over resources are framed, opening up space for policy dialogue centered on people's lives, and fighting against agrarian legislation biased in favor of corporate interests and formulating alternative legal frameworks.

We define the human right to land as *the right of every human being to access—individually or as a community—local natural resources in order to feed themselves sustainably, to house them-selves, and to live their culture.* The right to land is not a right to property and it does not refer to rights to buy or sell land. Nor it is a right to make a profit with land; the right is limited to its use for communities and individuals feeding themselves and nurturing their cultures. The human right to land does not provide a right to far away lands; the lands meant under the right to land are local. As with all other human rights, states have the obligation to respect, protect, and fulfill the right to land. The obligation to respect means that states must respect and not destroy existing access to and control over land by communities or individuals using it in the way described above. Civil codes and domestic property law (including also those that relate to international investment and investor protection) might need to be revised in order to fully recognize customary/ancestral/informal land rights and their governing systems and to overcome legal doctrines which deprive people of the lands they use to feed and house themselves and live their cultures. States must protect peoples' use of the land—and control over it—from interference by profit-seeking third parties whether they be other national elites, TNCs, or foreign states. States must also fulfill and facilitate sustainable access to, use of, and control over land for those who use it in the sense of the idea of a human right to land. This may require states to structure the land tenure system in a way that would allow all citizens access to land to feed themselves, to house themselves, and to provide an adequate standard of living for themselves. States must thus ensure policy environments which allow people to make sustainable use of the land to feed themselves, and to decide in a self-determined way how to develop their lands taking into account the right to land of future generations. In this sense, a sustainable use of land, conservation of soil fertility and biodiversity are also important components of the right to land.

Does the human right to land mean that everyone is entitled to get a piece of land? Obviously not. The right to housing does not mean that everyone gets a house; nor does the right to food mean that everyone gets free meals. The human right to land, as any other human right, is first and foremost for those who are deprived of a certain standard which is needed to be able to conduct a life in dignity.

The Significance of Extraterritorial Human Rights Obligations in an Era of Globalization

Globalization in general and the global land grab in particular make it necessary to pay particular attention to the international and transnational dimensions of the human right to land. FIAN has seen in its case studies that people on the ground increasingly face the challenge to defend themselves against powerful foreign actors like TNCs, institutional investors, agents of foreign states (e.g. development agencies, sovereign wealth funds, state-owned firms, and other partnership ventures), and multilateral institutions. Whereas we have a much better understanding of the international dimensions of land grabbing, such as that played by global finance (Sassen, 2013, pp. 25–46) and by state-sponsored acquisitions (McMichael, 2013, this volume), land grabbing scholarship has as yet underappreciated other dimensions such as that played by ODA. The case of Niassa province discussed earlier needs to be put into context: Mozambique, an extremely poor country, depends on ODA to fund half of its national budget; dependency results in a very unequal power relationship that virtually ensures that Mozambique gives into the pressures of its donors. Instead of the far too common kneejerk reaction to blame 'weak' states, Swedish government and business involvement in Niassa is an important part the story of why the government of Mozambique is actively promoting large-scale tree plantations while also disregarding its own national laws that exist to protect people's customary rights to land. Therefore, the responsibility for the human rights problems related to this type of 'development' cannot be pinned exclusively on Mozambique; Sweden, and other home states of investors, also carry responsibilities for the human rights impacts in Niassa (Windfuhr, 2005).

As economic globalization has deepened, so too has the power of TNCs and multilateral institutions. Neither of these is properly regulated at the global level. The regulation of TNCs was left to the host states under a peculiar legal construction that regards TNCs as separate legal entities under separate jurisdictions, even when de facto they are one business organism operating on a global scale but linked to place where they are headquartered—usually in an OECD country. With respect to many multilateral institutions, their activities in Southern states have often completely ignored the international human rights obligations, in many cases, these institutions encourage states to completely disregard these obligations (think structural adjustment programs). In fact, multilateral institutions have long rationalized this approach when it comes to their aid and financial programs on the basis of a doctrine that they (in particular the World Bank) are not mandated to deal with human rights and, hence, opted to ignore human rights altogether (Skogly, 2005). The IFIs, as well as many states, have long held the line that human rights are relations limited to national borders claiming human rights are relations between states and it residents.

Indeed, this particular view of who has human rights obligations and at which scale has been the subject of intense legal and political debate in the international human rights system. There is a crucial point at the heart of many globalization problems, although it may seem rather simple when expressed: states hold certain human rights obligations towards persons outside of their territories. These are known as extraterritorial obligations (ETOs); ETOs have often gone unrecognized in the law, policy, and practice of many states. This has undermined the regulatory capacities of the international community and has failed to uphold the universality of human rights.

The reductionism to territorial obligations has led to a vacuum of human rights protection in a number of international political processes and a paucity of regulations at the global level based on human rights in order to promote their protection. The situation is particularly challenging in the field of economic, social, and cultural rights (by comparison, states have been more supportive of applying ETOs in the realm of civil and political rights such as in the Responsibility to Protect or in granting asylum). Human rights proponents, including from the UN human rights system, NGOs, independent experts (such as the UN special rapporteurs), and academics have identified gaps in human rights protection that have become more severe in the context of globalization during the past 20 years, including: (1) the lack of human rights regulation and accountability of TNCs; (2) the missing human rights accountability of multilateral institutions, in particular the IFIs; (3) the current ineffectiveness in application of human rights law when compared to international investment and trade law; and (4) the failing implementation by states of the corresponding duties to protect and fulfill economic, social, and cultural rights abroad inter alia in their international cooperation and assistance policies.

Advancing Extraterritorial Obligations

The first steps to address these shortcomings and to mainstream states' ETOs have been taken. Since 1999, the UN Committee on Economic, Social and Cultural Rights (CESCR) has consistently referred to ETOs in its series of 'general comments' (i.e. authoritative expert legal opinion in the international human rights system) and elaborated in very sophisticated but pragmatic ways the human rights obligations in multilateral and bilateral contexts. NGOs have contributed to this work by regularly submitting parallel reports to the CESCR that have focused exclusively on the breaches of ETOs by states, which have served as a de facto monitoring of ETOs and increased the reputational pressure on states and non-state actors in the absence of direct mechanisms to do so. The expertise of academics (especially international legal scholars) and activists also play a significant role in expanding and adding precision to the concept of ETOs in what is now a voluminous literature on the subject (see, e.g. Coomans, 2011; Coomans and Künnemann, 2012; Langford et al., 2013).

A transnational experts network on ETOs now exists; in the summer of 2007 an 'ETO Consortium' was set up that now includes more than 70 NGOs and academics (see http://www.etoconsortium.org). The ETO Consortium's aim is to address the 'reductionism to territorial obligations' and 'to mainstream extraterritorial obligations with academia, community-based organizations and other CSOs, at the UN, at international, regional and national human rights bodies and with the States' (ETO Consortium, 2012). FIAN is a member of the ETO Consortium and one of the authors sits on its Steering Committee. As a transnational expert network, the ETO Consortium is primarily engaged in intellectual work, such as studying existing national and international case law and advancing the conceptual dimensions of ETOs. This work is particularly valuable for activists who see the strengthening of ETOs vis-à-vis economic, social, and cultural rights as an essential human rights response to the negative consequences of globalization and to steer the evolution of international human rights law towards progressive ends.

States have been reluctant to support integrating ETOs as legal practice in the sphere of economic, social, cultural rights. However, there are several ongoing initiatives at the global level that deal with ETOs directly. The negative impact that TNCs can have on human rights is not a new discovery.[3] In 2003, largely in response to growing public awareness of massive human rights abuses in the extractive sector and apparel industries, the UN Sub-Commission on the Promotion and Protection of Human Rights developed the *Norms on the Responsibilities of Transnational Corporations and Other Business Enterprises with Regard to Human Rights* (UNSCPHR, 2003). These 'Norms' were the first attempt within the UN system to go beyond mere recommendations, appeals, and invitations to TNCs, and instead to set out in legal terms the obligations for TNCs to respect human rights and to provide a regime of sanctions in case of non-compliance. The 'Norms' were unique in that it was a 'nonvoluntary initiative' to regulate business at the global level (see Ruggie, 2007, p. 820). However, the 'Norms' were not adopted by the Human Rights Commission, due to resistance by the International Chamber of Commerce, TNCs, and other global private sector lobbying groups.

Instead the UN in 2005 established a special procedure that eventually led to the recent *Guiding Principles on Business and Human Rights*, written by the international relations scholar John Ruggie in his capacity as special representative to the UN Secretary General, and which was adopted by the UN Human Rights Council in 2011 (Ruggie, 2011). Whereas the Guiding Principles have been lauded by many, in FIAN's view it largely remains on the level of recommendations, and as such, does not advance the human rights agenda by outlining regulation via binding obligations of corporations. However, the Guiding Principles do clearly spell out the state's obligation to protect against human rights abuses by business within the state's territory and/or jurisdiction. Moreover, it includes a responsibility of TNCs to respect human rights. However, it is not more than a strong recommendation by states for businesses to abstain from human rights abuses abroad.

One aspect of the Guiding Principles that is highly controversial is their claim that there is no direct legal obligation of TNCs under international law to respect human rights. This particular claim is rejected by considerable parts of global civil society and by numerous international legal experts.[4] The protect-obligation framework of the Guiding Principles is open to extraterritorial interpretation depending on the concept of jurisdiction used; however, in general it does not really meaningfully contribute to advancing ETOs. The comments included in the Guiding Principles document do not see a general obligation for states to regulate TNCs domiciled within their border abusing human rights abroad. States are merely asked to 'set out clearly the expectation' that such enterprises respect human rights throughout their operations.

Another global-level effort to address governance gap when it comes to ETOs has been spearheaded by the international legal community. In September 2011, Maastricht University and the International Commission of Jurists convened in September 2011 an international expert conference in order to issue an authoritative legal opinion document to offer a concise systematic presentation and summary of international legal standards on ETOs in the context of economic, social, and cultural rights available to national decision makers and at the UN. This expert opinion is in the tradition of agenda-setting and norm-building work in international human rights law such as the 1986 *Limburg Principles on the Implementation of the International Convention on Economic, Social and Cultural Rights* and the 1997 *Maastricht Guidelines on Violations of Economic, Social and Cultural Rights*. The Maastricht conference included the attendance of 40 experts from universities and organizations located in all regions of the world, among them current and former members of international human rights treaty bodies, regional human rights bodies, and former and current special rapporteurs of the United Nations Human Rights Council.

The conference outcome, *the Maastricht Principles on Extraterritorial Obligations of States in the area of Economic, Social and Cultural Rights,* (see Maastricht ETO Principles, 2011) provides clear legal guidance that a state carries in fact the obligation to protect against business abuses abroad when a TNC is registered or its controlling company has substantial business activities in the home state's territory. Furthermore the Maastricht Principles note that states have to take and enforce protective measures against abuses by TNCs, 'where there is a reasonable link between the state concerned and the conduct it seeks to regulate' (see Article 25d of the Maastricht ETO Principles).

More recently, the ETO Consortium set up a thematic working group on land grabbing, TNCs, and extractive industries with the aim to advance the application of Maastricht ETO Principles to land grabbing cases and advocacy work. To illustrate how this could be done, FIAN and other organizations are demanding that the Swedish government conduct a human rights impact assessment (HRIA) of the forest policy promoted by Swedish ODA in Niassa, Mozambique, and the Chikweti Forests of Niassa project in particular, and adopt effective measures to ensure cessation of violations of the right to food in Niassa as well as provide effective remedies (see Box 1 above). Moreover, FIAN and its allies have called on Sweden to also regulate the investment fund GSFF so that it is compelled to disclose all relevant information about the tree plantations projects, to compensate communities for the damages and losses suffered, and to introduce a complaint mechanism for the local population to provide remedy in cases of abuses by GSFF. FIAN is also demanding that Sweden and other home states of investors to the GSFF (i.e. the Netherlands and Norway) introduce a national complaints mechanism to investigate human rights abuses of TNCs and other business enterprises that would introduce monitoring mechanisms in the respective embassies of the states in Mozambique to track TNC activities and create a formal process where state officials would receive directly the complaints of local human rights defenders related to violations of legitimate tenure rights and human rights (in this case following the existing EU Guidelines on Human Rights Defenders). Furthermore, FIAN is also requesting Sweden, the Netherlands, and Norway to enact domestic laws (criminal or civil) that are applicable to extraterritorial human rights abuses (on the bases of companies and directors) and give foreign victims standing in national courts (FIAN, 2012).

Conclusion

FIAN's collected evidence on human rights violations related to land indicate that the current international responses to the global land grab are insufficient in the sense that they address some aspects of the problem but leave outside their scope many situations of human rights abuses. To address this governance gap, we argue for the promotion and application of the right to land as a human right. The human right to land will provide a more comprehensive response to the global land grab and to the increasing interference by international and transnational actors and policies on the local enjoyment of land by vulnerable peoples. The human right to land is a crucial missing element in the international human rights treaty framework necessary in order to stop and rollback the current drive to privatize and commodify the land that leads to the dispossession of local people. The human right to land fundamentally challenges the legal doctrines and frameworks that currently govern land. Existing laws were inherited from the era of colonialism, and today seem to give states unlimited power over land. These colonial-era legal ideas are impediments to implementing effective redistributive measures in the Global South and provide a framework for policy reforms conducive towards privatizing and commodifying land. Applying the right to land as a human right provides a powerful legal tool to support the mobilization of the myriad of rural and urban groups defending their lands or demanding land.

In the current situation, the international dimension of the right to land holds particular importance. ETOs in general—and the Maastricht ETO Principles in particular—help overcome some of the weaknesses in existing international human rights law and transnational governance. ETOs obligations may turn out to be the missing link for human rights to acquire the conceptual strength for upholding the legal primacy of human rights over all other legal regimes such as trade and finance in times of deepening globalization. Instead of expecting one single international organization or policy initiative to tackle the global land grab, ETOs are a range of norms that all states have to comply with in different policy fields, at different levels of operation (domestic, abroad, and when acting in international organizations) in order to ensure the realization of the right to land. The application of the Maastricht ETO Principles can close many of the key governance gaps in the international human rights framework. The biggest gap in protection, of course, remains the failure so far to establish a World Court on Human Rights to which victims can turn if they do not find remedy at national or regional levels. Such a court would also have to be open for complaints against TNCs. For the moment, human rights offer an important contribution to resist land grabbing and this essay has shown in the case of Niassa that there are many practical ways to address the gaps and limitations in the current application of human rights. After all, the history of human rights has been one of decades of struggle first for their recognition, and later for their implementation. The contemporary struggles around the human right to land are part of this evolving history and make clear that human rights are about protecting peoples' control of the resources that are essential for conducting a self-determined life in dignity and in community with others.

Acknowledgements

We would like to thank the anonymous peer reviewers and the editors for their helpful comments and suggestions.

Notes

1   FIAN conducts its investigation and documentation work according to the methodologies developed by UN human rights bodies and human rights organizations. See http://www2.ohchr.org/english/bodies/cescr/. FIAN relies on field

visits and first-hand information, such as testimonies from victims and authorities involved in the cases, legal complaints, and the like; as well as on secondary sources such as media and academic articles, NGO reports, etc. for its investigation and documentation work.

2   For a comprehensive interpretation of existing human rights standards backing the recognition of a right to land see Annex II to the CSO's Proposals for the FAO guidelines on responsible governance of land and natural resources tenure. Available at http://www.fian.org/resources/documents/others/civil-society-organizations-proposals-for-the-fao-guidelines-on-responsible-governance-of-land-and-natural-resources-tenure/pdf.

3   The UN Conference on Trade and Development (UNCTAD) attempted unsuccessfully to draft international codes for business in the 1970s. Early codification of 'corporate social responsibility' dates back to the 1976 OECD *Guidelines for Multinational Enterprises* and 1977 ILO *Tripartite Declaration of Principles Concerning Multinational Enterprises.*

4   For example those who signed a joint statement in January 2011: Companies' obligations to respect human rights abroad, available at http://www.fian.org/resources/documents/others/companies-obligations-to-respect-human-rights-abroad/pdf.

References

Alden Wily, L. (2012) Briefs on reviewing the fate of customary tenure in Africa (Washington: Rights and Resources).

APRODEV, CIFCA, FIAN, FIDH, Rel-UITA, & Via Campesina (2011) Human rights violations in Bajo Aguan, Honduras: International Fact-Finding Mission Report, http://www.fian.org/resources/documents/others/honduras-human-rights-violations-in-bajo-aguan/pdf.

Borras, S. & Franco, J. (2012a). Global land grabbing and trajectories of agrarian change: a preliminary analysis, *Journal of Agrarian Change,* 12(1), pp. 34–59.

Borras, S. & Franco, J. (2012b). A land sovereignty alternative? Towards a people's counter-enclosure (Amsterdam: Transnational Institute).

Borras, S., Hall, R., Scoones, I., White, B., & Wolford, W. (2011) Towards a better understanding of global land grabbing: an editorial introduction, *Journal of Peasant Studies,* 38(2), pp. 209–216.

Brot für die Welt, EED, & FIAN (2006) Germany's extraterritorial human rights obligations in multilateral development banks, http://www.fian.org/resources/documents/others/germanys-extraterritorial-human-rights-obligations-in-multilateral-development-banks/pdf.

Brot für die Welt, FIAN International, & Interchurch Organization for Development Cooperation (2010) Land grabbing and nutrition: challenges for global governance, http://www.rtfn-watch.org/.

Brot für die Welt, FIAN, GegenStrömung, Misereor, & Deutsche Komission Justitia et Pax (2011) Extraterritorial state obligations: parallel report in response to the 5th Periodic Report of the Federal Republic of Germany on the implementation of the International Covenant on Economic, Social and Cultural Rights (Cologne: FIAN Germany).

CESCR (1999) General Comment 12 on the right to adequate food (Geneva: CESCR).

Claeys, P. & Vanloqueren, G. (2013) The minimum human rights principles applicable to large-scale land acquisitions or leases, *Globalizations,* 10(1), pp. 193–198.

Committee on World Food Security (CFS) (2012) *Voluntary Guidelines on Responsible Governance of Tenure of Land, Fisheries and Forests in the Context of National Food Security* (Rome: FAO).

Coomans, F. (2011) The extraterritorial scope of the International Covenant on Economic, Social and Cultural Rights in the work of the United Nations Committee on Economic, Social and Cultural Rights, *Human Rights Law Review,* 11(1), pp. 1–35.

Coomans, F. & Künnemann, R. (2012) *Cases and Concepts on Extraterritorial Obligations in the Area of Economic, Social and Cultural Rights* (Antwerp and Oxford: Intersentia).

Cotula, L. (2012a) The international political economy of the global land rush: a critical appraisal of trends, scale, geography and drivers, *Journal of Peasant Studies,* 39(3–4), pp. 649–680.

Cotula, L. (2012b) *Human Rights, Natural Resource and Investment Law in a Globalized World: Shades of Grey in the Shadow of the Law* (London: Routledge).

Cotula, L., Vermeulen, S., Leonard, R., & Keeley, J. (2009) *Land Grab or Development Opportunity? Agricultural Investment and International Land Deals in Africa* (London: International Institute for Environment and Development).

ETO Consortium (2012) Report of the 5th Conference of the ETO-Consortium, Geneva, 6–7 March 2012, http://www.etoconsortium.org.

De Schutter, O. (2009) Report of the Special Rapporteur on the right to food, Olivier De Schutter. Addendum: Large-scale land acquisitions and leases: a set of minimum principles and measures to address the human rights challenge (Geneva: HRC).

De Schutter, O. (2010a) The emerging human right to land, *International Community Law Review*, 12(3), pp. 303–334.

De Schutter, O. (2010b) Access to land and the right to food: Interim Report of the Special Rapporteur on the Right to Food, Olivier De Schutter, to the 65th session of the General Assembly (New York: UN).

Fairhead, J., Leach, M., & Scoones, I. (2012) Green grabbing: a new appropriation of nature?, *Journal of Peasant Studies*, 39(2), pp. 237–262.

FAO (2004) Voluntary Guidelines to Support the Progressive Realization of the Right to Adequate Food in the context of national food security, adopted by the 127th session of the FAO Council, November 2004 (Rome: FAO).

FIAN (2006) La reforma agraria en Paraguay. Informe de la misión investigadora de FIAN y La Vía Campesina sobre el estado de la realización de la reforma agraria en tanto obligación de derechos humanos (Heidelberg and Tegucigalpa: FIAN).

FIAN (2010a) Land grabbing in Kenya and Mozambique. A report of two research missions and a human rights analysis of land grabbing (Heidelberg: FIAN).

FIAN (2010b). Desenvolvemento para quem? Impacto dos Projetos de Desenvolvimento sobre os Direitos Sociais da População Rural Moçambicana (Heidelberg: FIAN).

FIAN (2012) The human rights impacts of tree plantations in Niassa province, Mozambique (Heidelberg: FIAN).

FIAN Ecuador (2007) La lucha contra el secuestro del agua. El Proyecto Hidroeléctrico de Baba en Ecuador y su impacto en los Derechos al Agua y la Alimentación (Quito: FIAN).

FIAN & WACAM (2008) Submission of FIAN International, in cooperation with FIAN Ghana and the Wassa Association of Communities affected by Mining (WACAM) to the Office of the High Commissioner for Human Rights on human rights violations in the context of large-scale mining in Ghana (Geneva: OHCHR).

Gelbspan, T. & Nagaraj, V. (2012) Seeding hope? Land in the international human rights agenda: challenges and prospects (ESCR Net and International Council on Human Rights Policy).

Goetz, G. (2103) Private governance and land grabbing: the Equator Principles and the Roundtable on Sustainable Biofuels, *Globalizations*, 10(1), pp. 199–204.

GRAIN (2008) *Seized: The 2008 Land Grab for Food and Financial Security* (Barcelona: GRAIN).

Herre, R. (2010) German Investment Funds Involved in Land Grabbing (Cologne: FIAN Germany).

Housing and Land Rights Network (HLRN) (2010) Human rights, people and the land, paper presented to the Land Forum II: Middle East and North Africa (Cairo: Land Forum).

International Land Coalition (ILC) (2011) Tirana Declaration: Securing land access for the poor in times of intensified natural resources competition, http://www.landcoalition.org/about-us/aom2011/tirana-declaration.

ILO (2008) *Application of Convention N. 169 by Domestic and International Courts in Latin America: A Casebook*, http://www.ilo.org/wcmsp5/groups/public/—ed_norm/—normes/documents/publication/wcms_123946.pdf.

Kothari, M. (2007) *UN Basic Principles and Guidelines on Development-Based Evictions and Displacement: Annex 1 of the report of the Special Rapporteur on adequate housing as a component of the right to an adequate standard of living to the Human Rights Council* (Geneva: HRC).

La Via Campesina (2009). Declaration on the Rights of Peasants—Women and Men, http://viacampesina.net/downloads/PDF/EN-3.pdf.

Langford, M., Vandenhole, W., Scheinin, M., & Genugten, W. (2013) *Global Justice, State Duties: The Extra-Territorial Scope of Economic, Social and Cultural Rights in International Law* (Cambridge: Cambridge University Press).

Li, T. M. (2011) Centering labor in the land grab debate, *Journal of Peasant Studies*, 38(2), pp. 281–298.

Maastricht ETO Principles (2011) Maastricht Principles on Extraterritorial Obligations of States in the area of Economic, Social and Cultural Rights (Maastricht: University of Maastricht & International Commission of Jurists), http://icj.w-pengine.netdna-cdn.com/wp-content/uploads/2012/05/Maastricht-Principles-analysis-brief-2011.pdf.

McKeon, N. (2013) 'One does not sell the land upon which the people walk': land grabbing, rural social movements, and global governance, *Globalizations*, 10(1), pp. 105–122.

McMichael, P. (2013) Land grabbing as security mercantilism in international relations, *Globalizations*, 10(1), pp. 47–64.

Margulis, M. E. & Porter, T. (2013) Governing the global land grab: multipolarity, ideas, and complexity in transnational governance, *Globalizations*, 10(1), pp. 65–86.

Margulis, M. E., McKeon, N. & Borras, S. M. (2013) Land grabbing and global governance: critical perspectives, *Globalizations*, 10(1), pp. 1–23.

Monsalve Suárez, S. (forthcoming) Grassroots voices: the human rights framework in contemporary agrarian struggles, *Journal of Peasant Studies*.

OHCHR (2010) Consultation on Land and Human Rights: Background paper prepared by the Research and Right to Development Division (RRDD), Human Rights and Economic and Social Issues Section (HRESIS) (Geneva: OHCHR).

Peterson, L. E. (2009) *Human Rights and Bilateral Investment Treaties: Mapping the Role of Human Rights Law Within Investor-State Arbitration* (Montreal: Rights & Democracy), http://www.dd-rd.ca/site/_PDF/publications/globalization/HIRA-volume3-ENG.pdf.

PRAI (2010) Principles for Responsible Agricultural Investments that Respect Rights, Livelihoods and Resources. The World Bank, FAO, UNCTAD and IFAD, https://www.responsibleagroinvestment.org/rai/

Ruggie, J. G. (2007) Business and human rights: the evolving international agenda, *The American Journal of International Law*, 101(4), pp. 819–840.

Ruggie, J. G. (2011) *Guiding Principles on Business and Human Rights: Implementing the United Nations Protect, Respect and Remedy Framework* (New York: UN).

Sassen, S. (2013) Land grabs today: feeding the disassembling of national territory, *Globalizations*, 10(1), pp. 25–46.

Scott, J. D. (1998) *Seeing Like a State: How Certain Schemes to Improve the Human Condition Have Failed* (New Haven: Yale University Press).

Skogly, S. (2005) The Bretton Woods Institutions—Have human rights come in from the cold?, in M. Windfuhr (ed.) *Beyond the Nation State: Human Rights in Times of Globalization* (Uppsala: Global Publications Foundation), pp. 155–167.

UNSCPHR (2003) Norms on the responsibilities of transnational corporations and other business enterprises with regard to human rights, http://www.unhchr.ch/huridocda/huridoca.nsf/(Symbol)/E.CN.4.Sub.2.2003.12.Rev.2.En.

White, B., Borras, S., Hall, R., Scoones, I., & Wolford, W. (2012) The new enclosures: critical perspectives on corporate land deals, *Journal of Peasant Studies*, 39(3–4), pp. 619–647.

Windfuhr, M. (ed.) (2005) *Beyond the Nation State: Human Rights in Times of Globalization* (Uppsala: Global Publications Foundation).

World Bank, UNCTAD, FAO, & IFAD (2010), Principles for Responsible Investment in Agriculture, http://siteresources.worldbank.org/INTARD/214574-1111138388661/22453321/Principles_Extended.pdf.

Rolf Künnemann is the Human Rights Director of FIAN International and currently serves as the secretary to the ETO Consortium. He has 30 years of experience in human rights work around land issues in Africa, Asia, and the Americas.

Sofía Monsalve Suárez coordinates FIAN's program on Access to Natural Resources. She also coordinates the working group on agrarian reform and territory of the International Planning Committee for Food Sovereignty.

Certification Schemes and the Governance of Land: Enforcing Standards or Enabling Scrutiny?

ELIZABETH FORTIN* & BEN RICHARDSON**

*University of Bristol, Bristol, UK
**University of Warwick, Coventry, UK

ABSTRACT   *Given the challenges of upholding human rights in countries where land grabbing has been most acute, attention has turned to alternative regulatory mechanisms by which better land governance might be brought about. This essay considers one such approach: certification schemes. These encourage agricultural producers to adopt sustainability standards which are then monitored by third-party auditors. Used by the European Union to help govern its biofuel market, they now also have an important mandatory dimension. However, through a study of Bonsucro and the Roundtable on Sustainable Biofuels, we find both flaws in their standards and shortcomings in their ability to discipline the companies they are financially dependent upon. In sum, we suggest that the real value of these roundtable certification schemes might lie less in their ability to* enforce standards *than their (partially realised) role in* enabling scrutiny, *providing new possibilities for corporate accountability in transnational commodity chains.*

Introduction

'Buy land, they're not making it anymore.' Mark Twain's famous financial advice has been taken up in force during the last decade as over 200 million hectares of land have been sold, leased, licensed, or put under negotiation worldwide (International Land Coalition, 2011, p. 4). Much of this activity has taken place in countries with weak land tenure regimes, jeopardising the ability of the rural poor to block, or benefit from, this historic transformation of land control (Borras and Franco, 2012). Debates about how this should be interpreted have been marked by ideological division. Whereas some see it as bringing agricultural investment and development opportunity to the Global South, others see a further stage in the alienation of peasants from the land and the entrenchment of industrialised forms of farming that do little to reduce poverty or protect the environment (see McMichael, 2012; Robertson and Pinstrup-Andersen, 2010). Yet despite these divergent positions, consensus has arisen on the need to prevent certain *types* of acquisition, particularly those lacking effective participation of current land users and which result in forced evictions, inadequate compensation, and/or an absence of alternative livelihood opportunities for those displaced (Cotula et al., 2009; World Bank, 2011).

In the first instance, responsibility for preventing these worst forms of land grabbing has typically been placed with the legislatures and judiciaries of national governments. For example, the UN Special Rapporteur on the right to food has pressed home the need for governments to fully comply with their human rights obligations, much of which is already enshrined in domestic law, including the right of all peoples to freely dispose of their natural wealth and resources and not to be deprived of their means of subsistence (Claeys and Vanloqueren, 2013, pp. 193–198; De Schutter, 2011, p. 274; Künnemann and Monsalve Suárez, 2013, pp. 123–139). However, changing and enforcing national law is a slow, piecemeal, and indeterminate process, with reform and recognition of land rights often especially intransigent. Moreover, it has been noted that in most instances it has been national governments that have actively facilitated land grabs, acting as handmaidens to investors, both foreign and domestic, seeking large-scale plots for plantations and other export/enclave projects (Zoomers, 2010). Attention has thus turned to alternative regulatory mechanisms by which better land governance might be brought about, including corporate codes of conduct, donor conditionality, summit declarations, land reporting initiatives, and voluntary guidance on agricultural investment and land tenure management (Borras and Franco, 2010; Borras et al., 2013, pp. 161–179).

We focus our attention on yet another mode of global governance: certification schemes. These transnational, non-state initiatives pre-date popular concern with land grabbing, being largely focused on land stewardship issues related to biodiversity loss and environmental degradation. Nevertheless, they have since been touted as a means to protect land rights as well (Nuffield Council on Bioethics, 2011; Renewable Fuels Agency, 2008; WWF, 2010a). Their appeal rests on the claim that they offer a credible alternative to patchwork national law enforcement by tying the fortunes of corporations based in the Global North to the actions of their suppliers in the South. Others remain unconvinced, sceptical that private standards and certification schemes offer anything more than a novel form of corporate greenwash or a 'technical fix' to complex social problems (Friends of the Earth, 2008; Li, 2011).

This uncertainty over the effectiveness of non-state certification schemes has been mirrored in the hesitant treatment they have been given by international organisations. For example, in its principles for 'responsible agro-investment', the World Bank (2010) suggested that private standards offered 'potential value added' to traditional public standards but pulled up short of recommending their actual use. Meanwhile, in its *Voluntary Guidelines on the Responsible Governance of Tenure of Land, Fisheries and Forests*, the UN Committee on World Food Security (CFS) removed a statement from an earlier draft to 'promote the development of independent and voluntary quality certification schemes' and now makes no mention of them at all (FAO, 2011, 2012). Finally, in its 'Sustainability Indicators for Bioenergy', the Group of Eight's (G8) Global Bioenergy Partnership (GBEP) ignored earlier statements by its chairman that 'labelling and certification of origin of biofuels should be agreed internationally and introduced into the global energy market' and instead opted to provide only a best-practice guide to policymakers (Clini, 2007; GBEP, 2011). In short, the various institutional guidelines all finally returned to the principle of state sovereignty, reluctant to sanction novel mechanisms of rule that might impose mandatory requirements on national governments.

Not all public authorities have been so circumspect. Most notably, the European Union (EU) has formally integrated certification schemes into the EU biofuel regime through its 2009 Renewable Energy Directive (RED). This is significant since most of the recent land deals that have been concluded have been for the production of biofuel, with the EU as one of the biggest exports markets for this commodity (International Land Coalition, 2011, p. 24). In this way, certification schemes and their associated standards have gained importance as ways of monitoring and approving land acquisition in the Global South. As with other sites of governance within the emergent 'green economy', such as the Clean Development Mechanism and the Reduced Emissions from Deforestation and Degradation (REDD) initiative, these are changing the way in which land and resources are owned and exchanged through unorthodox market and legal mechanisms (Fairhead et al., 2012). It is therefore critical to consider how these schemes seek to regulate corporate activity in relation to land tenure/transfer and to what extent they succeed in these endeavours.

This essay attempts to do this by focusing on two case studies: Bonsucro (formerly the Better Sugarcane Initiative) and the Roundtable on Sustainable Biofuels (RSB). These have been chosen, firstly, because of their applicability to biofuels, which as we have argued are central to the dynamics of land grabbing, and, secondly, given their status as two of the most ambitious schemes currently in existence in terms of their coverage of land and resource rights (German and Schoneveld, 2011). The article proceeds in the following fashion. After outlining the emergence of certification schemes within the global governance architecture, it discusses weaknesses in the two schemes evident from close analysis of their standards and audit guidance. It then goes on to consider problems encountered by certification schemes beyond 'the text', namely the structural constraints posed by the very economic environment in which they operate. Taken together, these two sets of problems suggest that these schemes cannot deliver on their claim to protect the land rights of the rural poor. As a means of *enforcing standards*, then, we find them sorely tested as a means of land governance. However, by *enabling scrutiny* of transnational commodity chains, we suggest that they might have an important, and somewhat underplayed, role in providing new possibilities for corporate accountability.

Roundtable Certification Schemes and the Adoption of Their Standards

While a variety of public and private standards-setting bodies and certification schemes exist within the world of agriculture, Bonsucro and the RSB are examples of those that have been developed by commercial and non-profit organisations in concert (see Daviron and Vagneron, 2011; Fuchs et al., 2011). These 'roundtable' initiatives can be seen as distinct to those led either by companies and their trade associations (e.g. GlobalGAP, Sustainable Agricultural Initiative) or by conservation and development NGOs (e.g. Fairtrade International, Rainforest Alliance). The forerunner of these roundtables, the Forest Stewardship Council (FSC), was established in the 1990s and has since been followed by others focusing on particular sectors (aquaculture, fisheries, and biofuels) or commodities (palm oil, cotton, soy, sugarcane, cocoa, and beef). In each case the World Wide Fund for Nature (WWF) has acted as a founder member and through these schemes has sought to convince some of the world's biggest agro-industrial producers and consumer brands to implement standards which go beyond the comfort zone of those devised in self-regulatory initiatives. By targeting those companies with the biggest impact on the supply chain, the WWF aims to 'push commodity markets to a tipping point where sustainability becomes the norm' (WWF, 2012, p. 3).

Membership of the certification scheme's administrative unit—the roundtable itself—has typically been composed of retailers, manufacturers, traders, processors, and farmers, along with global and local NGOs. As well as devising the standard against which producers will be certified, these members also elect a governing body that then oversees revisions to the standard, acceptance of new members, the commission of consultations, and the resolution of complaints that arise through their (non-judicial) grievance mechanisms. The blend of different stakeholders is not only important in bringing in industry expertise and support to the roundtable; it also has a role in garnering legitimacy for the initiative. Whereas public standards-setting bodies derive authority from the democratic mandate of the (inter)governmental institution in which they are embedded, non-state bodies have not had this option. The roundtables have thus come to set themselves higher requirements for inclusiveness, transparency, and accountability than their state-based cousins. This has been reflected in governance structures designed to facilitate input from groups in developing countries and/or with smaller budgets, the open publication of assessment and audit reports carried out on members, and the tacit acceptance that NGOs would withhold or withdraw support should egregious environmental degradation and human rights violations be detected (Bernstein and Cashore, 2007).

While responsiveness to their community of interests has provided one leg of legitimacy for the roundtables, control of companies adopting the standard has given the other (Gulbrandsen, 2008). In other words, just as important as the ownership of the standard is compliance against it. Roundtables have sought to achieve this through on-site audits by independent third-parties 'based on objective and measurable performance standards' that are 'free of conflicts of interest from parties of interest' (WWF, n.d.). Consequently, as with other types of standard-setting schemes, roundtables have come to rely on the certification bodies that conduct the audits, as well as accreditation organisations that authorise and oversee the certification bodies and thereby 'regulate the regulators'. Since certification bodies and accreditation organisations are separate companies from those that devised the standard, they are considered *in principle* to have no stake in the outcome of the certification process and are cast accordingly as independent arbitrators of production processes (Hatanaka and Busch, 2008). Out of the formal separation of powers between these three groups, then, a 'tripartite standards regime' is constituted; an institutional arrangement which has enabled 'governing at a distance' to take root in everything from organic cultivation methods to fair-trade labour practices (Loconto and Busch, 2010).

Once established, roundtables have persuaded companies to adopt their standard in two distinct ways. The best-known has been through 'eco-labelling'. This uses a certificate logo to communicate to shoppers that the product they are buying has been sustainably sourced, which in turn convinces producers to sign up to the standard and satisfy this growing market demand. In effect, this attempts to rein in harmful business practices through the market itself, constructing 'alternative spheres of production, trade and consumption' in which the extra costs of avoiding pollution or paying decent wages are internalised within the product and paid for by the consumer (Hatanaka and Busch, 2008, p. 77). The other way has been through the integration of certification requirements into state policy on trade regulation, public procurement, and natural resource management—described as a form of public–private or 'hybrid' governance (Bernstein and Cashore, 2007).

As noted above, given the high proportion of land that has been acquired to grow crops for biofuel, of particular interest to us is the way this happened in the EU RED. Through this legislation, the EU required 10% of its transport fuel to come from biofuels by 2020, and because of concerns that this might actually encourage environmental degradation as plantations expanded into peat land and forested areas, also attached criteria as to what would be considered 'sustainable' biofuel. This specified that biofuels must provide at least 35% greenhouse gas emission savings compared to fossil fuels and must *not* come from crops cultivated on land with a high biodiversity value or carbon stock. Though these are not legal requirements, since biofuels sold in the EU can only be counted against Member States' binding energy targets and qualify for tax relief once they meet them, compliance does effectively constitute a de facto market access requirement (Lin, 2011). Building on the examples that had been set by the UK, Germany, and Netherlands in their national interpretations of EU biofuel law, the EU also specified that compliance would be monitored by certification schemes (including roundtables) rather than public agencies. Accordingly, the European Commission approved a number of schemes that met the EU's two criteria and demonstrated sufficiently credible auditing procedures—the RSB and Bonsucro being two of the first seven—and which would compete with one another to service the requirements of EU biofuel suppliers for certification.

A popular criticism of certification schemes has been that since the market-oriented method of enrolment is voluntary, there is nothing requiring companies to sign up to them (Harvey and Pilgrim, 2011). This is borne out by the low levels of coverage among even the established roundtables. Both the FSC and Marine Stewardship Council were launched in the 1990s yet still only cover 5% and 12% respectively of the timber and seafood industries (WWF, 2010a, p. 9). Related to this, even when companies do sign up to a particular scheme for eco-labelling purposes, they are not obliged to have all their suppliers audited. This means that buyers and producers can engage in 'selective certification' and choose to leave the sites/companies with more intractable problems aside. However, the mandatory requirements of the EU RED mean that this critique of voluntarism is no longer completely valid. Not all instances of land grabbing are undertaken to produce biofuel destined for the EU, but many certainly are, and, to the extent that the schemes approved by the EU adequately address land tenure issues, this may prove to be a compelling way to drive industry adoption of standards and better protect the rural poor. Bonsucro, for example, has expanded rapidly since its approval by the EU, certifying over 500,000 hectares of sugarcane in just its first two years of operation (Bonsucro, 2012; area calculated by authors). To assess these claims, we now consider the specific land-related criteria contained in the standards of Bonsucro and the RSB, the level of compliance producers must reach, and the way in which auditors verify this.

Assessing the Standards and Their Notion of 'Sustainable' Land Deals

Roundtable certification schemes have addressed two key aspects of land tenure, relating, firstly, to the ownership of land by certified producers, and, secondly, to the means by which any expansion/acquisition takes place. The argument presented is that if processors can only source from those farmers and estates which have legitimate title to their land, and that any land deals affecting the supply base have to take place with the 'free, prior and informed consent' of extant users and avoid conservation areas, then land grabbing becomes an unfeasible option for producers. Put simply, those investments dependent on improperly acquired land 'would never get off the ground' if the roundtable standards were applied (WWF, 2012, p. 25). Clearly this corresponds to a particular reading of land grabs, which emphasises the legality, transparency, and procedural justice of land tenure change over those issues relating to the privatisation of common land, concentration of ownership, and social justice for marginalised groups (Margulis and Porter, 2013, pp. 65–86; Margulis et al., 2013, pp. 1–23). Nevertheless, to the extent that this attempt to uphold tenure security and equitable agreements is considered normatively appealing, at least in preventing the worst forms of land grabbing, there is good reason to explore their ability to achieve this end.

Land Tenure Criteria

Although all roundtables share this core approach to land tenure, by virtue of their unique memberships and institutional histories, the precise way in which it has been expressed in their standards has differed between them. To illustrate this, we turn first to the Bonsucro standard. In terms of the ownership of land, Bonsucro's (2011a) provisions specify that producers must 'demonstrate clear title to land in accordance with national practice and law' and show that their right to use the land is not 'legitimately contested by local communities with demonstrable rights'. Importantly, then, this provision does permit recognition of communal and open access rights alongside private property rights, and suggests that simply having state-sanctioned land title is not necessarily enough to insulate suppliers from questioning. However, the burden of proof in establishing a 'legitimate contest' rests with those displaced or dispossessed.

In this respect, the provisions of the RSB are more onerous for companies. They state that no land under legitimate dispute can be used for biofuel operations, unless such disputes have been 'settled through Free, Prior and Informed Consent (FPIC) and negotiated agreements with affected land users' (RSB, 2011a, p. 30). Moreover, in speaking explicitly of land *users* rather than those with just land *rights*, protection is explicitly extended to (non-local) groups like pastoralists that frequently access land yet do not claim title to it (Vermeulen and Cotula, 2010). Unlike the Bonsucro provisions, then, this recognises that even the rights of those formerly living on and using the land in question may themselves have been contested, and that it is a prior condition of the company establishing its own land rights that it first determine what the existing rights are. This is hugely important given that in many parts of the world, legal recognition of land rights falls short of the negotiated and contested nature of land tenure (see Broegaard, 2005; Juul and Lund, 2002). This contributes to tenure insecurity, which is particularly acute in cases when land tenure arrangements are under threat from outside intervention (Peters, 2004).

Provisions related to the acquisition of land are again treated differently. In the Bonsucro standard, the most important criterion in this respect is the one that prohibits expansion into 'high conservation value' areas, which includes those areas 'fundamental to meeting the basic needs of local communities' and 'critical to their traditional cultural identity' (Bonsucro, 2011a, p. 11). Clearly a lot rests here on interpretations of what a high conservation value area actually is, and it is arguable that in those cases where a community (constituted here by its political representatives) has entered into negotiations to sell land, then by definition it is not essential. At this point, the provisions requiring 'transparent, consultative and participatory processes' become most relevant. These specify that for any expansion, an Environmental and Social Impact Assessment (ESIA) that involves stakeholder engagement must first be conducted and complied with, and that an ongoing mechanism for consultation with these stakeholders must be present and 'consensus-driven negotiated agreements' pursued. What issues these ESIAs should contain, however, and what checks should be carried out to ensure companies have acted on any stakeholder agreements, are both left unspecified. There are also important exceptions to this requirement: if the land expansion is less than 10% of total cane area or replaces land no longer providing cane to the mill, then an ESIA is no longer needed. Given the huge size that many cane farms reach, this enables significant amounts of unmonitored land acquisition 'via the back door'.

As before, the RSB provisions appear more onerous. Along with the explicit requirement that any deal must require the *consent* of affected land users and not just their consultation, the RSB also puts in place criteria designed to reconstruct lost livelihoods, compensate for lost assets and improve the socio-economic status of local communities (RSB, 2011a, p. 15). This is intended to help deliver on the promises of waged jobs and contract farming opportunities that typically accompany large agricultural investments, but which often fail to materialise once peasants have been alienated from their land and become, in Li's phrase, 'surplus people' (Li, 2011).

Compliance Levels

The other dimension of a standard that must be interrogated is the level and scope of compliance that companies are expected to reach to become certified. Standards schemes typically allow for some measure of failure, since it is unlikely that producers will meet every single one of their varied criteria. Bonsucro and RSB are no exception to this. For its part, Bonsucro asks that producers meet five compulsory criteria in the standard and 80% of the remainder (Bonsucro, 2011a, p. 3). This is problematic for land governance insofar as the two criteria discussed above, relating to land ownership and stakeholder engagement, respectively, are *not* compulsory. This means that producers can avoid complying with these requirements and yet still gain certification by meeting those easier criteria related to management practices and factory processes. As indicated by participants during a Bonsucro auditor training session in India attended by the author, this lack of emphasis on land rights will also affect the amount of time and effort that auditors dedicate to investigating them, since verifying the core criteria is considered a more important priority for the integrity of the scheme.

Consistent with our findings above, the RSB is also more stringent when it comes to compliance, setting a higher threshold for producers to meet. All of its criteria are compulsory in the sense that none can be failed as a 'major non-compliance', which includes violations which are systemic, uncorrected from previous audits, or compromise 'the good name of the RSB' (RSB, 2011b, p. 14). Nevertheless, auditors need only visit a representative sample of between 5% and 25% of the producer's subsidiaries and affiliates—5% of a company's operations if they have been classified as low risk and 25% if high risk. Although producers do not have a choice as to which percentage of operations are audited, the sampling approach does depend on the willingness of the certification body to seek out and fully investigate issues around land disputes ahead of/during the audit.

Auditors and Verification

Consideration of the role of the auditors brings us to our final point, which concerns the different forms of evidence that exist and the voices they embody. As noted in other studies of certification schemes, the implementation of standards ultimately depends upon their auditability and this in itself imposes a highly politicised schema upon its subjects (Ponte, 2008; Silva-Castañeda, 2012). For example, research into the Roundtable on Sustainable Palm Oil (RSPO) has shown how community evidence drawn from localised and personalised markers, such as graveyards and hunting areas, is discounted in assessments of land tenure because it cannot be translated into the 'language' used by auditors (Silva-Castañeda, 2012). While the use of quantifiable targets and 'objective' measurements against 'universal' science-based indicators may be necessary in order to score companies in the same abstract way, their very use also undermines contextual understandings and negotiated practices.

In respect of our two cases, this can be demonstrated in terms of the evidence that is permissible. As revealed during a Bonsucro auditor training session, in determining land tenure claims, readily available paper-based evidence is usually sought in the first instance. However, critics of certification have argued that documents obtained from land registries often fail to recognise communal and open access land tenure because they are biased towards property rights held in private or by the state, and are also often incomplete or out of date (Friends of the Earth, 2008). Another common form of proof called for by the schemes is company documents, used to verify details of community consultations. However, while a written record that a majority of people at a particular 'stakeholder meeting' raised their hand to indicate their consent to resettlement might provide 'objective evidence' for these purposes, it would hardly prove the absence of dispute, for example, from those who did not attend the meeting or not raise their hands. Nor would it prove that such consent was free or voluntary. Existing literature on land transfers has widely criticised the notion of 'willing-seller/willing-buyer' and it is doubtful in this case that stakeholder consultations are likely to include, let alone draw out the views of, those who do not have sufficient influence in 'affected communities' to come forward themselves (Borras, 2003; Fortin, 2005). Finally, though both Bonsucro and the RSB also require auditors to conduct on-site interviews, these are conducted primarily with farmers and workers. The guidance on speaking with those *outside* the supply chain is far less prescriptive and largely left to the discretion of the auditors. This is important since it is precisely these people who are most likely to raise concerns about current patterns of land use.

The course of action taken when disputes over a company's right to land *are* detected also suffers from biases. To decide whether these are legitimate, the Bonsucro scheme instructs its auditors to gather additional information from an 'independent authority such as government or local agencies' and to evaluate 'local level solution[s] on land ownership, access and use' (Bonsucro, 2011b, p. 11). This is highly problematic in that many of the most prominent land grabs in the sugar sector—from Cambodia to Uganda—have been state-sanctioned, meaning that 'independent' bureaucrats are acutely implicated in the process of alienation (Richardson, 2012). Moreover, since land tenure disputes tend to be entrenched, complex, and potentially irresolvable, it is exceedingly difficult for auditors to decide conclusively 'whose land it is' and, in this context, to judge decisively against a company for violation of the standard (Berry, 1992; Sikor and Lund, 2009).

What should by now be evident is that simply writing in references to land tenure in standards does not guarantee that they will be upheld through the process of certification. Notwithstanding the differences between the RSB and Bonsucro standards, by looking at the minutiae of their criterion and compliance thresholds, various loopholes and limitations become apparent that negate watertight and comprehensive coverage of land issues. Moreover, through the values inscribed in global standards-setting and auditing practices, we see how the notion of a 'sustainable land deal' is constructed by actors 'dislocated and distanced from the places they govern' (Fairhead et al., 2012, p. 247). Whether the specific criteria underlying it are met or not, this helps legitimise a particular form of land acquisition that favours those able to express and evidence their claims in a legalistic manner. This is crucial when considering the extent to which such schemes protect conventions of land use that are not already secured in law or in practice, and whether they unwittingly reinforce the asymmetry of power between companies and communities, or even within communities, of the powerful against the powerless.

Structural Constraints to the Adoption and Enforcement of Private Standards

Much of the commentary on the use of roundtable certification schemes has assumed a techno-cratic character, putting forward various suggestions on how the kinds of loopholes and limit-ations identified in the previous section could be closed and overcome (see IUCN, 2010; ISEAL Alliance, 2010; UNCTAD, 2008). This is very much the world of paper standards, focused on benchmarking one certification scheme against another with a view to 'ratcheting up' and harmonising the various criteria. However, in isolating the certification schemes from the context in which they are adopted and enforced, these approaches overlook the market and capitalist structures that hinder the upward progression of standards and the ability of their administrative bodies to avoid client relations with the producers they are meant to be monitoring. As we now explore in this section, where standards remain patchy and the ability of certification schemes to enforce them weak, then their utility as a mechanism of effective land governance must be doubted.

The Market for Certification

Since certification schemes are financially dependent on their members' subscription fees and on producers' certification fees, there is a need to 'sell' their standard to those companies they are endeavouring to discipline. This creates the incentive for schemes to lower the stringency of their standards in order to attract clients, a phenomenon known in the literature on eco-labels as 'a race to the bottom' (Bartley, 2012; Haufler, 2003). What is also important to recognise, however, is the way this also applies to certification schemes operating under the EU RED. Under this regime, the European Commission have approved a number of schemes that simply meet the minimum criteria on GHG emissions and conservation. So, while schemes like Bonsucro and RSB go beyond these to cover land tenure issues as well (albeit imperfectly) other approved schemes do not. As Table 1 shows, the seven schemes initially approved were highly uneven on the issues they covered, with some, namely those industry-led standards, con-taining no reference to land and resource rights whatsoever. An incentive to 'shop around' was thus created, as biofuel producers with contentious land claims would be able to opt for certifi-cation schemes with weaker standards. The dilemma this creates for the roundtables has been openly recognised by the RSB:

> How do we make compliance with RSB standards practical and cost-effective for companies while addressing complex issues such as biodiversity, food security or land rights? In other words, how can the RSB cope with fierce competition from a number of emerging schemes offering cheap and simple alternatives, while at the same time remaining true to its aspirations of comprehensively addressing sustainability? (RSB, 2012a, p. 1)

For its part, the WWF has called for European policymakers to raise the floor of permissible standards by including more mandatory criteria in the RED (WWF, 2012, p. 25; see also Oxfam, 2011a). Other NGOs have criticised the EU's decision to grant licenses to schemes that fail to protect local communities and prevent deforestation, with some even suing the Commission for failing to release details about the approval process (ClientEarth, 2011). In lieu of regulatory change, the RSB itself has responded through institutional innovation. It has spun out a separate sister company, 'RSB Services', from the original standards development organisation now known as 'RSB Standards'. The role of RSB Services, which is not 'multi-stakeholder' but simply a non-profit corporate entity, is to manage the certification scheme, market the standard, and expand its uptake.

Table 1. Land and resource rights addressed in EU-approved certification schemes

	Industry-led schemes				Roundtable schemes		
	Abengoa	Biomass, Biofuel, Sustainability Voluntary Scheme (2BSVs)	Greenergy	Bonsucro	International Sustainability & Carbon Certification (ISCC)	Roundtable on Sustainable Biofuels (RSB)	Round Table on Responsible Soy (RTRS)
Proof of legal ownership or lease	–	–	High	High	High	–	High
Proof that land tenure is not under dispute	–	–	–	High	–	High	–
Prohibition of involuntary land acquisition/resettlement	–	–	Low	–	–	High	–
Free, Prior and Informed Consent as the basis for decision-making on the relinquishment of rights by all land owners and users	–	–	Low	–	–	High	Low
Identification of customary land and resource rights	–	–	Med	–	Low	High	Low
Identification of potential impacts on customary rights, property and resources	–	–	High	Low	–	High	–
Livelihood baselines for affected land users	–	–	–	–	–	High	–
Mitigation of negative effects on rights, land and resources	–	–	Low	Low	Low	High	–
Compensation for lost assets (land, crops, economic trees, 'improvements')	–	–	–	–	–	High	Low
Compensation for loss of access rights to common property resources	–	–	–	–	–	–	–
Livelihood reconstruction for land/resource-losing households	–	–	–	–	–	High	–
Proof of effective compensation, livelihood reconstruction and impact mitigation efforts	–	–	–	–	–	High	–

Note: The ratings here are not conclusive but indicative of the uneven coverage between different schemes; it was suggested to us in personal correspondence that the RSB does require both proof of legal ownership and compensation for loss of access rights.

Source: German and Schoneveld, 2011: 12–13.

The thinking behind such separation is that with a more 'entrepreneurial' team RSB Services will be better placed to get companies signed up to the scheme, notwithstanding the rigour of the standard (RSB, 2011c). Yet it has struggled in this endeavour, having secured the certification of just two producers in its first year of operation. This helps explain RSB's second innovation, which is its decision to form an alliance with another (NGO-led) certification scheme, the Rainforest Alliance. To lower audit costs to producers and make certification more appealing, farms already certified according to the Rainforest Alliance standards will be able to receive RSB certification through a simplified audit process, simply adding on some requirements linked to GHG emissions and food security (LaChappelle, 2012). Yet in respect of land tenure, the weaker Rainforest Alliance criteria are left intact, meaning that the more demanding aspects of the RSB's standard will be avoided and the notion of a race to the bottom again given credence.

The market for certification not only affects the ability of schemes to enrol companies without undermining their standards but also their ability to discipline them effectively once they are signed up. In principle, this should happen through the suspension of a company's certificates or expulsion from the scheme, yet the risk of penalising influential firms and losing their business acts as a powerful constraint on such action (Pattberg, 2005). The RSPO, for instance, has been accused of this failing in relation to its handling of land-use violations by the major palm producer, the IOI Group. Even after it was found guilty by the RSPO's Executive Board, the roundtable still allowed IOI to sell palm oil from its existing certified plantations, extended the timeframes for complaint responses, and failed to speak out against the company's denial of wrongdoing. This left NGOs even within the RSPO itself calling its credibility into question (Fernandez, 2011). A similar example could be found at Bonsucro, where one of its founder members, Tate & Lyle, had been buying sugar from Cambodia grown on land illegally granted to private companies by the state (Inclusive Development International, 2012). Although the company had not certified its suppliers in Cambodia, complaints were lodged by local NGOs against Tate & Lyle for violation of the Bonsucro Code of Conduct, which asks (but does not require) members to endorse its objectives and implement its standard. Yet over a year later, and during which time thousands of people remained without land or livelihoods, Tate & Lyle had still not agreed to arbitration nor had it been asked to resign its membership of Bonsucro.

These cases also illustrate the difficulty in getting companies to resolve disputes through remedial action like the restitution of land or payment of compensation. Certification schemes can push them toward this end, but as non-judicial systems they must always seek to negotiate with the 'guilty party' over the terms of their infraction. Hence it is also problematic if companies simply decide to abandon a scheme which appears to be making excessive demands upon them. The trade association for European biodiesel producers publicly resigned its membership of the RSB after a disagreement over its 'excessively complex and theoretical' approach, while Bonsucro has suffered the loss of at three major sugarcane millers after being made the subject of complaints lodged by activists. The self-withdrawal of actors whose practices contravene a given standard could be interpreted as a boon for the integrity of the roundtable schemes. However, given their very purpose is to improve the sustainability of sugarcane/biofuels production, the withdrawal of recalcitrant producers from certification schemes underlines their limited ability to actually *enforce* their standards.

Conflicts of interest resulting from the power held by companies do not just affect the independence of certification schemes but also permeate the certification process itself. We noted earlier the division of powers within the tripartite standards regime between certification schemes, auditors, and accreditation bodies that was supposed to give it credibility as a means of governance. However, while audit firms possess organisational independence from the companies and certification schemes they work for, their need to establish a reputation conducive to repeat custom means that their *operational* independence and ability to do the job without any 'outside influence' on audit quality, intensity, and adjudication is less clear-cut (Fuchs et al., 2011; Hatanaka and Busch, 2008). This claim is given empirical weight by large-N studies highlighting variance between different auditors on the varying degrees of 'toughness' in how they judge companies, with one important factor being the reluctance of auditors to flag up problems lest other companies become reluctant to hire them for their certification in the future (Albersmeier et al., 2009).

In terms of land tenure, a prominent case involving the FSC also casts doubt on the assurances of the tripartite regime to 'regulate the regulators'. In 2011, Oxfam complained to the FSC about the veracity of an audit of the New Forests Company in Uganda, which, the NGO claimed, had overlooked the eviction of 22,500 people from their land to make way for the plantations. Since the accreditation body overseeing the process had previously given the auditors a clean bill of health for its certification of the New Forest Company, the FSC therefore had to ask the auditors to investigate themselves. Yet even *after* Oxfam had informed the auditors about the evictions and told them exactly who had attested to their forced displacement, in their internal review the auditors stuck by their original decision to award the certificate, partly justified by the positive findings of the accreditation body (Oxfam International, 2011b).

The Imperative to Expand

Some critics see certification as actually facilitating land expansion, in that it sanctions as 'sustainable' a particular model of production that involves large-scale acquisitions of land. This is especially important in the context of land grabbing, where it is precisely the expansion of monoculture production to feed/fuel 'the global consumer' that is held to be accelerating dispossession through new enclosures (McMichael, 2012). While the general validity of this argument may be contestable, since most agricultural markets make little, if any, use of certification schemes to legitimate their existence, within the context of EU biofuels it does have more appeal (McCarthy et al., 2012). Certainly in the eyes of NGOs critical of the very idea of mass-market biofuels, certification is 'little more than a green fig leaf' (World Rainforest Movement, 2008) which has been used instrumentally by European politicians to 'reduce opposition to the development of agrofuels' (Biofuelwatch et al., 2008). Notably, in both the Bonsucro and the RSB standards, there is no upper limit placed on the geographical size of individual farms or total supply areas. The reason is simple: while agro-industrial companies have submitted to the inclusion of (some) land and resource rights in the various roundtable standards, they have forcefully rejected any impediments on their ability to expand (see Mier y Teran, 2011).

Another dimension to the relationship between certification and expansion is the 'knock-on' effects seen in indirect land-use change (ILUC). This refers to the changes in land use caused by biofuel production, whereby an increase in demand for biofuel 'feedstocks' in one area results in farmers in other areas converting land to fill the resultant supply gap. For example, in Brazil, as sugarcane producers have bought up commercial crop/pasture land to increase their cane supply, it has been argued that the previous occupants have either moved their cattle ranches or soybean farms into environmentally sensitive and inhabited land themselves, or else turned their hand to cane farming and created economic incentives for others to do so instead (Friends of the Earth Europe, 2010).

Critics of this process have focused on the impacts this has had on the 'real' greenhouse gas emissions of biofuels (Searchinger et al., 2008). The debate has not, however, widened to consider other forms of ILUC so as to include the adverse impacts when people are displaced or concentrated into a particular portion of land as the indirect result of the expansion of a nearby plantation. The problem roundtables face here is that they only certify land used in the production of their particular crop, or, in the case of the RSB, any crop turned into biofuel. Hence for episodes of land alienation that are indirectly caused by the expansion of a roundtable producer, but which happen beyond the boundary of its supply area, then certification schemes run up against their spatial limits. As noted even by the RSB (2011a, p. 3): 'voluntary certification alone may not be the best tool to address indirect impacts, since these macro-level impacts are likely to be beyond the control of the individual farmer or biofuels producer seeking certification'.

Roundtables and their members have sought to square the circle of indirect impacts by encouraging producers to farm on idle land, improve productivity through higher yielding crops, and make better use of plant residues—a strategy of 'sustainable intensification' also put forward by the World Bank (see Shell and IUCN, 2010; World Bank, 2011). Establishing a set of criteria that would identify biofuels produced from these sources, the WWF have suggested that certification schemes could thus promote biofuels that are less likely to result in farmers being displaced and 'virgin' land brought under cultivation (WWF, 2010b; see also RSB, 2012b). Yet the notion of underused land that is 'idle' or 'marginal' remains highly contentious—needed, still, by unnoticed 'marginal peoples'—as does the claim that increasing per hectare output necessarily leads to an aggregate reduction in the demand for land (McMichael, 2010; Nalepa and Bauer, 2012). Together, this leaves certification schemes unable to resolve the ILUC question even in theory and suggests that much more bounded claims must be made for their utility in protecting the rural poor.

Roundtables Beyond Certification: Indirect Contributions to Land Governance

The previous section laid out two sets of structural constraints that cut across all certification schemes and created systemic impediments to their ability to control what companies do on the ground. In spite of these criticisms, in this section we discuss ways *beyond* the certification process in which roundtables can contribute, albeit indirectly, to the protection of land and resource rights. As part of this enquiry, we also forward suggestions as to how these alternative contributions may be improved to better support the interests of the rural poor.

First, it has been noted that investors and host governments have every incentive to shield the land deals they conclude from public scrutiny (De Schutter, 2011, p. 274). In this respect, through the public availability of their detailed certification and monitoring audits, roundtables can help expose the details of certain land acquisition processes and illuminate wider industry practices to advocates of agrarian communities. This could be furthered by promoting engagement between locally informed civil society actors and the auditing team, preferably prior to certification, in order to gather information about land conflict ahead of the audit and bring these accounts to light as well. This would require the same kind of awareness-raising and training for community associations and NGOs as the roundtables have carried out with potential producers and auditors, and essentially asks them to extend the 'multi-stakeholder' ethos of inclusive participation into the process of certification itself.

Second, land deals can be difficult to challenge because of the power wielded by investors, especially those acting as conduits to valuable foreign markets (Zoomers, 2010). Roundtables help address this asymmetry by leveraging the influence of campaign groups against 'big brand' transnational companies, explicitly using these companies' status as roundtable members to have them adapt their purchasing practices. In this way, campaigners have also been able to target those producers outside the scheme but linked, via the supply chain, to a member within it. One example would be the lobbying of Unilever, a founder member of the RSPO, to suspend purchases from Sinar Mas, a large palm oil group with many subsidiaries outside the palm oil roundtable (Schouten and Glasbergen, 2011). Another would be the additional pressure brought to bear on Shell as a member of Bonsucro and the RSB in its decision to discontinue purchases of sugarcane grown on indigenous land in Brazil (Shell, 2011, p. 13). Roundtables could further this kind of corporate accountability through the creation of 'resolution forums' in cases where land conflict is discovered in the audit process, bringing companies to the nego-tiating table to discuss land tenure cases with representatives of the affected groups and relevant public authorities. This would complement the call of the CFS to 'set up multi-stakeholder plat-forms and frameworks' to implement its guidelines on land tenure; a task currently left to states alone (FAO, 2011, p. 39; McKeon, 2013, pp. 105–122). Moreover, it would also help integrate the certification process with those existing regulatory networks that have a strong local charac-ter, rather than with those equally remote institutions like the UN's REDD with which the round-tables are exploring ties (cf. RT-REDD Consortium, 2012; Vandergeest, 2007).

Third and finally, recent scholarship points to the ways in which private regulatory schemes like roundtables are able to create 'pathways' to improved public policy (Bernstein and Cashore, 2012; Overdevest and Zeitlin, 2012). This could be in the form of test-beds for ideas and delib-erative spaces in which controversial issues of industry regulation, such as ILUC, may be aired. It is notable that the EU's 2012 proposal to cap the use of biofuel made from food crops and apply heavier carbon emissions weightings to certain feedstocks draws on very similar ideas to those discussed in the RSB's parallel work on 'low indirect impact biofuels', particularly the need to address the impacts of biofuels on food prices and biodiversity loss (Carrington, 2012; RSB, 2012b). Another kind of pathway involves the diffusion of governance mechanisms through adaptation and replication. The early certification schemes had demonstrated to states that getting industry buy-in to tougher standards of production was a feasible option, if not entirely problem-free, and that certification itself was a mode of governance that could be readily adapted to public regulatory systems. As certain countries in the EU now look to apply certification requirements to other commodities, and other states look to and learn from the EU's experience with certification (given Europe's status as a 'green normative power' within world politics) it is possible that this tougher type of trade regulation could be replicated beyond the EU biofuel sector (Falkner, 2007).

Conclusion

This article has considered the extent to which two global sustainability standards and certifica-tion schemes, Bonsucro and the RSB, are able to protect the land rights of those whose land tenure is insecure. This is crucial given the unprecedented scale of land deals in the Global South that have been concluded over the last decade—the majority for the production of biofuels. This transnational form of global governance, produced in these two cases by 'multi-stakeholder' roundtables, steps into a regulatory vacuum that persists at both national and intergovernmental levels. However, our analysis indicates that such an approach falls short in the protection it affords against land grabs by the powerful over the powerless.

The approach taken to land acquisitions by both schemes is predicated on the logic that if processors only source from suppliers which have legitimate title to land and if land deals take place with the free, prior, and informed consent of users, then land grabs will be prohibited. Not only have we found flaws in the way the two schemes endeavour to implement this approach but we have also criticised the approach per se. It provides scope for acquisitions of land currently being used by pastoralists or for subsistence farming, provided it is done 'by the book', and legitimises the language of 'objective evidence' and 'proof', changing the terms (literally) within which markets for land and resources are constructed and managed. This is particularly important given that those land rights which are most at risk are those subject to dispute or not secured in law (Peters, 2004).

That said, Bonsucro and the RSB are two of the more rigorous schemes approved by the European Commission under its RED legislation and could be used to challenge some types of land alienation, especially those that clearly contravene national law. However, even the though the EU RED criteria defines 'sustainable biofuels' for the purposes of attaining market access, it fails to include basic criteria related to land rights. As we have pointed out, this has undermined the limited protection roundtable certification schemes do offer since they can be undercut by competitors with less stringent criteria on land tenure. Coupled with economic dependencies of both the certification schemes and the auditors upon the very companies they are seeking to discipline, as well as the inability of certification to address the implications of ILUC, we find that as a mode of governance, its efficacy to protect against land grabbing cannot be assured.

In sum, we suggest that the real value of roundtables might lie less in their ability to *enforce standards* than their (partially realised) role in *enabling scrutiny*. In so doing, we do not overlook the other side of this political bargain, namely that roundtables 'provide lead firms [in commodity chains] with a pragmatic means of ameliorating reputational risk' (McCarthy et al., 2012, p. 564). However, notwithstanding the acceleration of land alienation over the last decade, we would maintain that its steady privatisation and the concomitant displacement of peasants has been a consistent feature of world agriculture (McMichael, 2012, p. 2). As such, the immediate opportunity to open up this process to contestation, first via scrutiny of these lead firms then via lobbying and regulation, should not be readily dismissed. While they cannot give assurances that violations of existing rights and of their own standards can be prevented, roundtables are in a position to help improve existing processes of land governance. What we do concede is that certification schemes in general must be situated in a pro-poor policy framework that advances land and agrarian reform (see Borras and Franco, 2010). Since roundtables can only preserve existing land rights rather than progress new ones, foremost among these policies must be to secure the underlying rights of farmers, herders, and fisherfolk to their land (De Schutter, 2011). While we believe that certification as a mode of governance is not necessarily inimical to such efforts, focused primarily on the governance of agribusiness it does not promote the kind of rural development that can provide more and better livelihoods in the Global South.

Acknowledgements

This work was supported by a British Academy Postdoctoral Fellowship (Fortin) and a Leverhulme Trust Early Career Fellowship (Richardson). The authors would like to thank participants at the Cabot Institute seminar in Bristol at which this paper was presented, as well as the journal editors and three anonymous reviewers. Any mistakes remain our own.

References

Albersmeier, F., Schulze, H., Jahn, G. & Spiller, A. (2009) The reliability of third-party certification in the food chain: from checklist to risk-oriented auditing, *Food Control*, 20(10), pp. 927–935.

Bartley, T. (2012) Certification as a mode of social regulation, in D. Levi-Faur (ed.) *Handbook on the Politics of Regulation* (Cheltenham, UK: Edward Elgar), pp. 441–452.

Bernstein, S. & Cashore, B. (2007) Can non-state global governance be legitimate? An analytical framework, *Regulation & Governance*, 1(4), pp. 1–25.

Bernstein, S. & Cashore, B. (2012) Complex global governance and domestic policies: four pathways of influence, *International Affairs*, 88(3), pp. 585–604.

Berry, S. (1992) Hegemony on a shoestring: indirect rule and access to agricultural land, *Africa: Journal of the International African Institute*, 62(3), pp. 327–355.

Biofuelwatch, Corporate Europe Observatory, Econexus, Grupo Reflexion Rural, & Friends of the Earth Denmark (2008) Sustainability criteria and certification of biomass—greenwashing destruction in pursuit of profit, *Joint Press Release*, 18 March 2008, http://www.biofuelwatch.org.uk/docs/jointngopressrelease180308.pdf.

Bonsucro (2011a) Bonsucro Production Standard: Version 3.0, http://www.bonsucro.com/assets/Bonsucro_Production_Standard_March_2011_3.pdf.

Bonsucro (2011b) Audit Guidance for the Production Standard: Version 3, privately obtained from Bonsucro Secretariat.

Bonsucro (2012) Welcome to Bonsucro, http://www.bonsucro.com/welcome.html.

Borras, S. J. (2003) Questioning market-led agrarian reform: experiences from Brazil, Colombia and South Africa, *Journal of Agrarian Change*, 3(3), pp. 367–394.

Borras, S. J. & Franco, J. C. (2010) From threat to opportunity? Problems with the idea of a 'code of conduct' for land grabbing, *Yale Human Rights and Development Law Journal*, 13(1), pp. 507–523.

Borras, S. J. & Franco, J. C. (2012) Global land grabbing and trajectories of agrarian change: a preliminary analysis, *Journal of Agrarian Change*, 12(1), pp. 34–59.

Borras, S. M., Franco, J. C. & Wang, C. (2013) The challenge of global governance of land grabbing: changing international agricultural context and competing political views and strategies, *Globalizations*, 10(1), pp. 161–179.

Broegaard, R. (2005) Land tenure insecurity and inequality in Nicaragua, *Development and Change*, 36(5), pp. 845–864.

Carrington, D. (2012) Biodiesel industry dealt a blow by EU policy changes, *The Guardian*, 21 September 2012.

Claeys, P. & Vanloqueren, G. (2013) The minimum human rights principles applicable to large-scale land acquisitions or leases, *Globalizations*, 10(1), pp. 193–198.

ClientEarth (2011) 'European Commission seven biofuels certification schemes', *ClientEarth Press Release*, 18 July 2011, http://www.clientearth.org/news/press-releases/seven-biofuels-certificates-1435.

Clini, C. (2007) Speech by the Chair of the Global Bioenergy Partnership, http://www.globalbioenergy.org/fileadmin/user_upload/gbep/docs/2007_events/NY_07_08/speech.Clini.ny.31-07-07.pdf.

Cotula, L., Vermeulen, S., Leonard, R. & Keeley, J. (2009) *Land Grab or Development Opportunity? Agricultural Investment and International Land Deals in Africa* (London: IIED, FAO, and IFAD).

Daviron, B. & Vagneron, I. (2011) From commoditisation to de-commoditisation . . . and back again: discussing the role of sustainability standards for agricultural products, *Development Policy Review*, 29(1), pp. 91–113.

De Schutter, O. (2011) How not to think of land-grabbing: three critiques of large-scale investments in farmland, *Journal of Peasant Studies*, 38(3), pp. 249–279.

Fairhead, J., Leach, M. & Scoones, I. (2012) Green grabbing: a new appropriation of nature? *Journal of Peasant Studies*, 39(2), pp. 237–261.

Falkner, R. (2007) The political economy of 'normative power' Europe: EU environmental leadership in international biotechnology regulation, *Journal of European Public Policy*, 14(4), pp. 507–526.

Fernandez (2011) IOI Corp's palm oil not green or sustainable, *MalaysiaKini Letters*, 27 May 2011, http://www.malaysiakini.com/letters/165286.

Food and Agricultural Organization (2011) Consolidated changes to the first draft of the 'Voluntary guidelines on the responsible govenrnance of tenure of land, fisheries and forests in the context of national food security', 12–15 July and 10–15 October 2011, http://www.fao.org/fileadmin/user_upload/nr/land_tenure/pdf/First_Draft_VG_with_changes_October_2011_English.pdf.

Food and Agricultural Organization (2012) *Voluntary Guidelines on the Responsible Governance of Tenure of Land, Fisheries and Forests in the Context of National Food Security*, (FAO: Rome).

Fortin, E. (2005) Reforming land rights: the World Bank and the globalization of agriculture, *Social & Legal Studies*, 14(2), pp. 147–177.

Friends of the Earth Europe (2010) *Sugar Cane and Land Use Change in Brazil* (Brussels, Belgium: FoE).

Friends of the Earth International (2008) *Sustainability as a Smokescreen: The Inadequacy of Certifying Fuels and Feeds* (Brussels, Belgium: FoE).

Fuchs, D., Kalfagianni, A. & Havinga, T. (2011) Actors in food governance: the legitimacy of retail standards and multi-stakeholder initiatives with civil society participation, *Agriculture and Human Values*, 28(3), pp. 353–367.

German, L. & Schoneveld, G. (2011) *Social Sustainability of EU-Approved Voluntary Schemes for Biofuels* (Bogor Barat, Indonesia: Center for International Forestry Research).

Global Bioenergy Partnership Secretariat (2011) *The Global Bioenergy Partnership for Sustainable Development* (FAO: Rome).

Gulbrandsen, L. H. (2008) Accountability arrangements in non-state standards organizations: instrumental design and imitation, *Organization*, 15(4), pp. 563–583.

Harvey, M. & Pilgrim, S. (2011) The new competition for land: food, energy and climate change, *Food Policy*, 36(1), pp. S40–S51.

Hatanaka, M. & Busch, L. (2008) Third-party certification in the global agrifood system: an objective or socially mediated governance mechanism?, *Sociologia Ruralis*, 48, pp. 73–91.

Haufler, V. (2003) New forms of governance: certification regimes as social regulations of the global market, in E. Meidinger, C. Elliott & G. Oesten (eds) *Social and Political Dimensions of Forest Certification* (Remagen-Oberwinter, Germany: Forstbuch), pp. 237–247.

Inclusive Development International (2012) Cambodia clean sugar campaign, http://www.inclusivedevelopment.net/sugar/.

International Land Coalition (2011) *Land Rights and the Rush for Land* (Rome, Italy: IIED, CIRAD, and ILC).

International Union for the Conversation of Nature (2010) Workshop summary: towards harmonization for biofuel sustainability standards, http://www.iucn.org/what/tpas/energy/key/biofuels/?5828/biofuelstandardsreport.

ISEAL Alliance (2010) Our credibility principles, http://www.isealalliance.org/codes-of-good-practice/defining-credibility.

Juul, K. & Lund, C. (2002) *Negotiating Property in Africa* (Portsmouth, NH: Heinemann).

Künnemann, R. & Monsalve Suárez, S. (2013) International human rights and governing land grabbing: a view from global civil society, *Globalizations*, 10(1), pp. 123–139.

LaChappelle, J. (2012) What makes a standard credible? An interview with RSB's Sébastien Haye on efficiency with other standards, *ISEAL Alliance Blog*, 13 August 2012, http://www.isealalliance.org/online-community/blogs/what-makes-a-standard-credible-an-interview-with-rsbs-s%C3%A9bastien-haye-on-efficiency-with.

Li, T. M. (2011) Centering labor in the land grab debate, *Journal of Peasant Studies*, 38(2), pp. 281–298.

Lin, J. (2011) Governing biofuels: a principal-agent analysis of the European Union biofuels certification regime and the Clean Development Mechanism, *Journal of Environmental Law*, 24(1), pp. 43–73.

Loconto, A. & Busch, L. (2010) Standards, techno-economic networks, and playing fields: performing the global market economy, *Review of International Political Economy*, 17(3), pp. 507–536.

McCarthy, J., Gillespie, P. & Zen, Z. (2012) Swimming upstream: local Indonesian production networks in 'globalized' palm oil production, *World Development*, 40, pp. 555–569.

McKeon, N. (2013) 'One does not sell the land upon which the people walk': land grabbing, rural social movements, and global governance, *Globalizations*, 10(1), pp. 105–122.

McMichael, P. (2010) Agrofuels in the food regime, *The Journal of Peasant Studies*, 37, pp. 609–629.

McMichael, P. (2012) The land grab and corporate food regime restructuring, *Journal of Peasant Studies*, 39(3–4), pp. 681–701.

Margulis, M. E. & Porter, T. (2013) Governing the global land grab: multipolarity, ideas, and complexity in transnational governance, *Globalizations*, 10(1), pp. 65–86.

Margulis, M. E., McKeon, N. & Borras, S. M. (2013) Land grabbing and global governance: critical perspectives, *Globalizations*, 10(1), pp. 1–23.

Mier y Teŕan, M. (2011) Strengths and limitations of the Round Table for Responsible Soy—RTRS in Mato Grosso, Brazil, Paper presented at the International Conference on Land Grabbing, University of Sussex, Brighton, UK, 6–8 April 2011.

Nalepa, M. & Bauer, D. M. (2012) Marginal lands: the role of remote sensing in constructing landscapes for agrofuel development, *Journal of Peasant Studies*, 39(2), pp. 403–422.

Nuffield Council on Bioethics (2011) *Biofuels: Ethical Issues* (Abingdon, UK: Nuffield Council on Bioethics).

Overdevest, C. & Zeitlin, J. (2012) Assembling an experimentalist regime: transnational governance interactions in the forest sector, *Regulation & Governance*, doi: 10.1111/j.1748-5991.2012.01133.x.

Oxfam (2011a) The EU must urgently fix biofuels policy driving scramble for land in poor countries, *Oxfam Press Release*, 29 September 2011, http://oxfameu.blogactiv.eu/2011/09/29/the-eu-must-urgently-fix-biofuels-policy-driving-scramble-for-land-in-poor-countries/.

Oxfam (2011b) Oxfam rejects SGS report findings into its Forest Stewardship Council certification of New Forests Company, *Oxfam Press Release*, 12 December 2011, http://www.oxfam.org/en/grow/pressroom/reactions/oxfam-rejects-sgs-findings-forest-stewardship-council-certification-new-forests-company.

Pattberg, P. (2005) The Forest Stewardship Council: risk and potential of private forest governance, *The Journal of Environment and Development*, 14(3), pp. 356–374.

Peters, P. (2004) Inequality and social conflict over land in Africa, *Journal of Agrarian Change*, 4(3), pp. 269–314.

Ponte, S. (2008) Greener than thou: the political economy of fish ecolabelling and its local manifestations in South Africa, *World Development*, 36(1), pp. 159–175.

Renewable Fuels Agency (2008) *Gallagher Review of the Indirect Effects of Biofuels Production* (St. Leonards-on-Sea, East Sussex: RFA).

Richardson, B. (2012) Sugarcane and the global land grab: a primer for producers and buyers, *Ethical Sugar Discussion Paper*, August 2012, http://www.sucre-ethique.org/Sugarcane-and-the-global-land-grab.html.

Robertson, B. & Pinstrup-Anderson, P. (2010) Global land acquisition: neo-colonialism or development opportunity? *Food Security*, 2(3), pp. 271–283.

RSB (2011a) *Consolidated RSB EU RED Principles and Criteria for Sustainable Biofuel Production: Version 2.0* (Lausanne, Switzerland: EPFL).

RSB (2011b) *Consolidated RSB EU RED Requirements for the Evaluation Of and Reporting On Participating Operators: Version 2.0* (Lausanne, Switzerland: EPFL).

RSB (2011c) RSB services: functioning and governance, *BioFuel for Thought: Newsletter of the Roundtable on Sustainable Biofuels*, 2(2), pp. 2–3.

RSB (2012a) Welcome, *BioFuel for Thought: Newsletter of the Roundtable on Sustainable Biofuels*, 2(4), p. 1.

RSB (2012b) Indirect impacts, http://rsb.epfl.ch/lang/en/iieg.

RT-REDD Consortium (2012) Slowing climate change through better farming: early results of the RT-RSEDD consortium, http://bit.ly/IPAM_P644.

Searchinger, T., Heimlich, R., Houghton, R. A., Dong, F., Elobeid, A., Fabiosa, J., Tokgoz, S., Hayes, D. & Yu, T.-H. (2008) Use of U.S. croplands for biofuels increases greenhouse gases through emissions from land-use change, *Science*, 319(5867), pp. 1238–1240.

Schouten, G. & Glasbergen, P. (2011) Creating legitimacy in global private governance: the case of the Roundtable on Sustainable Palm Oil, *Ecological Economics*, 70(11), pp. 1891–1899.

Shell (2011) Sustainability summary 2011, http://shell.com/sustainabilityreport.

Shell and IUCN (2010) Report of the Shell-IUCN indirect land use change workshop, Chatham House, London, 21–22 September 2010, http://cmsdata.iucn.org/downloads/shell_iucn_iluc_workshop_report___sept_2010.pdf.

Silva-Castañeda, L. (2012) A forest of evidence: third-party certification and multiple forms of proof—a case study of oil palm plantations in Indonesia, *Agriculture and Human Values*, 29(3), pp. 361–370.

Sikor, T. & Lund, C. (2009) Access and property: a question of power and authority, *Development and Change*, 40(1), pp. 1–22.

United Nations Conference on Trade and Development (2008) *Making Certification Work for Sustainable Development: The Case of Biofuels* (Geneva, Switzerland: UNCTAD).

Vandergeest, P. (2007) Certification and communities: alternatives for regulating the environmental and social impacts of shrimp farming, *World Development*, 35(7), pp. 1152–1171.

Vermeulen, S. & Cotula, L. (2010) Over the heads of local people: consultation, consent, and recompense in large-scale land deals for biofuels projects in Africa, *Journal of Peasant Studies*, 37(4), pp. 899–916.

World Bank, FAO, IFAD & UNCTAD (2010) Principles for Responsible Agricultural Investment that Respects Rights, Livelihoods and Resources, Discussion Note, 25 January 2010, http://siteresources.worldbank.org/INTARD/214574-1111138388661/22453321/Principles_Extended.pdf

World Bank (2011) *Rising Global Interest in Farmland: Can it Yield Sustainable and Equitable Benefits?* (Washington, DC: World Bank).

World Rainforest Movement (2008) Why certification of agrofuels won't work, *World Rainforest Movement Bulletin*, 135, pp. 5–6.

WWF (n.d.) WWF's view on biofuels: how to achieve sustainability?, http://www.sustainableethanolinitiative.com/Sve/Standardsidor/Filer/Peter%20Roberntz.pdf

WWF (2010a) *Certification and Roundtables: Do They Work?* (Gland, Switzerland: WWF).

WWF (2010b) New method emerges to deter 'indirect' land grab for biofuel production, WWF Press Release, 8 October 2010, http://wwf.panda.org/who_we_are/wwf_offices/brazil/news/?uNewsID=195535.

WWF (2012) *Better Production for a Living Planet* (Gland, Switzerland: WWF).

Zoomers, A. (2010) Globalisation and the foreignisation of space: seven processes driving the current global land grab, *Journal of Peasant Studies*, 37(2), pp. 429–447.

Elizabeth Fortin currently holds a British Academy Postdoctoral Fellowship in the School of Law of the University of Bristol. Her current research examines multi-stakeholder efforts to formulate sustainability standards and certification schemes for the biofuels industry, focusing on the Roundtable on Sustainable Biofuels. She has previously undertaken research on land reform, with a particular focus on Africa.

Ben Richardson is Assistant Professor in International Political Economy at the University of Warwick. He writes on trade and development and is the author of *Sugar: Refined Power in a Global Regime* (Palgrave Macmillan, 2009). He has worked with Bonsucro in a voluntary capacity via his position at the NGO Ethical Sugar.

The Challenge of Global Governance of Land Grabbing: Changing International Agricultural Context and Competing Political Views and Strategies

SATURNINO M. BORRAS JR*, JENNIFER C. FRANCO** &
CHUNYU WANG***

*International Institute of Social Studies, The Hague, the Netherlands
**Transnational Institute, Amsterdam, the Netherlands
***China Agricultural University, Beijing, China

ABSTRACT   *The emergence of 'flex crops and commodities' within a fluid international food regime transition, the rise of BRICS and middle-income countries, and the revalued role of nation-states are critical context for land grabbing. These global transformations that shape and are reshaped by contemporary land grabbing have resulted in the emergence of competing interpretations of the meaning of such changes, making the already complex governance terrain even more complicated. We are witnessing a three-way political contestation at the global level to control the character, pace, and trajectory of discourse, and the instruments in and practice of land governance. These are 'regulate to facilitate', 'regulate to mitigate negative impacts and maximize opportunities', and 'regulate to block and rollback' land grabbing. Future trajectories in land grabbing and its governance will be shaped partly by the balance of state and social forces within and between these three political tendencies. Given this an unfolding global development, this article offers a preliminary analysis by mapping under-explored areas of inquiry and puts forward initial ways of questioning, rather than firm arguments based on complete empirical material.*

Introduction: Changed Context for Global Land Governance

Reports of land grabbing from various parts of the world continue to come in. Media, international organizations, and non-governmental organizations (NGOs) remain the main sources of these reports. Estimates of the extent of land grabbing vary. There is no consensus as to how much land has been changing hands and on the methodologies of identifying, counting, and quantifying land grabs (see Margulis et al., 2013, pp. 1–23). But there is a consensus that land grabbing is underway and that is significant (White et al., 2012). Land grabbing occurs in Africa (Cotula, 2012), but also in the former Soviet Union and Central Asia (Visser and Spoor, 2011), Latin America (Borras et al., 2012a), and Asia. There are at least three important ways in which land grabbing manifests today. Grabbing land for purposes of using it as a factor of agricultural production to produce food, feed, biofuels, and other industrial products is probably the most common type. In addition, there is the emergence of 'green grabbing'—land grabbing for environmental ends (Fairhead et al., 2012). Water grabbing is another important dimension of contemporary land grabbing (Kay and Franco, 2012; Mehta et al., 2012; Woodhouse, 2012). The latter two require grabbing land in order to secure the resources they covet.

Global land grabbing is partly associated with the rise of what we call 'flex crops and commodities': crops and commodities with multiple and flexible uses—across food, feed, and fuel complexes and industrial commodities (think of corn which is eaten fresh, frozen, or canned; used to produce industrial sweeteners such as high-fructose syrup; processed into animal feed; and milled to produce ethanol, which is blended with conventional gasoline to fuel vehicles; and so on). These crops are produced in tropical and temperate countries, partly resulting in the rise of interest in land in both the South *and* North. Flex crops and commodities have implications on global governance as a single crop/commodity straddles multiple commodity sectors (food, feed, fuel, other industrial commodities), geographic spaces (e.g. North–South), and international political economy categories (e.g. OECD countries, non-OECD countries). The four currently most popular flex crops are maize, oil palm, soybean, and sugarcane. The increases in global aggregate production in terms of quantity and area harvested have been significant during the past 50 years, with greater increases during the past two decades. Many large-scale land investments are located in the flex crop and commodity sector.

Meanwhile, another sector where global land grabbing is implicated in is the fast-growing tree plantations. It is in a lot of ways a kind of 'flex crop/commodity'—these are trees and forests with multiple and flexible uses, the emergence of which is traceable to the same changes in the global political economy that ushered in the rise of flex crops. Tree plantations can be used for timber extraction for industrial purposes destined especially to the BRICS. But the same plantation can be anticipated for possible rise in wood chips-based biofuel complex, while at the same time it can be used to speculate on carbon offset schemes such as Reducing Emissions through Deforestation and Forest Degradation (REDD+). During the past decade, the rise in popularity of this sector, and the land use implication it has brought with it, has been observable. The sector is likely to expand even more in the coming time (see Kröger, 2012, 2013).

There is thus a significant change in the global political-economic context that has given rise to flex agricultural commodities (food and non-food) that are associated with the current land grabbing. The character of these political economic changes is relevant in understanding global governance of land grabbing.

The phenomenon of land grabbing has forced some national governments to pass laws and policies in order to regulate land deals, with varying initial outcomes. For example, several Southern American countries have tried to prohibit or control the 'foreignization' of land ownership, yet large-scale land deals remain widespread in this part of Latin America (Borras et al., 2012a, 2012b; Murmis and Murmis, 2012; Perrone, 2013, pp. 205–209; Urioste 2012; Wilkinson et al., 2012). Because of the international dimension of land grabbing, there has been increasing pressure for specifically *global* governance instruments to tackle the issue of land grabbing. Initiatives have proliferated, ranging from corporate self-regulation mechanisms around 'codes of conduct' (see von Braun and Meinzen-Dick, 2009; but see Borras and Franco, 2010, for an initial critique) to (inter)governmental measures, such as the FAO's Voluntary Guidelines for the Governance of Tenure of Land, Fisheries and Forest agreed to on 11 May 2012 (FAO, 2012).

Various state and social actors view land grabbing differently. Some look at it as opportunity, others as threat. This has led to what we identify as three competing political tendencies among state and non-state actors with regard to global governance of land grabbing: first is *regulate in order facilitate land deals*, second is *regulate in order to mitigate adverse impacts and maximize opportunities of land deals*, and third is *regulate to stop and rollback land deals*.

This article offers a *preliminary* analysis touching on key elements in the changing global political-economic context for land grabbing, including flex crops, food regime transition, and the role of the state, as well as the rise of three competing political tendencies in emergent global land governance. It maps under-explored areas of inquiry and offers initial ways of conceptualizing and questioning global land grabbing, rather than firm arguments based on solid and complete empirical material. The rest of the article is divided into two main parts: a discussion of the changing global context for governance, and an analysis of the three competing political tendencies. We end with a short conclusion.

Changing Food Regime, Flex Crops/Commodities, and the Role of National States

Recent changes in the global context relevant to global land grabbing have rendered existing international governance instruments such as those by FAO (various voluntary guidelines), Human Rights Council (human rights conventions), International Labour Organization (ILO), among others (see Edelman and Carwil, 2011; Monsalve Suárez, forthcoming; Sawyer and Gomez, 2008), including corporate self-regulation instruments useful to contemporary debates around land grabbing, but probably in a limited way. It is important to examine these international governance instruments within the context of pre-existing structural and institutional conditions and trends including the ongoing fluid transition towards a 'polycentric' food regime, the rise of flex crops and commodities, and the (changing) role of national states—and their implications for global governance of land grabbing.

A Fluid Transition Towards a Polycentric Food Regime?

Food regime is a powerful analytical framework developed by Harriet Friedmann and Philip McMichael (1989). An international food regime is the set of formal and informal rules that govern the production, distribution, and consumption of food on a world scale, embedded within the development of global capitalism. It is thus a huge concept covering a wide range of issues. For the purpose of this article, we are concerned with only a small aspect of food regime, and this is about the state anchoring these regimes in terms of rule-making.

In terms of institutional power holder, the food regimes that existed were first anchored by the British Empire starting in the 1870s and lasted until the eve of World War I. Food was inserted into global capitalist development by having colonial and settler economies produce cheap grains and meat via extensive agriculture and for export to the centers of capital in Europe to feed the working classes. The second food regime, which started in the 1930s and lasted until the early 1970s, was anchored by the United States (US). Chemical-based and mechanized agriculture produced food surpluses in the US and dumped them in developing countries largely through food aid, partly feeding working classes in these countries with cheap food (McMichael, 2009). There is no consensus among key scholars on whether there is a third regime, and if so, what it is and what is the power and institutional anchor, although they tend to agree that powerful transnational corporations (TNCs) tend to rule the regime in a neoliberal context (McMichael, 2012).

What we have witnessed recently seems to be the emergence of new players wanting to gain power in terms of reshaping international rules that govern the production, distribution, and consumption of food and other closely related commodities embedded within the ongoing reconfiguration of key hubs of global capital. These powerful actors seem to be seeking 'regime change'. Key actors in this context are BRICS countries, some powerful middle-income countries (MICs) and OECD countries (e.g. South Korea), and the Gulf states (see Lee and Muller, 2012; McMichael, 2012; Margulis and Porter, 2013, pp. 65–86; Woertz, 2013, pp. 87–104). There is a trend showing the increases in these countries' share in the production, distribution, and consumption of food and closely related commodities. Meanwhile, some powerful MICs, such as Argentina, Chile, Mexico, Indonesia, Malaysia, Thailand, and Vietnam, have posted similar trends in terms of their share in the production, distribution, and consumption of these commodities. This means that BRICS, collectively, are no longer just massive importer/consumer countries; at the same time, they are important producers of these key commodities. In this process, the states in these countries seem to be trying to reshape the international rules in the production, distribution, and consumption of food and related commodities. Many of these countries are trying to decrease their reliance on the North Atlantic power holders (via TNCs) for their food security, nor are the latter able to demonstrate continuing ability to wage hegemonic control over the food regime. Thus, we see increasing instances where the challengers to the regime try to secure footholds in the production of food and other agricultural commodities in distant territories (McMichael, 2012; see also Akram Lodhi, 2012).

This does not mean that the emergence of challengers to the traditionally North Atlantic-based food regime has marginalized the conventional power holders. Europe and the US remain key players in the global food systems and in the dynamics of regime rule-making. Especially in light of the financialization of (agricultural) production, North Atlantic-based finance capital has been increasingly involved in land deals. The fluid transition to what seems to be an emerging polycentric regime cautions us from either remaining fixated on the traditional imperialist powers or from getting overly obsessed of the new regime rule-makers (of China especially).

Whether these changes are going to lead to a full and stable regime remains to be seen. The transformation is dynamic and fluid for the time being. The fluidity of the transformation process, as well as the plurality, diversity, and distinct character of new key players, have made global governance more complicated than what existed in the past. For instance, how do we make US-headquartered pension funds accountable for the implications of their land investments? Civil society organizations (CSOs) and their transnational advocacy campaigns have been key to state–society interactions on global governance. However, historically they were used to interact with international institutions that have something to do with the North Atlantic powers and other key OECD countries. How are they going to interact with new players such as China, India, Gulf States, Vietnam, and others that are not the usual players in the transnational state–civil society interaction terrain, and with which there are no prior channels and patterns of interaction?

Initial scanning of the global political terrain tells us that there are no answers to these questions that are readily available to CSO campaigners, one of the key players in the global governance scene.[1] In our experience, CSOs have been trying to hard to implicate North Atlantic-based countries and companies to land grabbing, but find fewer cases that *directly* implicate these to land grabbing as compared to those that directly link China, India, South Korea, Brazil, South Africa and the Gulf states. There are three key issues that are potentially important to CSO campaigners to link, directly and indirectly, North Atlantic-based countries and companies to land grabs: (1) the US and European biofuel policy; (2) financialization of agriculture that involves finance capital that originates from and/or based in this region; and (3) green grabbing linked to North Atlantic-brokered or -influenced international climate change mitigation policies (carbon sequestration etc.) (Fairhead et al., 2012). (Inter)state–civil society interactions involving traditional key players are likely to revolve around these land grabbing subthemes.

But the emergence of BRICS countries, MICs, and the Gulf states as key players in food regime rule-making dynamics has rendered the traditional repertoire of international campaigning by CSOs inadequate in many ways, partly because there are no existing channels and rules of institutional interactions between them. It is not only that CSOs do not know how to deal with states like the Gulf states, it is also the other way around. As Woertz (2013, this volume) explains: 'Gulf states are ill prepared to engage with [CSOs]'. This situation is likely to make multilateral institutional spaces such as the UN and regional intergovernmental bodies such as the African Union, ASEAN, and the UN even more relevant to CSO campaigns (see McKeon, 2010, 2013, pp. 105–122). CSOs' interest and commitment to the Voluntary Guidelines process partly demonstrates this (refer to an initial discussion by McKeon, 2013, this volume, on the dynamics of negotiation process around the guidelines). Whether these spaces will be adequate and appropriate to tackle the issue of land grabbing is another matter, and requires careful empirical investigation.

The Rise of Flex Crops and Commodities

The BRICS countries have significant and increasing share in the world's total production of four flex crops (see Figure 1). If we bring in MICs into the mix, then Indonesia and Malaysia, together, corner the majority share in the production of palm oil worldwide. The BRICS countries have large economies—home to 43% of the world's population and have 26.3% of world's total agricultural land (FAOSTAT, 2010)—and as such constitute large markets for flex crops and commodities, as shown in Figure 2, which is the aggregated import data.[2] Some MICs are also important producers and exporters of flex crops and commodities, e.g. Argentina for soya, Malaysia and Indonesia as world's biggest exporters of palm oil, Vietnam for fast-growing trees and products, and so on. A trend to watch is the increasing *intra-BRICS/MICs* flex crop/commodity trade, and its implications for global agrarian transformation more generally.

The rise of flex crops and commodities has far-reaching and complicated implications for global governance. For one, there is a blurring of sectoral boundaries and sectoral governance instruments. Transnational governance mechanisms are generally structured by sector or theme, namely, food, feed, energy/fuel, forestry, climate change mitigation strategies, and so on. How then can one categorize soya that falls within three categories of food, feed, and energy/fuel, and which sectoral rules apply? How can one categorize palm oil that falls under the categories of food, fuel, industrial goods, and which sectoral rules apply? As a consequence, there is a complication in terms of framing a particular issue and policy advocacy campaign especially for CSOs. It fragments the political space and makes single-issue focus advocacy campaigns more difficult.[3]

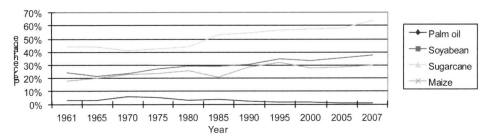

Figure 1. BRICS's share in selected flex crop production, world total (%). *Source*: FAOSTAT (2010).

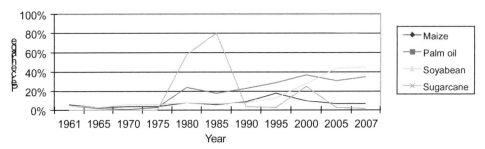

Figure 2. BRICS's share in selected flex crop imports, world total (%). *Source*: FAOSTAT (2010)

As mentioned earlier, when a CSO launches a campaign for biofuels-related governance around palm oil it is easy for oil palm industry players to claim that theirs has nothing to do with biofuels as it has to do more with food products (e.g. cooking oil) or other industrial commodities (e.g. shampoo), as the usual debate around Indonesian palm oil goes (White and Dasgupta, 2010). Indeed while oil palm plantation expansion has been inspired by market expansion of biofuels in the European Union (McCarthy, 2010), the immediate production in Indonesia remains largely for non-biofuel markets. Hence, it weakens policy advocacy campaigns by many CSOs using biofuels as an anchor issue.

This is even more complicated when we extend the issue to 'indirect land use change' (ILUC) in a global context. When rapeseed in Europe, which was previously used for food industry, was converted to feedstock for domestic biodiesel production, a substitute for the previous use was necessary: thus importing palm oil from Asia (Franco et al., 2010). It becomes more difficult for CSOs to directly pin down imported palm oil for the food sector as linked to biofuels (see also Fortin and Richardson, 2013, pp. 141–159). There is a similar complexity in other flex crops/commodities: corn, soya, sugarcane, and industrial trees.

One implication of the flex crop/commodity phenomenon is the complexity in understanding land grabbing. Observers tend to simplify data on land grabbing and the contexts for this phenomenon. An example is the claim by the International Land Coalition (ILC) that 60% of grabbed lands are devoted to biofuels (Anseeuw et al., 2011). Such an inaccurate reading may inadvertently lead to problematic propositions for policy reforms or demand framing in transnational policy advocacy campaigns. This is even more complicated if we bring in the concept of flex trees and forests and the various possibilities in it: forests are captured, some are planted with fast-growing trees: when there is a good market for timber products, timber products are produced and sold; if and when wood chips as feedstock to biofuel are required, biofuel feedstock these become; when REDD+ contracts are speculated, these tree plantations can be converted into conservation sites for cross-border carbon offset deals.

Key Role of National States

In our analysis of various country cases of land grabbing, we realize that national states are engaged in systematic policy and administrative initiatives aimed at capturing so-called 'marginal lands' for large-scale investments. The role of the state in facilitating land investments in these spaces includes some, or all, or a combination of the following: (1) 'invention/justification' of the need for large-scale land investments; (2) 'definition, reclassification and quantification' of what is 'marginal, under-utilized and empty' lands; (3) 'identification' of these particular types of land; (5) 'acquisition/appropriation' of these lands; and (5) 'reallocation/disposition' of these lands to investors. Only national states have the absolute authority to carry out these key legal-administrative steps to facilitate land deals. Most of these lands are within the legal-administrative-military control of national states. In some cases, coercion and violence have accompanied a state's effort at territorialization, enforcement of its sovereignty and authority, as well as its promotion of private capital accumulation (Grajales, 2011).

Stepping back, and looking at the big picture, there emerge three broadly distinct but interlinked areas of state actions that enable states to facilitate land grabs, namely, (1) state simplification process; (2) assertion of sovereignty and authority over territory; and (3) coercion through police and (para)military force to enforce compliance, extend territorialization, and broker for private capital accumulation. First, in order to administer and govern, states engage in a simplification process to render complex social processes legible to the state. The creation of cadastres, land records, and titles are attempts to simplify land-based social relations that are otherwise too complex for state administration (Scott, 1998). This requires the state's official powers to record land relations and (re)classifying lands. This in turn brings us back to the notion of 'available marginal, empty lands'. The trend in state discourse around land grabs seems to be: if the land is not formally privatized, then it is state-owned; if an official census did not show significant formal settlements, then these are empty lands, if the same official census did not show significant farm production activities, then these are unused lands. Second, beyond the economic benefits of land investment, land deals are also viewed as an essential component of state-building processes where sovereignty and authority are extended to previously 'non-state spaces' (ibid.). Third, coercion and violence usually with the use of police and (para)military to enforce compliance with the state simplification project and the broader state-building process have accompanied some of the land deals in various parts of the world (see, e.g. Grajales, 2011, on Colombia; Woods, 2011 on Burma; Peluso and Lund, 2011, more generally).

This threefold state role in land deals is carried out to a large extent on behalf of the dominant classes of capital, foreign or domestic. However, as Fox (1993) explains, the state's support for the capital accumulation process is always accompanied by the other task of the state to maintain a minimum level of political legitimacy. This makes capital accumulation and political legitimization inherently interlinked and contradictory, tension-filled, uneven, and contested, across space and time. The crucial role of national states in land grabbing has rendered attempts at the international governance of land grabbing a complicated undertaking. It will be a challenge for intergovernmental institutions to make these national governments responsive to international rules. This is doubly complicated in settings marked by 'land grabbed land grabbers', i.e. countries where land grabbing occurs, but where some land grabbers in other countries also originate. Brazil is a good example. The Brazilian state was quick to move to regulate foreign ownership of land in Brazil in response to popular sentiment against it, but at the same time it is actively supporting Brazilian companies grabbing lands in other countries such as Bolivia, Paraguay, and Mozambique (Galeano, 2012; Sauer and Leite Pereira, 2012; Urioste 2012; Wilkinson et al., 2012).

In short, the rise of flex crops and commodities within an ongoing fluid food regime transition, the rise of BRICS and MICs, and the revalued role of central states are the critical context for global land grabbing. While some may see this global restructuring as an opportunity, others may see it as a threat. This has led to the emergence of three political tendencies, each of which seeks to influence the nature, pace, and trajectory of global governance. We examine these three tendencies in detail in the next section.

Competing Tendencies in Global Governance of Land Deals

It is difficult to find any individual or institution engaged in the issue of land grabbing today that does not raise the issue of governance (for definitional discussion of global governance, refer to Margulis et al, 2013, this volume). Many of the contentious themes in current land grabbing are in fact governance-related, such as the Washington-based International Food Policy Research Institute's (IFPRI) early advocacy for 'codes of conduct' (von Braun and Meinzen-Dick, 2009), the World Bank's 'principles for responsible agricultural investments' (PRAI), the FAO's Voluntary Guidelines, advocacy for transparency in land investments, issues around community consultations (Vermeulen and Cotula, 2010), issues about contents of land deal contracts (Cotula, 2011), advocacy for a set of minimum human rights principles to address land grabbing (Claeys and Vanloqueren, 2013, pp. 193–198; De Schutter, 2011; Künnemann and Monsalve Suárez, 2013, pp. 123–139), calls to stop land grabbing by La Via Campesina and allies (Via Campesina, 2012), among others. There is a plurality of initiatives around and positions on the issue of governance of land grabbing. The differences between these positions can be significant, their political implications far-reaching.

Examining closely the emerging literature on land grabbing (i.e. academic, policy, and CSO activist materials) and observing the various unfolding policy and political processes,[4] we have come to an initial observation that the dynamic (re)positioning done by multiple (inter)state and non-state actors in terms of transnational governance of land grabbing seems to fall under three discernible political tendencies. These tendencies are not sharply defined and fixed, hence the use of the term 'tendency', and each is in turn internally variegated. The three tendencies are: (a) *regulate to facilitate* land deals; (b) *regulate to mitigate negative impacts and maximize opportunities*; and (c) *regulate to stop and rollback* land grabbing. These three tendencies have provenance in recent alignment of forces in at least two important agrarian fronts. The first was the political contestations around the World Trade Organization (WTO) negotiation in the 1990s. We saw more or less the same type of political groupings and trajectories: anti-WTO led by Via Campesina, pro-WTO led by neoliberal ideologues, and a huge grouping somewhere in between with some closer to the latter, others to the former, such as the now defunct International Federation of Agricultural Producers (IFAP). This has been examined by Desmarais (2007) and by Borras et al. (2008). The second was the emerging realignment of social forces among diverse food movements. Holt-Gimenez and Shattuck (2011) have examined the various groupings and political trajectories of these movements, and have identified more or less the same three broad trajectories, and they have identified nuances within each camp such as those between food justice and food sovereignty movements. More broadly, these political contestations are extensions of ideological struggles over the notion of 'development', and as such link back to relevant historical debates depending on one's particular academic discipline.

Coming back to our present three political tendencies: these trajectories are in turn embedded within the changing global context we discussed above: the rise of BRICS and MICs, rise of flex crops/commodities, and the repositioning of national states. The underlying ideological and political bases for these positions are markedly different.

Regulate to Facilitate Land Deals

The first current is premised on the belief that interest in large-scale land deals is a desirable phenomenon where states and the corporate sector have become interested in land (again) (Deininger, 2011). The basis in pushing for this development offensive is the fundamental assumption that there exist marginal, empty lands in the world (with an estimated area of some- where between 445 million and 1.7 billion hectares) that can be made available to address the multiple food–energy–financial–climate crises (World Bank, 2010). The anticipated positive outcomes of land deals can be achieved when such deals are carried out *well*. It can be surmised that part of the excitement in this camp can be linked back to the rise of flex crops (often also referred to as 'high value crops') which in turn attract the interest of investors. Governance, in this case, is based on two most fundamental assumptions in neoclassical and new institutional economics: clear property rights and functioning of free market forces (Deininger, 2011). Juergen Voegele, director of the Agricultural and Rural Development Department of the World Bank explained that:

> [W]hen done right, larger-scale farming can provide opportunities for poor countries with large agri-
> cultural sectors and ample endowments of land. To make the most of these opportunities, however,
> countries will need to better secure local land rights and improve land governance. Adopting an open
> and proactive approach to dealing with investors is also needed to ensure that investment contributes
> to broader development objectives. (World Bank, 2010, p. xv)

Governance tends to be seen from administrative and technical perspectives, for example, faster, cheaper, and clearer land titling. The concept of transparent land transaction builds primarily on mainstream economics' concern about efficiency and functioning of free market forces. Hence their call for strengthened property rights, environmental and labor standards, greater commu- nity consultation, and the use of some international governance instruments such as transparency mechanisms in land deals (e.g. free, prior, informed consent) (Deininger, 2011) is meant to facilitate capital accumulation within an efficient institutional context. This too links back to the context we discussed above: the changing role of the state. Here, mainstream economists who do not usually like the state coming into the picture are calling the state back in to facilitate the identification, quantification, acquisition, and disposition of so-called available marginal lands. In a way, this tendency is one of strategic thinking: overall, renewed large-scale land investment is good, and while some collateral damage may occur this can be tactically addressed by deploying a variety of 'good' governance instruments.

Regulate to Mitigate Negative Impacts and Maximize Opportunities

The second tendency around the position of mitigating negative impacts while harnessing oppor- tunities is based on the twin assumptions of the 'inevitability' of large-scale land deals and the 'impossibility' of redistributive land and rural development policies to promote small-scale farming-based development. The assumed 'inevitability' of land grabbing promotes a 'genie is out of the bottle' kind of argument—and so, we must live with it. The 'win–win–win' position's basis and justification are captured in IFPRI's earlier explanation (von Braun and Meinzen-Dick, 2009, p. 2): 'Because of the urgent need for greater development in rural areas and the fiscal inability of the developing-country governments to provide the necessary infusion of capital, large-scale land acquisitions can be seen as an opportunity for increased investment in agriculture.' This tendency also gravitates around the narrative that land deals are relatively a welcome development in the midst of state neglect of the rural sectors. Key to this position is the idea of linking small farmers to the corporate sector. This position is illustrated in the policy position by IFAP (released before its demise in October 2010) on biofuels and land use debate:

The production of food and feed remains paramount for the farmers of IFAP; however, biofuels represent a new market opportunity, help diversify risk and promote rural development. . . . Recently, biofuels have been blamed for soaring prices. There are many factors behind the rise in food prices, including supply shortages due to poor weather conditions . . . The proportion of agricultural land given over to producing biofuels in the world is very small: 1 percent in Brazil, 1 percent in Europe, 4 percent in the United States of America, and so biofuel production is a marginal factor in the rise of food prices. The misconceptions about biofuels are important to overcome for a farming community that has long suffered from low incomes. Bioenergy represents a good opportunity to boost rural economies and reduce poverty, provided this production complies with sustainability criteria. Sustainable biofuel production by family farmers is not a threat to food production. It is an opportunity to achieve profitability and to revive rural communities. (IFAP quoted in FAO, 2008)

This tendency also deploys a number international governance instruments to support its position: strengthened property rights to protect the land rights of people, environmental and labor standards, greater community consultation, and particularly the use of transparency instruments such as free, prior, informed consent. However, in contrast to the first current, which deploys these instruments clearly to strategically advance land deals, the second tendency deploys these governance instruments based on urgent tactical considerations: to mitigate negative impacts and maximize opportunities. Regular reports and policy positions from Oxfam are examples of this (see, e.g. Oxfam 2011, 2012). Explicitly and implicitly linked to the calculation of risks and opportunities by CSOs campaigning within this tendency are the same risks and opportunities brought about by flex crops/commodities, discussed earlier. The discussion on regulation within this political tendency also links back to the changing role of the state. It is clear here that the role of the state is identified as key in terms of mitigating risks and harnessing opportunities: enforceable rules that prevent people getting expelled from their land, delivering the promised jobs, and so on. This tendency is invested in global standards and 'best practices' to provide benchmarks for what states should do.

The urgency of the 'here and now' situations in many localities that require immediate concrete solutions inspires and mobilizes groups and individuals around the second tendency. Thus, in contrast to what seems to be the more strategic thinking underpinning the first tendency, this second current is more tactical: it is principally concerned with what is happening now and what can be done to protect poor people.

Regulate to Stop and Rollback

The third tendency is the 'stop and rollback land grabbing' position. The fundamental assumption in this current is that the contemporary expansion of production for food, biofuels, feed, and others is not really meant to solve the world's hunger, poverty, and environmental degradation, but to further capital accumulation for the insatiable corporate hunger for profits. For this camp, this process of capital accumulation advances a development model based on large-scale, fossil-fuel based, industrial, monocrop plantations that expels people from their land and degrades the environment. This camp's starting point is a stand against capitalism, often bringing in a strong anti-imperialist and anti-neocolonial dimension in its position. It sees the rise of flex crops more from a 'threat' perspective. In stark contrast to the IFAP position on biofuels, the transnational agrarian movement La Via Campesina declared:

> The current massive wave of investment in energy production based on cultivating and industrial processing of . . . corn, soy, palm oil, sugar cane, canola, etc., will neither solve the climate crisis nor the energy crisis. It creates a new and very serious threat to food production by small farmers and to the attainment of food sovereignty for the world population. It is claimed that agrofuels will help fight climate change. In reality, the opposite is true . . . If we take into account the whole cycle of production, transformation, distribution of agrofuels, they do not produce less greenhouse gases than fossil fuels, except in some cases. Meanwhile, the social and ecological impacts of agrofuel development will be devastating . . . They drive family farmers, men and women, off their land. It is estimated that five million farmers have been expelled from their land to create space for monocultures in Indonesia, five million in Brazil, four million in Colombia . . . (Via Campesina, 2008)

Like the first two tendencies, this third current takes on board similar international governance instruments: property rights for the people (although not limited to Western private property ideas, to include communal and community property regimes), environmental standards, community consultations, and transparency instruments, such as free, prior, informed consent. It links back again to our discussion earlier about the changing role of the state, although in this case it is quite clear that the appeal is for the state to intervene more forcefully on behalf of poor peasants. However, it is framed in a radically different way from the first two tendencies. This third tendency deploys these international governance instruments in order to 'expose and oppose', stop, and rollback land grabbing. The third tendency is captured by a statement of the 'Global Alliance Against Land Grabbing', which was convened by La Via Campesina and allies in November 2011 in Mali. It says partly:

> Land grabbing is a global phenomenon initiated by local and transnational elites, governments and multinational companies in order to control the most precious resources in the world . . . [It] exceeds the traditional North-South split that characterizes imperialist structures. Land grabbing displaces and dislocates communities, destroys local economies, cultures and the social fabric. It endangers the identity of communities be they peasants, small-scale farmers, pastoralists, fisherfolk, workers, indigenous peoples . . . Our land and identities are not for sale . . . There is no way to attenuate the impact of this economic model and of the power structures that defend it. Those who dare stand up to defend their legitimate rights and survival of their families and communities are beaten, imprisoned and killed . . . The struggle against land grabbing is a struggle against capitalism . . . (Via Campesina, 2012, pp. 21–22)

The third tendency is like the first tendency in that it is a strategic perspective, as if saying, 'this is not the kind of agriculture/development we want; another agriculture/development is possible.' Hence, alongside its general call to stop and rollback land grabbing is their call for an alternative, which in turn brings us to the currently most popular one: food sovereignty (see Patel, 2009, for background).

The three tendencies are more or less stable analytical constructs, but key state and non-state actors and their political stands are dynamic and constantly changing, often straddling two or three tendencies depending on the particular configuration of issues and alliances, over time.

This is partly because of the differentiated nature of relevant international/transnational actors; they are not monolithic entities. For instance, it is not very useful to think of a single position on global land grabbing within the World Bank, FAO, or IFAD (International Fund for Agricultural Development). Sub-groups within these institutions may gravitate around a particular tendency, and may also shuffle different positions over time. But for the time being, we argue that the World Bank probably hosts many of those inclined towards the 'regulate to facilitate' tendency, La Via Campesina and close allies represent the 'regulate to stop and rollback' position, while many groups, NGOs (such as Oxfam), aid donors, international development agencies, and community organizations, may be inclined to various shades of the 'regulate to mitigate negative impacts and maximize opportunities' tendency. Again, recall the earlier position of IFPRI.

These three tendencies are likely to compete with each other in their interpretations of key international governance instruments, how to use these, and for what purposes—in some ways similar to the political competitions around the WTO negotiations (Desmarais, 2007) and the range of positions on the food question among food movements (Holt-Gimenez and Shattuck, 2011). For example, all three tendencies identify community consultation and transparency instruments (e.g. free, prior, and informed consent) as critical, but have three competing interpretations and advocacies—all in support of their political positions. It is linked to how they perceive what the role of the state should be. The process of competing interpretations is inherently political and relational and is better understood from the (inter)state-(civil) society interactions perspective rather than through technical and administrative lenses. Hence, it would be wrong to look at the recently passed Voluntary Guidelines as a governance instrument that has uniform and standard meaning to the three tendencies. As explained by Franco (2008), once laws and policies are passed, they do not self-interpret or self-implement. It is the political interaction of various state and non-state actors that will shape how the Voluntary Guidelines will eventually be interpreted and implemented, from one setting to another (refer to McKeon, 2013, this volume, on the discussion on the Voluntary Guidelines; and Seufert, 2013, pp. 181–186, for initial examination of this process). We should then expect at least three versions of the actually existing Voluntary Guidelines and other global governance instruments (e.g. transparency, human rights) in the coming years.

Political contestations around the implementation of the Voluntary Guidelines will partly be an extension of the political contestations during the negotiations. Underlying the tensions during the negotiations was partly the ideological divide that underpins the three political tendencies discussed here. Foodfirst Information and Action Network (FIAN) was a key coordinator of CSOs working during the negotiations. In a brief, they raised the alarm and identified the fundamental source of tension:

> With the support of Canada, Australia and the private sector, the USA insisted that *economic growth, the strengthening of markets and investment are absolutely key* to eradicate poverty. Thus, they refused—or tried to weaken—any policy measures beyond market mechanisms such as restitution, redistribution and the establishment of regulations guaranteeing security of tenure . . . in favor of indigenous peoples, peasants, fishermen and women and nomadic pastoralists. (FIAN, 2011; emphasis added)

Did the negotiations lead to a consensus on the 'lowest common denominator', which could mean a set of Voluntary Guidelines that is not necessarily weak per se, but one that can be interpreted in many different ways? Most likely. BRICS countries were among those supporting the Voluntary Guidelines during the negotiations. Again, at the height of the negotiations, FIAN's observation was illuminating:

Particularly striking was the widespread hostility of states to recall their human rights obligations related to land, fisheries and forests. Fearing that the Guidelines will create new obligations or become too prescriptive, many governments did all they can to weaken the language and the recommendations of the Guidelines. For indigenous peoples this attitude is particularly worrying because the first draft of the Guidelines falls far behind the rights recognized in the UN Declaration on the Rights of Indigenous Peoples (UNDRIP). It took several hours of negotiation with Canada and the USA to move them to accept in the text of the Guidelines the incorporation of the indigenous peoples' right to free, prior and informed consent (FPIC) as enshrined in UNDRIP! (Ibid.)

Meanwhile, there seem to be no major internal contradictions within the first current, save for some unverified talks about tension within the World Bank between those who emphasize 'investment' and those who emphasize 'regulation' (probably underpinned by a purist neoclassical versus reformist new institutional economics fault line). But there are major dilemmas within and between the second and third tendencies. As mentioned earlier, the strength of the second tendency is its grave concern, quite rightly so, about the 'here and now' issues (expulsion of people from their land, shady land deals, and so on), placing them in a very good *tactical* political and policy position and enabling them to maneuver in global policy spaces. No wonder this is the most popular tendency of the three among key state and non-state actors at the international, national, and local levels. The potential pitfall of this tendency is, if and when it loses strategic perspective, getting engaged from one specific tactical policy and political battle to another, whether around specific land deals or around international policy instruments. The best scenario for this political tendency then is to win many tactical battles—i.e. special local land cases or specific governance instruments and processes—but in the end lose the strategic battle over development models.

The first two tendencies share several common features. If we take a closer look at the World Bank's position on governance of large-scale land deals and the role of key actors, we will realize that it is cast in a generic way so that both 'regulate to facilitate' and 'regulate to mitigate/maximize' tendencies will be able to identify with it:

Responsible investors interested in the long-term viability of their investments realize that adherence to a set of basic principles is in their interest; many have committed to doing so under a range of initiatives, including ones with a governance structure incorporating civil society and governments.

Civil society and local government can build critical links to local communities in three ways: educating communities about effectively exercising theirs rights; assisting in the design, negotiation, implementation, and monitoring of investment projects where requested; and acting as watchdogs to critically review projects and publicize findings by holding governments and investors accountable and providing inputs into country strategies.

International organizations can do more to support countries to maximize opportunities and minimize risks . . . First, they can assist countries to integrate information and analysis on large-scale acquisition into national strategies. Second, they can offer financial and technical support for capacity building. Third, there is scope for supporting stakeholder convergence around responsible agro-investment principles for all stakeholders than can be implemented and monitored. Fourth, they can help establish and maintain mechanisms to disseminate information and good practices on management of land acquisitions by incorporating experience and lessons from existing multi-stakeholder initiatives (World Bank, 2010, p. xliv).

The logistically superior first political tendency and the popular second political tendency are objectively allied. Both of them tend to emphasize *procedural* issues and corresponding governance to these. This can be seen in broad coalitions or initiatives that key players in both tendencies are present in, such as the ILC, which is a coalition of international financial institutions such as the World Bank and IFAD, intergovernmental institutions such as the FAO, NGOs such as Oxfam and the Asian NGO Coalition (ANGOC), funded by multilateral agencies such as the World Bank and by bilateral development agencies, with an international secretariat funded and housed by IFAD in Rome (see Borras and Franco, 2009, for background). The ILC's Tirana Declaration, for example, defines land grabbing mainly based on procedural questions. They declared:

> We denounce large-scale land grabbing . . . which we define as acquisitions or concessions that are one or more of the following: (i) in violation of human rights, particularly the equal rights of women; (ii) not based on free, prior and informed consent of the affected land-users; (iii) not based on a thorough assessment, or are in disregard of social, economic and environmental impacts, including the way they are gendered; (iv) not based on transparent contracts that specify clear and binding commitments about activities, employment and benefits sharing, and; (v) not based on effective democratic planning, independent oversight and meaningful participation (ILC, 2011, n.p.).

This is, arguably, not significantly different from the PRAI put forward by the World Bank or the code of conduct initially proposed by IFPRI. If this type of global governance instrument continues to be the dominant objective of this dominant alliance, it is reasonable to expect that the trend in and character of contemporary land grabs will continue, but that the *manner* in which land deals are done may change: from non-transparent and non-consultative to transparent and consultative land grabs—but land grabbing, just the same.

Meanwhile, the 'stop and rollback' tendency's strength is its firm commitment to strategic questions, treating the problematic within a framework of *competing development models*, firmly rooted within an anti-capitalist stance. It stays away from too procedure-centered advocacy work and emphasizes questions around *substance and meaning* of land deals. It is focused on explaining why there is global land grabbing, why it should be opposed, and why it is important to think of a strategic alternative. But what seems to be a serious limitation with this tendency is what seems to be its weak tactical political positioning. It is relatively less concerned and involved in tactical issues (local cases or governance instruments), in contrast to the second current. For instance, it seems to be silent on and stays away from tactical issues around labor standards in the emerging plantation enclaves, which is understandable as its analysis of the problem and framing of alternative is small farm-centered. It seems to be lukewarm toward some issues related to international governance instruments, such as transparency instruments. These issues (labor standards, transparency instruments) are important mechanisms for tactical mass mobilizations and campaigns. Defaulting on these issues is likely to result in less than vibrant international campaigns to stop and rollback land grabbing because mass campaigns usually need tactical foci and occasional tactical victories in order to agitate and mobilize mass participants and sustain mass participation. Campaigns that are very strategic in nature, advanced mainly via broadly cast issues and master frames may, at best, bring the issue onto the official agendas and occasional news but are unlikely to push for substantial reforms (see Keck and Sikkink, 1998, p. 201).

One dilemma in the context of global governance then is: if the 'regulate to mitigate' tendency remains quite popular and influential but overly tactical in its work, while the 'regulate to stop and rollback' tendency remains logistically weak (e.g. least funded among all groups campaigning around land grabs) and relatively politically isolated with strategically framed campaigns without much of a tactical component—in the context of the objectively allied first and second political tendencies, then we are likely to see continuation of land grabbing and its legitimization in global rule-making, only with possible changes in the *manner* of how it is being carried out. A transnational governance framework, or a transnational policy and political

174

advocacy work that aspires to have *substantial and procedural* changes in the current large-scale land investments is only likely when it is it is able to combine—and combine well—strategic and tactical issues and political master frames and maneuver. *This means an alliance, objective or otherwise, between key actors in the second and third tendencies.* Tension and conflict are likely to mark such an alliance because of the differences in their histories, class bases, ideological frameworks, and political perspectives.

Concluding Discussion

There have been important recent changes in the international political economy of agriculture and the environment This transformation has partly led to the rise of new international players— namely BRICS, some MICs, and the Gulf states—and alliances among them, the rise of flex crops and commodities, as well as the repositioning of the central state as a key actor in the development process. This has implications for international and national governance of land grabbing. What we have done in the article is to identify emerging key issues in global governance of land grabbing, albeit in very preliminary manner.

We raised a number of important points in terms of changing context. First, there is a regime transition, albeit still quite fluid, from North Atlantic-anchored global food regime towards a more polycentric global food and agro-commodity regime where rules, rule-making, and rule-makers are being contested and recast. Second is the blurring of boundaries between the sectors of food, feed, energy, climate change mitigation strategies, finance, and industrial/commercial complexes—and the subsequent blurring of governance boundaries between them, resulting in, among others, a far more complex terrain for social movements and civil society campaigners. Third is the complication in terms of area of jurisdiction and level of intervention in terms of global governance amidst the repositioning of the central state as a key actor in contemporary land grabbing. This is complicated because of the dual contradictory task of the central state in facilitating capital accumulation while maintaining a minimum level of political legitimacy. In several countries, such as Brazil and Argentina, this is doubly complicated because they are both the destination *and* the origin of land grabbers. What will international governance instruments aimed at addressing land grabbing look like when these hit the *national* political terrain of governance? This is one of the key empirical questions that needs to be answered in the future.

The recent global agrarian transformations that shape and are reshaped by contemporary global land grabbing have resulted in the emergence of competing interpretations of the meaning of such dynamic changes, making the already complex terrain of global governance around land grabbing even more complicated. What we have at the moment and what we are likely to witness in the future is a three-way political battle to control the character, parameters, and trajectory of discourse, as well as the instruments in and the practice of global governance of land grabbing. This struggle is between the three tendencies, namely, 'regulate to facilitate', 'regulate to mitigate negative impacts and maximize opportunities', and 'regulate to block and rollback' land grabbing. Each tendency has its own take on and interpretation of transnational governance policies and instruments. In this context, the recently passed Voluntary Guidelines and global governance instruments such as transparency mechanisms and human rights instruments (see, e.g. De Schutter, 2011; Edelman and Carwil, 2011; Monsalve Suárez, forthcoming) will become both objects and arenas of this three-way political contestation. It is therefore not about the technical and administrative *form* of governance instruments that are crucial especially since everyone endorses transparency, consultation, accountability, and the Voluntary

Guidelines. The more crucial points are inherently political: the actual interpretation of the meaning and the transformation into authoritative instruments of (inter)national governance mechanisms to tackle the problem of land grabbing. Therefore, implementation will be an even more contested and important site of struggle than the negotiations of the rules were.

Whether (trans)national agrarian movements and their allies will be able to mobilize, get connected to the communities at the local land grab sites, and interpret and influence the Voluntary Guidelines implementation and the use of various other global governance instruments such as FPIC in the direction of their ideological stand remains to be seen. It will depend partly on how, and how well, they are able to (re)frame their political actions around land grabbing to address some disconnect between the changing context and the movements' campaign master frames that have in turn implications on how well they are able to influence the broader global governance of land grabbing. This can be seen in a number of examples: (1) Campaigns around oil palm and land grabbing remain framed generally in the context of biofuels, which, as discussed earlier, is a politically weak framing. (2) Land reform, which is a national governance instrument, remains the main demand put forward in response to land grabbing. This is problematic for a number of reasons, including the fact that many land grab sites involve lands that were previously redistributed to small farmers via land reforms, many land grabs occur in indigenous peoples' lands and their historic demand has never been land reform, and so on. Hence, land reform as a master frame needs to be critically assessed (see Borras and Franco, 2012 for an initial discussion of this). (3) International campaigns remain narrowly focused on conventional principal targets: North Atlantic-based TNCs and governments, despite the more polycentric character of the emerging food and agro-commodity regime. How to integrate BRICS and MICs among the targets of campaigns and how to carry out policy advocacy campaigns in this new global political-economic context remain among the most difficult of the challenges confronting (trans)national agrarian, environmental, and human rights movements trying the influence global governance of land grabbing.

Acknowledgements

We thank the three anonymous peer reviewers, Matias Margulis, and Nora McKeon for their very critical but helpful comments and suggestions on an earlier rough draft of this article.

Notes

1 Based on participant-observation research by the authors.
2 Sugarcane is low most likely because of the fact that Brazil, India and South Africa are important producers of this crop).
3 We thank one of the reviewers for suggesting to us to make our point on this more specific.
4 During the past four years, the authors have participated in UN Committee on World Food Security process, engaged in various CSO activities around land grabbing, discussed with various national government officials, providing us important insights that in turn led us to our framing of the three political tendencies.

Referencess

Akram-Lodhi, H. (2012) Contextualising land grabbing: contemporary land deals, the global subsistence crisis and the world food system, *Canadian Journal of Development Studies*, 33(2), pp. 119–142.
Anseeuw, W., Alden Wily, L., Cotula, L., & Taylor, M. (2011) *Land Rights and the Rush for Land* (Rome: International Land Coalition).

Borras, S. M. & Franco, J. C. (2009). Transnational Agrarian Movements Struggling for Land and Citizenship Rights, IDS Working Paper 323 (Brighton: Institute for Development Studies).

Borras, S. M & Franco, J. C. (2010) From threat to opportunity? Problems with the idea of a 'Code of Conduct' for land grabbing, *Yale Human Rights & Development Law Journal*, 13(1), pp. 507–523.

Borras, S. M. & Franco, J. C. (2012) A 'Land Sovereignty' Alternative? Towards a People's Counter-Enclosure, Agrarian Justice Discussion Paper, July 2012 (Amsterdam: Transnational Institute).

Borras, S. M., Edelman, M., & Kay C. (eds) (2008) *Transnational Agrarian Movements Confronting Globalization* (Oxford: Wiley-Blackwell).

Borras, S. M., Franco, J. C., Gomez, S., Kay, C., & Spoor, M (2012a) Land grabbing in Latin America and the Caribbean, *Journal of Peasant Studies*, 39(3–4), pp. 845–872.

Borras, S. M., Gomez, S., Kay, C., & Wilkinson, J. (2012b) Land grabbing and global capitalist accumulation: key features in Latin America, *Canadian Journal of Development Studies*, 33(4), pp. 2–16.

Claeys, P. & Vanloqueren, G. (2013) The minimum human rights principles applicable to large-scale land acquisitions or leases, *Globalizations*, 10(1), pp. 193–198.

Cotula, L. (2011) Land deals in Africa: what is in the contracts? (London: International Institute for Environment and Development), http://pubs.iied.org/pdfs/12568IIED.pdf.

Cotula, L. (2012) The international political economy of the global land rush: a critical appraisal of trends, scale, geography and drivers. *Journal of Peasant Studies*, 39(3&4), pp. 649–680.

De Schutter, O. (2011) How not to think of land-grabbing: three critiques of large-scale investments in farmland, *Journal of Peasant Studies* 38(2), pp. 249–279.

Deininger, K. (2011) Challenges posed by the new wave of farmland investment, *Journal of Peasant Studies*, 38(2), pp. 217–247.

Desmarais, A. (2007) *La Via Campesina: Globalization and the Power of Peasants* (Halifax: Fernwood; London: Pluto).

Edelman, M. & Carwil, J. (2011) Peasants' rights and the UN system: Quixotic struggle? Or emancipatory idea whose time has come?, *Journal of Peasant Studies*, 39(1), pp. 81–108.

Fairhead, J., Leach, M. & Scoones, I. (2012) Green grabbing: a new appropriation of nature?, *Journal of Peasant Studies*, 39(2), pp. 237–261.

Food and Agriculture Organization (FAO) (2008) *Biofuels: Prospects, Risks and Opportunities* (Rome: FAO).

FAO (2012) *Voluntary Guidelines on the Responsible Governance of Tenure of Land, Fisheries and Forests in the Context of National Food Security* (Rome: FAO), http://www.fao.org/fileadmin/user_upload/nr/land_tenure/pdf/VG_Final_May_2012.pdf.

FAO Statistics (FAOSTAT) (2012) Raw data downloaded between 15 March and 15 April 2012, http://www.faostat.org.

Food first Information Action Network (FIAN) (2011) Negotiations of the Voluntary Guidelines to continue in October: civil society will have to redouble efforts (Heidelberg: FIAN), http://www.fian.org.

Fox, J. (1993). *The Politics of Food in Mexico: State Power and Social Mobilization* (Ithaca, NY: Cornell University Press).

Franco, J. C. (2008) Peripheral justice? Rethinking justice sector reform in the Philippines, *World Development*, 36(10), pp. 1858–1873.

Franco, J. C., Levidow, L., Fig, D., Goldfarb, L., Hönicke, M., & Mendonca, M. L. (2010) Assumptions in the European Union biofuels policy: frictions with experiences in Germany, Brazil and Mozambique, *Journal of Peasant Studies*, 37(4), pp. 661–698.

Friedmann, H. & McMichael, P. D. (1989) Agriculture and the state system: the rise and fall of national agricultures, 1870 to the present, *Sociologia Ruralis*, 29(2), pp. 93–117.

Galeano, L. (2012). Paraguay and the expansion of the Brazilian and Argentinian agribusiness frontiers, *Canadian Journal of Development Studies*, 33(4), pp. 458–470.

Grajales, Jacobo (2011) The rifle and the title: paramilitary violence, land grab and land control in Colombia, *Journal of Peasant Studies*, 38(4), pp. 771–792.

Holt-Gimenez, E. & Shattuck, A. (2011) Food crises, food regimes and food movements: rumblings of reform or tides of transformation? *Journal of Peasant Studies*, 38(1), pp. 109–144.

International Land Coalition (ILC) (2011) *Tirana Declaration*, http://www.landcoalition.org/about-us/aom2011/tirana-declaration.

Kay, S. & Franco, J. C. (2012) *The Global Water Grab: A Primer* (Amsterdam: Transnational Institute).

Keck, M. & Sikkink, K. (1998) *Activists Beyond Borders* (Ithaca, NY: Cornell University Press).

Kröger, M. (2012) The expansion of industrial tree plantations and dispossession in Brazil, *Development and Change*, 43(4), pp. 947–973.

Kröger, M. (2013) *Contentious Agency and Natural Resource Politics* (London: Routledge).

Künnemann, R. & Monsalve Suárez, S. (2013) International human rights and governing land grabbing: a view from global civil society, *Globalizations*, 10(1), pp. 123–139.

Lee, S. & Riel Muller, A. (2012) South Korean external strategy qualms: analysis of Korean overseas agricultural investment within the global food system, Paper presented at the Global Land Grabbing II conference at Cornell University organized by the Land Deal Politics Initiative (LDPI), 17–19 October.

McCarthy, J. F. (2010) Processes of inclusion and adverse incorporation: oil palm and agrarian change in Sumatra, Indonesia, *Journal of Peasant Studies*, 37(4), pp. 821–850.

McKeon, N. (2010) *The United Nations and Civil Society—Whose Voice?* (London: Zed).

McKeon, N. (2013) 'One does not sell the land upon which the people walk': land grabbing, transnational rural social movements, and global governance, *Globalizations*, 10(1), pp. 105–122.

McMichael, P. D. (2009) A food regime genealogy, *Journal of Peasant Studies*, 36(1), pp. 139–169.

McMichael, P. D. (2012) The land grab and corporate food regime restructuring, *Journal of Peasant Studies*, 39(3&4), pp. 681–701.

Margulis, M. E. & Porter, T. (2013) Governing the global land grab: multipolarity, ideas, and complexity in transnational governance, *Globalizations*, 10(1), pp. 65–86.

Margulis, M. E., McKeon, N., & Borras, S. M. (2013) Land grabbing and global governance: critical perspectives, *Globalizations*, 10(1), pp. 1–23.

Mehta, L., van Veldwisch, G., & Franco, J.C. (2012) Introduction to the special issue: water grabbing? Focus on the (re)appropriation of finite water resources, *Water Alternatives* 5(2), pp. 193–207.

Monsalve Suárez, S. (forthcoming) Grassroots voices: the human rights framework in contemporary agrarian struggles, *Journal of Peasant Studies*, 40(1).

Murmis, M. & Murmis, M. R. (2012) Land concentration and foreign land ownership in Argentina in the context of global land grabbing, *Canadian Journal of Development Studies*, 33(4), pp. 490–508.

Oxfam (2011) *Land and Power: the Growing Scandal Surrounding the New Wave of Investments in Land* (Oxford: Oxfam International).

Oxfam (2012) *Our Lands, Our Lives: Time Out on the Global Land Rush* (Oxford: Oxfam International).

Patel, R. (2009) Food sovereignty, *Journal of Peasant Studies*, 36(3), pp. 663–706.

Peluso, N. & Lund, C. (2011) New frontiers of land control, *Journal of Peasant Studies*, 38(4), pp. 667–681.

Perrone, N. M. (2013). Restrictions to foreign acquisitions of agricultural land in Argentina and Brazil, *Globalizations*, 10(1), pp. 205–209.

Sauer, S. & Leite Pereira, S. (2012) Agrarian structure, foreign investments on land, and land price in Brazil, *Journal of Peasant Studies*, 39(3–4), pp. 873–898.

Sawyer, S. & Gomez, T. (2008) *Transnational Governmentality and Resource Extraction: Indigenous Peoples, Multinational Corporations, Multinational Institutions and the State* (Geneva: UNRISD).

Scott, J. (1998) *Seeing Like a State: How Certain Schemes to Improve the Human Condition Have Failed* (New Haven, CT: Yale University Press).

Seufert, P. (2013) The FAO Voluntary Guidelines on the Responsible Governance of Tenure of Land, Fisheries and Forests, *Globalizations*, 10(1), pp. 181–186.

Urioste, M. (2012) Concentration and 'foreignization' of land in Bolivia, *Canadian Journal of Development Studies*, 33(4), pp. 439–457.

Vermeulen, S. & Cotula, L. (2010) Over the heads of the local people: consultation, consent and recompense in large-scale land deals for biofuels in Africa, *Journal of Peasant Studies* 37(4), pp. 899–916.

Via Campesina (2008) Small farmers feed the world, industrial agrofuels fuel hunger and poverty. A media release, 24 June (Jakarta: La Via Campesina).

Via Campesina (2012) La Via Campesina Notebook No. 3: International Conference of Peasant and Farmers: Stop Land Grabbing! (Jakarta: La Via Campesina).

Visser, O. & Spoor, M. (2011) Land grabbing in post-Soviet Eurasia: the world's agricultural land reserves at stake, *Journal of Peasant Studies*, 38(2), pp. 299–323.

Von Braun, J. & Meinzen-Dick, R. (2009) 'Land grabbing' by foreign investors in developing countries: risks and opportunities, IFPRI Policy Brief 13 (Washington DC: International Food Political Research Institute).

White, B. & Dasgupta, A. (2010) Agrofuels capitalism: a view from political economy, *Journal of Peasant Studies*, 37(4), pp. 593–607.

White, B., Borras, S. M, Hall, R., Scoones, I., & Wolford, W. (2012) The new enclosures: critical perspectives on corporate land deals, *Journal of Peasant Studies*, 39(3&4), pp. 619–647.

Wilkinson, J., Reydon, B., & di Sabbato, A. (2012) Concentration and foreign ownership of land in Brazil in the context of global land grabbing phenomenon, *Canadian Journal of Development Studies*, 33(4), pp. 417–438.

Woertz, E. (2013) The governance of Gulf agro-investments, *Globalizations*, 10(1), pp. 87–104.
Woodhouse, P. (2012) New investment, old challenges: land deals and the water constraint in African agriculture, *Journal of Peasant Studies*, 39(3&4), pp. 777–794.
Woods, K. (2011) Ceasefire capitalism: military–private partnerships, resource concessions and military–state building in the Burma–China borderlands, *Journal of Peasant Studies,* 38(4), pp. 747–770.
World Bank (2010) *Rising Global Interest in Farmland: Can It Yield Sustainable and Equitable Results?* (Washington DC: World Bank).

Saturnino M. Borras Jr. is Associate Professor at the International Institute of Social Studies (ISS) in The Hague, a fellow of the Transnational Institute (TNI) and Food First, and Adjunct Professor at the College of Humanities and Development (COHD) of China Agricultural University (CAU) in Beijing. He is co-coordinator of the Land Deal Politics Initiatives (LDPI; www.iss.nl/ldpi) which is an international network of academics doing research on global land grabbing. He is co-editor, together with Marc Edelman and Cristobal Kay of the book *Transnational Agrarian Movements Confronting Globalization* (Wiley-Blackwell, 2008).

Chunyu Wang is Associate Professor at the College of Humanities and Development of China Agricultural University in Beijing and was a China Scholarship Council postdoctoral fellow at International Institute of Social Studies (2011–2012) when she carried out her research on land grabbing and the politics of the negotiations on the Voluntary Guidelines on Land Tenure in the UN Committee for Food Security in Rome.

Jennifer C. Franco is coordinator of the Agrarian Justice Program of Transnational Institute and Adjunct Professor at the College of Humanities and Development (COHD) of China Agricultural University (CAU) in Beijing.

The FAO Voluntary Guidelines on the Responsible Governance of Tenure of Land, Fisheries and Forests

PHILIP SEUFERT

FIAN International, Heidelberg, Germany

ABSTRACT   *In May 2012, the UN Committee on World Food Security (CFS) endorsed the Voluntary Guidelines on the Responsible Governance of Tenure of Land, Fisheries and Forests. This article provides an overview on this new document. It puts the Guidelines in the context of the FAOs efforts to raise awareness on the importance of good governance of land and natural resource tenure, as emphasized in the 2006 final declaration of the International Conference on Agrarian Reform and Rural Development (ICARRD), as well as of the discussions on responses to the current new wave of land grabbing. The main objective of the Voluntary Guidelines is to provide practical guidance to governments to improve governance of natural resources, recognizing that secure tenure rights and equitable access to land, fisheries, and forests are crucial to achieve food security and the progressive realization of the right to adequate food. The article argues that despite being "voluntary" the Guidelines explicitly refer to existing human rights obligations related to natural resources and provide interpretation and guidance on how to implement them. It further looks back on the process that lead to the final document and analyses the roles of UN agencies, states and civil society. The article emphasizes that the inclusive and participatory character of the process gives the Guidelines a high level of legitimacy and political weight. Therefore all efforts are necessary to ensure implementation, with a special responsibility for states and UN agencies. The article further underlines the potential of the Voluntary Guidelines in improving accountability and monitoring on tenure issues. Finally, it addresses some controversial issues of the Guidelines, with a special attention to criticism raised by civil society. It concludes that despite these critiques the Voluntary Guidelines remain useful as a tool to advance progressive land tenure policies that are clearly anchored in existing international human rights obligations.*

Background and Scope of the Voluntary Guidelines

Since 2005, the Food and Agriculture Organization of the United Nations (FAO) has been working on raising awareness of the importance of good governance of land and natural resource tenure. The final declaration of the International Conference on Agrarian Reform and Rural Development (ICARRD, 2006) adopted by 92 FAO member states in 2006 highlighted the fundamental importance of secure and sustainable access to land, water, and other natural resources and of agrarian reform for hunger and poverty eradication. It further recalled the 2004 *Voluntary Guidelines to Support the Progressive Realization of the Right to Adequate Food in the Context of National Food Security*, and an approach based on economic, social, and cultural rights as essential considerations when dealing with land and natural resources issues. In 2009, the FAO built on these experiences and launched an initiative to adopt voluntary guidelines for the 'governance of land and other natural resources tenure' to develop a broad agreement jointly among governments, civil society organizations, and multilateral institutions, and to be approved by FAO member states and supported by other interested stakeholders. The process to negotiate these guidelines coincided with the global land rush by investors, commonly referred to as land grabbing.

According to their preface, the Voluntary Guidelines are intended to 'contribute to the global and national efforts towards the eradication of hunger and poverty' and pursue 'the overarching goal of achieving food security and the progressive realization of the right to adequate food in the context of national food security' (FAO, 2012). Recognizing that, in order to achieve this, secure tenure rights and equitable access to land, fisheries, and forests are crucial, they are intended to serve as a reference and to provide practical guidance to governments to improve governance of these resources.

The Voluntary Guidelines thus deal with the governance of tenure of land, fisheries, and forests, in other words: who decides which resources can be used by whom and under which conditions, and how this decision-making should be done.[1] In comparison to some other responses to land grabbing such as the Principles for Responsible Agricultural Investment (PRAI), the Voluntary Guidelines address the issue of land and natural resources tenure in a more comprehensive way, linking it with investment, agriculture, food policies, rural development, and with other international policies.

The document is divided into seven parts and contains recommendations on general principles of responsible governance of tenure, on the legal recognition and allocation of tenure rights, on transfers and other changes to tenure rights (such as restitution and redistributive reforms), administration of tenure, responses to climate change and emergencies (such as natural disasters and conflicts), as well as on the promotion, implementation, monitoring, and evaluation of the Guidelines. Overall, the guidelines constitute a framework for policies, legislation, and programs that actors can use when developing their own strategies, policies, legislation, and programs.

As their official name indicates, the Voluntary Guidelines are voluntary and thus do not establish new legally binding obligations nor replace existing national or international laws, treaties, or agreements (FAO, 2012, p. 2). However, they explicitly refer to existing binding international human rights obligations related to land and natural resources and provide interpretation and guidance on how to implement these obligations. Before, there was no such an authoritative international interpretation.

An Inclusive Negotiation Process

The Voluntary Guidelines have been developed in a process that lasted more than three years and that included regional consultations on all continents and several rounds of negotiations in the newly reformed CFS (see McKeon, 2013, pp. 105–122).

As already mentioned, the Voluntary Guidelines have been initiated and developed by the FAO, especially its Tenure Division. FAO is the UN agency in charge of normative issues related to food and agriculture and initiated this process in order to consolidate their normative work with respect to land administration policies. Several governments, mainly European ones, joined FAO in the process and supported the process with funding. At a later stage in the process, Brazil made it clear that the Voluntary Guidelines had to be understood as part of ICARRD follow-up, which was not the case at the beginning of the consultation process. The USA, who initially appeared resistant to the idea of the Voluntary Guidelines, eventually offered to chair the negotiations. Some African countries were hesitant from the outset about the usefulness of these guidelines, because in 2009 the African Union had only recently adopted a Land Policy Framework, and these countries were unsure how the two instruments would relate to one another. However, African states eventually became deeply engaged in the negotiations under the leadership of Zimbabwe. China carefully followed the entire process and was, along with Afghanistan, the only Asian country actively participating in the debates. The Office of the High Commissioner for Human Rights, the World Bank, and the International Fund for Agricultural Development (IFAD) participated in the negotiations, providing technical advice.

The Voluntary Guidelines negotiation process was substantially supported by global civil society, including non-governmental organizations (NGOs) and transnational peasant movements.[2] This was in order to continue the earlier multi-stakeholder dialogue that was institutionalized during the Parallel Forum to the ICARRD process. Global civil society also sought to incorporate into the FAO setting and the deliberations consideration of existing international human rights and environmental law provisions protecting the rights to land and natural resources of all rural peoples, including indigenous and non-indigenous peoples.[3]

Global civil society hoped that the multi-stakeholder consultation process could contribute to a more democratic decision-making process for global food and agriculture policies. To achieve this, global civil society made its participation conditional to applying FAO's 'Principles of Engagement' with civil society constituencies in global policy forums and demanded the same rules of participation as in the ICARRD process: autonomous and self-organized participation, especially of social movements, throughout all stages of the process. Once the new framework for the reformed CFS was in place in 2009 (see McKeon, 2013, pp. 105–122), civil society organizations (CSOs) pushed for an intergovernmental negotiation in this body.

CSOs also clearly emphasized the link between the Voluntary Guidelines and the growing privatization and commoditization of nature as exemplified in the case of global land grabbing, while taking into account that governments and FAO itself pointed out that the process was not about developing 'guidelines against land grabbing'.

Negotiating the Voluntary Guidelines comprised several steps. In a first phase, a consultation process took place through 2009 and 2010 during which government officials, CSOs, private sector representatives, and academics identified key issues, best practices, and possible policy options. This phase included 10 regional consultations, four consultations with civil society and one with the private sector. This first phase produced a zero draft document written by the FAO's Tenure Division that was then submitted for an open, web-based consultation in April and May 2011. This process permitted all interested parties and individuals, including global publics, to comment on the zero draft and make suggestions for alternative text and modifications. Based on these inputs, the FAO then elaborated a first draft that served as the basis for the intergovernmental negotiations at the CFS. The negotiation phase consisted of three rounds of talks in July and October 2011, and March 2012, when they were concluded and agreed to. The Voluntary Guidelines were formally endorsed by the CFS in a special session in May 2012.

The voluntary nature of the Voluntary Guidelines may raise questions about their effectiveness and performance. However, with respect to the negotiation process and its outcomes, the combination of the UN principle of one country, one vote and the institutionalized participation of CSOs throughout the process (including a special effort by FAO to facilitate the participation of the most marginalized groups affected by landlessness and tenure insecurity) points to one of the most democratic institutional frameworks for global decision-making for international agreements ever. It is this experiment in global democracy that ascribes a high level of legitimacy and political weight to the Voluntary Guidelines.

Implementation and Monitoring

As mentioned before, the Voluntary Guidelines set out principles and internationally accepted standards to provide practical guidance on the responsible governance of tenure. While in a broader sense they are targeted at all relevant actors including governments, private sector, CSOs, academia, as well as people and communities who hold tenure rights, they are primarily addressed to states, and set a framework for national policies, legislation, and programs. Given the fact that land and natural resource tenure issues vary considerably across countries, not all parts of the document apply in the same way to all states. One important element of the proposed implementation process contained in the Voluntary Guidelines is the setting up of national roundtables and platforms for dialogue with all stakeholders. These mechanisms are intended to identify the main problems and possible solutions regarding tenure and priorities when implementing the Voluntary Guidelines at the national level. At the global level, with the Voluntary Guidelines being an accepted standard set by the CFS, and because the CFS is supposed to foster international policy convergence in the field of food security and nutrition, this requires all relevant UN agencies to support the implementation of the Voluntary Guidelines in their work.

One area where Voluntary Guidelines have significant potential is to improve accountability and monitoring on tenure issues related to land, fisheries, and forests. The Voluntary Guidelines have built-in global monitoring processes in that they recommend that the CFS Secretariat work in collaboration with the Advisory Group[4] to report regularly in the future to the CFS on the progress of the implementation of the guidelines (FAO, 2012, p. 34). In addition, they call for CFS Secretariat and the Advisory Group to evaluate their impact and their contribution to the improvement of tenure governance at the national level. States and other CFS participants are currently discussing the potential design of a CFS-based monitoring mechanism with several proposals under consideration. For example, CSOs have proposed two options in this regard. One option is an independent body that reviews progress in improving governance of tenure and that uses the Voluntary Guidelines as a baseline. A second option is a process where states would present reports on their progress in implementing the Voluntary Guidelines that would be peer-reviewed by other states, CSOs, and other CFS participants. There is general support for establishing monitoring mechanisms at national level, however, the details remain under discussion.

Evaluation and Controversial Issues

While the adoption of the Voluntary Guidelines by the CFS has been generally acclaimed by all the parties involved in the negotiations, there has also been significant internal criticism.[5] This is not surprising if one considers that the final text of the Voluntary Guidelines was agreed by governments, and that in order to reach a final consensus the text had to accommodate conflicting views. As a result, several aspects of the Voluntary Guidelines were drafted in a general and/or ambiguous fashion. This section highlights these tensions. However, due to the confidential nature of the negotiations, these will be discussed in general terms.

From the onset of the negotiation process some issues were highly controversial. Take for example water, which from a very early stage was excluded outright for negotiation due to strong pressure from some governments. CSOs resisted this but were not successful in keeping water on the table. CSOs and their allies considered the omission of water from the final text as a major shortcoming of the Voluntary Guidelines. However, there may be some room for maneuver in the future because the preface mentions that states may wish to take the Voluntary Guidelines into account in the responsible governance of other natural resources that are 'inextricably linked to land, fisheries and forests, such as water and mineral resources'.

The Voluntary Guidelines' treatment of investment was one of the most controversial issues during the negotiations. Conflicting views on the issue of land grabbing became visible during the negotiation as CSOs pushed very strongly for an international ban on land grabbing. Several developing country governments asserted their belief that the large-scale acquisition of tenure rights (in other words, land grabbing) constituted investment essential for national economic development. While the final document accepts the latter position, there are several well-defined safeguards to control large-scale acquisition of tenure rights and their impacts (FAO, 2012, pp. 11–12). The issue of agricultural investment will be further and more thoroughly dealt with by the CFS in a separate process on responsible agricultural investment launched in late 2012.

CSOs, among others, were critical over the reluctance of some states to reiterate their existing human rights obligations in the context of the governance of natural resources. For example, CSOs representing indigenous peoples at the negotiations criticized the fact that several governments attempted to weaken the elements in the Voluntary Guidelines that contained explicit references to the *United Nations Declaration on the Rights of Indigenous Peoples* (UNDRIP). In particular, several states strongly opposed the inclusion of provisions related to restitution of ancestral lands into the Voluntary Guidelines but which is affirmed in the UNDRIP. As a result of this blocking strategy by states, some CSOs and indigenous peoples fear that the Voluntary Guidelines may constitute a step backwards in the recognition of their rights with respect to UNDRIP.

More generally, there has been harsh criticism of the Voluntary Guidelines from NGOs and social movements that consider the 'voluntary' guidelines as useless and inadequate to stop land grabbing. However, and as already mentioned, several CSOs and especially organizations of small-scale food producers—and thus those segments of the population most threatened and affected by land grabbing—expect to be able to refer to some of the more useful provisions in the Voluntary Guidelines to back their claims. Whereas these marginalized groups agree that a legally binding framework would have been preferable, they also point to the fact that the political reality is that it is extremely difficult, if not impossible, at the present moment to persuade governments to adopt binding international standards. Recognizing this political reality, the Voluntary Guidelines remain useful as a tool to advance progressive land tenure policies that are clearly anchored in existing international human rights obligations and thus have to be interpreted in full compliance with the highest international human rights standards.

Notes

1   FAO defines tenure as the relationship, whether defined legally or customarily, among people with respect to land (including associated buildings and other structures), fisheries, forests, and other natural resources. The rules of

tenure define how access is granted to use and control over these resources, as well as associated responsibilities and restraints. They determine who can use which resources, for how long, and under which conditions. Tenure systems may be based on written policies and laws, as well as on unwritten customs and practices (FAO, 2002).

2   During self-organized consultations CSOs developed their own proposal of the Guidelines, which was presented as input to the official process. For more information, see FIAN International (2011).

3   So far, only indigenous peoples have an international recognition of their rights to land and natural resources. Other rural groups like peasants, pastoralists, and fisherfolk see the international recognition of their rights to land and natural resources scattered in different instruments and in a precarious way.

4   The CFS Advisory Group is made up of representatives from the five different categories of CFS participants. These are: UN agencies and other UN bodies; civil society and NGOs, particularly organizations representing smallholder family farmers, fisherfolk, herders, landless, urban poor, agricultural and food workers, women, youth, consumers, and indigenous people; international agricultural research institutions; international and regional financial institutions such as the World Bank, the International Monetary Fund, regional development banks, and the World Trade Organization; private sector associations and philanthropic foundations.

5   For a more detailed assessment of the Tenure Guidelines from a civil society perspective, see Monsalve Suárez (2012).

References

Food and Agriculture Organization of the United Nations (FAO) (2002) *Land Tenure and Rural Development* (Rome: FAO), http://www.fao.org/DOCREP/005/Y4307E/y4307e00.htm#.

FAO (2012) *Voluntary Guidelines on the Responsible Governance on Tenure of Land, Fisheries and Forests in the Context of National Food Security* (Rome: FAO), http://www.fao.org/nr/tenure/voluntary-guidelines/en.

ICARRD (2006) Final Declaration of the International Conference on Agrarian Reform and Rural Development, http://www.icarrd.org/news_down/C2006_Decl_en.doc.

McKeon, N. (2013) 'One does not sell the land upon which the people walk': land grabbing, rural social movements, and global governance, *Globalizations*, 10(1), pp. 105–122.

Suggested Reading

FIAN International (2011) Civil Society Organizations' Proposals for the FAO Voluntary Guidelines on Responsible Governance of Land and Natural Resources Tenure (Heidelberg: FIAN), http://www.fian.org/resources/documents/others/cso-proposals-fao-land-guidlines?set_language=en.

Monsalve Suárez, S. (2012) The recently adopted guidelines on the responsible governance of tenure of land, fisheries, and forests: a turning point in the global governance of natural resources?, In *Right to Food and Nutrition Watch 2012: Who Decides about Global Food and Nutrition? Strategies to Regain Control* (Brot für die Welt/FIAN/Interchurch Organisation for Development Cooperation), pp. 37–42, http://www.rtfn-watch.org.

Philip Seufert is a program officer at FIAN International, a human rights organization for the right to food. He works on the access to natural resources and land grabbing. FIAN has a long history of documenting cases of agrarian conflicts and violations of the right to food linked to the loss of access to land and natural resources, as well as of supporting peasant communities in fighting for their rights. The author has closely followed the negotiation process of the Voluntary Guidelines, in which FIAN facilitated the working group of the Civil Society Mechanism (CSM) to the CFS.

The Principles of Responsible Agricultural Investment

PHOEBE STEPHENS

Independent Researcher, Toronto, Canada

ABSTRACT   *In 2009 the Group of Eight called for the development of principles to promote responsible agricultural investment as a means to regulate foreign investment in land. This essay contextualizes the development of principles for responsible agricultural investment within the global land grab. In particular, the essay examines the Principles that Respects Rights, Livelihoods and Resources proposed by multilateral organizations in 2010 and the decision by the Committee on World Food Security in 2012 to initiate a multi-stakeholder process to develop principles for responsible agricultural investments.*

In January 2010, the World Bank, the Food and Agriculture Organization of the United Nations (FAO), the International Fund for Agricultural Development (IFAD), and the United Nations Conference on Trade and Development (UNCTAD) published a document entitled *Principles for Responsible Agricultural Investment that Respects Rights, Livelihoods and Resources* (PRAI). As stated in the introduction to this volume (Margulis et al., 2013, pp. 1-23), these Principles were developed in reaction to the 'sharp increase in investment involving significant use of agricultural land, water, grassland, and forested areas in developing and emerging countries' prompted by factors such as 'the 2008 price spike in food and fuel prices, a desire by countries dependent on food imports to secure food supplies in the face of uncertainty and market volatility, speculation on land and commodity price increases, search for alternative energy sources, and possibly anticipation of payments for carbon sequestration' (FAO et al., 2010, p. 1).

Background

In light of how rapidly the land grabbing phenomenon was coming to public attention following the publication of the civil society denunciation of land grabbing (GRAIN, 2008), in 2009 the

Group of Eight (G8) committed at its summit in L'Aquila, to 'work with partner countries and international organizations to develop a joint proposal on principles and best practices for international agricultural investment' (G8, 2009). This commitment quickly translated into intergovernmental action to develop tools and guidelines for best practices. In September 2009 the government of Japan, along with the World Bank, FAO, IFAD, and UNCTAD, hosted a roundtable entitled 'Promoting Responsible International Investment in Agriculture' at the margins of the UN General Assembly which aimed at launching an intergovernmental response to land grabbing. Representatives from 31 governments and 13 organizations, including a private bank and a multinational agri-food corporation, attended the roundtable where the basic outlines for principles and a framework for responsible global agricultural investment were agreed. The report urged the four multilateral organizations to undertake work on policy options in consultation with states, investors, and civil society, however, the actual drafting process was a top-down endeavor tightly managed by international organizations.

A first version of PRAI was made public in January 2010 in a discussion paper jointly prepared by the World Bank, FAO, IFAD, and UNCTAD (FAO et al., 2010). This inter-agency discussion paper, *Principles for Responsible Agricultural Investment that Respects Rights, Livelihoods and Resources* (PRAI) outlined seven principles (see Box 1). The PRAI discussion paper report was intended to encourage discussion over regulating land grabs from a broad selection of stakeholders including civil society organizations, multilateral and bilateral donor agencies, and all major investor categories. As a point of departure, the PRAI emphasized the important role of investment, especially private investment, in agriculture as central to increase smallholder farm productivity and its potential to contribute to economic

---

Box 1. The Principles for Responsible Agricultural Investment are:

Principle 1 (Respecting land and resource rights): existing rights to land and associated natural resources are recognized and respected.

Principle 2 (Ensuring food security): investments do not jeopardize food security but rather strengthen it.

Principle 3 (Ensuring transparency, good governance, and proper enabling environment): processes for accessing land and other resources and then making associated investments are transparent, monitored, and ensure accountability by all stakeholders, within a proper business, legal, and regulatory environment.

Principle 4 (Consultation and participation): all those materially affected are consulted, and agreements from consultations are recorded and enforced.

Principle 5 (Responsible agro-enterprise investing): investors ensure that projects respect the rule of law, reflect industry best practice, are viable economically, and result in durable shared value.

Principle 6 (Social sustainability): investments generate desirable and distributional impacts and do not increase vulnerability.

Principle 7 (Environmental sustainability): environmental impacts due to a project are quantified and measures taken to encourage sustainable resource use while minimizing the risk/magnitude of negative impacts and mitigating them.

---

growth and poverty reduction. Despite its favorable disposition to private investment, the discussion paper also noted that the surge in agricultural investment in the form of land grabs undermined growth and poverty reduction when 'large tracts of land are shifted from production of food crops to non-food crops' (e.g. biofuels and animal feed), when food produced in areas that suffer food shortages is destined mainly for export markets, and when conversion to mono-cropping undermines the resilience of local ecological system (FAO et al., 2010, pp. 6–7).

The above discussion foregrounds the framing of the principles as risk-minimizing mechanisms and the importance of industry-led forms of governance. The prominence of risks—risks to investors, risks to capital, risk to land rights—is notable throughout the inter-agency discussion paper. This is why the authors of the paper seek to expand upon existing industry self-regulation initiatives like the Extractive Industry Transparency Initiative (EITI), the Equator Principles, and the Santiago Principles to develop a mix of guidelines, codes of good or best practices in the context of land grabbing (Inter-Agency Panel, 2010; see also Margulis and Porter, 2013, pp. 65–86).

Since the introduction of the PRAI in 2010, it has received substantial attention at the global level. On one end of the spectrum, the PRAI are championed not just by their authors, the multilateral institutions, but endorsed by the G8 and subsequently the Group of Twenty (G20). In November 2010 at the G20's Seoul Summit, world leaders referred to PRAI as part of the *Seoul Development Consensus for Shared Growth*, and called for states and companies to uphold the principles (G20, 2010, p. 6). However, there has also been major political backlash against these principles. For example, the UN Special Rapporteur on the Right to Food, Dr Olivier De Schutter, has been highly critical of PRAI even arguing it is 'providing policy-makers with a checklist of how to destroy the global peasantry responsibly' (De Schutter, 2011, p. 254). Significant transnational advocacy has been directed against the PRAI by civil society and social movements, such as the campaign 'Why We Oppose the Principles for Responsible Agricultural Investment', led by an increasingly vocal global food sovereignty movement rejecting PRAI as a 'long-term corporate takeover of rural people's farmlands' (GCAR, 2010, p. 2).

World Bank's Defense of PRAI

The World Bank's land grabbing study, *Rising Global Interest in Farmland* (Deininger et al., 2011) constituted an effort to shape the debate about land and investment, especially in regard to informing policymakers' understanding of land grabs and the desirability of PRAI as a regulatory response. The study report was self-identified as a 'dialogue with governments to define principles, provide guidance, and assess the magnitude of ongoing trends through empirical research' and to agree on 'a definition of issues, best practices, decision tools, guidelines and codes of practice for governments and investors in land-extensive agriculture' (World Bank, 2010).

The World Bank study seeks to build a case for PRAI. The stakeholders that the report considers integral to achieving positive outcomes with respect to land grabbing are governments in target countries, investors, civil society, and international institutions and the report addresses recommendations to each category. Ultimately, the Bank identifies the RAI as the best way forward in terms of regulating land grabs.

The Bank calls on recipient countries to improve administrative structures, provide infrastructure, clarify and secure local rights, and protect critical natural resources. Investors are considered to be highly sensitive to reputational risk and thus it is taken as a given that they will engage in activities that minimize social dislocation and environmental destruction. Civil society organizations are called upon to educate communities on their rights, provide specific assistance in negotiation and monitoring, and perform a watchdog function to draw attention to noncompliance with existing policy or 'globally agreed norms' (Deininger et al., 2011, p. 137). Finally, the Bank regards international organizations as performing a bridging function that encourages stakeholders to agree on a standard set of principles.

Initially, the World Bank planned on piloting the RAI principles with six case studies (Ibid., p. 138). However, the Bank has chosen to 'retrofit' the principles to pre-existing projects. Forty land investment projects are being been chosen for initial study, two-thirds of these in Africa with the rest in Asia. After the preliminary stages, investors and community members associated with the projects are being interviewed and 15 cases will be retained for more in-depth analysis. Conclusions from the case studies are expected to be made available by May 2013.

Consideration of the PRAI in the context of the Committee on World Food Security

Conscious of the lack of legitimacy from which the PRAI suffered since they had been developed without any sort of meaningful consultative process, its promoters sought to obtain the endorsement of the Committee on World Food Security (CFS). This CFS had been reformed in October 2009 to constitute the foremost inclusive global forum deliberating on food security issues (McKeon, 2013, pp. 105–122). The discussion document prepared for the Policy Roundtable on 'Land Tenure and International Investment in Agriculture' at the 37th Session of the CFS in October 2010 proposed that the CFS 'endorse the on-going elaboration' of the PRAI initiated by the four agencies. This discursive formulation of an endorsement was strongly contested by the civil society participants, by the G77 countries who resented the fact that they had not been consulted in formulating the PRAI, and by others who considered that the CFS would lose its authority if it simply ratified instruments developed in other forums for which food security is not the primary mission. The decision finally adopted the CFS used the wording 'taking note of the on-going process' rather than 'endorsing'. In addition, the Committee decided to start a new and 'inclusive process of consideration of the principles within the CFS' consistent with and complementary to the *Voluntary Guidelines on the Responsible Governance of Tenure of Land, Fisheries and Forests* (hereinafter 'Voluntary Guidelines') which the same session agreed to negotiate. It was subsequently agreed that the investment in agriculture consultation would begin only once the Voluntary Guidelines had been adopted, which occurred on 11 May 2012. Provisions on investment in the Voluntary Guidelines were among the most strongly debated (McKeon, 2013, this volume; Seufert, 2013, pp. 181–186).

Terms of Reference for the consultation were adopted by the 39th Session of CFS in October 2012 following a highly contentious debate regarding the scope and purpose of the PRAI and the format of the consultation. Some G8 nations, principally the US and Canada, along with Australia, the corporate sector, and the World Bank and IFAD fought to take the current PRAI as the basis for the consultation, to focus it exclusively on foreign investment, and to conduct it as rapidly as possible. Civil society and social movements, allied with a number of G77 countries, insisted instead on starting anew from small-scale producers' own investments, recognized to account for the bulk of all investments in agriculture. In their view, the objective would be to develop principles within a human rights framework that would support investments targeted at small-scale producers and defend them from potentially negative impacts of corporate and speculative investments. In addition, African states, the region most targeted by large-scale investments, underlined their need for clear guidance to set in place national frameworks which would mobilize domestic investments in the first instance, and ensure that foreign investments be supportive of domestic dynamics and processes. A decentralized, inclusive two-year consultation process was considered to be essential in order to involve all stakeholders and raise awareness of the importance of using sustainable and resilient food security objectives as a reference point for investment frameworks. The Terms of Reference as adopted take most of these points into consideration, and consultations will be carried out over the next two years. The results of the consultation will be submitted to the CFS for debate and adoption at its 41st Session in October 2014. In the meantime the World Bank is continuing to pilot the PRAI, with support from the G8-led New Alliance for Food Security and Nutrition.

The PRAI is indicative of new regulation for land grabbing that does not stand alone but that falls within the wider governance framework for the global food and agricultural system. Cohen and Clapp (2009, p. 6) point out the incoherent global governance architecture of food and agriculture: 'Many international institutions claim a role, mandates overlap, and power structures within the relevant institutions vary considerably.' The contrast between the PRAI, championed by the G8, and the principles under development in the CFS is exemplary in this regard.

References

Buffett, H. (2010) *(Mis)Investment in Agriculture: The Role of the International Finance Corporation in Global Land Grabs* (Oakland, CA: Oakland Institute).

Cohen, M. J. & Clapp, J. (2009) *The Global Food Crisis: Governance Challenges and Opportunities* (Waterloo: Centre for International Governance Innovation and Wilfrid Laurier University Press).

Deininger, K., Byerlee, D., Lindsay, J., Norton, A., Selod, H., & Stickler, M. (2011) *Rising Global Interest in Farmland* (Washington, DC: World Bank).

De Schutter, O. (2011) How not to think about land-grabbing: three critiques of large-scale investments in farmland, *Journal of Peasant Studies*, 38(2), pp. 249–279.

FAO, IFAD, UNCTAD, & World Bank (2010) Principles for responsible agricultural investment that respects rights, livelihoods and resources: discussion note prepared to contribute to an ongoing global dialogue, http://siteresources.worldbank.org/INTARD/214574-1111138388661/22453321/Principles_Extended.pdf.

Farmlandgrab.org (2009) Promoting responsible international investment in agriculture, 29 September, http://farmlandgrab.org/post/view/8002.

Global Campaign for Agrarian Reform (CGAR) (2010) Why We Oppose the Principles for Responsible Agricultural Investment, http://www.fian.org/resources/documents/others/why-we-oppose-the-principles-for-responsible-agricultural-investment.

G8 (2009) Responsible leadership for a sustainable future, http://www.canadainternational.gc.ca/g8/summit-sommet/2009/declaration.aspx.

GRAIN (2008) Seized! The 2008 Land Grab for Food and Financial Security, http://www.grain.org/briefings_files/landgrab-2008-en.pdf.

GRAIN (2012) Responsible farmland investing? Current efforts to regulate land grabs will make things worse, http://www.grain.org/article/entries/4564-responsible-farmland-investing-current-efforts-to-regulate-land-grabs-will-make-things-worse#sdfootnote5sym.

McKeon, N. (2013) 'One does not sell the land upon which the people walk': land grabbing, rural social movements, and global governance, *Globalizations*, 10(1), pp. 105–122.

Margulis, M. E. & Porter, T. (2013) Governing the global land grab: multipolarity, ideas, and complexity in transnational governance, *Globalizations*, 10(1), pp. 65–86.

Margulis, M. E., McKeon, N., & Borras, S. M. (2013) Land grabbing and global governance: critical perspectives, *Globalizations*, 10(1), pp. 1–23.

Seufert, P. (2013) The FAO Voluntary Guidelines on the Responsible Governance of Tenure of Land, Fisheries and Forests, *Globalizations*, 10(1), pp. 181–186.

Verbist, H. (2012) Proposal for process of consultation on principles for responsible agricultural investments within the CFS (Rome: FAO).

World Bank (2010) Large-scale land acquisition study, http://web.worldbank.org/WBSITE/EXTERNAL/TOPICS/EXTARD/0,,contentMDK:22173916~pagePK:148956~piPK:216618~theSitePK:336682,00.html#Insights.

Phoebe Stephens holds a BA in international development studies from McGill University and an MA in global governance from the Balsillie School of International Affairs at the University of Waterloo. Her Master's research focused on the global governance of land grabs. Phoebe currently lives in Toronto and is researching the future path of energy production and consumption in East Asia.

The Minimum Human Rights Principles Applicable to Large-Scale Land Acquisitions or Leases

PRISCILLA CLAEYS & GAËTAN VANLOQUEREN

University of Louvain, Louvain-La-Neuve, Belgium

ABSTRACT *In June 2009, Olivier De Schutter, the United Nations Special Rapporteur on the right to food, put forward a set of 11 principles to address 'the human rights challenge' of large-scale acquisitions and leases of land. This article briefly outlines the main elements of the Minimum Principles, their objective, as well as the context in which they were released. It also presents a critical analysis of their impact, based on the controversies that they sparked among various stakeholders.*

In June 2009, Olivier De Schutter, the United Nations Special Rapporteur on the right to food, put forward a set of 11 principles to address 'the human rights challenge' of large-scale acquisitions and leases of land. The call by the Special Rapporteur to discipline land grabbing came at a time when there was no clear guidance from the international community as to how to address the emerging phenomenon of land grabbing. It was also unclear whether new norms were needed, or whether existing national laws and international standards were sufficient to regulate what some observers viewed as a simple resurgence of investments typical of the colonial era.

The Human Rights Issues Raised by Land Grabs

Large-scale investments in land emerged as a key trend during the 2008 global food crisis. They rapidly proved to pose important threats, primarily to the food security of populations living in areas targeted by large-scale acquisitions—such as smallholder farmers or pastoralists—but also to the ability of consumers in those regions to access food at decent prices, as a significant proportion of the local food production could be diverted from domestic markets.

Land grabs soon received the attention of a large number of stakeholders involved in the global governance of food security, including multilateral institutions, developing countries, social movements and non-governmental organizations (NGOs), and investors themselves. Media interest was tremendous, and, as a result, stakeholders with divergent views engaged in a polarized debate on the advantages and risks of large-scale investments in land.

A process was initiated at the global level to address the issue of land grabs, but this process was fragmented and its general direction unclear. At the July 2009 L'Aquila Summit, G8 governments expressed their readiness to initiate negotiations on the governance of investments in agriculture (see Stephens, 2013, pp. 187–191). The World Bank was closely associated to this initiative, but did not publicly circulate a proposal for 'Principles for Responsible Agro-investment' until September 2009, before issuing, in 2010, the *Principles for Responsible Agricultural Investment that Respects Rights, Livelihoods and Resources* (PRAI), in conjunction with the Food and Agriculture Organization of the United Nations (FAO), the International Fund for Agricultural development (IFAD) and the United Nations Conference for Trade and Development (UNCTAD) (FAO et al., 2010). Earlier on, in 2008, the FAO had initiated a process to develop the *Voluntary Guidelines on the Responsible Governance of Tenure of Land and other Natural Resources* (VGs) (see McKeon, 2013, pp. 105–122; Seufert, 2013, pp. 181–186), but the initiative addressed a much broader scope of land issues such as access to land and the governance of land tenure.

Thanks to his mandate as independent expert under the Human Rights Council of the United Nations, the Special Rapporteur on the right to food was able to move swiftly. He issued his set of *Minimum Principles and Measures to Address the Human Rights Challenge of Large-Scale Land Acquisitions or Leases* (hereafter 'Minimum Principles') before the multilateral institutions above finalized and presented their proposals (De Schutter, 2009a). The Minimum Principles, targeted at host states and investors alike, presented a clear interpretation of existing international norms applicable to large-scale land investments agreements, with a view to set a baseline for the various governance initiatives that were about to be released by dominant institutional actors. The Minimum Principles were issued just six months after the Special Rapporteur on the right to food released his report on the World Trade Organization that demonstrated how international trade should be reformed so as to respect and integrate the human right to adequate food (De Schutter, 2009b). With the Minimum Principles the Special Rapporteur on the right to food sought to demonstrate that international human rights law, and in particular the normative and analytical framework provided by the human right to adequate food, applied to concrete food security issues, which were usually addressed without taking into account human rights. Indeed, while acknowledging the importance of investments in agriculture for the realization of the right to food, the Minimum Principles interpreted the possible negative impacts of land grabbing as a human rights issue. They made clear that the human right to food would be violated if communities depending on land for their livelihoods lost access to land, without suitable alternatives; if local incomes were insufficient to absorb the increases in food prices that might result from the shift to export crops; or if the revenues of local small food producers were to fall as a result of the arrival on local markets of cheaply priced food, produced on more competitive large-scale plantations (De Schutter, 2009a, p. 3).

Key Features of the Minimum Principles

The Minimum Principles are grounded in the right to self-determination, the right to development, and the right to food. They insist that negotiations leading to investment agreements be conducted in a transparent fashion, with the participation of potentially affected local communities, and that host governments explore whether other uses could be made of the land available, that could better contribute to the food security of local populations (principle 1). The principles emphasize that forced evictions should only be allowed to occur in the most exceptional circumstances, and that shifts in land can only take place with the consent of the local communities concerned (principle 2). To protect communities against the appropriation of their land and ensure their full judicial protection, the principles advise states to assist individuals and communities in obtaining individual titles or collective registration of the land they use (principle 3), while recognizing the limits of individual titling schemes (De Schutter, 2009a, p. 11).

The principles are progressive in that they extend the principle of free, prior, and informed consent—already recognized in international human rights law for indigenous peoples (principle 10)—to non-indigenous rural constituencies (principle 3). The principles urge host states to impose clear and enforceable obligations for investors, with attached sanctions in case of non-compliance of the commitments made in the agreement, such as the generation of local employment and compliance with labor rights (principle 7). But the Minimum Principles go beyond the negotiation and adequate monitoring of land deals. They urge host states and investors to establish and promote, in priority, agricultural development models that respect the environment (principle 6), increase the food security of local populations (principle 8), and are sufficiently labor-intensive to contribute to employment creation (principle 5).

The Minimum Principles are not the result of an international negotiation process. They were built independently by the Special Rapporteur on the right to food following a series of exchanges held in 2008 and 2009 with various experts and constituencies. The Minimum Principles can be seen as summarizing and aggregating the relevant and applicable existing human rights obligations of states. In that sense, they differ from the voluntary nature of the PRAI, which are not grounded in human rights, and the VGs, which were adopted by the Committee on World Food Security (CFS) in May 2012 (and are grounded in human rights and the result of an intergovernmental negotiation process). The Minimum Principles do not contain any type of new implementation mechanism at the national or international level. At national level, compliance with the Minimum Principles is the responsibility of states, which are called to set up appropriate institutional frameworks to ensure that laws and policies governing land investments will not be curtailed by corporate interests (De Schutter, 2009a, p. 14). At the international level, the Minimum Principles describe some of the extraterritorial obligations and duties that apply to states and investors involved in the negotiation of agreements and that need to be taken into account.

The influence of the Minimum Principles, as well as the other new global land governance instruments to emerge in the last few years, is difficult to assess. In our view, it has been relatively modest so far: the PRAI failed, for example, to acknowledge the binding nature of certain principles, such as the necessity to respect the rights of existing land users. However, the CFS is now launching its own broad and inclusive consultation process on principles guaranteeing responsible investment in agriculture from a food security viewpoint, and the Minimum Principles have already been invoked in that context. The Minimum Principles were also referred to, as a baseline, during the negotiations of the VGs, mostly by civil society organizations.

Controversial Issues

Although the Minimum Principles were repeatedly discussed in a number of international arenas and intergovernmental processes, their endorsement by states has been limited. This is not surprising considering the high requirements they place on both investor and host states when negotiating and implementing land deals. Opposition to the Minimum Principles by some actors can be explained by their grounding in international human rights law and the right to food in particular, and by their focus on the extraterritorial dimensions of states' obligations—and the fact that they insist quite strongly on the obligations of investors to respect the human rights of local populations.

Endorsement by civil society organizations too has been limited. Transnational agrarian movements such as La Vía Campesina, NGOs such as GRAIN, and several human rights groups (including FIAN, see Künnemann and Monsalve Suárez, 2013, pp. 123–139) feared that the Minimum Principles would 'legitimize' the very practice of land grabs rather than block it. Whereas most social movements and NGOs working on land issues adopted a strong oppositional stance to land grabbing,[1] the Minimum Principles were interpreted as falling within the dominant 'win–win' narrative argued elsewhere by Borras and Franco (2010, p. 510) on investments in land. Indeed, the Minimum Principles were perceived by social movements as indirectly and indiscriminately encouraging foreign investments in agriculture (without expanding much on the type and scale of the investments at stake) and as suggesting that it was possible for investments to respect the criteria outlined in the Minimum Principles. Civil society's skepticism was strong despite the fact that the Special Rapporteur on the right to food insisted that large-scale investment in land was not to be considered justified simply because it complied with the Minimum Principles (De Schutter, 2009a, p. 5). The stance taken by the Special Rapporteur on the right to food was also considered by many CSOs to be naïve—considering the weak governance mechanisms in place at the national level and the power relations between investors, host states, and local land users—and strategically dangerous.

A second tension that was sparked by the Minimum Principles was the controversial issue of whether or not contract farming schemes (and other similar business models) represented a viable or desirable alternative to the transfer of rights over land. Despite the fact that the Special Rapporteur on the right to food later spelled out criteria that contract farming and similar business models should be required to meet in order to support the realization of the right to food (De Schutter, 2011b), his message was understood by social movements as promoting contract farming as an alternative to large-scale investments of land (De Schutter, 2009a, p. 5). The Special Rapporteur on the right to food's position on this issue was criticized by several CSOs, which generally argued against the incorporation of small farmers into global supply chains, and alerted to the unfair repartition of risks and benefits that these schemes often imply.

These two areas of tensions find their source in the obviously distinct institutional roles held by the various actors involved and hence in distinct strategies. Yet, they also point to diverging conceptions of social change. Social movement activists tend to be quite skeptical as to the possibility that states or global institutions could be vectors of social change, while not shying away from institutional goals. In reaction to the global land grab phenomenon, organizations such as FIAN and La Vía Campesina have demanded new human rights. For example, they have advocated for a Declaration on the Rights of Peasants to be discussed at the UN system (see Claeys, 2012; Edelman and James, 2011) and for the recognition of a human right to land (Künneman and Monsalve Suárez, 2013, this volume).

For his part, the Special Rapporteur on the right to food and many right to food defenders have directed their efforts into making the right to food 'operational'. The right to food has become increasingly associated with a number of criteria against which global and national development, trade, financial and agricultural policies are to be tested. This is evident in the advocacy efforts for states to undertake human rights impact assessments. At the same time, efforts have been made to apply the right to food framework to a broad range of issues pertaining to agricultural and rural development, touching on the very issue of which economic model best serves the realization of human rights. The positions outlined by the Special Rapporteur on the right to food in his reports on agroecology (De Schutter, 2011a), on access to land (De Schutter, 2010b, 2011c) and on international trade (De Schutter, 2010) point to the importance of a paradigm shift and of reinvesting in smallholder agriculture (De Schutter and Vanloqueren, 2011). The Minimum Principles should be interpreted in light of such reports, which situate the land grabbing phenomenon within the broader issue of rural development. Nevertheless, the Principles raise the issue of the extent to which small-scale, relocalized, equitable food systems can co-exist with large-scale intensive/industrial agriculture.

Note

1   This position was announced by La Vía Campesina and GRAIN in their statement 'Les paysans et les mouvements sociaux disent non à l'accaparement des terres' delivered at a press conference in Rome on 16 November 2009.

References

Borras, S. & Franco, J. C. (2010) From threat to opportunity? Problems with the idea of a 'Code of Conduct' for land-grabbing, *Yale Human Rights & Development Law Journal*, (13), pp. 507–523.

Claeys, P. (2012) The creation of new rights by the food sovereignty movement: the challenge of institutionalizing subversion, *Sociology*, 46(5), pp. 844–860.

De Schutter, O. (2009a) *Large-Scale Land Acquisitions Leases: a Set of Minimum Principles and Measures to Address the Human Rights Challenge. Addendum to the Report of the Special Rapporteur on the Right to Food to the Human Rights Council (A/HRC/13/33/Add.2)* (Geneva: Human Rights Council).

De Schutter, O. (2009b) *Mission to the World Trade Organization: Report of the Special Rapporteur on the right to food to the Human Rights Council (A/HRC/10/5/Add.2)* (Geneva: Human Rights Council).

De Schutter, O. (2010) *Report of the Special Rapporteur on the Right to Food Presented to the 65th General Assembly of the United Nations (a/65/281): Access to Land and the Right to Food* (New York: United Nations).

De Schutter, O. (2011a) *Report of the Special Rapporteur on the right to food presented at the 16th Session of the United Nations Human Rights Council (A/HRC/16/49): Agroecology and the right to food* (Geneva: Human Rights Council).

De Schutter, O. (2011b) *Towards More Equitable Value Chains: Alternative Business Models in Support of the Right to Food: Report Presented at the 66th Session of the United Nations General Assembly (A/66/262)* (New York: United Nations).

De Schutter, O. (2011c) How not to think about land-grabbing: three critiques of large-scale investments in farmland, *Journal of Peasant Studies*, 38(2), pp. 249–279.

De Schutter, O. & Vanloqueren, G. (2011) The new green revolution: how twenty-first-century science can feed the world, *Solutions*, 2(4), pp. 33–44.

Edelman, M. & Carwil, J. (2011) Peasants' rights and the UN system: Quixotic struggle? Or emancipatory idea whose time has come?, *Journal of Peasant Studies*, 38(1), pp. 81–108.

FAO, IFAD, UNCTAD, & World Bank (2010) Principles for responsible agricultural investment that respects rights, livelihoods and resources: discussion note prepared to contribute to an ongoing global dialogue, http://siteresources.worldbank.org/INTARD/214574-1111138388661/22453321/Principles_Extended.pdf.

Künnemann, R. & Monsalve, Suárez S. (2013) International human rights and governing land grabbing: a view from global civil society, *Globalizations*, 10(1), pp. 123–139.

McKeon, N. (2013) 'One does not sell the land upon which the people walk': land grabbing, rural social movements, and global governance, *Globalizations*, 10(1), pp. 105–122.

Seufert, P. (2013) The FAO Voluntary Guidelines on the Responsible Governance of Tenure of Land, Fisheries and Forests, *Globalizations*, 10(1), pp. 181–186.

Stephens, P. (2013) The Principles for Responsible Agricultural Investment, *Globalizations*, 10(1), pp. 187–191.

Priscilla Claeys is a doctoral candidate in social and political sciences at the University of Louvain, Belgium and advises the United Nations Special Rapporteur on the human right to food. Her research is on the use of human rights by contemporary transnational agrarian movements using concepts from the sociology of law and the sociology of social movements. She also teaches on the right to food at the Open University of Catalunya in partnership with the Food and Agriculture Organization of the United Nations (FAO). Before joining the team of the United Nations Special Rapporteur on the right to food in May 2008, she worked for a number of human rights and development NGOs.

Gaëtan Vanloqueren is an agro-economist by training and a research associate at the University of Louvain, Belgium. He advises the United Nations Special Rapporteur on the right to food and coordinates the support team. He also lectures at ICHEC-Brussels Management School on development economics. Currently he is part of research groups on Agroecology and Redefining Prosperity at the National Fund for Scientific Research in Belgium. Before joining the team of the United Nations Special Rapporteur on the right to food, he completed a Ph.D. on the innovation dynamics within agro-food chains and the democratic choices to be made on scientific progress in agriculture.

Private Governance and Land Grabbing: The Equator Principles and the Roundtable on Sustainable Biofuels

ARIANE GOETZ

Wilfrid Laurier University, Waterloo, Canada

ABSTRACT   *Goals, norms, and rules negotiated and implemented by the private sector are one of the global governance approaches under debate for regulating land grabbing. This paper looks at two private governance instruments that are especially relevant: the Equator Principles (EPs) and the Roundtable on Sustainable Biofuels (RSB). Both instruments promote and introduce sustainability meta-standards in the decision-making and risk management process of signatory firms, financial institutions, and non-governmental organizations (NGOs) with regard to land use and access. And they aim to govern two sectors of international investment, namely biofuels and project finance, that are associated with highly land consuming economic activity. Against the background of key features, the paper concludes that the imprecise and voluntary nature, lack of effective sanction and compensation mechanisms, and bias towards client interests highlight that both governance approaches provide insufficient protection of communities or the environment in weak regulatory settings and in view of the intense commercial pressure on land.*

The Equator Principles

Project finance, that is essentially a bundle of long-term loans, insurance, and financial guarantees provided by banks and/or international financial institutions, makes possible many of the large-scale investment projects in the extractive industries, power generation, and infrastructure characterized by massive up-front costs and requiring financing support over very long time horizons (Daniel, 2010; Schepers, 2011). Such mega-projects have come under scrutiny over the past decades, especially when they lead to human rights violations, namely forced evictions, and also massive environmental damage. Indeed, these type of mega-projects have become sites of international 'naming and shaming campaigns' by NGOs, some of which are quite well known internationally such as the campaign led by the Rainforest Action Network in the early 2000s against CitiGroup's involvement in the Three Gorges dam project in China (Spitzeck, 2007). The EPs are a voluntary, private industry-led governance system that emerged in 2003 out of concern over reputational damage associated with large-scale infrastructure, such as the Three Gorges dam.

The EPs build directly on the World Bank 1998 Safeguard Policies and Performance Standards, which set standards to protect nature and people from adverse effects of projects financed by the World Bank and its subsidiary, the International Financial Corporation (IFC). The EPs were negotiated by nine international banks in conjunction with the IFC in 2002, launched in 2003, and subsequently updated in 2006 and again in 2012. The EPs are self-identified as a credit risk management framework for determining, assessing, and managing environmental and social risk in project finance transactions. Their two key stated goals are to ensure that the large-scale projects meet specified social and environmental requirements throughout their operation and thereby, reduce risk of operations in developing and non-high income OECD countries where adequate state regulation is not in place. The EPs apply to projects where capital costs exceed US$10 million.

Since their inception, the number of participating financial institutions (referred to as 'Equator Principles Financial Institutions' [EPFI]) has increased from an original group of 4 to 77 in 2012. The actual number of EP-compliant debt offerings is in fact significantly higher than the number of participant institutions because the EPs apply to all loans involving EPFI participates, which can involve multiple parties and projects (Schepers, 2011).

At present, EPFI must comply with 10 principles. These include the commitment by EPFIs to (see EP, 2006):

- Review and categorize social and environmental risks and impacts, based on the Performance Standards of the IFC;
- Conduct a social and environmental assessment and develop solutions to mitigate negative impacts at the project design stage;
- Apply social and environmental standards depending on the host country's categorization by the World Bank Group (non-OECD, low income OECD, high income OECD);
- Develop an action plan and management plan to mitigate assessed impacts of the project;
- Consult with and disclose information to affected communities from project planning through construction and operation of the project;
- Establish grievance mechanisms that ensure the good social and environmental performance of the project;
- Ensure an independent review of their own project assessment, action plan and consultation process documentation;
- Ensure compliance with host country laws, action plan solutions, regular reporting;
- Support independent monitoring and reporting over the life of the loan as demanded by the lending EP financial institutions; and
- Report to the lender (EPFIs) on an annual basis.

The EP system functions as an unincorporated association, characterized by a highly constrained and weak governance structure. This includes a steering committee of 13 elected members, whose chair rotates annually (and is elected), and which administrates and coordinates the further development of the EP standards and guidelines for the member EPFIs with assistance of the Secretariat. While the EP provides basic principles and criteria, their operationalization, implementation, and oversight is governed and managed by each EPFI individually. EFPI pay an annual fee and publish an annual report about relevant projects. Since 2010, and in order to ensure the EPs credibility, the association of EPFI introduced delisting provisions for members that failed to provide public reporting requirements laid out in the governance rules.

EPs are relevant to the global governance of land grabbing in several ways given that project finance is already playing a role in facilitating some land grabs (Daniel, 2010). First, due to the EPs' focus on evolving processes of long-term investments instead of one-time transaction, they provide one established framework to try to facilitate a (more) transparent, low-impact and accountable project planning, design, and operation for longer-term projects (Lawrence, 2009). The EPs are therefore relevant to land grabbing because most land deals are long-term investments and may involve project financing or similar forms of long-term financing that involve multilateral banks and private banks.

With the IFC's 2012 *Updated Performance Standards* now built into the EPs, the EPs contain very specific standards about land use and access, as well as guidance for investors and financiers on how to best interact with affected communities. Of particular interest here are Performance Standard 5 on land acquisitions and involuntary resettlement, Performance Standard 7 on indigenous peoples, and Performance Standard 8 on cultural heritage. Take Performance Standard 7, which states that projects with potential significant adverse impacts on indigenous peoples shall apply the principle of Free, Prior and Informed Consent (FPIC) in the context of 'Lands and Natural Resources Subject to Traditional Ownership or Under Customary Use' (IFC, 2012). However, this approach is different from that found in the RSB (see Fortin and Richardson, 2013, pp. 141–159), which, at least in text form, forbids going through with a project that would result in involuntary resettlement. In contrast, the EP never takes a restrictive stance on a project with adverse effects, which can be argued to nullify the intention of the FPIC. Certainly, the EPs' approach mirrors that of the IFC standards, which is to apply mitigation, compensation, and negotiation strategies to reduce the negative repercussions, even in the case of involuntary resettlement.

Another well-known criticism of the EPs is related to their weak governance structure and the general vagueness of the principles. This leaves operationalizing, monitoring and grievance mechanisms to the discretion and interpretation of each EPFI. In its current form, the EPs do not fundamentally address the problem of the lack of external accountability and transparency related to its very limited disclosure requirements. Returning to land grabbing, the EPs may seem of limited use to pressure EPFIs that are directly or indirectly involved in land deals since non-complying EPFIs might have little to lose given that the operationalization of EP is often done poorly with few staff and resources allocated to its management. More broadly, this tendency of EPFI banks to focus on client complaints more than stakeholder or civil society concerns remains a significant obstacle (Schepers, 2011).

The Roundtable on Sustainable Biofuels (RSB)

The RSB is much a more recent form of private governance, created in 2007 in response to the mounting global criticism directed at the alleged sustainability of biofuels. Growing empirical evidence increasingly highlighted that biofuels production poses severe ecological challenges. Moreover, the economic viability of many biofuel projects is much more circumspect when its highly problematic challenges for the socio-economic development in host countries are taken into account, including the displacement of people and local food production, insufficient job creation or the creation of low wage jobs (e.g. contract farming, daily wage labor) and/or endangering of wildlife habitat and local water security (Dornbusch and Steenblik, 2007; RFA, 2008).

As a 'roundtable' type of global governance initiative, the RSB founding steering board in 2007 comprised industry, global civil society, and public sector that share an interest to support the creation of 'clean energy' (see also Fortin and Richardson, 2013, this volume). Prominent actors associated with the RSB include the World Wide Fund for Nature (WWF), Mali FolkCenter, United Nations Environment Program (UNEP), Swiss and Dutch governments, UNICA (the Brazilian sugarcane growers association), Royal Dutch Shell, British Petroleum, Toyota, and Petrobas (RSB, 2011). RSB's goals are twofold: establish criteria for sustainable biofuel production and a voluntary certification scheme for produced and processed biofuels based on these criteria.

The RSB began certification activity in 2011. Certification is a multi-step process (i.e. application, third party verification and formal licensing/issuing of certificate) that in essence depends on whether applying firms can prove they satisfy the 12 *Principles and Criteria for Sustainable Biofuel Production* (see Box 1).

Box 1. Roundtable for Sustainable Biofuels: Principles and criteria for sustainable biofuel production

- Principle 1 (Legality): Biofuel operations shall follow all applicable laws and regulations.
- Principle 2 (Planning, Monitoring and Continuous Improvement): Sustainable biofuel operations shall be planned, implemented, and continuously improved through an open, transparent, and consultative impact assessment and management process and an economic viability analysis.
- Principle 3 (Greenhouse Gas Emissions): Biofuels shall contribute to climate change mitigation by significantly reducing lifecycle GHG emissions as compared to fossil fuels.
- Principle 4 (Human and Labor Rights): Biofuel operations shall not violate human rights or labor rights, and shall promote decent work and the well-being of workers.
- Principle 5 (Rural and Social Development): In regions of poverty, biofuel operations shall contribute to the social and economic development of local, rural and indigenous people and communities.
- Principle 6 (Local Food Security): Biofuel operations shall ensure the human right to adequate food and improve food security in food insecure regions.
- Principle 7 (Conservation): Biofuel operations shall avoid negative impacts on biodiversity, ecosystems, and conservation values.
- Principle 8 (Soil): Biofuel operations shall implement practices that seek to reverse soil degradation and/or maintain soil health.
- Principle 9 (Water): Water: Biofuel operations shall maintain or enhance the quality and quantity of surface and ground water resources, and respect prior formal or customary water rights.
- Principle 10 (Air): Air pollution from biofuel operations shall be minimized along the supply chain.
- Principle 11 (Use of Technology, Inputs, and Management of Waste): The use of technologies in biofuel operations shall seek to maximize production efficiency and social and environmental performance, and minimize the risk of damages to the environment and people.
- Principle 12 (Land Rights): Biofuel operations shall respect land rights and land use rights. *Source*: RSB (2010).

With regard to the governance of land grabbing, RSB purports to have created standards for producers and processors on *how to use land* sustainably, based on legal, social and environmental criteria (i.e. Principles 2–11); and on *how to access land* sustainably (Principles 1, 2, 4, and 12). In the latter case, the RSB scheme goes beyond the soft land access criteria embedded in other private governance instruments (e.g. IFC Performance Standards) and takes a more restrictive stance with regard to conflicts of interest. For instance, RSB's principle 12 on land rights states that no involuntary resettlement shall be allowed for biofuel operations and also in cases of unresolved land tenure disputes biofuel operations shall not be approved (see also Fortin and Richardson, 2013, this volume).

The RSB promotes its standards to be applicable to all crops; it presents itself as a simple, efficient, and low-cost approach that can be implemented globally by all actors in the supply chain and that is in accordance with WTO rules. The RSB is not a standalone set of rules but builds upon already existing initiatives for biofuel crops such as the other roundtables on palm oil, soy, and sugar. However, the RSB distinguishes itself by its self-presentation as a 'Global Sustainability Standard for biomass and biofuel production' (RSB, 2010). As the RSB framework is primarily targeted towards the food industry, it additionally includes verification criteria, such as greenhouse gas (GHG) emissions and indirect CO_2 effects of biofuel production (e.g. land use change).

To gain broader legitimacy, a new membership-based governance structure was introduced in January 2009. Accordingly, stakeholders now participate in the RSB decision-making and revision process through a chamber system. Stakeholders can apply to the RSB steering board, the decision-making body, for approval to join one of seven chambers, namely: (1) farmers and growers of biofuel feedstock; (2) industrial biofuel producers; (3) retail/blenders, transportation industry, bank/investors; (4) rights-based NGOs and trade unions; (5) rural development or food security organizations and smallholder farmer or indigenous people organizations; (6) environment conservation and climate change organizations; and (7) intergovernmental organizations, specialist agencies, governments. Within the chambers, contents of the RSB standard are reviewed, and each chamber (except chamber 7) participates in the RSB decision-making process through two elected representatives at the RSB steering board.

The decision-making process follows the *Code of Good Practice for Setting Social and Environmental Standards* developed by ISEAL, the global association for sustainability standards, which requires venues for stakeholders to provide input and the transparency during the development and implementation of the RSB standards. For monitoring and certification, participating operators are required to verify that their production fulfills the RSB standards through a third party audit conducted by a Certification Body that has been accredited by RSB's Accreditation Body.

Major criticism of this certification schemes points at the mostly vague standards, the assumption of 'unused land', or the failure to account for indirect effects of biofuel projects and policy, arguing that it provides mainly 'a veneer of sustainability' (Leopold, 2010; see also Fortin and Richardson, 2013, this volume). Moreover, RSB's input legitimacy seems problematic: not only have critical groups such as FIAN not participated in the standard setting and revision process but also the membership is quantitatively clearly skewed to industrial sector representatives. At the same time, key stakeholders in the process of biofuel production, such as the European Biodiesel Board, have withdrawn their support for the scheme, weakening its potential to reach the actual producers of biofuels/biomass.

Concluding Thoughts

Their imprecise and voluntary nature, lack of effective sanction and compensation mechanisms, and bias towards certain industry interests, highlight that the EPs and RSB provide insufficient protection of communities or the environment in weak regulatory settings in the context of a global commercial pressure on land. Instead, both instruments engage in the construction of an understanding of sustainability (e.g. biofuels, risk) that frames debates around *how* investments shall take place, while removing from consideration the far-reaching questions of *whether* these investments should occur at all. In this context, FIAN (2012) has pointed out that the RSB standard, for instance, is primarily facilitating the further expansion of large-scale biofuels projects in spite of empirical evidence about inefficacy of biofuels, especially first generation biofuels that do not meet environmental or technical requirements for a sustainable energy policy and its indirect land use change effects. This leads to an interpretation by human rights NGOs that RSB is part of a general tendency of private governance to weaken/crowd out human rights-based approaches to governance and, as such, should be approached with caution as a potential regulatory tool to address land grabbing (e.g. Partzsch, 2011).

References

Daniel, S. (2010) *(Mis)Investment in Agriculture: The Role of the International Finance Corporation in Global Land Grabs* (Oakland, CA: The Oakland Institute).

Dornbusch, R. & Steenblik, R. (2007) Biofuels: is the cure worse than the disease?, Paper presented at the OECD Round Table on Sustainable Development, Paris, France, 11–12 September.

EP (2006) The Equator Principles, http://www.equator-principles.com/resources/equator-principles.pdf.

FIAN (2012) Email communication with FIAN Germany, 1 August 2012.

Fortin, E. & Richardson, B. (2013) Certification schemes and the governance of land: enforcing standards or enabling scrutiny? *Globalizations*, 10(1), pp. 141–159.

International Finance Corporation (IFC) (2012) IFC Performance Standards on Environmental and Social Sustainability (Washington, DC: IFC/World Bank Group).

Lawrence, P. (2009) Equator Principles: or how I learned to stop worrying and love sustainability, *Impact Assessment and Project Appraisal*, 27(1), pp. 3–6.

Leopold, A. (2010) The changing constellation of power and resistance in the global debate over agrofuels, *The European Journal of Social Science Research*, 23(4), pp. 389–408.

Partzsch, L. (2011) The legitimacy of biofuel certification, updated version of, Paper originally presented to the Symposium on the Private Governance in the Global Agro-Food System, Münster, Germany, 23–25 April 2008.

Renewable Fuels Agency (RFA) (2008) *The Gallagher Review of the indirect effects of biofuels production* (London: RFA).

Roundtable for Sustainable Biofuels (RSB) (2010) *RSB Principles & Criteria for Sustainable Biofuels Production* (Lausanne: EPFL Energy Center).

RSB (2011) *RSB Stakeholder Mapping* (Lausanne: EPFL Energy Center).

Schepers, D. H. (2011) The Equator Principles: a promise in progress?, *Corporate Governance*, 11(1), pp. 90–106.

Spitzeck, H. (2007) Innovation and learning by public discourse: Citigroup and the Rainforest Action Network, Center for Responsible Business, http://escholarship.org/uc/item/6z99m2zr.

Ariane Goetz is a Ph.D. candidate in global governance at Wilfrid Laurier University/Balsillie School of International Affairs. Her current research focuses on international land acquisitions in the context of the political economy and ecology of major investor countries and in view of global restructuring and crisis.

Restrictions to Foreign Acquisitions of Agricultural Land in Argentina and Brazil

NICOLÁS MARCELO PERRONE

London School of Economics, London, United Kingdom

ABSTRACT   *This review examines the recent reactions of the governments of Argentina and Brazil to land grabbing by foreign actors. In these two countries, national political parties, small and medium farmers, and the overall population perceive the recent surge of foreign acquisitions of land as a threat to national sovereignty. This political support translated into new regulations that restrict foreign acquisitions of agricultural land and aim to determine the amount of land that is presently in the hands of foreigners.*

In the Southern Cone, agriculture has returned to the political and economic frontline. The rise in food prices has increased the importance of agricultural commodities, in particular soya, for both the private and public sectors in these countries. On the one hand this translates into new business opportunities in a region where agricultural exports are already a significant contributor to national income, especially in Argentina. On the other hand, extending the land frontier for producing commodities is not without significant economic and social problems (Borras et al., 2012). This review examines the recent reactions of the governments of Argentina and Brazil to land grabbing by foreign actors. In these two countries, national political parties, small and medium farmers, and the overall population perceive the recent surge of foreign acquisitions of land as a threat to national sovereignty. Indeed, the discourse of national sovereignty has dominated the media and the political debate about land.

Argentina and Law 26,737

In Argentina, Federación Agraria Argentina, the association of small and medium agricultural producers, has long advocated a limitation of foreign acquisitions of agricultural land. The present left-wing government took the issue as a national priority in 2011, promoting a new law to restrict these transactions. This proposal gathered important support from most political forces, including the most popular newspaper in Argentina, *Clarín*, which has been the most vocal critique of Kirchner's administration (Clarín, 2011). The representatives of the big land-owners, the agribusiness sector, and a right-wing party (Propuesta Republicana (PRO)) posed limited opposition to this initiative (Colombres, 2011).

After a political debate that took much of 2011, and overlapping with a presidential election that October, the Argentine Congress passed Law 26,737 (Rural Land Law) with a strong majority vote: 152 votes in favour to 26 against in the Lower House and 62 votes in favour to 1 against in the Senate. The main objective of Law 26,737 is to determine the exact number of hectares currently in foreign hands and to regulate foreign control of agricultural land with an aim to curb it. In spite of the law's evidently narrow scope, this change represents a major break from the liberal policy on foreign investment and agriculture that has been in place since the country adopted its first national constitution in 1853. In the recent past, the liberal land framework has allowed foreigners, including wealthy individuals such as Luciano Benetton, Joe Lewis, Ted Turner, and Douglas Tompkins to acquire very large areas of land (*Tiempo Argentino*, 2011).

At present there is a major lack of adequate information regarding how much land foreigners own, partially because this was a not a concern until the recent wave of land grabbing. There are two important surveys that provide a general picture. First is the private Pensar Foundation, which suggests that somewhere between 3.4% and 9.9% of the total arable land in the country is held by foreign owners (Pensar, 2011). This is equivalent to a figure of about 5.8 to 17 million of hectares of land. A second estimate is drawn from a recent research sponsored by the Food and Agriculture Organization of the United Nations (FAO) that points to a much higher figure; it suggests somewhere between 8.29% and 15.45% of the total arable land in Argentina is foreign owned (Murmis and Murmis, 2011). The new land ownership accounting introduced by Law 26,737 is expected to provide some certainty on this point.

Law 26,737 objective to limit foreign ownership of agricultural land depends on a new set of restrictions that have a subjective, general, and individual scope. First, new limits on land ownership apply to foreign individuals, foreign corporations, and domestic corporations under foreign control. In the case of the latter, the law establishes a set of criteria to determine when a firm is under the control of foreigners. This is driven by a concern to address practices of registering fake 'national companies' and other forms of legal manipulation to hide the real foreign beneficiary owners. Such cases are well known in Brazil and the Argentine government is actively seeking to prevent clever exploitation of loopholes.

Second, the law sets fixed limits on foreign ownership of agricultural land. Under the law, foreigners can own up to a maximum of 15% of all agricultural land in Argentina. This is also why the creation of a national register is all the more pressing. This latter provision is to address concerns about hyper-concentration of land; high levels of land concentration are a major political reality and historical legacy in Argentina. Restrictions on foreign ownership apply also at the provincial and municipal level, in an effort to ensure political elites distant from Buenos Aires do not circumvent the rules and create free-rider problems. Furthermore, the law prohibits foreign ownership in designated security and border areas such as those where the borders of Argentina, Brazil, and Paraguay meet, and in locations with large and permanent water sources.

The new land law also includes very strict individual limits on land ownership. In a break with past practices the law forbids foreigners to own more than 1,000 hectares in any one location, although there is some ambiguity here and scope for this to be adjusted in particular regions of the country.

Law 26,737 delegates authority to a new federal agency, the *Registro Nacional de Tierras Rurales* (National Registry of Agricultural Lands), to determine the process for classifying of areas where limits apply taking into account, for example, the availability and quality of the land in a specific area (i.e. on a municipal, provincial, and/or deferral level). This new national register will operate within the Ministry of Justice because this office is in charge of the existing land registry. However, other related federal ministries will participate under a new high-level consultative body, the *Consejo Interministerial de Tierras Rurales* (Inter-ministerial council for agricultural land), given the political sensitivity of foreign land ownership, which will be chaired by the minister of justice and include the ministers for agriculture, defence, interior, and environment and sustainability.

Brazil and Legal Opinion CGU/AGU n 01/2008-RVJ

In Brazil, earlier in 2010, Lula da Silva's administration decided to restrict foreign acquisitions. Relying on a law dating from 1971, the government reintroduced limitations applicable to land acquisitions by Brazilian corporations under foreign control. These limitations had been considered unconstitutional by a Legal Opinion issued in 1994 (and ratified in 1998). As in Argentine, there are diverging opinions about these restrictions. However, in Brazil, big landowners, agribusiness, and some political representatives have adopted a stronger critical view (Ávila, 2011). Brazil's journey to develop new land ownership laws shows a different trajectory compared to Argentina. According to the federal statute 5,709, established in 1971, Brazil had already put in place several restrictions on foreign acquisitions of agricultural land. These limitations apply to foreign individuals, foreign corporations, and Brazilian corporations under foreign control. However, this statute was substantially modified by the Legal Opinion of 1994 that established that the limitations applicable to Brazilian corporations, even those under foreign control, were against the 1988 Constitution. This change in the understanding of land ownership statutes permitted foreigners to acquire agricultural land through purchasing or partnering with Brazil-based corporations. One consequences of the Legal Opinion is that it became very difficult to monitor how much agricultural land is under foreign control in Brazil.

During the recent (re)introduction of the restrictions on land use, the use by foreign actors of Brazil-based and registered firms to hide foreign ownership is considered a serious problem that makes it very difficult for the state to determine how much land is under foreign control (State of Sao Paulo, 2011). Some public research in Brazil estimates that foreign-owned land is over 4 million hectares or about 1.7% of the total arable land in Brazil (Wilkinson et al., 2011). This all remains guesswork, but the Instituto Nacional de Colonização e Reforma Agrária (INCRA), Brazil's agrarian reform agency, has suggested the figure is likely in the range of 5.5 million hectares (Estado do Norte, 2010).

In 2010, during a surge of foreign acquisitions of Brazil land, the Brazilian government initiated new national rules on foreign land ownership. This work was led by the General Attorney of Brazil, under direct instructions form then President 'Lula' da Silva. The first step included the drafting of new Legal Opinion that would define national regulation and restrictions on land ownership applicable to Brazilian corporations under foreign control that would be consistent with the 1988 Brazilian Constitution. In short, the 'new' Legal Opinion provided an alternative interpretation of Article 190 of the Constitution, which the Attorney General argued provides the government with authority to establish limitations to foreign ownership of agricultural land. A critical factor was the manner in which the new Legal Opinion utilized the reasons of national sovereignty, independence, and national development goals to justify limits on foreign ownership. As a result, the 'new' Legal Opinion, which was ratified by the Brazilian congress, meant the reestablishment of the restrictions created under the 1971 statue.

Thus the 'new' Brazilian legislation on land ownership sets out general and individual limitations. At the municipal level, foreign ownership cannot exceed 25%. In addition, on an aggregate basis, foreign owners of the same nationality cannot own more than 10% of the total area of a municipality. At the individual level, foreign individuals and corporations (either foreign or Brazilian under foreign control) cannot acquire more than 50 and 100 units of land in total, respectively. What constitutes a 'unit' of agricultural land is to be determined by the National Institute of Colonisation and Agrarian Reform (INCRA from its abbreviation in Portuguese). Together with the minister of agriculture, this agency plays a crucial role in the regulation of foreign ownership of agricultural land. First, INCRA monitors compliance with the general limitations established by the law. For this reason, foreign individual acquisitions of up to three units of land, which are exempt from authorisation must be notified to this agency. Second, INCRA is in charge of authorising any acquisitions between 3 and 50 units (for individuals) and up to a 100 units (for corporations). This process is not simply bureaucratic because the authorisation of an acquisition requires the approval of a project by the minister of agriculture (See INCRA, Instrução Normativa No. 70–12 December 2011). Finally, the legislation in Brazil establishes an exemption: foreign individuals and corporations can acquire areas beyond the existing limitations with the approval of the National Congress.

Some Concluding Remarks

The new regulations on foreign land ownership recently introduced by the governments of Argentina and Brazil are binding and legally powerful. In accordance to international law, a foreign investment is valid and recognised as such for the protection of investors only when investments are established in accordance with host state laws. This means that foreign investors who circumvent or are in non-compliance with the existing limitations may lose protection of international law.[1] Arguably, these types of laws should play a decisive role in regulating land grabbing to the extent they pressure financial actors investors to comply, given that losing protection under international law is highly undesirable. At the same time, Brazil and Argentina are middle-income developing countries with strong national governments and legal institutions. Such laws may be less effective in 'weak' or fragile states.

The new laws are too recent to say anything definitive about their effectiveness. Of course we can expect problems of implementation and monitoring given the new responsibilities for national governance apparatus. In the case of Brazil, INCRA is a long-standing institution with a very broad mandate on agriculture and land issue. In Argentina, the National Registry of Agricultural Land and the Inter-Ministerial Council are new entirely new regulatory bodies, although with a more limited mandate than their Brazilian neighbour. The political economy and flavour of domestic politics in Argentina are highly unpredictable; whether such dynamics may facilitate or hinder the goal of the new legislation is unknown. Thus far, however, the new limits on foreign land ownership have currency across the Argentina political class. Therefore, there appears to be little appetite to repeal or modify the new restrictions in Brazil and Argentina.

It is worth mentioning that these initiatives have not been exempt from criticisms. Opposing actors have tended to be large landowners and agribusiness sector that have stated concerns that new limits on foreign land ownership may discourage further international investment in the sector. This criticism has been stronger in Brazil. One complaint has been that these rules preclude individuals and domestic firms from offering land as collateral to obtain credit and financing. Indigenous peoples and rural workers groups continue to criticise the existing agricultural policy. These groups find that the controls on foreign ownership do not focus on their situation, which they see as exploitative, unfair, and precarious. They are affected by the proliferation of large-scale farms regardless if they are under domestic or foreign control. In Argentina and Brazil, land concentration is already very high and while the restrictions may limit foreign ownership, they still promote modes of scale and efficiency. That is, they support in principle the process of land ownership concentration rather than challenging it.

These two cases of limits on foreign land ownership reveal two important dimensions of land grabbing. The first is that Brazilian and to a lesser extent Argentine firms are land grabbers themselves. This does open some political space to highlight the hypocrisy of these states' domestic and foreign policy and use the hypocrisy argument to target land grabbers based in these states. The second is that rules on foreign ownership of land are subject to continuous change. Not only do policies vary during different administrations for ideological reasons, they also vary due to external global political economy conditions such as Argentina and Brazil's concerns. The case of concerns about excessive foreign ownership by Chinese and private investors is an example.

Note

1   For a more developed discussion on this point, see Perrone (2010).

References

Ávila, V. (2011) Xenofobia Verde, http://revistadinheirorural.terra.com.br/secao/agroeconomia/xenofobia-verde.
Borras, S. M., Franco, J. C., Goméz, S., Kay, C. & Spoor, M. (2012) Land grabbing in Latin America and the Caribbean, *Journal of Peasant Studies*, 39(3–4), pp. 845–872.
Colombres, M. (2011) La propiedad divide opiniones, *La Nación*, 18 June, http://www.lanacion.com.ar/1382316-la-propiedad-divide-opiniones.
Estado do Norte (2010) JORNAL—Proibida venda de terras da Amazônia para estrangeiros, 2 February, http://www.incra.gov.br/index.php/noticias-sala-de-imprensa/incra-na-midia/739-proibida-venda-de-terras-da-amazonia-para-estrangeiros.
Murmis, M. & Murmis, M. R. (2011) *Dinámica del mercado de la tierra en América Latina y el Caribe: El caso de Argentina* (Santiago: FAO).
Perrone, N. (2010) Governing foreign investments in agriculture: is the International Investment Regime suitable?, *Perspectivas* 01/10, http://www.lasil-sladi.org/webdav/site/lasil-sladi/shared/Perspectivas/perspectivas26.pdf.
State of Sao Paulo (2011) *CNJ denuncia uso de laranjas para compra de terra*, 16 September, http://www.estadao.com.br/noticias/impresso,cnj-denuncia-uso-de-laranjas-para-compra-de-terra,773235,0.htm.
Pensar (2011) *Propiedad extranjera de la tierra* (mimeo).
Tiempo Argentino (2011) El 10% en otras manos, 28 April, http://tiempo.infonews.com/notas/10-otras-manos.
Wilkinson, J., Reydon, B. & Di Sabbato, A. (2011) *Dinámica del mercado de la tierra en América Latina y el Caribe: El caso de Brasil* (Santiago: FAO).

Nicolás Marcelo Perrone is a doctoral candidate at the London School of Economics and Political Science. He has worked as a consultant for the OECD Directorate for Financial and Enterprise Affairs and as a fellow at the UNCTAD Division on Investment and Enterprise. His main research interests are international investment and economic law, and international investment governance, in particular foreign investment in agriculture.

Index

Note:
Page numbers in **bold** type refer to figures
Page numbers in *italic* type refer to tables
Page numbers followed by 'n' refer to notes

Related titles from Routledge

Green Grabbing: A New Appropriation of Nature

Edited by James Fairhead, Melissa Leach and Ian Scoones

Green grabbing builds on well-known histories of colonial and neo-colonial resource alienation in the name of the environment. Yet it involves novel forms of valuation, commodification and markets for pieces and aspects of nature, and an extraordinary new range of actors and alliances. This book draws together seventeen original cases from African, Asian and Latin American settings to ask: To what extent and in what ways do 'green grabs' constitute new forms of appropriation of nature? What political and discursive dynamics underpin 'green grabs'? How and when do appropriations on the ground emerge out of circulations of green capital? Are the ecologies, landscapes and livelihoods gaining or losing? How are agrarian social relations, rights and authority being restructured, and in whose interests?

This book was published as a special issue of the *Journal of Peasant Studies*.

James Fairhead is Chair in Social Anthropology at the University of Sussex.

Melissa Leach is a Professorial Fellow at the Institute of Development Studies, University of Sussex.

Ian Scoones is a Professorial Fellow at the Institute of Development Studies, University of Sussex.

July 2013: 246 x 174: 112pp
Hb: 978-0-415-64407-5
£95 / $155